The Critical Reader

The Complete Guide to SAT Critical Reading

by

Erica L. Meltzer

Sentence completion explanations by
Elizabeth Foster

Dedication

To Ricky, who pestered me to write this book until I finally acquiesced

Table of Contents

Preface

I did not want to write this book. No matter how much you don't want to take the SAT, I assure you that I didn't want to write this book just as badly. In fact, I resisted writing it for as long as I possibly could. So why, you ask, did I do it? After all, I didn't *have* to. No one was going to refuse my college application if I didn't. Well, there are a couple of reasons. First, one of my students badgered me incessantly for months, insisting that there wasn't a single prep book out there for smart, motivated, high-scoring students that accurately explained in a straightforward, no-nonsense manner exactly what Critical Reading was testing and how to ace it. The other reason, however, was that I kept encountering smart, motivated, high-scoring students who nevertheless had surprising and significant gaps in their knowledge – gaps that had never been addressed or even noticed in school, and that prevented them from dealing with the test at the level of what it was actually testing and thus from getting those last 50-150 points. What often looked like a simple case of getting down to two answers and then picking the wrong one consistently turned out to be something much deeper. So to put it bluntly, I wrote this book because it had to be written. Critical Reading tests skills so different from – and, I would argue, more important than – those emphasized in American schools that most high school students quite simply don't even have a vocabulary for understanding it. Besides, there didn't seem to be anyone else who was crazy enough (or had enough time on their hands) to do it. And once I got started, I simply kept going, determined to get it over with as quickly as possible. I knew that if I stopped, I would immediately become so overwhelmed by the sheer immensity of the project that I simply wouldn't be able to bring myself to start again.

Although I was initially concerned that the book would be too sophisticated for high school students (devoid as it was of references to video games and reality television), when I showed the book to the student who had begged me to write it, he reassured me that the style was perfect. It would, he said, come as a relief to serious, highly motivated teenagers who were sick of being talked down to and just wanted to know what Critical Reading questions were really asking. That said, I realize this is a less accessible book than *The Ultimate Guide to SAT Grammar*, and I am aware of the inevitable criticisms that it will bring: It's too dry. The language is too hard. It doesn't have any fun pop-culture references. It makes Critical Reading seem too complicated. I can only imagine the grimaces that the section on pronouns will incur. I can almost hear people wondering, "Could this book *possibly* get any more pedantic?" But here's the thing: I've tutored a lot of kids in Critical Reading. And I've seen the sometimes very considerable misconceptions about reading that they bring to the test – even the ones consistently scoring above 700. This book represents my attempt to address those misconceptions directly. The fact is that most high school students do not read or write like adults (if you're a teenager reading this, no offense!). That's why they're in high school and not writing for, say, *The Journal of International Affairs*. Most American teenagers do not regularly use words such as *assertion* or *notion* in their own writing, nor do they, unprompted, spend half a page addressing the subtleties of viewpoints they don't agree with. As a result, they have an awful lot of trouble understanding what's going on when they read writing jam-packed with those elements. And if they have consistent difficulty recognizing passage topics, they need to be given specific tools for identifying them. Naming and discussing – not to mention trying to remedy – problems that already exist is not the same thing as creating those problems. If that's dry and boring, so be it.

Introduction

Note: this part is primarily intended for parents and tutors. If you're a student preparing for the SAT, you're welcome to read it too, but you can also start on p. 15.

Eight years elapsed between my last SAT, which I took as a senior in high school, and the first time I was asked to tutor Critical Reading. I distinctly remember sitting in Barnes and Noble, hunched over the Official Guide, staring at the questions in horror and thinking, "Oh wow, this test is *hard*. How on earth did I ever get an 800 on this thing when I was seventeen?" Mind you, I felt completely flummoxed by Critical Reading *after* I had earned a degree in literature.

Somehow or other, I managed to muddle through my first Critical Reading tutoring sessions. I tried to pretend that I knew what I was doing, but to be perfectly honest, I was pretty lost. I had to look up answers in the back of the book. A lot. I lost count of the number of times I had to utter the words, "I think you're right, but give me one second and let me just double-check that answer…" It was mortifying. No tutor wants to come off as clueless in front of a sixteen year-old, but I was looking like I had no idea what I was doing. Grammar I could handle, but when it came to teaching Critical Reading, I was in way over my head. I simply had no idea how to put into words what had always come naturally to me. Besides, half the time I wasn't sure of the right answer myself.

Luckily for me, fate intervened in the form of Laura Wilson, the founder of WilsonPrep in Chappaqua, New York, whose company I spent several years writing tests for. Laura taught me about the major passage themes, answer choices patterns, and structures. I learned the importance of identifying the main point, tone and major transitions, as well as the ways in which that information can allow a test-taker to spot correct answers quickly, efficiently, and without second-guessing. I discovered that the skills that the SAT tested were in fact the exact same skills that I had spent four years honing.

As a matter of fact, I came to realize that, paradoxically, my degree in French was probably more of an aid in teaching Critical Reading than a degree in English would have been. The basic French literary analysis exercise, known as the *explication de texte linéaire*, consists of close reading of a short excerpt of text, during which the reader explains how the text functions rhetorically from beginning to end – that is, just how structure, diction, and syntax work together to produce meaning and convey a particular idea or point of view. In other words, exactly the skills tested on Critical Reading. I had considered *explications de texte* a pointless exercise (Rhetoric? Who studies *rhetoric* anymore? That's so nineteenth century!) and resented being forced to write them in college – especially during the year I spent at the Sorbonne, where I and my (French) classmates did little else – but suddenly I appreciated the skills they had taught me. Once I made the connection between what I had been studying all that time and the skills tested on the SAT, the test suddenly made sense. I suddenly had something to fall back on when I was teaching, and for the first time, I found that I no longer had to constantly look up answers.

I still had a long way to go as a tutor, though: at first I clung a bit too rigidly to some methods (e.g. insisting that students circle all the transitions) and often did not leave my students enough room to find their own strategies. As I worked with more students, however, I began to realize just how little I could take for granted in terms of pre-existing skills: most of them, it turned out, had significant difficulty even identifying the point of an argument, never mind summing it up in five or so words. A lot of them didn't even realize that passages contained arguments at all; they thought that the authors were simply "talking about stuff." As a result, it never even occurred to them to identify which ideas a given author did and did not agree with. When I instructed them to circle transitions like *however* and *therefore* as a way of identifying the key places in an argument, many of them found it overwhelming to do so at the same time they were trying to absorb the literal content of a passage – more than one student told me they could do one or the other, but not both at the same time. In one memorable gaffe, I told a student that while he often did not have to read every word of the more analytical passages, he did need to read all of the literary passages, only to have him tell me that he couldn't tell the difference. He thought of all the passages as literary because the blurbs above them all said they came from books, and weren't all books "literary?" It never occurred to me to tell him that he needed to look for the word "novel" in the blurb above the passage in order to identify works of *fiction*. When I pointed out to another student that he had answered a question incorrectly because he hadn't realized that the author of the passage disagreed with a particular idea, he responded without a trace of irony that the author had spent a lot of time talking about that idea – no one had ever introduced him to the idea that writers often spend a good deal of time fleshing out ideas that they *don't* agree with. And this was a student scoring in the mid-600s!

Eventually, I got it: I realized that I would have to spend more time – sometimes a lot more time – explaining basic contextual pieces of information that most adult readers took for granted and, moreover, I would have to do so at the same time I covered actual test-taking strategies. Without the fundamentals, all the strategy in the world might not even raise a score by 10 points.

Unfortunately, the focus of most high school English classes in the United States has very little to do with the skills that get tested on the SAT; most of the students I've worked with had barely even heard the term "rhetoric," and if they had heard it, they weren't really sure what it was. Reading rhetorically – reading to understand the structure of an argument and the roles that various pieces of information played within it – was a skill they had simply never been asked to develop. Only the very strongest readers, the ones who had read extensively on their own since childhood, were able to intuit on their own just what they were expected to do. It was no wonder that the rest of them were baffled by the kind of reading the SAT required and concluded that since the only place they had ever been asked to do it was on the SAT, the test was therefore stupid and pointless and utterly irrelevant to everything else in life.

That is, incidentally, a criticism I hear a lot. Truth be told, defending a test that nearly everyone over the age of 16 in the United States loathes is not exactly pleasant (although at this point I'm so accustomed to it that it no longer really fazes me). So that said, why on earth *should* anyone care about Critical Reading, especially since the only thing that SAT scores have ever been demonstrated to correlate with is freshman college grades – and even then the correlation isn't particularly strong? Well, if you'll bear with me, there are a few reasons I find particularly compelling.

First, the kind of reading required on the SAT, while very different from the kind of reading typically done in high school, is essentially the same kind of reading required in college – even if college assignments (hopefully!) bear no resemblance to the kind of multiple-choice questions that appear on the SAT. High school students typically do two kinds of reading: on one hand, they read textbooks, which are dry, factual, and generally devoid of any obvious point of view. Important information is often clearly marked, and there is little room for critical engagement or consideration of why the information is presented in the way that it's presented. Many textbooks are also written well *below* grade level: beginning in the late 1940s, when school enrollments rose dramatically, there was a precipitous drop in the level of language used in textbooks[1] – a drop reflected in the abrupt decline of SAT Verbal scores between the mid-1960s and late 1970s, when the baby boom generation applied to college. Students may occasionally be assigned supplemental material intended for older readers (in History class, for example), but otherwise, they have minimal exposure to the class of adults engaged in serious ongoing written conversation and debate about *ideas*. And because of their limited experience with this type of writing, they have difficulty identifying arguments (especially when they are couched in unfamiliarly dense language), keeping track of points of view, and differentiating between what authors think vs. what authors say "other people" think.

In English class, on the other hand, high school students read classic works of fiction – but there, too, they are taught to read descriptively rather than analytically. They are taught to focus almost entirely on the content of what they read (themes, symbols, characters) and are never asked to consider texts as constructions made up of rhetorical moves deliberately intended to convey particular ideas and impressions, and to elicit particular reactions from the reader. The rhetorical purpose or *function* of words, phrases, and even punctuation is all but ignored. Furthermore, their teachers tell them that the mark of great literature is that it is ambiguous and open to interpretation, and they are encouraged to come up with their own unique interpretations of what they read – interpretations that often involve either relating the book to their own lives or speculating about the underlying motivations or psychology of the characters in ways not always directly supported by the text. Because they are so used to focusing on their *own* ideas, they do not know how to identify the *author's* intention, nor are they accustomed to reading with the word-for-word precision that Critical Reading demands. While I would never dispute the fact that great literature is in fact ambiguous and open to interpretation, there is plenty of reading out there that is not fiction and that is not quite so open to interpretation. Although non-fiction authors may encourage their readers to reflect on particular ideas or experiences, they are writing primarily to convey a point. And usually

---

[1] A study by Hayes, Wolfer, and Wolfe found that the level of contemporary twelfth grade reading is often below that of *seventh or eighth grade* reading from the 1940s. See "Schoolbook Simplification and Its Relation to the Decline in SAT Verbal Scores." Donald P. Hayes, Loreen T. Wolfer, and Michael F. Wolfe. *American*

they're not particularly shy about telling the reader what that point is. Sometimes they're even nice enough to say flat-out "the point is…" or "my goal in writing this is…" It's up to the reader to identify and pay attention to what the author indicates is important, not to pick out the bits and pieces they happen to like and invent their own idea of what they might mean. That tendency to read "around and beyond" the text explains why so many students who earn straight A's in English, even in so-called "AP courses," are unable to break 700 – or sometimes even 600 – in Critical Reading.

The problem is not, however, just confined to the SAT. The vast majority of the reading assigned in college is almost guaranteed to be the type of non-fiction reading that appears on the SAT; even in a literature class, non-fiction criticism is regularly assigned to accompany the primary text. And sometimes there's a lot of it: as part of a challenging liberal arts curriculum, professors will often assign hundreds and hundreds of pages per week. While they do not expect their students to absorb and beautifully annotate every single word of their reading, they do expect that students will be able to skim through very large quantities of information and get the gist of it without too much trouble; that means recognizing when to slow down and pay attention (when an author is making an important point) and when to skim (when an author is giving a tenth example), even when the topic isn't 100% familiar and the reading is less than fully engaging. Academic writing isn't always good writing – sometimes it's overblown, jargon-laden, and pretentious – but whether or not students like it or agree with it, they have to be able to understand it. Plenty of students don't acquire this skill until they get to college – that's why most schools have a required freshman seminar – but those who get it down earlier will find their transition to college much smoother.

In addition, one of the most common SAT passage structures, "they say/I say," is the basic model for most serious texts students will encounter in the sciences, social sciences, and humanities. Academics and professional writers do not focus exclusively on their own arguments, ignoring nuances and failing to consider potential objections the way high school students often do.[2] They "converse" with influential figures in their field, both past and present, review the background of their research, and spend a good amount of time discussing prevailing explanations and their strengths and weaknesses before they even begin to discuss their own ideas. A student who becomes comfortable with keeping track of multiple arguments and points of view in high school is far less likely to feel overwhelmed by college-level reading.

Furthermore, a major difference between high school and college is the shift from summarizing other people's arguments to actually "dialoguing" with and evaluating those arguments and deciding whether or not they have merit – and there's really no way to evaluate an argument critically or formulate a cogent response without understanding precisely what it's literally saying – rather than what one merely *imagines* it might be saying – and how it's put together. An author who continually relies on "personal anecdote" to support a point is probably on much shakier ground than one who repeatedly cites specific facts and figures or the opinions of multiple experts in a field (although those can certainly

---

[2] A major difference between twelfth graders and professional writers is that the former rarely use concession words (e.g. *however*) to recognize others' viewpoints. See Bill Williams, "Rhetorical and Grammatical Dependency," *Syntax in the Schools*, Vol. 12 no. 1, Sept. 1995.

be manipulated as well to suit an argument). If a reader can't recognize personal anecdote vs. citation of an expert, they can't even begin to make a judgment about whether an argument is reliable. As Gerald Graff, Cathy Birkenstein, and Russell Durst point out in *They Say/I Say: The Moves that Matter in Academic Writing*, their superb introduction to college-level writing, the ability to "converse" with people who hold opposing viewpoints – without reducing those viewpoints to parody – is a crucial skill for members of a democracy.[3]

Studying for Critical Reading teaches students to think, well, critically – to move beyond taking a piece of writing at face value and actually consider how its component parts work together to convey a particular idea. That may seem obvious, but it's actually an extraordinarily important component of media literacy. Given the sheer quantity of information with which most twenty-first century teenagers are constantly bombarded, the ability to focus on important information and filter out irrelevant details is crucial, as is the ability to understand how written and visual media are put together to persuade people to buy a product, vote for a candidate, or take part in a social movement. An advertisement, for example, consists of images and texts specifically chosen to elicit specific emotions. The ability to break it down and understand how it is intended to seduce/inspire/flatter makes people less likely to take it at face value and consider whether a product, a social media trend, or a political movement is truly worth buying into. And given the simplistic level of most political and media discourse in the United States, the ability to recognize nuances and understand that arguments are not necessarily black and white is an increasingly vital ability.

Moreover, the use of rhetorical devices such as euphemism – the replacement of a harsh or offensive word or phrase with a more innocent-sounding one – can have profound social and political implications. It may be mildly amusing when someone says "vertically challenged" rather than "short," but a newspaper that blandly refers to civilians killed in war as "collateral damage" is doing something considerably less innocuous (for a student interested in that idea, I would recommend George Orwell's essay "Politics and the English Language"). Someone who can't recognize a euphemism probably won't think about why an author used one instead of saying flat-out what they meant, and what they *didn't* want the reader to think about.

None of this, of course, is directly covered on the SAT; the passages on the test are carefully chosen and edited to be as inoffensive as possible. But there's no fundamental difference between reading an SAT passage critically and a *New York Times* article critically. Rhetoric is rhetoric is rhetoric is rhetoric.

Erica Meltzer
New York City
March 2013

---

[3] Gerald Graff, Cathy Birkenstein, and Russell Durst. *They Say/I Say: The Moves that Matter in Academic Writing*. New York: W.W. Norton and Co., 2009, p. 13.

A Quick Note About This Book (for Students)

This book has two main goals: the first goal is, of course, to help you improve your score on the Critical Reading section of the SAT. The second goal, however, is to prepare you for the type of reading you'll be asked to do in college. College reading is fundamentally different from high school reading in that it is primarily based on non-fiction texts that require you to keep track of multiple points of view held by scholars and professionals in various disciplines, and to understand the relationships between those points of view. In college, you will also be expected to read many more pages and in much less time than you are given in high school – staying on top of your work will, to a large extent, depend on your ability to read "from the top down," focusing primarily on the big picture and understanding details in relation to main points. You simply cannot read a 500 page book about political science or anthropology or sociology the same way you would read a work of literature. You'll need to know how to figure out which information you need to pay attention to and which information you can skim past. If you try to get every last word, you'll never finish. If you can get an accurate gist, on the other hand, you don't have to worry about knowing every last detail because you'll understand how things fit together. This is the type of reading that the SAT tests.

Unlike many of the other SAT guides out there, this book treats you like an adult. Its goal is to bring you up to the level of the authors you'll encounter on the SAT, not bring them down to the level of some hypothetical average teenager. It does not sugarcoat Critical Reading or claim that it's easy enough to be "outsmarted" with a few simple tricks. It does, however, aim to give you the tools necessary to approach Critical Reading with a sense of mastery. Although there are many patterns you can use to make educated guesses even if you're not totally sure what a passage or an answer choice is saying, there are few 100% hard and fast rules. Critical Reading is, in some ways, an intellectual game, but it's an adult game, one based on a very dry, subtle humor. If you get to know the test well enough, you can spot when the test-writers were clearly having a good time, either because an answer choice is blatantly absurd or because an answer that has all the characteristics of a typical right answer is indisputably wrong. So yes, Critical Reading does have the potential to be "fun," but probably not in a way that you're accustomed to.

While some of the passages here are reasonably straightforward and perhaps even mildly interesting to read, other are dry and very challenging. Whenever possible, I have chosen excerpts from works by the same authors used on College Board exams; some of them discuss concepts and include language that are probably unlike anything you've encountered in school. But that's the point: Critical Reading is a test of whether you are *already* reading at a college level. So if you have difficulty understanding some of the passages and answers, don't panic! After all, you're still in high school. But that said, you might have to put in a lot of work if you really want to catch up to the kids who devour hundreds of books for pleasure, the ones who magically absorbed the skills the SAT tests somewhere along the way – although granted if you've been struggling with this Critical Reading for a while, you probably already know that.

The fact that this book *recognizes* that the SAT is hard does not, however, mean that it tries to *make* things hard; on the contrary, it tries to teach you to simplify texts and recognize patterns that will get you to the answer as quickly and confidently as possible. But unlike other prep books, this book also deals with the nitty-gritty of the underlying comprehension skills – the things that most college educated adult readers do automatically but that you might not yet know how to or think to do. Although some of those things may seem quite challenging at first, the goal of this book is to teach you to actually answer the questions, competently and confidently, rather than simply play process of elimination and hope for the best. For that reason, this book primarily focuses on helping you understand just what Critical Reading questions are actually asking, as well as their relationships to answers that seem vague or confusing or just plain weird. This book also heavily emphasizes close reading skills, teaching you to identify authors' intentions and beliefs through careful attention to and analysis of their language and rhetorical forms. At every step, I have done my best to emphasize the underlying logic on which Critical Reading is based, and to make that logic seem as straightforward and accessible as possible.

Each chapter of this book covers a particular type of Critical Reading question, moving from most concrete (literal comprehension) to most abstract (paired passage relationships). If you are already scoring around 700 and have consistent difficulty only with a particular type of question (e.g. tone, inference), I strongly recommend that you begin by focusing on the corresponding chapter. If, however, your errors are more random and encompass a variety of question types, you may simply be best served by working through the chapters in order. There is unfortunately no single "trick" guaranteed to raise a score those last 50-150 points. Almost inevitably, even my students in the mid-700s are typically missing important pieces of contextual knowledge simply because they haven't yet read extensively enough to be able to recognize the conventions of "serious" non-fiction writing, and haven't yet learned to use their knowledge of those conventions to gain the sort of rapid and accurate "big picture" understanding that translates into immediate recognition of correct answers. This book attempts to help you recognize and understand many of those conventions – conventions that you will encounter again and again in college and beyond.

Provided that you have solid comprehension skills, success in Critical Reading is also largely a question of approach, or method. Because the test demands a certain degree of flexibility – part of what makes Critical Reading so difficult is the fact that no single strategy can be guaranteed to work 100% of the time – I have also tried to make this book a toolbox of sorts. My goal is to provide you with a variety of approaches and strategies that you can choose from and apply as necessary, depending on the question at hand. That ability to adapt is what will ultimately make you unshakeable – even at eight o'clock on a Saturday morning.

1. Overview of Critical Reading

There are three Critical Reading sections, containing a total of 67 questions, distributed more or less evenly throughout the test. In the case that an Experimental section consists of Critical Reading, however, two consecutive sections may appear.

- The first two sections last 25 minutes and contain 24 questions (although very occasionally one will contain 25).

- The third section lasts 20 minutes and contains 19 questions.

- The beginning of each section contains between 5 and 8 sentence completions, which test vocabulary and the ability to determine words logically from context.

In total, sentence completions comprise slightly less than one-third of Critical Reading. The remainder of each section is devoted to passage-based reading questions.

The breakdown of passages per test is typically as follows:

- Two short (10-20 line) passages, always presented consecutively. 2 questions each.

- One short paired passage set. 4 questions.

- One medium passage (approximately 50 lines), social science, science or art. 5-7 questions.

- One long passage (approximately 85 lines), social science, science or art. 9-12 questions.

- One long fiction passage from either a classic (nineteenth century) or modern novel written either originally in English or translated into English . 9-12 questions.

- One long paired passage set. 9 12 questions.

Although sentence completions are arranged in order of difficulty, passage-based reading questions are arranged according to the order of information of the passage itself, and the difficulty level is entirely random. A question rated level 5 (most difficult) may therefore be placed next to a level one (easiest) question, and there is no way to predict when or where either will occur. For that reason, it is very much to your advantage to skip around, answering all the questions that you can answer easily before turning to the ones that are more difficult and time-consuming.

Passages cover a wide range of topics, themes, and genres, with most passages drawn from "serious" recent works of non-fiction written for an educated adult audience. (For an overview of common passage topics and themes, see p. 92).

Scoring and Strategies

Because Critical Reading contains more questions than either Math or Writing, and because it is traditionally the most difficult section for most test-takers to obtain a high score on, the Critical Reading curve is noticeably more generous than the curves for the other two sections. While it is usually necessary to answer every single Math question and nearly every Writing question correctly to score an 800, it is sometimes possible to miss up to three or skip up to four Critical Reading questions and still receive the highest possible score.

That said, the distance between a 700 and an 800 is larger than the distance between a 600 and a 700. To earn a 600, it is only necessary to obtain a raw score (the number of questions correct minus .25 times the number of questions incorrect) of about 45-47, slightly more than 2/3 of the total points. It is therefore possible to skip more than 20 questions, or 6-7 per section, and still score a very respectable 600. If you consistently miss around 6 questions per section and are looking for a quick fix to get your score just over the 600 mark, it is well worth your while to experiment with skipping some of the questions you are genuinely uncertain how to answer.

To earn a 700, on the other hand, you must generally attain a raw score of about 57-58, which requires you to answer just over 85% of the questions correctly. To do so, you can attempt to answer every question and get no more than 7 wrong (67-7 = 60), with an additional two points subtracted for the incorrect questions (7 x .25 = 1.75, which rounds to 2). Alternately, if you are a strong reader and feeling very brave, you can attempt to simply skip the 10 questions you find most difficult. If that feels too risky, you can also try skipping three or four questions. That way, if you get four questions wrong, you'll end up with a raw score of 58 or 59, which usually translates into a 700 or 710.

Regardless of what sort of score you are aiming for, you should not attempt to answer a question if you have absolutely no idea what the answer could be – and no tools for making even a slightly educated guess – even if you can narrow the answer down to two possibilities. I understand that this is a controversial position, but while I am in no way a statistician, I *have* seen firsthand many, many, many times (did I say that enough?) what happens when people make wild guesses, and my own thoroughly anecdotal and completely unscientific observation is that they almost always get those questions wrong. If you think you're the exception, you're welcome to ignore my advice; just don't say you weren't warned.

What Does Critical Reading Test?

It is important to understand that that the Critical Reading is so named for a reason. It is not a reading comprehension test, nor is it a test of literary analysis and interpretation. **It is rather a test about the construction of arguments and the ways in which specific textual elements (e.g. words, phrases, punctuation marks) work together to convey meaning. The focus is on moving beyond <u>what</u> a text says to understanding <u>how</u> the text says it. Comprehension, in other words, is necessary but not sufficient.**

To sum up, the SAT does not simply test the ability to find bits of factual information in a passage, but rather the ability to do the following:

Sentence Completions

- Use contextual clues to recognize words that would fit logically within a sentence.

- Use roots to make educated guesses about the meaning of unfamiliar words.

Passage-Based Reading

- Distinguish between main ideas and supporting detail.

- Understand how the diction (word choice), syntax, structure, and rhetorical devices convey meaning and tone/attitude.

- Understand the rhetorical role (e.g. supporting, emphasizing, criticizing) that various pieces of information play within an argument.

- Keep track of multiple viewpoints and understand relationships between arguments, perspectives, and attitudes.

- Make logical inferences and generalizations from information not explicitly stated.

- Understand nuances of arguments and recognize that it is possible for an author to agree with some aspects of another person's idea while rejecting others.

- Draw relationships between specific wordings and general/abstract ideas.

- Use contextual information to determine the meanings of unfamiliar words, and recognize when common words are being used in uncommon ways.

The skill that the SAT requires is therefore something I like to call **"rhetorical reading."** Rhetoric is the art of persuasion, and reading rhetorically simply means reading primarily to understand an author's argument as well as the rhetorical role or *function* that various pieces of information play in creating that argument. **Reading this way is an acquirable skill, not an innate aptitude. It just takes practice.**

The Answer Isn't Always *in* the Passage

One of the great truisms of SAT prep is that "the answer is always in the passage," but in reality this statement is only half true: **the information necessary to answer the questions is always provided in the passage, but not necessarily the answer itself.** The SAT tests the ability to draw relationships between specific wordings and general ideas – so while the correct answer will always be *supported by* specific wording in the passage, the whole point is that you are responsible for making the connection. That, in essence, is the test.

As a rule, therefore, the correct answers to most questions will virtually never be stated word-for-word in the text. In fact, **the more directly the phrasing in an answer choice mimics the phrasing in the passage, the more likely it is to be wrong!** The correct answer choice, on the other hand, will refer to an **idea** that has been discussed in the passage and that has simply been **rephrased**. Your job is therefore to identify that idea and look for an answer choice that rewords it with **synonyms**. Same idea, different words.

Understanding Incorrect Answer Choices

Each Critical Reading question is accompanied by five answer choices, labeled (A) through (E). Despite the multiple-choice format, the presence of multiple answers does not somehow make incorrect answers any more valid or make correct answers any less so.

Although one or more incorrect answers may sound convincing, there are always specific textual elements that prevent an incorrect answer from being acceptable. Incorrect answers are written to sound plausible. Often, they describe a situation that *could* be true but that is *not necessarily true* according to the information explicitly stated in the passage. They also tend to employ relatively sophisticated vocabulary and highly abstract language that many test-takers find confusing or difficult to comprehend. That said, incorrect answers typically fall into the following categories:

- Off-topic

- Too broad (e.g. the passage discusses *one* author while the answer refers to *authors*)

- Too extreme (e.g. the passage is slightly negative but the answer extremely negative)

- Half-right, half-wrong (e.g. right information, wrong point of view)

- Could be true but not enough information

- True for the passage as a whole, but not for the specific lines in question

- Factually true but not stated in the passage

On most questions, many test-takers find it relatively easy to eliminate two or three answers but routinely remain stuck between two plausible-sounding answers. Typically, the incorrect answer will fall into either the "could be true but not enough information" or the "half-right, half-wrong" category. In such cases, you must be willing to read very carefully in order to determine which answer the passage truly supports.

How to Work Through Critical Reading Questions

While your approach may change depending on the question, in general I recommend the following strategy:

1) Read the question <u>slowly</u>

Put your finger on each word of the question as you read it; otherwise you may miss key information, and every letter of every word counts.

When you're done, take a second or two to make sure you know exactly what it's asking. If the question is phrased in an even slightly convoluted manner, rephrase it in your own words in a more straightforward way until you're clear on what you're looking for. If necessary, scribble the rephrased version down.

This is not a minor step. If, for example, the question asks you the purpose of a particular sentence, you need to be prepared to re-read it with the goal of understanding what role the sentence plays within the argument or impression the author is trying to convey; if you re-read it with a different goal, e.g. understanding what the sentence is literally saying, you can't do any meaningful work toward answering the question that's actually there.

2) Go back to the passage and re-read the lines given in the question. If the question seems to call for it, read from a sentence or two above to a sentence or two below.

"Purpose" or "function" questions often require more context and, as a result, you should be prepared to read both before and after the line reference. In contrast, inference and "support/undermine" questions typically involve only the information in the line reference itself. If the line reference begins or ends halfway through a sentence, however, make sure you back up or keep reading so that you cover the entire sentence in which it appears. If a line reference begins close to the beginning of a paragraph, you should automatically read from the first sentence of the paragraph because it will almost always give you the point.

There is unfortunately no surefire way to tell from the wording of a question whether the information necessary to answer that question is included in the line reference. Most of the time it will be there, but sometimes it will appear either before or after, and very occasionally in another paragraph entirely.

If you read the lines referenced and have an inordinate amount of difficulty identifying the correct answer, or get down to two answers and are unable to identify which is correct, that's often a sign that the answer is actually located somewhere other than in the line reference. Go back to the passage, and read from a sentence or two above to a sentence or two below.

For long line references: a long line reference is, paradoxically, a signal that you *don't* need to read all of the lines. Usually the information you need to answer the question will be in either the first sentence or two, the last sentence or two, or in a section with key punctuation (dashes, italics, colon). Start by focusing on those places and forgetting the rest; they'll almost certainly give you enough to go on.

3) Answer the question in your own words, and write that answer down

The goal is not to write a dissertation or come up with the exact answer ETS has written. You can be very general should spend no more than a few seconds on this step; a couple of words scribbled down in semi-legible handwriting will suffice. The goal is to identify the general information or idea that the correct answer must include, keeping in mind that the correct answer may present that idea worded in a way that you're not entirely expecting.

It is, however, important that you write down something in your own words because that answer serves to focus you. It reminds you what you're looking for and prevents you from getting distracted by plausible-sounding or confusing answer choices.

Again, make sure you're answering the question that's actually being asked, not just summarizing the passage.

You should take **no more than a few seconds** to do this. If you can't come up with anything, skip to step #4.

4) Read the answers carefully, (A)-(E), in order

If there's an option that contains the same essential idea you put down, choose it because it's almost certainly right. If it makes you feel better, though, you can read through the rest of the answers just to be sure, but make sure you don't get distracted by things that sound vaguely plausible and start second-guessing yourself.

When you cross out an answer, put a line through the entire thing; do not just cross out the letter. As far as you're concerned, it no longer exists.

If you can't identify the correct answer…

5) Cross out the answers that clearly don't work; leave <u>everything</u> else

Try not to spend more than a couple of seconds on each answer choice. If an option clearly makes no sense in context of the question or passage, get rid of it.

Any answer that could even slightly work, even if you're not quite sure how it relates to the passage or question, you should leave. Remember: your ability to understand an answer choice has no bearing whatsoever on whether it's right or wrong, so you should never cross out anything simply because you don't fully grasp what it's saying.

When you get down to two or three answers, go back to the passage again and start checking them out. Whatever you do, do not just sit and stare at them. The information you need to answer the question is in the passage, not in your head.

There are several ways to approach the remaining answers.

First, when you go back to the passage, see if there are any major transitions or strong language you missed the first time around; you may have been focusing on the wrong part of the line reference. If that is the case, the correct answer may become clear once you focus on the necessary information.

Very often, the correct answer will also contain a synonym for a key word in the passage, so if a remaining choice includes this feature, you should pay very close attention to it.

You can also pick one specific word in each answer to check out when you go back to the passage. For example, if the lines in question focus on a specific author and the answer choice mentions "authors," then the answer is probably beyond the scope of what can be inferred from the passage. Likewise, if an answer focuses on a specific person, thing, or idea not mentioned in the lines referenced, there's also a reasonable chance that it's off-topic.

Remember: that the more information an answer choice contains, the greater the chance that some of that information will be wrong. Function questions often have correct answers that are short "vague," and general, and you should give them careful consideration.

Finally, you can reiterate the main point of the passage or paragraph, and think about which answer is most consistent with it. That answer will most likely be correct.

6) If you're still stuck, see whether there's a choice that looks like a right answer

If you still can't figure out the answer, you need to switch from reading the passage to "reading" the test. Working this way will allow you to make an educated guess, even if you're not totally sure what's going on. Does one of the answers you're left with use extremely strong or limiting language (*no one, always, totally incompatible*)? There's a pretty good chance it's wrong. Does one of them use a common word (e.g. *qualify, conviction*) in its second meaning? There's a pretty good chance it's right. Is one answer very long and detailed and the other very broad and general? You might want to pay particularly close attention to the latter.

In addition, ask yourself whether all of the answers you're left with actually make sense in context of both the test and the real world. For example, an answer choice that states an author is "criticizing the prominent role of the arts in society" is simply out of keeping with the SAT's humanistic bent. No author who seriously believed that the arts should not play an important role in society would ever be approved for inclusion on the test. Likewise, an answer containing information that is historically false (e.g. it suggests that a man who lived during the eighteenth century held radically feminist views) is equally unlikely to be right. Yes, you should be very careful about relying on your outside knowledge of a subject, but it's okay to use common sense too!

7) If you're still stuck, skip it

You can always come back to it later if you have time.

Understanding and Marking Line References

One of the major advantages of the SAT as opposed to the ACT is that Critical Reading questions are always organized chronologically in order of the passage, *and* the test-writers are nice enough to tell you what lines to focus on. But line references aren't nearly as much of a gift as many people think. The most important thing to understand is that a line reference simply tells you where in the passage a particular word, phrase, or set of lines is located. Consider a question that reads: "The author's attitude toward 'that alternative' (line 35) can be best be described as..." This question is telling you that the words "that alternative" appear in line 35. That's it. The answer is not necessarily in line 35. It could be in line 33 or line 37 or line 40. If the author is playing "they say/I say," it could even be suggested in line 5. Yes, much of the time, the information you need to answer the question will in fact appear in the lines provided, but sometimes it will also be in a neighboring line, either before or after. Occasionally it may be in a different paragraph entirely.

In one popular Critical Reading strategy, the test-taker goes through all of the questions and marks all of the line references in the passage before reading it so that she or he will "know where to focus." While this can be a very successful strategy for helping people whose minds would otherwise wander, and I would not discourage anyone from using it if they find it particularly helpful, it does have some pitfalls. First, as discussed above, the answer may not actually be in the lines provided in the question. If it doesn't occur to you to read elsewhere when you can't figure out the answer, you'll often get stuck between two options and have no clear-cut way of figuring out which one is correct. And that's a shame since often the answer will be fairly straightforward; it will simply be somewhere else.

Second, this strategy can drain significant amounts of time that could be better spent answering questions. If you have difficulty finishing sections on time, you probably shouldn't be using it. There's no reason you can't go back and block off the lines as you come to them.

Third, this strategy is to some extent based on a misunderstanding of how Critical Reading works: **the most important places in the passage, the ones that you need to pay the most attention to, are not necessarily the ones indicated by the questions**. Remember: the details are only important in context of the point. Focusing excessively on a particular set of lines can therefore cause you to lose sight of the big picture – and often it's the big picture you actually need to answer the questions. At the other extreme, only a small part of the line reference may sometimes be important. There's no point in meticulously blocking off eight lines if all you need to focus on is the first sentence or a set of dashes.

I've worked with a number of students who diligently marked line references and who, not coincidentally, were stuck around 700. They were good students and fairly strong readers, but they lacked flexibility – they insisted on working through every question the same way. They did fine when the information they needed was present in the lines referenced, but when it wasn't, they floundered. It didn't occur to them how much they needed to consider ideas and parts of the passage not explicitly mentioned by the question. At some level, they also didn't really understand what the test was asking them to do. The ones who were willing to approach questions from a variety of angles improved; the ones who insisted on staying in their comfort zone and only reading the lines they were given did not.

Now let's actually look at an example:

There's a certain way jazz musicians from the 1930s
pose for photographs, half-turned to face the camera, symmetrically arrayed around the bandleader, who can be
identified by his regal smile and proximity to the microphone.
5   Publicity stills of the period were the equivalent of English
court paintings, hackwork intended to exalt their subjects and
attract admiration to their finery. Band-leaders often took
titles borrowed from the aristocracy: Duke Ellington, Count
Basie, Earl Hines . . . well, Earl was actually the man's given
10   name, but he lived up to it in a way no modern celebrity
could approach.
There's a picture of Hines with his hand on the stage at
the Pearl Theater in Philadelphia, exuding swank. Their suit
pants, which bear stripes of black satin down the seams, break
15   perfectly over their gleaming shoes; their jacket lapels have
the span of a Madagascar fruit bat; their hair is slicked. They
were on top of their world. The year was 1932, and about one
in four Americans was out of work.

The author mentions the "given name" (lines 9-10)
in order to

(A) characterize the appearance of English court
      paintings
(B) praise Earl Hines for his elegance and style
(C) promote a particular type of music
(D) criticize the practice of borrowing titles from the
      aristocracy
(E) indicate an exception to a common occurrence

If we're going to try to answer the question on our own, the first thing we need to do is make sure we understand what it's actually asking. The phrase "in order to" indicates that it's a "purpose" or "function" question. We could therefore rephrase as it, "Why does the author use the phrase 'given name' right there," or "What's the point of using the phrase 'given name' right there?" Although you might be rolling your eyes right now and saying, "Duh, yeah, that's *obviously* what it's asking," taking a moment to rephrase the question is crucial because it forces you clarify your thinking and allows you to approach the passage with a precise idea of what you're looking for.

The fact that it's a "purpose" question tells us that we need to establish **context**, so we're *not* going to start reading where the line reference tells us to read – we're going to start reading **before** it, where the sentence begins, all the back to line 7. (The colon in line 8 tells us that there's important information there.) What do we learn from that sentence? That "band leaders often took titles borrowed from the aristocracy." In other words, they took names that weren't their own (i.e. their **given names**). So the fact that Earl Hines used his own name meant that he was *different* from other musicians. The correct answer must therefore have something to do with that idea. When we scan through the choices, we see that (E) is the only option that goes along with that idea – "exception" is the only word in any of the answers that captures the idea of being different. And (E) is in fact correct.

If that seems like a reasonable – not to mention simpler – way to work, great. Although it's true that the above question was not written by ETS, you can use this method of working to answer many real SAT questions. The test is set up so that you can often jump immediately to the right answer if you've taken the time to identify the idea it must contain.

You might, however, also be thinking something like, "Well *you* make it seem easy enough, but *I'd* never actually be able to figure that out on my own." Or perhaps you're thinking something more along the lines of, "Ew… that seems like way too much *work*. I just want to look at the answer choices." So for you, here goes. One by one, we're going to consider the answer choices – very, very carefully.

(A) characterize the appearance of English court paintings

This is pretty obviously not the answer. The author does draw a comparison between the pictures of jazz musicians and English court paintings, but the mention of Hines' given name clearly has nothing to do with that. Besides, it's just not the focus of the passage. So it's wrong because it's **off topic.**

(B) praise Earl Hines for his elegance and style

It would be pretty easy to assume that this was the answer. After all, the author talks about Earl Hines, and he clearly likes him and his style a whole lot. There's only one little problem, though: the question isn't asking what the author is doing throughout the passage as a whole – it's asking **why** the author uses the particular phrase "given name" at the particular spot in the passage. And unfortunately, that little detail isn't included to support the overall point of the passage; it's included to support a different point: that Earl Hines, unlike Duke Ellington and Count Basie, truly did have a name (*Earl*) that was also an aristocratic English title.

So it's *a* right answer. It just isn't *the* right answer to this particular question.

(C) promote a particular type of music

Yes, the author does talk about "a particular type of music" (i.e. jazz), but he isn't really "promoting" anything in the sense that *promote* = try to get people to listen to jazz. Now, it might seem reasonable to infer that since the author thinks these musicians were so amazing, he must be promoting their music, but there's nothing in the passage that explicitly supports that idea. He's just talking about how sleekly jazz musicians presented themselves during the 1930s, and even though he's clearly impressed by them, being impressed with something is not *by definition* the same thing as trying to get other people to do it. It's too much of a leap.

This type of answer plays on **associative thinking**, which involves making connections between ideas even when no direct relationship between them is indicated by the passage, and it can get you in a lot of trouble on Critical Reading.

Besides, when the word "promote" appears in an answer choice, that answer is pretty much always wrong. But we'll get to that later.

(D) criticize the practice of borrowing titles from the aristocracy

Like (A), this is an answer choice that's also relatively easy to get rid of, mostly because it's so far away from the focus of the passage. Notice, however, that this answer includes a phrase taken directly from the passage ("borrowed from the aristocracy") – it's the first part of the answer, the word "criticize," that makes the whole thing incorrect. If you really didn't understand (or think about) either 1) what the passage was saying, or 2) what the question was asking, however, you could get fooled by the fact that the answer choice contains identical wording to that of the passage.

You could also fall prey to associative thinking again: you might assume that since the SAT is an American test and America is a democracy, the author would probably be against a form of social organization that gave people status based purely on family background, and so it would make sense for him to be criticizing it. Unfortunately, there is absolutely nothing whatsoever in the passage to support that interpretation. It's also completely unrelated to the question. Being aware of the SAT's biases *can* be useful in some instances, but that goes way, way too far. **Right words, wrong idea.** It's also **too broad**. The passage only talks about jazz musicians who named themselves after aristocratic titles; it says nothing about the practice in general.

Remember: when the exact same words appear in the answer as appear in the passage, that answer is most likely wrong.

(E) indicate an exception to a common occurrence

If you're like many test-takers, you probably eliminated that answer almost immediately. After all it doesn't really seem to have anything to do with the passage – but in fact, that's precisely why you should pay extra-close attention to it.

Don't forget that the question asked us to consider *why* the author used the particular phrase "given name." In other words, how does the use of that phrase support the idea that the author is trying to convey? As we saw in (B), the point is that Earl Hines was *different* (i.e. an exception) from other jazz musicians in that his real name was an aristocratic title (*Band-leaders often took titles borrowed from the aristocracy: Duke Ellington, Count Basie, Earl Hines . . . well, Earl was actually the man's given name, but he lived up to it in a way no modern celebrity could approach.*) The word "often" tells us that it was **common** for jazz musicians to take such names (taking such names = an occurrence).

So (E) is right because it simply restates what's going on in the passage, albeit in very, very different language – language that you probably weren't expecting and might not have been sure how to connect to the question or the passage. We'll look at that issue later on, in Chapter Two, but for now, just one more thing to point out: although the question tells you to look at line 9, the information you need to answer the question actually comes *earlier*. If you start at the line you're given, you have no way of figuring out the answer, whereas if you back up and start in line 7 at the beginning of the sentence, you at least have a chance.

And now, before we get started for real, some tidbits of test-prep wisdom:

Vocabulary counts. A lot. Make time to study it.

One of the biggest mistakes that people studying for the SAT make is to ignore vocabulary. While it is true that the SAT is not a conventional vocabulary test – the ability to understand when words are not being used to mean what they typically mean is just as important as knowing lots of words – vocabulary is not just tested via sentence completions. Most passages include at least one question, occasionally two or three, that asks about a word in context. While you do not necessarily need to know the word already in the passage, you do need to know the words in the answer choices – and sometimes they'll be high-frequency words such as *unsubstantiated, didactic,* and *convoluted.* It doesn't matter if you can answer the question in your own words if you can't recognize the right answer when it's in front of you!

If you're a native English speaker with a basic knowledge of roots, you probably don't need to memorize thousands of words; however, there is a core group of about very 300 high-frequency words that you absolutely need to know. If you don't already have a strong vocabulary and can't be bothered to spend the time learning them, you'll probably top out at 650, 700 if you're very lucky.

SAT vocabulary isn't as esoteric as you might imagine

One of the most common complaints from people studying for the SAT is that no one really uses the words that are tested on the exam. What they actually mean, however, is that no one in their daily lives uses those words. In reality, you'll probably find a sprinkling of them on any given page of *The New York Times* or *The Economist* or any other "serious" adult publication. Many of the hardest sentence completions involve topics such as political candidates and writers are lifted almost verbatim from articles about upcoming elections or reviews of well-known authors' latest books. If you read the paper on a regular basis, these types of sentences will become much more familiar to you. You'll also learn that yes, people really do write that way. So as a matter of fact…

If you're not in the habit of reading things written for educated adults, start. Now.

The College Board states flat-out that the SAT is a test of college-level reading, and college reading is adult reading. If you struggle to understand material at that level, you'll have to spend some time getting comfortable with it. You don't have to read Dickens or Austen; you can read about black holes if you want. If you're unsure where to start, check out Arts & Letters Daily (http://www.aldaily.com), which has links to dozens of publication written at SAT level and above. You cannot, however, read passively and expect your Critical Reading score to magically rise. Rather, you must **actively** and **consistently** practice the skills introduced in this book. Circle/underline the point, major transitions, and words that reveal tone; pay close attention to the introduction and conclusion for the topic and the author's opinion (see how *little* you can read while still getting the gist); look for phrases that reveal the "they say" and the "I say;" identify rhetorical strategies such as anecdotes and direct quotations; notice when words are used in non-literal ways, and look up unfamiliar words; and practice summarizing arguments in only a few words. The more you develop these skills independently, the easier it will become to apply them to the actual test.

The SAT isn't really just about the SAT

One of the most frequently repeated truisms about the SAT is that you have to forget all of your outside knowledge and just worry about what's in the passage. That's mostly true… but not completely. First, just to be clear, an answer can be both factually correct and wrong if that particular fact is not discussed in the passage. That's what most people mean when they say to forget about outside knowledge. The reality, however, is that Critical Reading, unlike Math, does not exist in a vacuum. It is always dependent upon ideas and debates that exist outside of the SAT. Many of those topics are quite foreign – and boring – to high school students, but they're not boring to the adults who write and argue about them seriously.

Let me give you an example: one recent SAT passage dealt with the seventeenth-century French philosopher Descartes and his role in the debate over how the mind processes physical sensation – something that most American high school students know next to nothing about, not least because cognitive science and philosophy are two subjects they generally don't encounter until college. Even for someone who is familiar with Descartes and knows that he set off a debate about the relationship between the body and the mind that has lasted for nearly 400 years, that passage is pretty challenging – but a person who knows the basics of the so-called "body-mind problem" has at least a basic frame of reference and can thus more easily understand the "big picture" of what the author is trying to say. For someone who's never heard of Descartes or the body-mind problem, the passage is still doable, but it's much, much harder.

The more you know about the world, the more easily you'll be able understand what you're reading. And if you see an answer you know is factually correct, it can't hurt to check it first.

Read exactly what's on the page, in order, from left to right

This piece of advice may seem overwhelmingly obvious, but I cannot stress how important it is. When people feel pressured, they start grabbing onto random bits of information without fully considering their context. While it is not necessary to read every word of a passage to get the gist of it, skipping around randomly does not constitute effective skimming. Pay attention to what the author is telling you to pay attention to: when you see italics or words like "important" or "the point is," you need to slow down and go word by word. **Put your finger on the page, and bracket or underline as you read; the physical connection between your eye and your hand will force you to focus in a way you wouldn't if you were just looking at the page. You're also far less likely to miss key information.**

Be as literal as you possibly can

While your English teacher might praise you for your imaginative interpretations, the College Board will not. Before you can understand the function of a piece of information or make a reasonable inference about it, you have to understand exactly what it's saying – otherwise, you'll have a faulty basis for your reasoning. When you sum things up, stick as closely as possible to the language of the passage. People often get themselves into trouble because they think that there's a particular way they're supposed to interpret passages that they just don't "get," when in reality they're not supposed to interpret anything. **In short, worry about what the author is actually saying, not what she or he might be trying to say.**

Answering Critical Reading questions is a process

Sometimes you need to go back and forth between the passage and the questions numerous times: you need to remember that the test is set up so that you can figure out the answer, and that if you stick to it and think things through logically, you'll eventually hit on the answer. No, this is not easy to do when you're under pressure, but that's the mindset with which you have to approach the test. If you look at the answers with an assumption about what the correct one will say but don't see a choice that says it, you need to be willing to revise your original assumption and re-work through the question from scratch from a different angle. This is particularly true for sentence completions that don't give you a lot of information about the words that belong in the blanks, and for passage-based "function" questions whose answer can be based either on the lines provided in the question or on an entirely different line. Yes, reworking through questions from the beginning does take some time, but if you can get through most of the questions quickly, having to slow down occasionally won't make much of an impact.

Draw a line through the entire answer, not just the letter

Your goal is to deal with the smallest amount of information possible at any given time, and looking at answers you've already eliminated is an unnecessary distraction. If you get down to one option and it doesn't seem to work, you can always erase the lines, but only if you…

Always work in pencil

It's a lot harder to re-consider answer choices when you've crossed them out in ink.

Flexibility is Key

To obtain a very high score, you need to be able to adapt your approach to the question at hand. People who insist on approaching every question the same way tend to top out at 700, while those who start out scoring in the 750+ range tend to adjust automatically (even if they think they're just reading the passage and answering the question every time). Sometimes you'll be able to answer a question based on your general understanding of the passage and won't even need to reread any portion of it. Sometimes you'll be able to go back to the passage, answer the question on your own, and then easily identify the correct answer when you look at the choices. Other times the answer will be far less straightforward and you'll have to go back and forth between the passage and the questions multiple times, eliminating answers as you go. Yet other times – for example when you are answering tone questions, whose answer choices tend to be highly formulaic – it might make more sense for you to begin by looking at the answer choices and eliminating those that are clearly wrong, then going back to the passage and seeing which remaining choice best fits. It's up to you to stay flexible and find the strategy that will get you to the answer fastest and most easily. For that reason, I have done my best, whenever possible, to offer multiple ways of approaching a given question.

The path to 800 is not linear

Whereas Math or Writing can often be improved those last 100 or so points if you spend time internalizing just a few more key rules, the same cannot be said for Critical Reading. Often, students scoring in the 650-720 range must reconsider their entire approach in order to see a significant increase. If you want a 750+ score, you *cannot skip steps* and start guessing or skimming through answers – you'll keep making just enough mistakes to hurt yourself. The SAT is a standardized test: if you keep approaching it the same way, you'll keep getting the same score. It's designed very effectively to work that way. If you want your score to change radically, you have to approach the test in a radically different way. Raising your score is also not just about how much practice you do: you improve your score by improving your reasoning skills, not just by memorizing. Getting into the right mindset can take five minutes or five months, but until you've absorbed it, your score will probably stay more or less the same – no matter how many tests you take.

Don't rush

I took the SAT twice in high school: the first time, I raced through Critical Reading, answering questions mostly on instinct, not thinking anything through, and finishing every section early. I was an incredibly strong reader and even recognized one of the passages from a book I'd read for pleasure (a passage that was incidentally re used in 2005), but I got a 710.

The second time I understood what I was up against: I broke down every single question, worked through it step-by-step, wrote out my reasoning process, and worked every question out meticulously as if it were a math problem. It was one of the most exhausting things I'd ever done, and when I stumbled out of the exam room, I had absolutely no idea how I'd scored. I'd literally been focusing so hard I hadn't left myself the mental space to worry about how I was doing. Working that way was *hard*, but it got me an 800.

Summoning that level of focus is not easy. It's also terrifying because you don't have the "well, I maybe didn't try as hard as I could have" excuse. If you bomb, you have nowhere to put the blame. If you have excellent comprehension and can stand to do it, though, working that precisely is almost foolproof. It might take you longer than you're used to in the beginning, but the more you go through the process, the more accurate you'll become and the less time you'll take. Skipping steps may take less time, but your score will suffer as a result.

Every passage has two authors – the author of the passage and the author(s) of the test – and you need to be able to read both of them.[*]

The highest scorers are often able to use a combination of close reading skills and knowledge about the test itself (themes, biases, types of answers likely to be correct), and they are able to employ both of those skills as needed in order to quickly identify the answer choices most likely to be correct and then check them out for real.

When I was in high school and uncertain about an answer, I trained myself to always ask, "What would the people at ETS consider correct?" It didn't matter that I couldn't put the patterns into words then; the point was that I was able to convince myself that what *I* personally thought was irrelevant, and that was the part that counted. To score well on Critical Reading, you have to think of the test in terms of what ETS wants – not what you want. You have to abandon your ego completely and approach the test with the mindset that *The College Board is always right and what you think doesn't matter.* Even if that thought makes you want to throw up, you have to get over it and put yourself at the mercy of the test. Then, once you've gotten the score you want, you can put it out of your mind and never have to worry about it again (or at least until your own children take it).

The ability to do this is really important: occasionally the logic on certain questions will not be airtight, or in *very* rare cases even particularly solid. In those instances, you need to be able to consider the choices on their own and ask which one looks most like the sort of answer that ETS usually makes correct. It's not fair that ETS can get away with being sloppy, but sometimes the test does work that way, and when it happens, you need to be prepared.

Be willing to consider that the test might break its own "rules"

For example, you can usually assume that answers containing extreme language such as *always, never, awe, incomprehensible, impossible,* etc. are incorrect and cross them off as soon as you see them. But you can't *always* assume that a particular pattern holds without carefully considering what the passage is actually saying. Correct answers, especially to inference questions, will very occasionally contain words such as *always* or *only*. If you're trying to score 800 or close to it, you need to stay open to the possibility that an answer containing one of those words could on occasion be correct.

Remember: provided that doing so won't result in a lawsuit, the College Board is free to ignore its own rules. General patterns are just that: general. That means you will sometimes encounter exceptions.

---

[*]I need to thank Debbie Stier for putting this idea into words so eloquently. They're hers, not mine, and thanks to her, I've spent a lot more time thinking – and talking – about the necessity of reading the test at two levels.

Fit the answer to the passage, not the passage to the answer

If an answer could only *sort of kind of maybe possibly be true if you read the passage in a very specific way*, it's not right. Don't try to justify anything that isn't directly supported by specific wording in the passage.

Every word in the answer choice counts

One incorrect word in an answer choice is enough to make the entire answer wrong. It doesn't matter how well the rest of the answer works; it doesn't matter how much you like the answer or think it should be right. If the author of the passage is clearly happy about a new finding in, say, particle physics, and an answer choice says "express skepticism about a recent finding," the answer choice is wrong. The fact that the words "a recent finding" might have appeared in the passage is irrelevant if the answer does not correctly indicate the author's attitude toward it. On the other hand...

Just because information is in the passage doesn't mean it's important

One of the things the SAT tests is the ability to recognize important information and ignore irrelevant details. Reading SAT passages is not about absorbing every last detail but rather about understanding what you need to focus on and what you can let go. And that means...

Most time problems really aren't

I certainly do recognize that some very bright students are simply slow readers who, given an extra ten or so minutes, would have no problem answering every question correctly. If you're one of those people, I don't mean to dismiss your experience. But from what I've observed, those cases are far less common than they are generally assumed to be. Usually people have difficulty finishing because either 1) they get hung up on a particular part of the passage that they find confusing – sometimes an irrelevant part because they don't know how to identify important information – and waste a lot of time reading and re-reading it, or 2) they get stuck between two answer choices and sit there staring at them, trying to figure out how to decide which one is right.

If something confuses you, ignore it and focus on what you do understand

You have a limited amount of time to get through each section, and that means you need to be constantly figuring things out. **Don't be afraid to skip around**: if you don't know how to work through a problem, you need to leave it and work on something you *can* answer. It doesn't matter if you have to leave a couple of the most time-consuming questions blank if doing so allows you to answer everything else correctly. Inference, analogy, strengthen/weaken, and "all of the following EXCEPT" questions take time, and sometimes there's no way to make them go quickly. If they take too much time, don't do them. The curve is substantial; you can still do very well without answering every single question.

Critical Reading is not a guessing game

If you consistently get down to two choices and always pick the wrong one, that's a sign that you either don't really know how to answer the questions or that you're not reading carefully enough. I've had a lot of students tell me they always got down to two and then guessed wrong when in fact they were missing the entire point of the passage. That's not a test-taking problem; that's a comprehension problem.

If you are just not reading carefully enough, slow down, put your finger on the page, make sure you're getting every single word, and make a concerted effort to think things through before you pick an answer.

On the other hand, if you really aren't sure how to choose between answers, you need to figure out what particular skills you're missing and work on them. If you're misunderstanding the passage because you don't know vocabulary words, you need to drill vocabulary; if you're getting thrown by complicated syntax, you need to spend more time reading SAT-level material; if you can't figure out what the author thinks, you need to focus on key phrases and places (e.g. last sentence of the first paragraph, end of the conclusion).

You also need to spend some time getting familiar with the kinds of answers that usually appear as correct and incorrect choices: if you know, for example, that *apathetic* and *ambivalent* are often wrong answers to tone questions, and that *emphatic*, *appreciative*, and *disdainful* often appear as correct answers, you'll be a lot less tempted to pick one of the former – even if you thought you *might* be able to argue for an interpretation that made one of them work. **Remember: just because an answer is there doesn't mean it can be correct.** If you look for reasons to keep answers, you'll never get down to one. But on the other hand…

Don't assume you'll always recognize the right answer when you see it

Incorrect answers are deliberately written to sound both reasonable and plausible. You might get away with jumping to the answers on easy and medium questions, but you'll almost certainly fall down on at least some of the hard ones, unless you do some legwork upfront. The test is designed that way. The fact that there are answer choices already there does not excuse you from having to think.

This is especially true for "function" or "purpose" questions. Because correct answers are phrased in a more general manner than the text itself, they do not always initially appear to be correct – or even directly related to the passage. **Confusing does not equal wrong.** If there's any chance an answer could work, you have to leave it until you see something better. Sometimes the right answer just won't say what you're expecting it to say, and in those cases, you need to keep an open-enough mind to consider that you've been thinking in the wrong direction and be willing to go back and revise your original assumption.

In addition, correct answers – especially those to questions about what Passage 1/Passage 2 authors agree on – may occasionally depend on a seemingly minor detail or less important facet of an author's argument; consequently, many test-takers eliminate them automatically, without stopping to actually consider whether they do in fact answer the question. This does not make the response any less correct – it just makes it harder to identify at first glance.

There are no trick questions

Before you start howling with laughter, hear me out. Critical Reading questions may be "tricky" – that is, they may require you apply very careful logic or make fine distinctions between ideas – but they're also set up so that you can figure them out logically. If they weren't, the test would be useless. The right answer might something that you're not expecting, but it can still be reasoned out. Wrong answers are wrong because they are based on various kinds of faulty reasoning. If you think your way carefully through a question and put the answer in your own words, then see an option choice that truly says the same thing, it's almost certainly correct.

Go back to the passage and read

Even if you are absolutely, incontrovertibly 100% certain of what the passage says in the lines cited, you probably need to go back and read it anyway (unless you can find the answer based on the main point). Stress makes memory unreliable; don't assume you can trust yours. You could be absolutely certain that you remember the author mentioning a particular idea in line 15 when in fact it doesn't show up until five or ten lines later and refers to something that *someone else* thinks. Don't play games or be cocky. Just take the extra few seconds and check.

Don't ever read just half a sentence

Context counts. If you only read the first (or last) half of a sentence, you might miss the fact that the author thinks exactly the *opposite* of what that half of the sentence says.

If the answer isn't in the lines you're given, it must be somewhere else

A line reference simply tells you that a particular word in the question appears in line so-and-so; it doesn't mean that the answer to the question is there. It might be, but if you read the lines you're given and can't figure out the answer, chances are it's located either before or after. Don't just assume you're missing something and guess. Again: be willing to revise your original assumption and start over. Yes, this will take time (although probably not as much as you think), but you're a whole lot more likely to get the correct answer.

When in doubt, reread the end of the conclusion

The point of the passage is more likely to be located at the end of the conclusion, usually the last sentence or two, than it is just about anywhere else. If you get lost and start to panic, stop and reread it to focus yourself. It won't work all the time, but it will work often enough.

Writing things down is not a sign of weakness

Most people don't have a huge problem writing down their work for Math problems; the same, alas, cannot be said for Reading. Unfortunately, one of the biggest differences between people scoring 650-720 and 750-800 is often their degree of willingness to write down each step of a problem. The very highest scorers tend to view writing each step down as a crucial part of the process necessary to get the right answer, whereas lower scorers often resent having to write things down, viewing it as a drag on their time or a sign of weakness that they should be above. It's not either of those things. Writing things down does not have to take a long time – you should abbreviate as much as possible, and the only person who has to read your handwriting is you. Writing also keeps you focused and takes some pressure off of your memory; everything you write down is one less thing your brain has to manage. If you're really certain what you're looking for, you probably don't need to spend the time. If you have any hesitation, though, it's worth your while. When you're under a lot of pressure, having even one less thing to worry about is a big deal. Besides, you probably wouldn't try to work the hardest Math problems out in your head, so why on earth would you for Reading?

The order in which you read the passage and do the questions doesn't really matter

While I would never encourage anyone to skip the passage entirely and jump straight to the questions (having even a general sense of the big picture makes it much, much easier to answer many of the questions), I certainly acknowledge that some people, especially those with serious timing issues, find it helpful to do the questions as they read the passage, saving the "big picture" questions for last. What truly matters is that you have the necessary close reading and reasoning skills to figure out or recognize the correct answers. **Strategy is not a substitute for skill**; rather, it's a way of leveraging the skills you do have to work efficiently and with the least possible amount of second-guessing.

Don't fight the test

It doesn't matter how much you want the answer to be (C) instead of (B). It never will be, and unless you want to file a complaint with the College Board, you're stuck. Instead of arguing about why your answer should have been right, try to understand why it was wrong – chances are you misunderstood something or extrapolated a bit too far along the way. If you're serious about improving, your job is to adapt yourself to the mindset of the test because it certainly won't adapt itself to yours. Who knows, you might even learn something.

And finally, a word of caution…

If you think Critical Reading is easy, you're probably doing something wrong

I'm only half-joking about this. I got an 800 on Critical Reading at the age of 17, have spent more time than anyone I've ever met analyzing it and writing questions, and I still think it's hard sometimes. Not impossible, but definitely a challenge. Consider that. If you do think it's easy and you're scoring above 750, good for you; you probably don't need this book in the first place (unless you want to be an SAT tutor). But otherwise, it might be worth your while to get just a little bit nervous. When that happens, it's a sign you're ready to deal with the test on its own terms. Which is exactly what this book is designed to teach you to do.

2. Vocabulary and Sentence Completions

For many test-takers, the vocabulary portion of the SAT is one of the most daunting aspects of the test. Although sentence completions comprise less than one-third of the total questions on the Critical Reading section, they test words that many high school students will never have encountered before.

One of the most important things to understand, however, is that the SAT is not a conventional vocabulary test – that is, what's tested is the ability to use the information you do have to figure out the information you don't have, and to make reasonable assumptions based on a careful and logical process of elimination. The ability to memorize hundreds or thousands of words is ultimately just as important as being able to use contextual clues and a basic knowledge of roots to make educated guesses about the meanings of unfamiliar words.

Believe it or not, the College Board does not intend for you to spend huge amounts of time trying to memorize 5,000 words; that's just not what the test is about. (If you're not a native English speaker or come from a home where the primary language spoken is not English, that's a little different, however.) Some of the most challenging questions actually test second or third meanings of very common words – words like "bent" and "conviction," which would be highly unlikely to appear on any SAT vocabulary list because they run exactly counter to most people's notion of what an "SAT word" is.

This is in no way to suggest that you do not need to study vocabulary: many of the core group of 300 or so "hard" words tested will in fact be unfamiliar and have the potential to cost you quite a few points, especially if you're getting most of the passage-based questions right. You need to put in the time and learn them.

The other reason that studying vocabulary is so important is that it will improve your comprehension of both the passages and the answer choices. Many of the same words tested in the sentence completions will also appear in the passages themselves. Furthermore, a number of passage-based questions do test vocabulary, some indirectly and some quite directly. Occasionally, all of the answer choices to a passage-based question will consist of SAT vocabulary words – if you don't know the meaning of the words, you simply can't answer the question with any degree of certainty.

Overview of Sentence Completions

Sentence completions appear at the beginning of each Critical Reading section. Each sentence contains either one or two blanks accompanied by five answer choices, all of which will be in the correct form (e.g. all verbs or all adjectives) necessary to complete the sentence in a grammatically correct manner.

Although the number per Critical Reading section and even the overall number of sentence completions per test can fluctuate slightly, the most common configuration is as follows:

-First Critical Reading section = 8 sentence completions

-Second Critical Reading section = 5 sentence completions

-Third Critical Reading section = 6 sentence completions

Each set of sentence completions is arranged in order of least to most difficult, but the difficulty is not cumulative from section to section. In other words, #8, the last sentence completions of the first Critical Reading section may have a difficulty level of 5 (most difficult), but the first sentence completion of the next Critical Reading section will start over at a difficulty level of 1.

Since memorizing vocabulary for the SAT is a rite of passage and one of the most talked-about aspects of the test, many students are surprised to discover that the SAT contains only about 20 sentence completions out of 67 questions. As a result, they sometimes underestimate the impact it can have on their score, particularly at the higher end. A test-taker who misses two vocabulary questions per section on each of three Critical Reading section can generally only miss *one* additional Critical Reading question on the entire test and still score above 700. As a result, anyone who does not already possess an exceptional vocabulary and wants to obtain a high Critical Reading score should expect to spend a significant amount of time learning words likely to appear on the SAT.

There is no "best" way to study vocabulary. Some people find pre-made flashcards helpful; others learn by writing definitions. Regardless of preferences, you should plan to spend at least 15 minutes or so per day reading a challenging contemporary publication (e.g. *The Economist, The New York Times*) and keep a running list of unfamiliar vocabulary words and their definitions. As a general rule, any word whose meaning you are not 100% certain of, or that you cannot define out of context, should be looked up and written down.

Types of Sentence Completions

Sentence completions test vocabulary in two ways: the first kind simply requires you to use contextual clues to determine meaning. While the words themselves may be challenging, the intended meaning is fairly clear. For example:

> Elvis Presley is regarded as one of the most important figures in twentieth-century popular music because of his unusually ------- repertory, <u>which encompassed genres ranging from country to pop ballads and blues.</u>
>
> (A) rebellious
> (B) noxious
> (C) eclectic
> (D) impulsive
> (E) somber

The phrase "which encompassed genres ranging from country to pop ballads and blues," tells us that we're looking for a word that means "containing lots of different types of things." The answer is (C) because that's exactly what "eclectic" means. This is a medium-level question since it's fairly straightforward but contains some choices that many high school students are unlikely to know (*noxious, eclectic,* and *somber*).

The second type of sentence completion is less about the words and more about the logic of the sentence itself. Often, these types of questions will contain **negations** so that you will be looking for a word that means the *opposite* of the idea being conveyed. For example:

> Because migrant workers experience a variety of cultures and see the world from ------- cultural perspectives, they are often capable of identifying opportunities easily overlooked by their **less** ------- counterparts.
>
> (A) eclectic . . provincial
> (B) diverse . . ambivalent
> (C) heterogeneous . . astute
> (D) myriad . . cosmopolitan
> (E) restricted . . pragmatic

For the first blank, the phrase "variety" of cultures suggests that the correct word means "many," but that only gets rid of (E). The second part of the sentence tells us that these workers are fortunate because they can spot opportunities that people who *haven't* experienced a variety of cultures would miss. But the word *less* means that the word in the blank must mean the **opposite** of *haven't experienced a variety of cultures*. In other words, the right answer means *have experienced a variety of cultures*. Which leaves only (D), cosmopolitan.

Occasionally, the most difficult questions will test the ability to follow the logic of a sentence as well as knowledge of advanced vocabulary, but the majority involve only one skill.

How to Work Through Sentence Completions

As is true for everything on the SAT, working carefully and systematically through sentence completions is the key to answering every question correctly that you are capable of answering correctly. I repeat: it does not matter how strong a vocabulary you have. Working this way ensures that you will not overlook crucial information or make careless errors. The scantron does not care whether you knew the answer – it just scores what you put down.

1) Identify and circle/underline the key words or phrases

Sentences will always contain built-in clues to either the definition of one or both words, or to the relationship between the words.

For a discussion of how to identify key words, please see the following page.

2) Plug your own words into the blank(s)

If you do this and one of the words is contained in an answer choice, check it first. There's no guarantee that it'll be right, but when it is, you can save yourself a lot of time.

Very often, the second blank is easier to figure out than the first, either because you simply won't have enough information about the first blank until you read further into the sentence or because the meaning of the first blank is dependent upon the meaning of the second. If that's the case, forget the first blank for the moment and start with the second one.

You should spend no more than a couple of seconds attempting to fill in your own word. It also doesn't matter if you just scribble down an approximate definition or even draw an arrow from the key part of the phrase to the blank. The point is to save time by getting an idea, even a general one, of what belongs in the blank – not to think of the perfect word (although if you can do that, great). Spending a lot of time on this step defeats its whole purpose.

Important: If you can't define with certainty the word that belongs in a blank, do NOT try to plug in something that might only sort of work. Plugging in a word when you're not really sure what belongs is a great way to set yourself up to overlook the right answer. If you're not sure exactly what belongs in a blank, skip this step and go to step #3.

3) Play positive/negative

Determine whether the word(s) in question are positive or negative – it won't always be clear, but when it is, this is an incredibly effective strategy. If the first blank is positive, draw a (+); if it's negative, draw a (–). Do not try to rely on your memory.

If you know that one blank is negative, for example, go through each answer from (A) to (E) looking *only* at the second blank. Do not skip around. Going in order keeps you thinking logically and systematically and reduces the chances that you'll overlook something important.

If the answer fits, keep it; if not, cross out the whole answer. If it's half-wrong, it's wrong.

If you're unsure of whether an answer fits, keep it.

Repeat for the other blank.

By now you should have gotten rid of at least two answers, sometimes three, and if you're really lucky, four. Plug the remaining options in and see which works best.

When to Guess and When to Skip

If you are left with more than one answer and are truly unsure of how to determine which one is correct, you should plan to skip the question. Wild guessing will not usually work in your favor, even if you've already eliminated several choices.

If, on the other hand, you can make an educated guess by using a root word (see p. 47 for a discussion of roots and p. 65 for a list of common SAT roots) or by relating a word you are uncertain of to a word you already know, you should answer it. For example, if you don't know what *alleviate* means but can relate it to the painkiller Aleve™, you can make a very good guess about its meaning. In fact, *alleviate* does mean "to lessen pain" or "make better."

As a general rule, any logical process you use to figure out an answer will be at least somewhat effective because it is precisely your ability to reason logically that the SAT is testing. You may not always get the answer for sure, but you'll usually get somewhere close enough to make a reasonably confident assumption.

Important: worry about what a word means, not how it sounds

While some words can clearly be eliminated immediately because they sound thoroughly incorrect in context, you need to consider things much more closely once you get down to a couple of answers.

At that point, you need to ignore the fact that a particular word, one whose meaning is consistent with what the sentence requires, may sound odd or unusual to you. Whether you yourself would think to use a given word is irrelevant – you are simply responsible for identifying the word with the most appropriate meaning. The right answer will not always be the answer you're expecting it to be or the answer you'd like it to be, and you need to realize that you may not be sufficiently well-read to always judge whether a word is truly strange in a particular context.

Using Context Clues to Predict Meanings

Whenever you read a sentence, one of the first things you should look for is the presence of **transition words:** words that indicate logical relationships between parts of the sentence.

Transitions fall into three basic categories:

Continuers

Continuers are words that indicate an idea is continuing in the direction it began.

> **Key words:**   and, also, in addition, as well as, furthermore, moreover, similarly, like(wise), even, not only…but also, just as

When they appear, you need to look for **synonyms** for other key words in the sentence, or for words that are generally consistent with those key words. For example:

> One of the ------- types of grain, sorghum can withstand harsh
> conditions and is especially important in regions where soil is poor
> **and** resources are -------.

Let's just focus on the second blank. The fact that the continuer "and" links the blank to the phrase "soil is poor" tells us that the word we're looking for goes along with the idea of poor soil and must be a negative.

Continuers also include **cause, effect, and explanation** words, which indicate that something is causing a particular result or explain why something is occurring.

> **Key words:**   so, because, in that, therefore, consequently, as a result
>
> **Punctuation:**   colons, dashes, semicolons (sometimes)

The presence of one of these words or punctuation marks also indicates that you are looking for a word consistent with other key words in the sentence.

> The first astronauts were required to undergo <u>mental</u> evaluation
> before their flight **because** the ------- danger inherent in space
> travel was judged to be as important as the physiological one.
> .

The transition "because" indicates that the word in the blank must go along with the idea of "mental evaluation" – it must mean something like "psychological."

Contradictors

Contradictors are words that indicate that a sentence is shifting directions, or that contrasting information is being introduced.

> **Key words:** but, however, while, whereas, despite/in spite of, nevertheless,
> for all (= in spite of), in contrast, unlike, belies

When these words appear, you need to look for **antonyms** for other key words in the sentence, or for words that are generally inconsistent with those key words. For example:

> **Although** the southern part of Tunisia is covered by the Sahara <u>desert</u>,
> the remaining areas of the country contain exceptionally ------- soil and
> hundreds of miles of coastline.

The word "although" tell us that the two parts of the sentence contain opposite ideas, and "Sahara desert" tells us that the word in the blank must mean the opposite of "dry" or "barren" – something along the lines of "healthy" or "good."

Parallel Structure

Parallel structure is an idea that you may be familiar with from studying for the multiple-choice Writing section, but it also applies to sentences completions. In such cases, the structure of the sentence itself tells you what sorts of words belong in the blanks. For example:

> The new translation is both -------- and -------: it captures the clarity of the
> original without sacrificing any of its subtlety or complexity.

Alternately, the sentence could be phrased in this way:

> Because it captures the clarity of the original without sacrificing any of its
> subtlety or complexity, the new translation has been praised for its --------
> as well as its --------.

In both cases, the two blanks are intended to run parallel to the two ideas expressed in the sentence. Blank 1 = clarity, Blank 2 = subtlety and complexity.

The colon in the first version and the word "because" in the second indicate the words in the blanks explain or elaborate on the idea that the translation is both subtle and complex.

Important: Two key phrases that sometimes confuse test-takers are *for all*, which means "despite," and *all but*, which means "essentially" or "more or less," not "everything but." These appear frequently, and if you don't know what they mean, it's very easy to misinterpret an entire sentence.

Let's work through a full question now and see how all the pieces fit together:

> Some butterfly species are regarded as **pests** <u>because</u> in
> their larval stages they can ------- crops or trees; <u>however,</u>
> other species play a more ------- role because their cater-
> pillars consume harmful insects.
>
> (A) infect . . detrimental
> (B) destroy . . nefarious
> (C) ruin . . dangerous
> (D) damage . . beneficial
> (E) fertilize . . helpful

The words "pest" and "because" tell us that the word that belongs in the first blank is negative and means something like "harm"

The word "however" indicates that the meaning of the word in the second blank will be the opposite of the meaning of the word in the first blank and will mean something like "nice."

In this case, both blanks are fairly straightforward, so it doesn't really matter which one we start with. Let's start with the first one.

We know it has to be negative, which means we can **eliminate** answers that contain **positive** or **neutral** words for the first blank. Unfortunately, *infect*, *destroy*, *ruin*, and *damage* are all fit. Only (E), *fertilize*, is positive.

We're going to put a line through the entire answer. Out of sight, out of mind.

> (A) infect . . detrimental
> (B) destroy . . nefarious
> (C) ruin . . dangerous
> (D) damage . . beneficial
> (E) fertilize . . helpful

Now we look at the second blank. We're looking for something positive:

-(A) Detrimental? Negative.

-(B) Nefarious? Maybe you're not sure. Leave it.

-(C) Dangerous? Negative.

-(D) Beneficial? Positive. Definitely works.

So now we're left with this:

    (A) ~~infect . . detrimental~~
    (B) destroy . . nefarious
    (C) ~~ruin . . dangerous~~
    (D) damage . . beneficial
    (E) ~~fertilize . . helpful~~

Both words clearly work for the first blank; the problem is the second blank.

This is a very common situation: often you can easily get rid of three answers but will be left with two answers choices. You'll know both words for one of the choices, but for the other choice will know only one. Even if you do know what "nefarious" means and can answer this question easily, please bear with me here because this is important.

The rule is that you always work from what you **do** know to what you **don't** know.

If the choice with the words you do know really works – which means that you don't have to "twist" the words at all or understand them in an unusual way to make them fit – then it's the answer. If that choice doesn't work, it's not the answer, and you need to go with the other option.

In this case, *damage . . beneficial* works, so it's the answer. The fact that you might not know what *nefarious* means is irrelevant.

And one more:

> Maria Elena Fernandez is considered an ------- in her field <u>because</u> <u>unlike nearly all present-day journalists</u>, she has a prose style that readers find <u>highly distinctive, even</u> -------.
>
> (A) anomaly . . unmistakable
> (B) iconoclast . . redundant
> (C) anachronism . . insipid
> (D) equivocator . . unforgettable
> (E) autocrat . . flippant

The first thing to notice about this sentence is there is no information about the first blank at the beginning of the sentence; its meaning does not become clear until we read further.

That means it's easier to start with the second blank.

The word "even" tells us that we're looking for a word that is a more extreme form of "distinctive." It's also a positive word because in American culture, standing out or doing something unusual is considered a good thing. I mention this because some of my students who grew up outside the United States or came from cultures that placed a stronger emphasis on conformity have been inclined to view such words negatively.

Going in order, we can eliminate (B), (C), and (E) entirely because *redundant* (repetitive), *insipid* (boring and unoriginal) and *flippant* (not taking something seriously) do not go along with the idea of "distinctive." (A) and (D) both fit.

> (A) anomaly . . unmistakable
> (B) iconoclast . . redundant
> (C) anachronism . . insipid
> (D) equivocator . . unforgettable
> (E) autocrat . . flippant

At this point, we need to consider the relationship of the first blank to the rest of the sentence, which tells us that Fernandez is *unlike* nearly all other present day journalists – in other words, she's unusual.

So which one means unusual, *anomaly* or *equivocator*? Well, if you're not sure how to figure it out (and even if you are), keep reading.

Using Roots to Make Educated Guesses

As we've just seen, a familiarity with roots will allow you to make educated guesses about the meanings of words and to quickly identify answers likely to be correct. In fact, learning how to take words apart in order to make reasonable assumptions about their meanings is just as important as memorizing lots of vocabulary words.

In some ways, it is actually far *more* important: if you've simply memorized a lot of definitions, you'll have no way of figuring out whether an unfamiliar word works or not and will be much less certain about the answer you choose. Knowing how the components of a word can reveal its meaning, however, gives you much more flexibility as well as more control, which in turn can give you a lot more confidence.

One of the most important things to remember about the SAT is that it's set up so that you can figure things out. That's what makes it a test of verbal reasoning rather than just an English test. If you have a little background knowledge and think calmly and logically about what's being asked, you can usually come to a reasonable conclusion. It doesn't matter if you're 100% percent sure – that's not the point.

So if you haven't been paying attention in foreign-language class, you might want to start (although admittedly it won't make much of a difference if you study Mandarin). An enormous number of high-frequency words on the SAT have Latin roots, which means that even though the English words being tested may be somewhat esoteric, they are in fact very similar to some extremely *common* French and Spanish and Italian words (everyday words in English tend to have Germanic, or Anglo-Saxon, roots).

If someone uses the word *facile* in English, they'll probably raise some eyebrows. But *facile* means *easy* in French – it's a word that gets used all the time. And if you know what *facile* means, you can make a pretty good assumption about *facility* ("ease"). Likewise, most people don't go around saying *arboreal* in English, but if you know that *arbre, arból,* or *albero* means *tree*, you can probably figure it out without too much trouble.

Let's come back to our question from the previous section:

> Maria Elena Fernandez is considered an ------- in her field <u>because unlike nearly all present-day journalists</u>, she has a prose style that readers find <u>highly distinctive, even</u> -------.
>
> (A) anomaly . . unmistakable
> (B) iconoclast . . redundant
> (C) anachronism . . insipid
> (D) equivocator . . unforgettable
> (E) autocrat . . flippant

Since both *unmistakable* and *unforgettable* fit, we need to decide between *anomaly* and *equivocator*. The root *equi-* means *equal* or *same*, which is the opposite of unusual, so we can make an educated guess that (D) won't work. On the flipside, the prefix *a-* means "not," and we're looking for something that means *not usual*. And in fact the answer is (A). An *anomaly* is something that's highly unusual (*a* = not + *nom* = name → without a name. It doesn't fit exactly, but it's in the same general area).

Let's look at one more example:

> Because he has authored numerous books that draw upon a
> wide range of fields, including many that he has never
> formally studied, Jared Diamond has earned a reputation
> as -------.
>
> (A) a heretic
> (B) a pedant
> (C) a polymath
> (D) an iconoclast
> (E) a pioneer

It's relatively easy to figure out that the word in the blank goes along with the idea of doing a lot of different things: Diamond has written books in a "*wide* range of fields," including "*many* that he has never formally studied." The problem is that when most test-takers look at a set of answers like the one above, they don't recognize any of the words except "pioneer" and maybe "heretic," and then they panic.

In reality, however, the question is much easier than it looks (something that the SAT specializes in) – if you can recognize that the prefix *poly-* means "many." It doesn't actually matter whether you know the exact definition of "polymath," or even the definitions of the other words; it's the ability to draw the logical connection between the wording of the sentence and that particular prefix – and to make an educated guess based on that understanding – that's really being tested. No, *poly-* isn't a Latin root (it's actually Greek), but it's still a very common prefix (think of a *polyhedron*), and if you know that, you have all the information you need to answer the question.

But, you say, that's only one part of one word. Aren't there a lot of other words there, and couldn't they be important too? In principle, yes; in reality, probably not. One of the other major things that the SAT tests is the ability to distinguish relevant from irrelevant information – just because an answer is there doesn't mean it's necessarily relevant. It could just be a plausible-sounding placeholder. Your job is to focus on the information that the question tells you is important and to ignore everything else. (This is an incredibly important concept for understanding passage-based reading questions as well.) If a root in an answer choice is consistent with a key word in the sentence, you need to pay attention.

You can also use roots to figure out whether words are positive or negative – even if you're not certain of the word itself. Sometimes that's the only information you even need. Remember this question?

> Some butterfly species are regarded as **pests** because in
> their larval stages they can ------- crops or trees; <u>however,</u>
> other species play a more ------- role because their cater-
> pillars consume harmful insects.
>
> (A) ~~infect . . detrimental~~
> (B) destroy . . nefarious
> (C) ~~ruin . . dangerous~~
> (D) damage . . beneficial
> (E) ~~fertilize . . helpful~~

Let's say for a moment that you weren't sure what *beneficial* meant. In that case, you could use the root *bene-*, which means "good" and always signals a positive word, to help you determine that the answer would fit. Even if you didn't know the definition of *nefarious*, you could still make an educated guess that (D) was the correct answer. To confirm your hunch, you could also observe that *nefarious* starts with *ne-*, like *negative*, and is therefore most likely wrong. And in fact, *nefarious* does mean "cruel."

Roots Can Be Misleading

While roots can generally help you figure out the meanings of unfamiliar words, they can occasionally be deceptive, too. Words with typically negative roots can sometimes be positive, and vice-versa. For example:

Though ------- and even attractive in appearance, nightshade has long been recognized as one of the most poisonous plants grown in the western hemisphere.

(A) stoic
(B) innocuous
(C) toxic
(D) disquieting
(E) ephemeral

The phrase "and even attractive in appearance," tells us that the word we're looking for must be positive. "Toxic" is pretty obviously wrong, but after that you might be a little bit stuck.

Here's where playing roots can get you into trouble: if you just go by the fact that *-in* and *-dis* are negative, you'll end up crossing out the right answer. Although words that begin with those prefixes *are* generally negative, in this case, "innocuous" is actually negating a negative: *in* = not + *noc* (Latin *nocere*) = harm → **not** harmful, which is positive and makes perfect sense in the sentence (it is in fact the answer). But to put that together, you have to know two roots – and chances are anyone who knows those roots probably already knows what "innocuous" means as well.

Unfortunately, aside from actually knowing what the words mean, there's no guaranteed strategy for recognizing these exceptions – you simply need to be aware that they exist. In general, though, your best bet is to simply use the rules you know: the exceptions are few, and using roots *will* get you the correct answer the vast majority of the time. Worrying about the exceptions can hurt you a lot more than it can help. If you start to view everything as a potential trick, you're much more likely to second guess yourself, even when your logic is solid. You also risk losing sight of the fact that the test is set up so that you can reason your way toward the answer, even if you're not 100% certain of what every word means. Given the choice between missing an occasional sentence completion and turning your back on an essential component of the test, you're much better off with the former.

Using Relationships to Determine Meanings

Sometimes, a sentence will give you no direct information about the meanings of the words in the blanks. In such cases, however, it will often give you information about the relationship between the words (same/opposite meanings, one a result of the other).

You therefore start by determining that relationship. Is one word the result of the other (both positive or both negative), for example, or is there a transition such as "but" that indicates the words have opposite meanings (one positive, one negative)?

Go through the answer choices looking only at that relationship: if it fits, keep it; if not, cross it out. If you can get down to two or three answers, plug in them and check them in the context of the sentence.

Here again, using roots can be a very effective way of determining relationship if you're not certain of the meanings of the words themselves. You will not be able to apply this strategy to every question, but when you are able to do so, it can be very effective.

For example:

> Far from being -------, the patterns woven into kente cloth, the traditional fabric of the Asante people, are created with a great deal of -------, with each symbolizing a key value such as family unity and collective responsibility.
>
> (A) dogmatic . . wariness
> (B) irrelevant . . candor
> (C) haphazard . . deliberation
> (D) trite . . banality
> (E) esoteric . . efficiency

Since there's no information in the sentence itself that tell us directly what we're looking for, we need to ignore it and just consider the relationship between the words in each choice. (Although if you happen know that kente cloth comes from Africa and that the SAT is generally positive toward all things African and African-American, you *can* make an educated guess that the second blank is positive and that the first blank is negative.)

Notice that most of the answer choices are "hard" words – this question tests both your ability to follow the logic of the sentence and your knowledge of the words themselves.

(A) dogmatic = holding rigidly to a belief; wariness = suspicious. Yes, opposites.

(B) irrelevant = not relevant; candor = openness, directness. No relationship.

(C) haphazard = by chance; deliberation = on purpose, with great care. Yes, opposites.

(D) trite and banality = unoriginal. No, same.

(E) esoteric = beyond normal understanding; efficiency = without waste. No relationship.

Now we're down to (A) and (C). *Dogmatic* is really only used to talk about a person's adherence to a belief or idea. And *wariness*? There's nothing in the sentence to explain why someone would be suspicious of cloth.

So the answer is (C). Logically, it makes sense that cloth-makers would use great care in choosing patterns that symbolize *key values*.

If you had no idea whether the words in (C) were opposites, though, and had been paying close attention in French class, you could figure it out this way: you probably know that *deliberately* means "on purpose," so the question is *haphazard*. *Hap-* is like "happen," and in French, *hasard* means "chance," hence *haphazard* means "happens by chance."

Will figuring out the answer that way be too big a stretch for most people? Yes, of course. But that's beside the point. The point is that there is an underlying logic to the answer choices, and you can use that logic to help you figure things out. If you approach studying for sentence completions with that idea in mind, you'll already be ahead.

Second Meanings are Usually Right

One of the cardinal rules of SAT sentence completions is that the closer you get to the end of the section, the less you can take for granted. On #1 or 2, or even #3, you can be pretty sure that if a word doesn't initially appear to fit the sentence, it's not going to be the answer. The same does not hold true at the end of the section, however. Mindlessly eliminating words that seem obviously – perhaps too obviously – wrong can get you in a good deal of trouble.

Sometimes the word that you want to show up just won't be among the answer choices, and sometimes the right answer is something that never would have occurred to you – even if you'd spent ten minutes staring at the question. That's why #8 is #8 and not #2. And that's also why, as you get close to the end of a section, you need to be particularly on the lookout for words that are being used in their second or third meaning. Why? Because the people at ETS know that those are the last words that it would occur to most test-takers to pick – which is precisely why they're likely to be correct. (Those psychometricians at the College Board may be nasty, but after hearing dozens of students say, "I never ever would have thought to pick that," I have to admit that they're remarkably accurate.)

But here we have a problem: it's not much help to know that second meanings are usually right if you can't recognize them! Admittedly, there's no surefire way around it. **As a general rule of thumb, though, you need to pay particular attention to "easy" words on hard questions, especially on the last question of a section, where second meanings are most likely to appear**. If you're on question #8 and see a simple word that seems too obviously wrong, you might need to think again. There's a pretty good chance it's being used in some other way. And if it's being used in some other way, there's a good chance it's correct. For example:

> Because the Symbolists believed that art should ------- absolute
> truths that can only be described indirectly, they wrote in a highly
> metaphorical and ------- manner.
>
> (A) suggest . . garrulous
> (B) convey . . lucid
> (C) represent . . elliptical
> (D) resist . . fervent
> (E) insist on . . cantankerous

Since the sentence provides relatively little information about the first blank, the key to the question is the second phrase. The word "and" tells us that the meaning of the second blank is a general synonym for "highly metaphorical." Scanning just the second side, a lot of people would, however, immediately jump to cross out *elliptical* because they associate ellipses with math or physics class and assume that they couldn't possibly have anything to do with art. The problem is that *elliptical* can also mean *obscure*, *cryptic*, or *impenetrable* – synonyms for "highly metaphorical." So in fact it fits perfectly; the answer is (C).

Important: words used in their second meanings also tend to be correct when they appear as answers to passage-based questions. You should therefore pay close attention to answers that contains words like "qualify" and "conviction."

Sentence Completion Exercises

Directions:

1) Identify and <u>underline or circle</u> the sentence "clues" that provide information about the word(s) required to complete each sentence.

2) Either fill in your own word or, if you are unable to do so, indicate whether each blank requires a positive or a negative word by <u>writing a (+) or a (−) in the blank.</u> Note that this strategy will not be applicable to every sentence.

3) For sentences that contain two blanks, consider each side separately, eliminating the <u>entire</u> answer when one side does not fit.

4) When you have completed steps 1-3, look at the answer choices provided, select the answer that logically fits the sentence.

1. In Ancient Egyptian art, human figures are presented in a rigid and ------- manner; in contrast, animals are often very well-observed and lifelike.

Circle or underline key words

Definition or (+/-): _____

(A) dazzling
(B) artificial
(C) revolutionary
(D) satirical
(E) realistic

2. The outwardly ------- appearance of the Afar Triangle, one of the world's most geologically active regions, belies the presence of fiery pools of lava lying just beneath its surface.

Circle or underline key words

Definition or (+/-): _____

(A) placid
(B) noxious
(C) cavernous
(D) belligerent
(E) ludicrous

3. Though well-done and expressive, Van Gogh's early drawings never succeed in approaching the level of ------- that marks his most celebrated works.

Circle or underline key words

Definition or (+/-): _____

(A) mediocrity
(B) instability
(C) virtuosity
(D) serenity
(E) efficiency

4. Because female hyenas remain within their clan and inherit their mother's rank, sisters must compete with one another to obtain a ------- position in the hierarchy.

Circle or underline key words

Definition or (+/-): _____

(A) relative
(B) cumbersome
(C) dominant
(D) surreptitious
(E) peripheral

5. Because music plays an essential role in facilitating social functions and is more effective than speech at improving people's moods, researchers are beginning to question whether it truly is as ------- as they once believed.

Circle or underline key words

Definition or (+/-): _____

(A) aesthetic
(B) mellifluous
(C) demanding
(D) invigorating
(E) frivolous

6. Paradoxically, the attainment of creative success nearly always requires the ------- of a cherished ideal or familiar way of working.

Circle or underline key words

(A) stipulation
(B) renunciation
(C) embellishment
(D) repetition
(E) dissemination

Definition or (+/-): _____

7. The camera obscura was perhaps the earliest known imaging device, --------- of the modern-day photographic camera.

Circle or underline key words

Definition or (+/-): _____

(A) a descendant
(B) a forerunner
(C) a relic
(D) a proponent
(E) an heir

8. To recreate the daily activities of Renaissance merchants as well as their worldview, the exhibition includes paintings and mercantile -------, from weighty ledgers to nautical maps.

Circle or underline key words

Definition or (+/-): _____

(A) diatribes
(B) paraphernalia
(C) caveats
(D) foibles
(E) euphemisms

9. English botanist James Edward Smith demonstrated a ------- interest in science, exhibiting an intense fascination with the natural world from the earliest years of his childhood.

Circle or underline key words

Definition or (+/-): _____

(A) cursory
(B) trivial
(C) hackneyed
(D) precocious
(E) circumspect

10. The company's leaders have a poor record of keeping their promises, raising the risk they will not be able to meet the most recent set of --- set out by union officials in the new contract.

Circle or underline key words

Definition or (+/-): _____

(A) innovations
(B) quandaries
(C) stipulations
(D) enigmas
(E) dichotomies

In the following questions, the answer choices for the two blanks have been separated so that you must consider each side separately. Do not mix and match answer choices (i.e. if you determine that (A) is the correct answer for the first blank, you must also choose (A) for the second blank.)

11. For centuries, ------- have questioned the authorship of Shakespeare's plays, ------- no fewer than fifty alternative candidates that include Francis Bacon, Queen Elizabeth I, and Christopher Marlowe.

Circle or underline key words

1st Definition or (+/-):

_____

2nd Definition or (+/-):

_____

First Blank:

(A) partisans
(B) detractors
(C) skeptics
(D) naysayers
(E) zealots

Second Blank:

(A) rejecting
(B) exonerating
(C) proffering
(D) embellishing
(E) detaining

Remaining Possibilities:

Answer:

_____

12. If it is to succeed, any new ------- for resolving disputes between workers and management must include a less ------- review board, one with members who are independent and neutral experts.

Circle or underline key words

1st Definition or (+/-):

_____

2nd Definition or (+/-):

_____

First Blank:

(A) paradigm
(B) proposal
(C) construct
(D) idea
(E) consensus

Second Blank:

(A) partisan
(B) erudite
(C) adept
(D) disinterested
(E) litigious

Remaining Possibilities:

Answer:

_____

13. All of the factors that allowed the Great Barrier Reef to ------- are changing at unprecedented rates and may cause it to ------- below a crucial threshold from which it cannot recover.

Circle or underline key words

1st Definition or (+/-):

_____

2nd Definition or (+/-):

_____

First Blank:

(A) grow
(B) diminish
(C) exist
(D) thrive
(E) flourish

Second Blank:

(A) evolve
(B) recover
(C) forestall
(D) deteriorate
(E) crest

Remaining Possibilities:

Answer:

_____

14. Although traditional historians and historical filmmakers differ in their choice of medium, the most respected ones share a ------- regard for facts and the rules of evidence that ------- their acceptability.

Circle or underline key words

1st Definition or (+/-):

_____

2nd Definition or (+/-):

_____

First Blank.

(A) blatant
(B) capricious
(C) pedantic
(D) sporadic
(E) scrupulous

Second Blank:

(A) mock
(B) determine
(C) derive
(D) underlie
(E) dictate

Remaining Possibilities:

Answer:

_____

Now try it on your own:

15. Although psychologists once ------- fiction as a way of understanding people, they have recently developed a new ------- for the insight that stories can provide into human behavior.

(A) pored over . . empathy
(B) condescended to . . preference
(C) scoffed at . . appreciation
(D) insisted on . . penchant
(E) wondered about . . disregard

16. Japanese artist Okakura Kakuzo is credited with ------- Nihonga, or painting done with traditional Japanese techniques, at a time when Western-style painting was threatening to ------- it.

(A) inventing . . emphasize
(B) salvaging . . supplant
(C) domesticating . . subsume
(D) demonstrating . . lionize
(E) perpetuating . . divert

17. Even as a child, Linnaeus never failed to be -------- by the presence of plants: when he grew upset, the sight of a flower would immediately ------- him.

(A) soothed . . placate
(B) angered . . mollify
(C) perplexed . . calm
(D) elated . . infuriate
(E) invigorated . . enervate

18. The space station is intended to ------- scientific progress, speeding the development of new technologies and ------- their integration into industry and medicine.

(A) hinder . . enabling
(B) accelerate . . facilitating
(C) permit . . mitigating
(D) enhance . . impeding
(E) debilitate . . simplifying

19. Though he occasionally experimented with ------- topics, the director always acquiesced to the demands of his audience and returned to more ------- subjects.

(A) controversial . . interesting
(B) recondite . . elaborate
(C) eclectic . . heterogeneous
(D) esoteric . . mundane
(E) somber . . bucolic

20. Like many of the surgeons general before her, Joycelyn Elders became an outspoken advocate for a variety of controversial health issues and quickly established a reputation for being a -------.

(A) pragmatist
(B) dichotomy
(C) conundrum
(D) polemicist
(E) sycophant

21. The whale is a remarkably ------- navigator, migrating thousands of miles each year without a compass and always arriving in precisely the same spot.

(A) belligerent
(B) compliant
(C) intractable
(D) ingenuous
(E) adept

22. Until well into the nineteenth century, most Europeans ------- the majority of their nutrients from bread, devoting half of their revenue to it and living in constant dread of -------.

(A) obtained . . abundance
(B) rejected . . excess
(C) derived . . scarcity
(D) consumed . . innovation
(E) tolerated . . famine

23. At its peak, roughly corresponding to the Middle Ages, Constantinople was the richest and largest European city, ------- a powerful cultural pull and ------- economic life in the Mediterranean.

(A) rejecting . . sustaining
(B) exerting . . dominating
(C) denying . . simplifying
(D) extolling . . thwarting
(E) renouncing . . determining

24. Beginning in 1900, Yeats renounced the transcendental beliefs of his youth and began to display a greater interest in ------- topics, writing about everyday cares and concerns.

(A) controversial
(B) insignificant
(C) abstruse
(D) quotidian
(E) tedious

25. Proponents of the Arts and Crafts movement claimed that its simple but refined aesthetics would ------- the new experience of industrial consumerism, making individuals more rational and society more harmonious.

(A) elevate
(B) differentiate
(C) quell
(D) assuage
(E) substantiate

26. In contrast to some of the more ------ children in his class, Michael is generally ------- and speaks only when prompted to do so by his teacher.

(A) gregarious . . vociferous
(B) diligent . . reticent
(C) indolent . . lazy
(D) jovial . . placid
(E) loquacious . . taciturn

27. Sharply criticized for his weak leadership and for his failure to create jobs and ------- poverty, the country's president was forced to ------- as a result of widespread protest.

(A) reduce . . conform
(B) perpetuate . . resign
(C) stimulate . . flee
(D) mitigate . . abstain
(E) alleviate . . abdicate

28. In the two-dimensional world of maps, sharp lines are used to indicate where one country ends and another begins, but in reality borders are typically much more -------.

(A) dense
(B) rigid
(C) fluid
(D) ephemeral
(E) identifiable

29. Thomas Jefferson believed that in order to ------- the horrors of war, enemy prisoners should be treated humanely and with -------.

(A) reduce . . aspersion
(B) mitigate . . compassion
(C) propagate . . joviality
(D) dilute . . scrutiny
(E) condone . . sympathy

30. Growing from several hundred residents in 1830 to nearly two million only eighty years later, Chicago epitomized the remarkable ------- of urbanization during the nineteenth century.

(A) mastery
(B) dilution
(C) rebuttal
(D) velocity
(E) moderation

31. While good metaphors can help us see the world in fresh and interesting ways, many others are simply -------, utterly lacking in originality and -------.

(A) hackneyed . . torpor
(B) superfluous . . decorum
(C) cloying . . boredom
(D) abstruse . . determination
(E) banal . . insight

32. Traffic engineers are rather ------- characters: although they determine the way we move through many kind of public space, we are rarely ------- the influence that they wield over our daily lives.

(A) obscure . . cognizant of
(B) effusive . . absent from
(C) ostentatious . . suspicious of
(D) didactic . . ignorant about
(E) protean . . impatient with

33. Although the building has many admirers who ------- its groundbreaking design, it also has numerous detractors who are far less ------- its construction.

(A) disparage . . enthusiastic about
(B) laud . . wary of
(C) praise . . resistant to
(D) extol . . enamored of
(E) impugn . . resigned to

34. The ancient Greeks ------- Orpheus as the greatest of all poets and musicians, often holding festivals to celebrate his art.

(A) symbolized
(B) venerated
(C) scrutinized
(D) disregarded
(E) challenged

35. Because the remote islands were settled
------- over a span of two centuries, their
cultures, dialects, and traditions are remarkably
-------.

(A) randomly . . esoteric
(B) rapidly . . substantive
(C) sporadically . . heterogeneous
(D) inconsistently . . profound
(E) separately . . cohesive

36. Smallpox, believed to have emerged human
populations around 10,000 B.C., is one of only two
infectious diseases to have been fully --------; the last
natural case occurred in 1977.

(A) exonerated
(B) emaciated
(C) eradicated
(D) exculpated
(E) exhorted

37. Even in pristine condition, the Balinese
carved doors would appear fragile and -------,
an impression that is heightened by the delicate and
feathery wooden blossoms that decorate
their edges.

(A) malleable
(B) diaphanous
(C) unwieldy
(D) specious
(E) indigenous

38. Although readers of Mark Twain's autobiography
may occasionally become bored with some of the more
------- references to nineteenth century scandals, the
work as a whole is seldom less than -------.

(A) opaque . . engaging
(B) daunting . . tedious
(C) dated . . stultifying
(D) obscure . . militant
(E) infallible . . enthralling

39. Famed for his ability to produce breathtaking
illusions, Houdini was also a notorious skeptic who set
out to expose ------- purporting to truly create
supernatural phenomena.

(A) misanthropes
(B) charlatans
(C) pugilists
(D) zealots
(E) adversaries

40. Until the swing era, jazz had been internationally -------
by serious musicians, who viewed it as a form of high art;
swing, on the contrary, was regarded as an industry to sell
records to the masses, all but devoid of ------- value.

(A) rejected . . artistic
(B) supported . . cacophonous
(C) lauded . . aesthetic
(D) criticized . . original
(E) censured . . harmonic

41. In order to ------- the demonstrations, government
officials finally agreed to ------- a number of the protestors'
demands.

(A) halt . . disparage
(B) perpetuate . . agree to
(C) denounce . . withhold
(D) prevent . . refuse
(E) quell . . acquiesce to

42. Historians often hold ------- views about when the
Harlem Renaissance began and ended: while some believe it
ended in the early 1930s, others argue that many of its ideas
-------, influencing artists and thinkers decades later.

(A) contrasting . . dissolved
(B) concurrent . . dissipated
(C) unshakeable . . endured
(D) divergent . . persisted
(E) incomprehensible . . declined

43. New knowledge about creatures that thrive in seemingly
hostile environments has made scientists less ------- to
accept the notion that life may persist on Mars.

(A) eager
(B) inclined
(C) reticent
(D) elated
(E) available

44. Although opposition to the creation of a park based on
Modernist principles has been limited, the criticism leveled
against city officials is nevertheless striking for the level of
its stridency and -------.

(A) vitriol
(B) parsimony
(C) equivocation
(D) restraint
(E) diffidence

45. J.R.R. Tolkien, who captivated millions of readers with his fantasy stories, was ironically ------- as a professor because his lectures were so dull as to be -------.

(A) celebrated . . byzantine
(B) tolerated . . unintelligible
(C) disdained . . soporific
(D) mistrusted . . unique
(E) reprimanded . . whimsical

46. True moral ------- is entirely absent from his writings: good characters are very good and bad ones very bad, their struggles untouched by doubt or -------.

(A) ambivalence . . hesitation
(B) interest . . obstinacy
(C) clarity . . uncertainty
(D) conflict . . jubilation
(E) engagement . . whimsy

47. While early experiences are not solely responsible for ------- an individual's personality, they do set pathways that can either be changed or ------- by later experiences.

(A) fostering . . altered
(B) shaping . . victimized
(C) determining . . reinforced
(D) molding . . simplified
(E) changing . . impacted

48. Because people generally overestimate how ------- their preferences are, they are frequently ------- to discover how much they have in common with those around them.

(A) trite . . puzzled
(B) common . . astonished
(C) distinct . . impatient
(D) eclectic . . perturbed
(E) unique . . surprised

49. A fondness for humble subjects and homely details characterizes much of Dutch art, and Rembrandt's paintings ------- this tradition in their focus on representations of daily life.

(A) analyze
(B) epitomize
(C) amplify
(D) subvert
(E) guarantee

50. The association between cultural values and economic outcomes is hardly ------- because economic success is dependent on numerous shifting political and historical factors.

(A) despicable
(B) immutable
(C) perplexing
(D) convoluted
(E) meticulous

51. Biologist Lynn Margulis's revolutionary theory of cell development was initially met with almost unanimous ------- because it built upon ideas that had largely been -------.

(A) ridicule . . integrated
(B) reverence . . rejected
(C) interest . . compromised
(D) befuddlement . . embraced
(E) skepticism . . discredited

52. Much like particular physics, modern medicine has become far too subtle and complex to offer -------; with so many different kinds of therapies available, it is often impossible to say which one will be most effective.

(A) solace
(B) immunity
(C) variety
(D) certainty
(E) elaboration

53. Because television has become the primary medium through which many people learn about past events, best-selling books about history are now seen as -------.

(A) anomalies
(B) harbingers
(C) diatribes
(D) paradigms
(E) heretics

54. Although historians working in prose may choose to write in the narrative tradition, many prefer to ------- scientific rather than literary models by exposing their subjects to intense ------- and thoroughly analyzing them.

(A) rely on . . indifference
(B) mock . . punditry
(C) emulate . . scrutiny
(D) defer to . . contempt
(E) eschew . . description

55. A scientific theory is presumed to be ------- until it is challenged by a hypothesis that explains the current data equally well and also accounts for ------- that the prevailing one cannot.

(A) useful . . quantities
(B) objective . . solutions
(C) unreliable . . anomalies
(D) duplicitous . . biases
(E) sound . . inconsistencies

56. The chronological scope of a memoir is determined by the work's context and is therefore more flexible than the ------- arc of birth to old age found in most autobiographies.

(A) convoluted
(B) ambitious
(C) concise
(D) linear
(E) redundant

57. Although Martina is typically outgoing and -------, in larger groups she becomes uncharacteristically -------.

(A) frank . . candid
(B) vociferous . . sympathetic
(C) gregarious . . diffident
(D) assiduous . . taciturn
(E) laconic . . aloof

58. Plans for the bridge's replacement have been ------- by ------- over the path the proposed structure would take across the river.

(A) facilitated . . arguments
(B) hindered . . squabbles
(C) dismantled . . consensus
(D) simplified . . discord
(E) suspended . . agreements

59. By breeding dogs to suit their tastes, the Victorians ------- created genetically isolated populations, little knowing how useful they might be to scientists in the future.

(A) inadvertently
(B) repeatedly
(C) deliberately
(D) strategically
(E) paradoxically

60. Authenticating a centuries-old work of art is seldom an ------- process; ego, personal tastes, and the desire to avoid error all inevitably influence the final judgment.

(A) observable
(B) efficient
(C) intuitive
(D) abstract
(E) objective

61. As human societies developed and people became increasingly connected to one another, the struggle for survival, mating and, reproduction became less dependent on physical abilities and more on social -------.

(A) stigma
(B) rebellion
(C) buoyancy
(D) acumen
(E) profligacy

62. The air we breathe is not an ------- physical phenomenon, like gravity or magnetism, but rather a precise combination of gases whose balance can be ------- by human actions.

(A) absolute . . venerated
(B) idiosyncratic . . reinforced
(C) arbitrary . . altered
(D) immutable . . upset
(E) effective . . contradicted

63. Although Emmy Noether's conceptual approach to algebra eventually proved to have many practical applications, it was at first controversial because many mathematicians then favored a ------- as opposed to a ------- method of investigation.

(A) theoretical . . an abstruse
(B) utilitarian . . an impulsive
(C) pragmatic . . an abstract
(D) philosophical . . a specific
(E) methodical . . a derivative

64. Voters who admire the candidate for the strength of her ------- are likely to ignore her well-publicized foibles and offer her their ------- support.

(A) principle . . tenuous
(B) beliefs . . theoretical
(C) convictions . . unqualified
(D) constituencies . . capricious
(E) ideas . . ruthless

65. Because it is highly organized and capable of carrying out sophisticated tasks by breaking them into simpler parts, ant society often serves as a ------- for understanding how complex jobs get done with small parts and minimal instructions.

(A) paradigm
(B) antidote
(C) doctrine
(D) tribunal
(E) catalyst

66. More than a week after the announcement that the university's president had been forced to resign after less than two years in office, the controversy over her removal continued to ------- and showed no sign of -------.

(A) increase . . amplifying
(B) diminish . . dwindling
(C) multiply . . aggregating
(D) intensify . . abating
(E) improvise . . subsiding

67. In order to bring an end to the country's internal struggles, the government must seek a comprehensive solution rather than settle for a ------- fix.

(A) malicious
(B) piecemeal
(C) creative
(D) nebulous
(E) permanent

68. Because new technologies are ------- established models of business and communication, companies must remain flexible in order to ------- their customers' evolving needs.

(A) disrupting . . adapt to
(B) encouraging . . undermine
(C) overturning . . detract from
(D) fostering . . stabilize
(E) subverting . . validate

69. Much as he loved fine craftsmanship, architect Arne Jacobsen held ------- principles; that is, he believed every element of a design project should be determined by its intended purpose.

(A) aesthetic
(B) deterministic
(C) utilitarian
(D) inscrutable
(E) complex

70. Because the international court is -------, composed of both foreign and domestic officials, it cannot escape the laws of the country that hosts and achieve true -------

(A) a conglomerate . . integration
(B) an amalgam . . ratification
(C) a monolith . . equivocation
(D) a paragon . . judiciousness
(E) a hybrid . . autonomy

71. Finding a way to prevent or delay certain diseases has become a priority for researchers because decades of research have resulted in only a few treatments that become all but ------- after just a few months.

(A) ineffective
(B) essential
(C) baffling
(D) magnanimous
(E) advantageous

72. Forming alliances and sharing gossip are two of the ways people ------- power from friendships; as a result, tyrannies are sometimes very ------- toward them.

(A) extract . . conducive
(B) derive . . hostile
(C) obtain . . obstinate
(D) mitigate . . menacing
(E) ascertain . . amicable

73. For all its flaws, the book is the product of a well-informed and ------- thinker and lacks many of the more objectionable aspects that often -------- works of its kind.

(A) astute . . embellish
(B) hackneyed . . substantiate
(C) lucid . . mar
(D) vacuous . . detract from
(E) erudite . . elevate

74. Standing aloof from academic squabbles, the author is able to put scholarly findings in perspective and ------- them in a language that is remarkably free of impenetrable -------.

(A) convey . . jargon
(B) disparage . . neologisms
(C) analyze . . colloquialisms
(D) discuss . . jaundice
(E) promote . . sophistries

75. The ------- of the tormented writer in his own life, Tolstoy nonetheless succeeded in producing fictional masterpieces of ------- introspection and humane insight

(A) alias . . enigmatic
(B) demagogue . . trite
(C) antithesis . . negligible
(D) epitome . . serene
(E) pseudonym . . marginal

Common Roots and Prefixes

Positive

Ama - Love
amiable = easy to get along with

Amic - Friend
amicable = friendly

Ana - Not, without
Anarchy = without rule

Bene - Good
beneficial = helpful, good
(bene + fic = do, something that does good)

Eu - Happy
Euphoria = joyful exhilaration
Euphonic = pleasant sounding

Fid - Loyal
perfidy = disloyal
(per = through or beyond+ fid = literally "beyond loyalty")

Lev - Light (weight)
alleviate = to relieve from pain, literally "to make lighter"

Luc, Lux - Light (absence of dark)
lucid = clear

Magna - Large
magnanimous = very generous
(magna + anim, soul/spirit = greatness of spirit)

Moll - Soft
emollient = substance that softens
mollify = pacify, calm down, literally "make soft"

Multi - Many
multifarious = complex, having many different aspects

Pac, Plac - Peace
placate = to soothe, make peaceful

Poly - Many
polymath = person knowledgeable about or accomplished in many different areas

Pro - In favor of
prolong = make longer

Val - Value
Valid = True, literally "having value"

Vener - Worship, Love
venerate = hold in high regard

Ver - True
verisimilitude = appearance of truth
(ver + simil, similiar = similar to the truth)

Vig Energy
vigorous = energetic, full of life

Negative

A - Not, Without
anomalous = unusual, literally "without name"

Anti - Against
antipathy = dislike

Bell - War
belligerent, bellicose = threatening, violent

Contra - Against
contrast = difference

Culp - Guilt
exculpate = free from guilt
(ex = from + culp)

Deb - Weak
debilitate = to make weak, cripple

Dis - Not
disparage = to put down, insult

Err - Wrong
erroneous = wrong

Fall - Wrong
fallacious = false

Fict - False
fictitious = fake, false

Im, In - Not
ineffable = inexpressible

Neb - Cloud
nebulous = cloudy, unclear

Pej - Bad
pejorative = insulting

Pug - Violent
pugnacious = violent, looking for a fight

Vac - Empty OR Waver
vacuous = empty, meaningless

Neutral or positive/negative based on context

Ambi - Both
ambivalent = having mixed feelings, unable to choose between two sides

Ante - Before
antebellum = before the war
(ante + bellum, war)

Anthro - Human
Misanthrope = one who hates people

Auto - Self
autonomous = independent

Bi - Two
Bifurcate = split down the middle

Chron - Time
anachronism = in the wrong time period (a record player is an anachronism in the 21st century)
(ana = not + chron = not in time)

Circum - Around
circumspect = careful, cautious
(circum + spect, look = to look around)

Co, Con - With
condescending = looking down on, disdainful

Cog - Think
cognition = thought

Corp - Body
corporeal = having a body

Di - Two
dichotomy = contradictory, separated into two mutually exclusive groups or ideas

Dia - Through
dialect = regional or local form of a language
(dia + lect, read = read through)

Dict - Say
dictum = saying, cliché

Dom - Mastery
dominate = have power over

Dur - Hard, Lasting
endure = last

E, Ex - From
extemporaneous = done without preparation
(ex + temp, time = away from time)

Equi - Equal, Same
equivocal = unclear or using ambiguous
language, sometimes with the intention to
mislead
(equi + voc, voice = literally "equal voice")

Fac, Fic - Make, do
facile = easy (literally "doable")

Gen - Knowledge, Innate, Type
ingenuous = naive
(in = not + gen = not having knowledge)
genre = type, category
genetic = from the genes, innate

Grav - Weight, Serious
gravity = seriousness

Hetero - Different
heterogeneous = varied, multifaceted
(hetero + gen = different types)

Homo - Same
homogeneous = same
(homo + gen = same type)

Inter - Between
interrupt = come between

Lib - Free OR Book
liberate = to set free

Loc, Loq - Words, Speech
loquacious = talkative

Mal - Bad
malicious = cruel, evil

Ment - Mind
mentality = mindset

Morph - Shape
amorphous = shapeless

Mut - Change
immutable = fixed, unchanging
(im = not + mut)

Nerv - boldness, courage
enervate – to sap of energy
(e = from + nerv = take away courage)

Nom - Name
nominal = literally "in name only"

Ob - Against
obdurate, obstinate = extremely stubborn

Os - Bone
ossify = become hard, like bone

Para - Alongside, Contrary to
Paradox = contradiction, two seemingly
contradictory ideas

Ped - Foot OR Child
pedestrian = boring, unoriginal (literally,
"like a child would do")

Pend - Hang
pendulous = hanging, heavy

Per - Through
perspicacious = perceptive
(per + spic = look, look through)

Peri - Around
periphery = border

Phon - Sound
euphony = pleasing sounds
(eu, happy + phon)

Port - Carry
portentous = significant, amazing, (literally "carrying a lot of weight")

Pot - Power
potent = powerful, potentate = a powerful person

Re - Again
revive = bring back to life
(re + viv, live = make live again)

Scrut - Look, Examine
Scrutinize = Look very closely

Sens, Sent - Feel
sentimental = emotional, displaying or appealing to tender feelings

Seq - Follow
obsequious = follower, toady

Spec/Spect - Look
spectator = one who watches

Stat - Stand
static = unmoving, literally "in a state of standing"

Sub - Below
substantiate = support, prove (literally "stand below")

Super - Above
supercilious = condescending
(super + cil = eyelash, literally looking down from above)

Tac - Silence
taciturn = silent, not talkative

Temp - Time
temporize = procrastinate, take too much time

Ten - Hold
tenacious = stubborn, literally "holding on"

Terr - Earth
terrestrial = having to do with the earth

Tract - Move
intractable = stubborn

Trans - Through
intransigent = stubborn, unmovable

Vap - Air, Steam
evaporate = to become air

Ven - Come
advent = beginning, literally "coming of"

Vid - See
invidious = envious
(in = not + vid = see, literally "unable to see," i.e. jealousy is blinding)

Vit, Viv - Life
convivial = merry, lively
(con = with + viv = with life)
vitiate = to sap of life, tire out

Voc, Vox - Voice
vociferous = loud

Vol - Desire, Fly (v.), Volume
volatile = unstable, having the potential to explode (literally "ready to fly off")

Volut - Turn, Twist
convoluted = extremely intricate or complex
(con = with + volut = turn, literally "with lots of turns")

Vocabulary Lists

List 1

Adroit
Capricious
Circumspect
Didactic
(Un)Equivocal/equivocate
Esoteric
Ineffable
Magnanimous
Obsequious
Pedantic
Pedestrian
Pragmatic
Quixotic
Sycophant
Tacit(urn)

List 2

Aloof
Banal
Censure
(Dis)ingenuous
Disparage
Duplicitous
Eschew
Extol
Heterogeneous
Iconoclast
Innocuous
Laconic
Meticulous
Mitigate
Substantiate/Unsubstantiated

List 3

Alleviate
Assiduous
Bellicose
Convoluted
Cosmopolitan

Deleterious
Ephemeral
Obstinate
Paradigm
Transitory
Scrutinize
Superfluous
Undermine
Venerate
Wary

List 4

Abstruse
Ascetic
Bombastic
Candid
Contemptuous
Derivative
Gregarious
Hackneyed
Motley
Penchant
Provincial
Supercilious
Tout
Vitriolic
Whimsical

List 5

Acumen
Acquiesce
Aesthetic
Assuage
Benign
Bucolic
Caustic
Diligent
Eclectic
Flippant
(In)tractable
Laud

Munificent
Trite
Vernacular

List 6

Anomaly
Capitulate
Charlatan
Heretic
Immutable
Insipid
Intrepid
Lucid
Mundane
Obdurate
Partisan
Penury
Surreptitious
Tenacious
Vindicate

List 7

Adept
Alacrity
Diffident
Disseminate
Enigmatic
Erudite
Loquacious
Mirthful
Prosaic
Reticent
Sedulous
Soporific
Succinct
Tangential
Vapid
Zealot

List 8

Abate
Belligerent
Cacophony
Circumscribe
Dilettante

Euphemism
Garrulous
Jovial
Misanthrope
Parochial
Perfidy
Protean
Pugnacious
Vacuous
Venerate

List 9

Beguiling
Byzantine
Chary
Dearth
Dogmatic
Exculpate
Expedient
Fervid/Fervent
Forestall
Harbinger
Interminable
Obtuse
Paragon
Prolific
Serendipity

List 10

Amiable
Cloying
Condone
Contentious
Digression
Dormant
Idiosyncratic
Inchoate
Infallible
Myriad
Peripheral
Placate
Recondite
Revere
Zenith

List 11

Amorphous
Arbitrary
Benevolent
Elated
Enthrall
Impugn
Ludicrous
Marginal
Paucity
Perfunctory
Polemical
Sanguine
Sardonic
Terse
Vacillate

List 12

Aplomb
Augment
Cantankerous
Disdain
Epitome
Foible
Haphazard
Indignant
Mellifluous
Obstreperous
Predilection
Redolent
Renounce
Sanction
Stoic

List 13

Abeyance
Astute
Audacious
Castigate
Circumvent
Diaphanous
Diatribe
Incredulous
Maverick
Maudlin

Prurient
Rectitude
Utilitarian
Veracity

List 14

Adversary
Anachronistic
Cavalier
Dispel
Idealistic
Indelible
Jingoistic
Mercurial
Palliate
Perspicacious
Platitude/Platitudinous
Profligacy
Quotidian
Stipulate
Voracious

List 15

Admonish
Amalgam
Ambivalent
Arduous
Buoyant
Captious
Copious
Dichotomy
Evade
Lackadaisical
Permutation
Propensity
Pundit
Quibble
Subvert

List 16

Ancillary
Belabor
Callous
Dilatory
Fortuitous

Germane
Ingenious
(In)temperate
Intransigent
Malignant
Mendacious
Prescient
Recalcitrant
Vestige
Wistful

List 17

Austere
Bemused
Conciliatory
Converge
Deride
Exonerate
Galvanize
Hapless
Indigent
Nonplussed
Onerous
Renege
Seminal
Spurious
Stilted

List 18

Averse/Aversion
Baleful
Chicanery
Compunction
Discrete
Fallacious
Forestall
Frenetic
Incendiary
Indigenous
Itinerant
Rancor
Repudiate
Specious
Trenchant

List 19

Appease
Bolster
Cajole
Fleeting
Implacable
Impromptu
Mercenary
Officious
Ostentatious
Peripatetic
Philanthropist
Preclude
Proliferate
Unprecedented
Volatile

List 20

Adulation
Conjecture
Cursory
Expurgate
Exultant
Florid
Malleable
Mimetic
Multifarious
Nominal
Portentous
Propitiatory
Spurn
Sybaritic
Vituperate
Voluble

List 21

Eulogy
Euphony
Excavate
Exhort
Dispassionate
Facetious
Mawkish
Nadir
Ostensible

Panache
Plasticity
Prognosticate
Rapacious
Stagnate/Stagnant
Treacly

List 22

Denizen
Divulge
Expedite
Extemporaneous
Imperious
Judicious
Libel
Myopic
Polymath
Proclivity
Ruminate
Sheepish
Sophistry
Torpid/Torpor
Voluptuous

List 23

Acrimony
Apprise
Bashful
Beguile
Conflate
Delectable
Edify
Empiricism
Explicate
Fickle
Inculcate
Rebut
Reiterate
Resuscitate
Simulate

List 24

Blunder
Connoisseur
Equanimity
Expunge
Forbearance
Imperturbable
Meld
Nullify
Ratify
Reconcile
Rhetoric
Solvent
Synthesize
Truncate
Watershed

List 25

Aspersion
Becalm
Denigrate
Denounce
Disquiet
Flustered
Humbuggery
Indispensable
Phlegmatic
Picayune
Protégé
Quackery
Serene
Untenable
Unwieldy

Top Words by Category

Unoriginal/Lacking in Substance - Prosaic, Pedestrian, Banal, Cliché, Trite, Hackneyed, Vapid, Vacuous, Quotidian, Mundane, Insipid, Derivative

Stubborn - Obstinate, Obdurate, Intransigent, Intractable, Tenacious

Brief - Fleeting, Ephemeral, Transitory, Cursory, Transient

Beyond normal human understanding - Esoteric, Recondite, Abstruse, Arcane

To Make Better/Relieve Pain - Ameliorate, Alleviate, Assuage, Mitigate, Palliate

Varied, Diverse - Heterogeneous, Eclectic, Motley, Multifarious

Talkative/Outgoing - Loquacious, Garrulous, Gregarious

Using few words - Laconic, Terse, Perfunctory, Spare, Economical

To Insult - Impugn, Disparage, Deprecate, Malign, Censure (also means punish), Decry, Vilify, Vituperate

To Praise/Hold in high regard - Tout, Extol, Revere, Laud

Generosity - Munificence, Magnanimity (Adj. = Magnanimous), Largess

Greed - Avarice, Cupidity

Poor - Indigent, Penurious, Impecunious

Inclination toward - Penchant, Proclivity, Predilection, Affinity, Bent

Prevent - Forestall, Preclude, Thwart

Highly decorated - Florid, Ornate, Baroque

Shy - Reticent, Aloof, Diffident, Reticent

Hardworking - Assiduous, Diligent, Sedulous

Cheerful - Jovial, Jocund, Mirthful

Overjoyed - Exultant, Elated, Jubilant, Ebullient

Lazy - Indolent, Slothful

Arrogant - Condescending, Supercilious

Complicated - Byzantine, Convoluted, Intricate

Clear - Lucid, Perspicuous

Harsh, Burning - Caustic, Vitriolic

Sickeningly Sweet - Cloying, Treacly, Maudlin, Mawkish

Mystery - Enigma, Conundrum

Unpredictable - Mercurial, Capricious

Narrow-Minded - Provincial, Insular, Parochial

Broad-Minded - Cosmopolitan

Small Amount - Paucity, Dearth

Large Amount - Myriad, Copious, Plethora

Fake - Spurious, Specious

Suspicious of - Wary of, Chary of

Fraud, Trickery - Charlatanism (Person who is a fraud = Charlatan), Chicanery

Naive - Ingenuous, Guileless

Calm - Phlegmatic, Placid (Verb: To Placate), Serene

Easily Angered - Irascible, Cantankerous

Violent - Bellicose, Pugnacious

Supplementary, not of central importance - Ancillary, Peripheral, Tangential

Irrelevant, Unimportant - Picayune, Trivial

Free from blame, find innocent - Exonerate, Exculpate, Vindicate

Practical - Pragmatic, Prudent

Common Second Meanings

Afford – Grant (e.g. an opportunity)

Appreciate – To take into account, recognize the merits of, OR to increase in value

Arrest – To stop (not just put handcuffs on a criminal)

Assume – To take on responsibility for, acquire (e.g. to assume a new position)

Austerity – Financial policy to reduce excess spending on luxury or non-essential items

Badger – To pester or annoy (e.g. reporters repeatedly badgered the candidate after the scandal broke)

Bent – Liking for. Synonym for *penchant, predilection, proclivity*

Capacity – Ability

Chance – To attempt

Check – To restrain, control, or reduce (e.g. *The vaccine checked the spread of the disease*)

Coin – Invent (e.g. coin a phrase)

Compromise – To endanger or make vulnerable (e.g. to compromise one's beliefs)

Constitution – Build (e.g. a football player has a solid constitution)

Consummate – Total, absolute (e.g. a consummate professional)

Conviction – Certainty, determination. Noun form of *convinced.*

Couch – To hide

Discriminating – Able to make fine distinctions (e.g. a *discriminating* palate)

Dispatch – Speed, efficiency (e.g. *She completed the project promptly and with great dispatch*)

Doctor – To tamper with

Economy – Thrift (e.g. a writer who has an *economical* style is one who uses few words)

Embroider – To falsify, make up stories about

Execute – To carry out

Exploit – Make use of (does not carry a negative connotation)

Facility – Ability to do something easily (e.g. *a facility for learning languages*)

Foil – To put a stop to (e.g. to foil a robbery), OR a secondary character in a play/novel

Grave/Gravity – Serious(ness)

Grill – To question intensely and repeatedly (e.g. *The police officers grilled the suspect thoroughly*)

Hamper – To get in the way of, hinder

Harbor – To possess, hold (e.g. to harbor a belief)

Hobble – Prevent, impede

Mint – To produce money, or as an adjective = perfect, like new

Plastic – Able to be changed, malleable (e.g. brain plasticity)

Provoke – Elicit (e.g. a reaction)

Realize – To achieve (a goal)

Reconcile – To bring together opposing or contradictory ideas

Relay - To pass on to someone else (e.g. to relay information)

Relate – To tell, give an account of (a story)

Reservations – Misgivings

Reserve – To hold off on (e.g. to reserve judgment)

Ruffled – Flustered, nonplussed

Sap – To drain (e.g. of energy)

Scrap – To eliminate

Shelve/Table – To reject or discard (e.g. an idea or proposal)

Solvent – Able to pay all debts (usually used in a business context)

Sound – Firm, stable, reliable, valid (e.g. a sound argument)

Spare, Severe – Unadorned, very plain

Static – Unchanging (i.e. in a state of *stasis*)

Sustain – To withstand

Uniform – Constant, unvarying

Unqualified – Absolute

Upset – To interfere with an expected outcome

Commonly Confused Words

Adverse – Difficult, challenging
Averse – Disliking for

Amused – Happily entertained
Bemused – Puzzled

Anecdote – Story
Antidote – Substance that neutralizes a poison

Ascetic – One who rejects worldly pleasures
Aesthetic – Related to beauty

Censor – To restrict or remove offensive information
Censure – To punish or limit

Diffident – Aloof, standoffish
Different – Unlike

Discreet – Secretive
Discrete – Separate, distinct

Elicit – To draw out, provoke
Illicit – Illegal

Exceptional – Out of the ordinary
Exceptionable – Unpleasant

Eminent – Distinguished, well-respected
Imminent – About to happen

Ingenious – Clever
Ingenuous – Naïve

Perspicacious – Perceptive, astute
Perspicuous – Clear

Uninterested – Not interested
Disinterested – Objective

Words that Look Negative But Aren't

Critic/Criticism – A critic is a person who writes commentary about literature or art. That commentary can be either positive or negative.

Discern/discerning – To recognize or distinguish; perceptive

Ineffable – Indescribable, sublime, beyond words

Infallible – Unable to be wrong

Ingenious – Clever, brilliant

Ingenuous – Naïve

Inimitable – Unique, one-of-a-kind

Innate – Inborn, natural

Innocuous – Harmless

Intrinsic/Innate – Inborn, a natural part of

Invaluable – Having immense value, priceless

Unassuming – Modest

Unqualified – Absolute

Explanations: Sentence Completion Exercises

1. The correct answer is **(B)**. The word "rigid" is a clue word for this question; it lets you know that the blank will mean something similar to rigid. The second half of the sentence tells you that *in contrast* to the human figures, animals are lifelike: in other words, the human figures are NOT lifelike. Thus, for the blank, you want a negative word that means "rigid" or "not lifelike." "Dazzling," "revolutionary," "satirical," and "realistic" don't mean "not lifelike," so cross them off. "Realistic" is a tempting choice, but remember: you want a word that means the *opposite* of "lifelike," not the same thing. Choice (B) is the only word that fits, so (B) is correct..

2. The correct answer is **(A)**. In this sentence, the word "belies" signals a contradiction, letting you know that the outer appearance will somehow form a contrast to the "fiery pools of lava." Good words to fill in the blank here might include "peaceful" or "safe." Choice (A) is the only answer that logically contrasts with fiery pools of lava (placid means "peaceful;" think of the root PLAC-, meaning "peace"), so (A) is the right answer. "Cavernous" might seem to fit because it logically fits with underground pools of lava, but remember that you want a contrasting word for the blank. "Noxious," "belligerent," and "ludicrous" don't mean "peaceful," so cross them off. Even if you aren't sure about "noxious" and "belligerent," you can use the roots NOC/NOX- (harm) and BELL- (war), to figure out that they're both negative.

3. The correct answer is **(C)**. The sentence tells you that his early drawings are "well-done and expressive," but they don't quite reach the "level of _____" of his "most celebrated" works. This lets you know that the second blank will be a better or more emphatic version of "well-done and expressive." For your own word, try filling in "genius" or something similar. "Mediocrity" and "instability" are negative, so cross them off. Even if you don't know what "mediocrity" means, look for the root MED-, which has to do with the middle: something in the middle isn't likely to be outstanding or genius. "Serenity" and "efficiency" are positive, but neither one of them is a stronger way of describing something "well-done and expressive." Answer choice (C) is correct because "virtuosity" means "genius."

4. The correct answer is **(C)**. "Compete with one another" is a key phrase in this sentence; it tells you that word in the blank will be something positive (something that the sisters want to compete for). "Hierarchy" lets you know that the word will have something to do with status or power, because a hierarchy is a way of ranking individuals according to authority or superiority. "Relative" seems to fit with "position" at first, but remember that you want a word describing a *good* kind of position; "relative" only means "in relation to something else," so it could be good or bad. Thus, you can cross off "relative," "cumbersome," "surreptitious," and "peripheral" because these words all have negative or neutral connotations. Even if you aren't sure what "peripheral" means, you can use the root word PERI- (around) to help you: you want a word that means "on top," not "around the outside." The only answer choice left with a strong positive connotation is "dominant," and since "dominant" also refers to superiority and power, (C) is the correct answer.

5. The correct answer is **(E)**. Key words in the first part of the sentence include "essential role" and "effective." These positive qualities are the reasons why scientists are doubting the characterization of music "as _____." Therefore, you know that the word in the blank has to be a negative word, the opposite of "essential" or "effective." "Useless" or "silly" might be good words to fill in the blank. "Aesthetic" is a tempting choice because music *is* aesthetic, but this doesn't fit in the context of the sentence. "Invigorating" is also tempting, because it means almost the same thing as "more effective than speech at improving people's moods," but remember that you want a word that means the *opposite* of this. "Mellifluous" is positive (think of the same root in "melody"), so you can cross off (B). "Demanding" is negative, but doesn't mean "useless." "Frivolous" means "having no practical purpose," so (E) is correct.

6. The correct answer is **(B).** The key word "paradoxically" tells you that the two parts of the sentence will contrast with each other. So, since "creative success" in the first part is a positive idea, it will require something negative in the second part.

"Stipulation," "embellishment," "repetition," or "dissemination" of a cherished ideal aren't negative. If you aren't sure what "dissemination" means, note the roots DIS- (apart) and SEM- (seed): to disseminate is to spread something around. The "renunciation" (giving up – notice the prefix RE-, "back") of something precious is negative, so (B) is correct.

7. The correct answer is **(B).** The key word in this sentence is "earliest known;" this clues you in that you could fill in "an early form" or something similar for the blank. (A) and (E) are both trap answers because they give you the opposite of what you want: the modern-day camera is a "descendant" or an "heir" of the camera obscura, not the other way around. A "relic" is a leftover, so (C) is also backwards. "Proponent" makes no sense: look at the root words PRO- (supporting) and PON- (put): a proponent is a supporter. Since "forerunner" means "early form," choice (B) is the right answer.

8. The correct answer is **(B).** The key phrase here is "*from* weighty ledgers *to* nautical maps." Even if you aren't sure exactly what a ledger is, the construction "from…to" lets you know that you're looking for a word describing many different kinds of physical things. "Diatribes" (rants), "caveats" (warnings), "foibles" (faults), and "euphemisms" (nicer ways of saying unpleasant things – note the root EU-, "good" or "well") aren't physical things that you could show off in an exhibition. The only word that fits in the blank is (B), paraphernalia.

9. The correct answer is **(D).** The key words are "from the earliest years of his childhood:" you want a word in the blank that refers to a very young age. "Cursory," "trivial," "hackneyed," and "circumspect" don't have anything to do with a young age. For "circumspect," note the roots word CIRCUM (around) and SPEC- (look at), which can give you a clue that this isn't the word you want. "Precocious" means "starting unusually young" (the root PRE-, "before," will give you a clue about this even if you aren't sure what "precocious" means), so the answer is (D).

10. The correct answer is **(C).** A key word here is "promises." The question specifies that because the leaders have trouble keeping their promises, they'll also have trouble meeting the "_____ set out…in the new contract." You know that the word in the

blank will be something that could logically be set out in a contract, and something similar to promises. A good word for the blank might be "agreements" or "rules." For "innovations," look at the root word NOV- (new): an innovation is a new invention, which doesn't make sense as a synonym for "promises." "Quandaries," "enigmas," and "dichotomies" also don't fit. Since "stipulations" means "terms" or "rules," (C) is correct.

11. The correct answer is **(C).** For the first blank, the key word is "questioned" – the word must refer to a type of person who questions something. A "partisan" is someone with a strong bias toward one side or another, so (A) doesn't fit. "Detractors" (note the prefix DE-) are people who argue *against* something. "Naysayers" literally means "people who say nay (no)," so this doesn't fit either. A zealot is someone who is unreasonably enthusiastic about a cause, so this is definitely the wrong choice. "Skeptics" are people who question what they're told, so (C) makes sense for the first blank. For "proffering," look at the root word PRO- (forward) + "offering:" this word means "offering to someone" or "putting forward for consideration," which makes sense in the second blank, so (C) is correct.

12. The correct answer is **(A).** Start with the second blank because you have a stronger clue word: "independent and neutral." You want "less _____" to mean "independent and neutral," so the blank will mean the opposite. "Erudite" means wise, and "adept" means "skillful," so these words don't fit. "Disinterested" ("objective") is clearly wrong. Both "partisan" and "litigious" might work in the second blank, so check the first blank to see which one is correct. For the first blank, you could fill in your own word – "process" or "way" might be good choices. "Paradigm" fits, but "consensus" means agreement (note the root word CON-, meaning "together"), which doesn't make sense. Thus, (A) is correct.

13. The correct answer is **(D).** Again, start with the second blank. The clue for the second blank is "from which it cannot recover," so you know you want a negative word that means something like "be damaged." To "evolve" is to change in a good way, so this doesn't make sense. The clue actually says "cannot recover," so "recover" is clearly wrong. Looking at "forestall," note the root FORE-

(before): this word means to stop something before it starts. That doesn't mean "be damaged," so cross it off. To "crest" is to reach the top of something, which is the opposite of the word you want. Thus, even if you aren't sure what "deteriorate" means, it's the only answer choice left. The negative prefix DE- should give you a hint; this word means "become worse" or "become damaged." "Thrive" (be healthy) fits in the first blank, so (D) is correct.

14. The correct answer is **(E)**. For the first blank, the clue word "respected" lets you know that you need a positive word. "Scrupulous" is the only word in the list with a positive connotation. For the second blank, you want a word that gives the relationship between evidence and facts: a good word to fill in might be "prove" or "show." "Mock" is clearly wrong. "Determine" and "dictate" could both work for this blank, but (B) is wrong because "capricious" (changing one's mind often) doesn't work for the first blank. Thus, (E) is correct.

15. The correct answer is **(C)**. The key word "insight" tells you that the second blank will be positive. Thus, you can cross off (E) because "disregard" (notice the negative prefix DIS-) doesn't fit. For the first blank, "Although…once _____" lets you know that this blank will be the opposite of the second blank, so you want a negative word that means something like "rejected." "Insisted on" isn't negative, so cross off (D). "Pored over" is also positive, so cross off (A). "Condescended to" is indeed negative, but it doesn't mean "rejected," so it isn't the word you want. (To condescend means "to lower yourself to someone else's level"). "Scoffed at" is negative, and "appreciation" is positive, so the correct answer is (C).

16. The correct answer is **(B)**. The fact that Kakuro is "credited" with something indicates that word in the first blank must be positive, and the fact the something was "threatening" traditional Japanese painting indicates that the word in the second blank must be negative. Unfortunately, all of the first words are relatively positive, but you can eliminate "emphasize" and, if you know it, "lionize" (celebrate) on the second side. You could also eliminate (A) because Kakuro couldn't "invent" a traditional technique. So (A) and (D) are out. Now think about the meaning of the sentence. Logically, the word in the first blank must mean something like "saving," whereas the word in the second blank must mean

something like "destroying." "Salvaging" works perfectly, and "perpetuating" could work as well, but "domesticating" makes no sense in context. So (C) is out. Now look at the second side for (B) and (E). "Supplant" means "overtake" or "displace," so that makes sense. "Divert," on the other hand, means "redirect" or, in an alternate meaning, "amuse." Neither of those things quite fits, so (B) is the answer.

17. The correct answer is **(A)**. In this sentence, the colon tells you that the two parts of the sentence are essentially similar, or saying almost the same thing. Both blanks are describing the effect of plants on Linnaeus' mood, so the words should be similar. "Angered" is the opposite of "mollify" (think of the root word MOLL-, soft), "perplexed" (confused) is the opposite of "calm," "elated" (overjoyed) is the opposite of "infuriate," and "invigorated" (notice the root VIG-, lively) is the opposite of "enervate." For (A), "soothed" and "placate" (notice the root word PLAC-, peace) have the same connotation of peacefulness and calm. Thus, the only plausible answer is (A).

18. The correct answer is **(B)**. Here, the key words "speeding the development" are the key to the first blank: the word should have something to do with speed or quickness. "Hinder" means to impede or hamper, so (A) doesn't make sense. "Permit" doesn't have to do with speed, and "debilitate" means "to make weak" (think of the negative prefix DE- + "ability"), so (C) and (E) are incorrect. "Accelerate" means to speed up, which makes sense with the key words. For the second blank, the same key words apply. "Facilitating" (think of the root word FACIL-, easy) makes sense with "speeding the development," but "impeding" (preventing) is incorrect. Thus, (B) is correct.

19. The correct answer is **(D)**. In this sentence, the key word "though" tells you that the first blank will be the opposite of the second blank. "Controversial" isn't the opposite of "interesting," so (A) is incorrect. "Recondite" means "esoteric," which isn't the opposite of "elaborate." "Eclectic" and "heterogeneous" are synonyms (notice the root HETERO-, meaning "other;" both of these words describe a group of different things), so (C) is not correct. "Somber" (gloomy) and "bucolic" (related to country life) are completely unrelated, so this is not the pair you're after. Only (D) fits.

20. The correct answer is **(D)**. In this sentence, the clues are "outspoken advocate" and "controversial:" you want a word that describes someone who strongly supports very controversial topics. "Pragmatist" means a practical person, so (A) isn't right. "Dichotomy" (notice the prefix DI-, meaning "two;" this word means "division into two parts") doesn't fit, either. A conundrum is a problem, so (C) is wrong. A "sycophant" is someone who slavishly praises another person, so (E) isn't right. A "polemicist" is someone with strong opinions on touchy subjects, so (D) is correct.

21. The correct answer is **(E)**. The sentence makes it clear that the whale is a *good* navigator ("arriving in precisely the same spot"), so the word in the blank must be positive. For "belligerent," look at the root word BELL- ("war") to eliminate it. "Compliant" means "agreeing" (look at the prefix COM-, meaning "with," as in "communication") so (B) is wrong. For "intractable," think about the root word TRACT- (which means "move" as in "retract," "detract," or "extract"): "intractable" means "stubborn" (unable to be moved), so (C) is wrong. "Ingenuous" means "sincere:" think of the same root in "genuine." Don't get confused with the similar-sounding word "ingenious," meaning "very clever." Thus, (D) is also incorrect. "Adept" means "skillful," so (E) is the correct answer.

22. The correct answer is **(C)**. Start with the second blank: if people live in "constant dread" of something, the word will be strongly negative. Thus, you can cross off (A) because "abundance" is positive, (B) because an "excess" (too much) of bread isn't anything to live in dread of, and (D) because "innovation" (inventing new things; look the root word NOV-, new) isn't negative. For the first blank, "most of their nutrients" is a key word that tells you to look for a positive word. "Tolerated" has a slightly negative connotation, and "derived" (got) makes much more sense in context, so (C) is correct.

23. The correct answer is **(B)**. Start with the second blank: the key words are "powerful cultural pull," so the word in the blank should have something to do with power. "Sustaining" (supporting) and "dominating" might both work, but "simplifying," "thwarting" (preventing), and "determining" are wrong. Looking at the first blank, "rejecting a powerful cultural pull" doesn't make sense, so (B) is correct.

24. The correct answer is **(D)**. The key phrase is "everyday cares and concerns." These are unlikely to be "controversial," so cross off (A). "Abstruse" means the *opposite* of "everyday" (think of the same roots in "abstract") so cross it out. "Tedious" (long and boring) doesn't fit with the clue. "Insignificant" means "unimportant" – this is tempting because "everyday" things are often seen as being unimportant, but it doesn't make sense in the context of the sentence, because if Yeats thought these subjects were unimportant, he wouldn't be writing about them. Between "insignificant" and "quotidian" (which literally means "daily" or "everyday"), (D) is more strongly related to the clue, so (D) is correct.

25. The correct answer is **(A)**. The key phrase is "making individuals more rational and society more harmonious." Thus, the blank will be a positive word, so "quell" (suppress) is incorrect. To "differentiate" is to distinguish between (think of the word "difference"), so (B) doesn't mean "rational and harmonious" and you can cross it off. To "assuage" means to "make less severe," which doesn't make sense. To "substantiate" means "verify" or "prove," so (E) doesn't fit either. Thus, (A) is the right answer.

26. The correct answer is **(E)**. Start with the second blank, since the meaning is easier to figure out. The key phrase is "speaks only when prompted," so you want a word that means "quiet." Looking at the answer choices, "vociferous" ("loud;" think of the root word VOC/VOX- meaning "voice"), doesn't make sense; neither does "lazy" or "placid" (think of the root word PLAC-, which means "peace"). So you can eliminate (A), (C), and (D). For the first blank, the sentence *contrasts* "speaks only when prompted" with "the more _____ children," so the first blank should mean something like "loud" or "talkative." "Diligent" means hardworking, so (B) doesn't fit. For "loquacious," think of the root word LOQU-, to speak, the same word found in "eloquent." Since you've eliminated the other answers, (E) is correct.

27. The correct answer is **(E)**. For the first blank, "_____ poverty" describes something the president was expected to do, so the word should mean something like "stop." Thus, you can eliminate (B), because "perpetuate" means "continue" (think of the same root used in words

like "perpetual"). (C) is also wrong because "stimulate" means the exact opposite of "stop." For "alleviate," think of the root word LEV- (light); it makes sense that the president would want to lighten the burden of poverty. The second blank should describe a logical action for a president to take "as a result of widespread protest:" it will clearly be negative and probably mean something like "step down" or "leave office." "Conform" doesn't make sense, so (A) is incorrect. "Abstain" might look tempting because of the prefix AB- (away), but this word means to hold off from doing something, so "abdicate," which means "leave" (note the same prefix) is the best choice. Since you can eliminate (A)-(D), (E) is correct.

28. The correct answer is **(C)**. In this sentence, "sharp lines" are *contrasted* with real borders, which are "more _____." Thus, the blank should be the opposite of "sharp." For your own word, try filling in something like "flexible." "Dense" is clearly wrong. "Rigid" is tempting because it means the same thing as "sharp," but remember that you want an antonym, not a synonym. "Ephemeral" means "lasting only a short time," so (D) is also wrong, and "identifiable" doesn't mean "flexible," so you can cross off (E) as well. Thus, (C) is correct.

29. The correct answer is **(B)**. For the second blank, the key word is "humanely:" if you aren't sure what this means, think of the Humane Society or other words with the same root like "humanity" or "human." For your own word, try filling in something like "kindness." The second blank will clearly be positive, so "aspersion" (criticism) is clearly wrong, and "scrutiny" (close attention – think of the root word SCRUT-, to look) doesn't work either. For the second blank, treating enemy prisoners well would reduce the horrors of war, so you want a word that means "lessen" or "reduce." (A) looks tempting, but remember that you already crossed it off because "aspersion" doesn't fit. "Propagate" (think of "propaganda") means "to spread," so (C) is incorrect. "Condone" means "approve of," so (E) is also wrong. Thus, the correct answer is (B).

30. The correct answer is **(D)**. The key phrase here is "only eighty years later:" the sentence is emphasizing that this process took a very short time. Thus, the word in the blank should mean something like "speed" or "quickness." "Mastery" clearly doesn't work. For "dilution," think of the word "dilute:" this

doesn't mean "speed," so cross of (B). "Rebuttal" means "response, "so (C) is incorrect, and "moderation" doesn't mean speed, so you can cross off (E) as well. "Velocity" does mean speed (which you might recognize from the root word VEL-), so (D) is correct.

31. The correct answer is **(E)**. For the first blank, the clue is "fresh and interesting ways," which is *contrasted* with "simply _____." Thus, the word in the blank should be the opposite of "fresh and interesting." "Superfluous" means "more than enough" (think of the root word SUPER, as in "superhero" or "superstar"), so (B) is incorrect. "Banal" means "common" or "unoriginal," which works for this blank. For the second blank, the key word is "originality:" "torpor" means "sluggishness," so (A) is incorrect. "Boredom" is not the same as "originality," and neither is "determination," but "insight" does logically fit with "originality," so (E) is correct.

32. The correct answer is **(A)**. For this sentence, start with the second blank. The second part of this sentence establishes a contrast between engineers being important ("they determine…") and most people not being "_____" their influence. Thus, a good word to fill in might be "aware of." Absent from" doesn't mean "aware of," so cross off (B). "Suspicious of" might seem tempting, but it has a negative connotation, so (C) is also wrong. "Ignorant about" means the *opposite* of the word you want, so (D) is wrong. Even if you don't know what "protean" means, "impatient with" does not mean "aware of," so (E) must also be wrong. For "cognizant," think of the root word COG/COGN-, to know (as in recognize): this word means "aware of." "Obscure" makes sense in the first blank, since this means "hidden," a logical description for a group that most people aren't aware of. Thus (A) is correct.

33. The correct answer is **(D)**. For the first blank, "admirers" is a key word that tells you the word will be positive and mean something like "admire" or "appreciate." Thus, you can cross off "disparage" (think of the prefix DIS-, as in "dismay" or "dislike") and "impugn" (think of the root word PUG-, which means "fight"). The key word for the second blank is "detractors." Even if you aren't sure what this means, the word "although" lets you know that the sentence is setting up a contrast between

84

"admirers" and "detractors," so "detractors" is likely to mean something like "critics." The critics are "less _____," so the blank word will be something positive. "Wary of" and "resistant to" are both negative, so (D) is the only answer choice left. "Extol" means "praise," which works for the first blank, and "enamored of" (think of the root word AMOR-, love) means "positive about," so (D) is correct.

34. The correct answer is **(B)**. The key words are "the greatest of all poets:" clearly the blank will be very strongly positive. "Symbolized" and "scrutinized" are neutral (for "scrutinized," think of words like "scrutiny" that share the same root SCRUT-, meaning to see or look at), so (A) and (C) are both wrong. "Disregarded" (notice the prefix DIS-) means "ignored," which is negative, so (D) is wrong. "Challenged" is also negative, so (E) is incorrect, and (B) must be the correct answer, even if you aren't sure what "venerated" means.

35. The correct answer is **(C)**. For the first blank, the key phrase "over a span of two centuries" lets you cross off (B), since this certainly isn't rapid. The key word "because" lets you know that the second half of this sentence will be something that logically follows from the first half, so you want two words with similar meanings. "Randomly" and "esoteric" are incorrect, because "esoteric" ("abstruse" or "arcane") isn't similar to "random." "Inconsistently" and "profound" are also incorrect, because they don't mean the same thing. "Separately" and "cohesive" (joined together) are opposites. For "cohesive," think of other words that share the same root HES- (stick together), like "adhesive." Thus, (C) must be the correct answer. "Sporadically" means "bit by bit," so "heterogeneous" (having many different kinds) is indeed a logical consequence. For the meaning of "heterogeneous," think of the root word HETERO-, which means "different."

36. The correct answer is **(C)**. The key phrase "the last natural case occurred in 1977" lets you know that the word in the blank should mean something like "wiped out" or "eliminated." This question is tricky because three of the answers start with "EX-," which is a prefix that means "out of," so it's hard to cross off answer choices using root words. "Exonerated" means "freed from guilt," so (A) is wrong. "Emaciated" means "very thin," so (B) is also incorrect. "Eradicated" means "wiped out entirely"

(think of the root word RAD, which means "root"), so (C) fits. "Exculpated" is a synonym for "exonerated," (think of EX- plus the root word CULP-, harm or fault) so (D) is incorrect, and "exhorted" means "strongly urged," so (E) doesn't work either. Thus, (C) is correct.

37. The correct answer is **(B)**. In this sentence, the key words "fragile" and "delicate and feathery" let you know that the word in the blank will mean something similar. "Malleable" means "flexible" or "able to be shaped," so (A) is incorrect. "Unwieldy" means awkward, "specious" means "false," and "indigenous" means "native," so (C), (D), and (E) are incorrect. "Diaphanous" means "thin and delicate," so (B) is correct.

38. The correct answer is **(A)**. For the first blank, "bored" is a key word that signals the word in the blank will be negative. Thus, you can eliminate (E) because "infallible" means "incapable of failing," which is positive (note that this word is positive despite the prefix IN-). The word "although" signals that the second blank will be the opposite of "boring," so try plugging in "interesting" for your own word. "Tedious" means the same thing as boring, so (B) is incorrect. "Stultifying" means "exceedingly boring" (think of the root word STULT-, meaning stupid) so C is also wrong. For "militant," think of the same root word in "military:" (D) is also wrong, so (A) is correct.

39. The correct answer is **(B)**. From the key words in the sentence, you know that the word in the blank will mean a person who claims to create magic ("supernatural phenomena"), but that this person is lying (otherwise, there would be nothing to "expose"). Thus, "faker" or "liar" would be a good word to fill in the blank. For "misanthropes," think of the prefix MIS and the root word ANTHRO- (human): this is someone who dislikes other people, but not a faker. For "pugilists," think of the root PUG-, meaning "fight:" (C) is also incorrect. A "zealot" is someone excessively enthusiastic about a cause, so (D) doesn't fit, and "adversary" is not the same as "liar," so (E) is also wrong. IN choice (B), "charlatans" does mean "fakers," so (B) is correct.

40. The correct answer is **(C)**. In this sentence, the phrase "who viewed it as a form of high art" is a clue that the first blank will be positive. Thus, you can cross off (A), (D), and (E), because these words are negative. The sentence then creates a contrast ("on the contrary"), describing swing as "devoid of _____." Since "devoid of _____" must be negative, the word in the blank should be positive. "Cacophonous" is tempting because of the root word PHON-, meaning "sound," but "CAC-" means "bad," so this is actually a negative word. For choice (C), "lauded" means "praised," and "aesthetic" means "artistic," so both words fit with the clues and choice (C) is correct.

41. The correct answer is **(E)**. Start with the second blank. For this word, you want something that means "give in to," so you can cross off "disparage" (look at the prefix DIS), "withhold," and "refuse." Giving in to the protestors' demands would stop the protest, so for the first blank, you want a word like "stop." "Perpetuate" means "continue" (think of the root word PERPET-, meaning "forever," as in "perpetual"), so (B) is incorrect. Thus, even if you aren't sure what "quell" (stop) or "acquiesce to" (give in to) mean, you know that (E) is correct.

42. The correct answer is **(D)**. This sentence sets up a contrast between "some" and "others," so the word in the first blank should mean something like "different." "Concurrent" means "occurring at the same time" (look at the prefix CON-, meaning "with"), so (B) is incorrect. "Unshakeable" is also wrong, as is "incomprehensible" (think of the prefix IN-, not, plus the same root in "comprehension" and "comprehend;" this word means "not understandable"). For the second blank, "influencing artists and thinkers decades later" is a clue, letting you know that the word will mean something like "lasted for a long time." "Dissolved" doesn't mean this, so you can cross off (A). In choice (D), "divergent" (look at the prefix DI-, meaning "two" or "separate") means "different," and "persisted" means "lasted for a long time," so the correct answer is (D).

43. The correct answer is **(C)**. The new information about creatures living "in seemingly hostile environments" would suggest the possibility of life on Mars (also a hostile environment), so the scientists should be more open to accepting the idea. Since "more open" means "less _____," the word in the blank should mean "unwilling." (A) and (B) are

trap answers: these are the opposite of the words you want. "Elated" means "overjoyed," so (D) is also incorrect, and "available" clearly doesn't fit with the idea of "unwilling." "Reticent" means "holding back" or "unwilling," so (C) is correct.

44. The correct answer is **(A)**. The clue for this sentence is "stridency" ("shrillness") which tells you that the word in the blank will mean something similar. "Parsimony" means "stinginess," which is not the same. For "equivocation," think of the root word EQUI- (equal): to "equivocate" is to waver back and forth without making up one's mind. "Restraint" also does not mean "loudness;" neither does "diffidence." "Vitriol" means "severity" or "bitterness," which fits with the idea of "stridency," so (A) is correct.

45. The correct answer is **(C)**. The sentence uses the word "ironically" to set up a contrast between "captivated…readers" and the way Tolkien was as a professor. Thus, the word in the blank should mean something like "disliked." "Celebrated" is clearly wrong, so cross off (A). "Tolerated" is also not the same as "disliked," so (B) is incorrect. For the second blank, the clue word "dull" tells you that the blank will mean something like "boring." "Unique" is the opposite of "boring," and "whimsical" is unrelated (it means "lighthearted.") In choice (C), "disdained" is a negative word (notice the prefix DIS-) that means "looked down on" or "disliked." "Soporific" means "something that puts you to sleep," which does make sense, so (C) is correct.

46. The correct answer is **(A)**. The key phrase "good characters are very good and bad ones very bad" suggests that his writing has no gray areas, so "ambiguity" or "uncertainty" might be good words for the blank. "Interest" doesn't mean the same thing as "uncertainty, and "clarity" is exactly the opposite. "Engagement" is also not the same, so cross off (B), (C), and (E). For the second blank, the clue is "doubt." "Hesitation" means the same thing as doubt, but "jubilation" means "joy", so (D) is incorrect and (A) is the correct answer.

47. The correct answer is **(C)**. Start with the second blank. The sentence sets up a contrast between "changed" and the blank word using "either…or…," so the word in the blank should mean something like "kept the same." "Altered" means changed, so (A) is incorrect. "Victimized"

and "simplified" don't mean "kept the same," so (B) and (D) are also wrong. "Impacted" is tempting, because it might seem to mean the same as "changed," but remember that this is the opposite of the word you want: the blank should mean "kept the same." Thus, (E) is incorrect. For choice (C), "determining" works with the clue "set pathways" for the first blank, and "reinforced" means "kept the same," so (C) is correct.

48. The correct answer is **(E).** The clue for the second blank is "overestimate," which tells you that the "discovery" will be news. So "shocked" or "confused" might be good words to plug in the blank. "Impatient" doesn't mean "confused," so (C) is incorrect. For the first blank, if people were shocked to discover their commonalities, this implies that they were expecting to be very different. Thus, "different" or "strange" would be good words for the first blank. "Trite" means "commonplace," so cross it off (A). "Common" is the opposite of "different," so (B) is also incorrect. "Eclectic" means "having a variety of sources," so (D) might be tempting, but ultimately "unique" is a stronger antonym for "common," so (E) is a stronger fit with the clues. Thus, (E) is correct.

49. The correct answer is **(B).** The two parts of this sentence work together ("humble objects and homely details" are the same as "daily life;" there is no contrast between the two parts of the sentence.) Thus, "are examples of" would be a good word to fill in the blank. "Analyze," "amplify," "subvert," and "guarantee" don't mean "are examples of," so these choices are wrong. "Epitomize" does mean "exemplify," so (B) is correct.

50. The correct answer is **(B).** The key phrase "numerous shifting…factors" lets you know that "hardly _____" will mean something like "unstable." Thus, the blank will mean something like "stable." For "despicable," think of the same root in the word "despise:" "hateful" doesn't mean "stable," so (A) is incorrect. "Perplexing" ("confusing"), "convoluted" ("complicated") and "meticulous" ("careful") don't mean "stable," so these are all incorrect and (B) is correct.

51. The correct answer is **(E).** The key word "because" tells you that the second part of the sentence is an explanation or clarification of the first, so the two blanks will be very similar in meaning. "Ridicule"

(think of the same root in the word "ridiculous") would not meet an "integrated" theory, so (A) is incorrect. "Reverence" and "rejected" are also opposite in meaning, so (B) is not correct. "Interest" suggests a positive response, while "compromised" would be negative, so cross out (C). "Befuddlement" (confusion) is a negative response, which doesn't work with the positive connotations of "embraced." "Skepticism" is a negative response that goes with "discredited" (think of the negative prefix DIS- plus the root word CRED-, believe), so (E) is correct.

52. The correct answer is **(D).** Modern medicine is "too subtle and complex" for the blank word, so that word should carry the idea of simplicity. "Impossible to say" is another clue, letting you know that the word in the blank will have something to do with knowing for sure. "Clear answers" might be good as your own suggestion for the blank. "Solace" (comfort) doesn't fit; "immunity" is tempting because most people recognize the word as being related to medicine, but remember that you're looking for a word that modern medicine *doesn't* offer. "Variety" is the opposite of what you want, since it means the same thing as "subtle and complex." Similarly, "elaboration" logically follows from subtlety and complexity, so (E) is also wrong. "Certainty" fits with the clues (remember that you wanted something involving simplicity and effectiveness), so (D) is correct.

53. The correct answer is **(A).** The sentence contrasts television and books. Television is described as the "primary medium," so books should logically be described as less important or relevant. "Harbingers" are "warnings", which doesn't fit. "Diatribes" means "rants," so (C) is out. "Paradigms" means "examples," and "heretics" refers to people who break from traditional religious belief, so (D) and (E) are incorrect. An "anomaly" is something out of the ordinary, which fits with the contrast between television (the "primary medium") and books. Thus, (A) is correct.

54. The correct answer is **(C).** Start with the second blank. The key words "thoroughly analyzing" give you an idea of what word should fit here; try plugging in "analysis" or "research" for the blank. "Indifference" (think of the prefix IN-, "not," + "difference:" something that doesn't make a difference) means an attitude of not caring, which doesn't fit. "Contempt" is an attitude of scorn or

strong disdain, which clearly doesn't fit, so (D) is also out. The clue for the first blank is "write in:" this lets you know that the word will mean something like "follow" or "use." "Eschew" means "reject," which is the opposite of the word you want. "Mock" means "make fun of," which doesn't fit, so you can cross off (B). "Emulate" means "imitate," and "scrutiny" means "close examination" (think of the root word SCRUT-, "look at"), so (C) is correct.

55. The correct answer is **(E).** In this sentence, the key words "until it is challenged" let you know that the blank will be a positive word. Thus, you can cross of "unreliable." "Duplicitous" means "false" or "deceptive" (think of the root word DUPL-, meaning "two," as in "two faced" or "double dealing") so (D) is also wrong. For the second blank, "accounts for _____" lets you know that the blank will be negative, so you can cross off "quantities," which is neutral, and "solutions," which is positive. In choice (E), "sound" is positive, and "inconsistencies" are negative, so (E) is correct.

56. The correct answer is **(D).** "More flexible" is a key phrase that tells you that the word in the blank will mean "inflexible" or "rigid." "Convoluted" means "extremely complicated," but even if you don't know the definition, you can use the root VOLUT- ("turn") to cross it out, since "turning" has the opposite meaning of "rigid." "Ambitious" doesn't mean "rigid." "Concise" (short) is also incorrect, as is "redundant." Thus, "linear" ("in a straight line") is correct.

57. The correct answer is **(C).** For the first blank, "outgoing" is a key word that tells you that the blank will be a similar word. "Assiduous" means "careful," which doesn't fit, and "laconic" is exactly the opposite: it means quiet. Thus, you can cross off (D) and (E). For the second blank, the key words "although" and "uncharacteristically" clue you in that this will be the opposite of "outgoing," so you can cross off "candid" (which means "open" or "honest" – think of a candid photo) and "sympathetic." For choice (C), even if you aren't sure what "gregarious" means, think of the root words GREG-, which means "group:" this fits with "outgoing." "Diffident" means "withdrawn," so (C) is correct.

58. The correct answer is **(B).** In this sentence, the key word "by" lets you know that the second blank will be a logical cause of the first. "Arguments" don't

cause something to be "facilitated" (think of the root word FACIL-, easy: this word means "made easier"), so (A) is out. "Consensus" ("agreement") is not a logical cause of something being "dismantled" (torn apart); even if you aren't sure what these words mean, you can see that the prefixes CON- ("with") and DIS- ("not" or "against") are opposites. "Discord" (the prefix DIS- will again let you know that this word is negative; it means "argument" or "disagreement") would not cause anything to be "simplified," so (D) is also wrong. "Agreements" would also not cause a plan to be "suspended," so (E) is wrong. "Squabbles" (arguments) would cause plans to be "hindered" (delayed), so (B) makes sense.

59. The correct answer is **(A).** The key phrase "little knowing" tells you that the blank will mean something like "by accident." "Repeatedly" is incorrect, "deliberately" is exactly the opposite of "by accident," and "strategically" and "paradoxically" are completely unrelated. "Inadvertently" does mean "by accident:" think of IN-(not) + AD- (towards) + VERT- (turned): if you weren't turned towards something, you weren't intending to do it. Thus, (A) is correct.

60. The correct answer is **(E).** This sentence contrasts "an _____ process" with "ego, personal tastes, and the desire to avoid error." Thus, the blank will mean something positive like "perfectly rational" or "logical." "Observable" is clearly wrong. "Efficient" is tempting, because it's related to being rational or logical, but it isn't exactly a synonym, so (B) is not correct. "Intuitive" is the opposite of rational, and "abstract" is unrelated. "Objective" does mean "rational," so (E) is correct.

61. The correct answer is **(D).** This sentence compares "physical abilities" and "social _____," which lets you know that the word in the blank will mean something positive like "abilities" or "skills." "Stigma," "rebellion," and "profligacy" (wastefulness) are all negative, so you can cross off (A), (B), and (E). "Buoyancy" is positive but doesn't mean "abilities," so (C) doesn't fit with the clue. "Acumen" means "skill," so (D) is correct.

62. The correct answer is **(D)**. In this sentence, "an _____" in the first blank is contrasted ("not...but rather") with being "_____ by human actions" in the second blank. Thus, the two words will have opposite meanings. "Absolute" and "venerated" (highly respected) aren't opposites, so (A) is incorrect. "Idiosyncratic" (think of the same root in "idiom") means "specific to a particular person," which isn't the opposite of "reinforced," so (B) is also wrong. "Arbitrary" means "at will," which isn't the opposite of "altered," so (C) doesn't work. "Contradicted" doesn't make sense at all (look at the root words CONTRA-, against, and DICT-, speak), because it means "talked back to," or "disagreed with" and it doesn't make sense to talk back to a balance of gasses. For choice D, look at the root words "IM-" (not) and "MUT" (change): "immutable" means "not changeable," which is the opposite of "upset." Thus, (D) is correct.

63. The correct answer is **(C)**. In this sentence, "as opposed to" tells you that the two blanks will be opposites. The first blank must also be something opposite of "conceptual," since the conceptual approach was "controversial" among mathematicians who favored the first blank. Thus, the first blank will mean something opposite to "conceptual" ("practical" might be a good word to fill in the blank), and the second will mean something like "conceptual." For the first blank, "theoretical" and "philosophical" are antonyms for "practical," so (A) and (D) are incorrect. For the second blank, "impulsive" and "derivative" don't mean the same as "conceptual," so you can cross off (B) and (E). "Pragmatic" means "practical," and "an abstract" fits with "conceptual," so (C) is correct.

64. The correct answer is **(C)**. "Admire" and "strength" indicate that the first blank will be a strongly positive word that describes some kind of personal quality of the candidate. Since "constituencies" are just the groups that vote for someone and not a personal quality, (D) doesn't make sense. For the second blank, "ignore her...foibles" gives you a clue that the blank will mean something like "complete" or "unquestioning." Even if you aren't sure what "foibles" means, you can tell that this will also be a positive word, since these are the same voters who "admire" the candidate. "Tenuous" doesn't make sense, since this is a negative word. "Theoretical" is neutral, and "ruthless" is negative, so you can cross off (B) and (E). "Unqualified" might look negative at

first: this is a confusing word because it has both positive and negative meanings. In this case, it's a strongly positive word (if you "qualify" something, you put conditions on it, so "unqualified" means "unconditional" or "complete"). Thus, (C) is correct.

65. The correct answer is **(A)**. In this sentence, the society is described as having the same qualities as the "complex jobs." Thus, it could be used as a "model" or a "tool" for understanding them. "Antidote" (look at the root word ANTI-, "against") refers to a medicine taken to counteract a poison, so (B) is incorrect. "Doctrine" is official teaching, a "tribunal" is a court, and a "catalyst" is something that sparks a change, so none of the other answer choices mean anything like "model" or "tool." A "paradigm" is a perfect example of something, so (A) is correct.

66. The correct answer is **(D)**. "showed no sign of" is a key phrase telling you that the first blank and the second blank will be opposites. "Increase" and "amplifying" (think of an "amp" at a rock concert) are synonyms, so (A) is incorrect. "Diminish" and "dwindling" both refer to getting smaller, so (B) is also wrong. "Multiply" and "aggregating" are almost synonyms ("aggregating" means "collecting" or "gathering together" – think of the root word GREG-, group), so cross off (C). "Improvise" doesn't make sense for the first blank because only people (not controversies) can improvise something. In choice (D), "intensify" is the opposite of "abating" (dying down – look at the prefix AB-, away), so (D) is correct.

67. The correct answer is **(B)**. This sentence contrasts "a comprehensive solution" with the word in the blank, so you might fill in "incomplete" or "partial." The word will definitely be negative, so "creative" and "permanent" are incorrect. "Malicious" is strongly negative, but it doesn't mean "partial" (look at the root word MAL-, which means "evil"), so (A) is incorrect. "Nebulous" means "vague" (think of a nebula, which is just a big cloud of floating gas in space), so (D) also doesn't fit. "Piecemeal" means "randomly in little pieces," which works well as an opposite for "comprehensive," so (B) is correct.

68. The correct answer is **(A)**. The first blank describes the effect of "new technologies" on "established models," so you want a word that means something like "changing." "Encouraging" doesn't mean

"changing;" neither does "fostering," (think of foster care: this word means "nurturing" or "supporting"), so you can cross off (B) and (D). For the second blank, "evolving needs" and "flexible" are key phrases: try filling in "meet" or "keep up with" for your own word. "Detract from" doesn't fit; neither does "validate" (think of "valid"), so you can cross off (C) and (E). "Disrupting" means "changing," and "adapt to" fits with the idea of flexibility, so (A) is correct.

69. The correct answer is **(C)**. In this sentence, the blank is defined by the second part of the sentence. Thus, the word will have something to do with using an object for an intended purpose. "Aesthetic" (related to beauty) is tempting because it's a word commonly associated with design, but this doesn't have anything to do with purpose, so (A) is incorrect. "Deterministic" refers to a philosophy that all events are caused (determined) by natural laws, so you can cross off (B). For "inscrutable," look at the root words SCRUT-, which means "look at:" this word means "not clear" or "not visible," which isn't what you want. "Complex" clearly doesn't have anything to do with using something for a practical purpose, so (E) is also wrong. "Utilitarian" (think of the same root in "utility") means "focused on practical use," so (C) is correct.

70. The correct answer is **(E)**. For the first blank, the key words "both foreign and domestic" give you a clue that the word will refer to some kind of mixture or combination. Thus, you can cross off (B) because a "monolith" is something uniform or unvarying (MONO-, one). You can also cross off (D), because "a paragon" means "an example" and doesn't have anything to do with combination. For the second blank, the key phrase "escape the laws of the country that hosts it" lets you know that the word will mean something like "freedom" or "independence." "Integration" means the opposite of "independence," so (A) is incorrect. "Ratification" and "judiciousness" are both words associated with courts, so they're tempting choices, but they don't mean "independence," so cross them out. "Equivocation" (think of the root word EQUI-, equal) means "wavering back and forth," so (C) is also wrong. "A hybrid" is a mixture of two or more things, and "autonomy" (look at the root word AUTO-, self) means "independence," so (E) is correct.

71. The correct answer is **(A)**. In this sentence, scientists must be looking for ways to "prevent or delay" diseases because the cures are not good (otherwise, why would they be turning to new alternatives?). Thus, you want a strongly negative word that means "useless" or "not effective." "Essential," "magnanimous," (think of the root words MAGN-, great, and ANIM-, spirit: this word means "generous" or "great-hearted") and "advantageous" are all positive, so you can eliminate (B), (D), and (E). "Baffling" is negative, but it means "confusing" which is not the same as "useless," so (C) doesn't fit. "Ineffective" is the opposite of "effective;" this works in the blank, so (A) is correct.

72. The correct answer is **(B)**. For the first blank, the sentence clearly requires a word like "get." Thus, you can cross off "mitigate" (which means to "make less bad") and "ascertain," which means "make certain." Tyrannies would be unfriendly toward people getting power, so the word in the second blank should be strongly negative. Thus, you can cross off "conducive" (think of the prefix CON-, with, and the root word DUC, lead). "Obstinate" means "stubborn," which is negative, but doesn't quite mean "unfriendly." "Hostile" does mean "unfriendly," and "derive" means "figure out" or "obtain," so (B) is correct.

73. The correct answer is **(C)**. For the first blank, "well-informed" is a key word that lets you know the blank will be positive and have a similar meaning to "well-informed." Try plugging in "smart" or "convincing" for your own word. "Hackneyed" means "clichéd," which is negative, so (B) is wrong. "Vacuous" is exactly the opposite of what you want (think of a vacuum, which is an empty space: "vacuous" means "empty-headed" or "stupid"), so cross off (D) as well. For the second blank, "more objectionable" is a clue that the word in the blank will be negative, so try "spoil" or "ruin" for your own word. "Embellish" is positive, so (A) is incorrect. "Elevate" is also positive, so "E) doesn't work. For choice (C), "lucid" (think of the root word LUC-, light) is positive, and "mar" is negative, so (C) is correct.

74. The correct answer is **(A)**. Start with the second blank. The key words "language" and "impenetrable" tells you that the word will be negative and have something to do with language. "Jaundice" is negative, but this refers to a type of disease, so (D) doesn't fit. "Colloquialisms" are related to language (colloquialisms are things people say in everyday conversation, as opposed to formal language) but they aren't "impenetrable," so (C) doesn't fit. For the first blank, the key phrase "put…in perspective" lets you know that the blank will mean something positive like "tell." Thus, you can cross off "disparage" (look at the prefix DIS- if you aren't sure what the word means; this is definitely a negative word). "Promote" is tempting, but "convey" is a better word because the sentence describes the author as "aloof from academic squabbles," which implies a *lack* of bias. "Promote" contains the idea of supporting one side, so it isn't as good of a fit as "convey." Thus, (A) is correct.

75. The correct answer is **(D)**. The key word "nevertheless" lets you know that this sentence has a contrast between "the tormented writer" and "_____ introspection." Thus, you could fill in "calm" or "peaceful" for the second blank. At the very least, "masterpieces" lets you know that the word will be strongly positive. "Enigmatic" means "mysterious," which doesn't fit. "Trite" means "clichéd" or "unoriginal," so it's exactly the opposite of what a masterpiece would be. "Negligible" is negative, so (C) is wrong. "Marginal" means "minor" or "unimportant" (think of the margin of a page), so (E) doesn't fit. "Serene" does mean peaceful, and "epitome" (example) works in the first blank, so (D) is correct.

3. Passage Content and Themes

When it comes to Critical Reading, one of the most frequent admonitions is that test-takers should base their answers to every question on the passage, only the passage, and nothing but the passage; outside knowledge of or opinion about a subject should never affect answer choice. While this piece of advice is of course true – every Critical Reading question *can and should* be answered based only on the information in the passage – and often uttered with the best of intentions, it nevertheless fails to take into account an important point: many test-takers find Critical Reading difficult not because they cannot resist injecting their opinion into their answers but rather because they have so little context for what they are reading. Consequently, they end up wasting significant time and energy simply trying to understand what the passages are literally saying. And just as often, they misunderstand what roles particular pieces of information play within the argument because they either cannot figure out the argument itself or fail to even recognize that an argument is being made.

This difficulty is hardly a surprise: numerous studies have shown that familiarity with a subject improves reading comprehension and that, conversely, a lack of familiarity with a subject impedes comprehension. Since the vast majority of American high school students have had no formal exposure to subjects such as art history and criticism, animal cognition, media studies, and superstring theory – all of which have appeared on recent SATs and some of which appear regularly – it is entirely unsurprising that so many test-takers have difficulty sifting through all of the various points of view presented and distinguishing between primary information, secondary information, and irrelevant detail. Acquiring even some basic background knowledge about these subjects can thus make certain passages, even dense ones written in unfamiliar and seemingly impenetrable academic jargon, feel less overwhelming and increase comprehension, concentration and speed. Furthermore, the ability to "place" a given passage within a particular category or identify its important themes can also make the process of drawing relationships between specific details and abstract categories – and thus of recognizing correct answers – more straightforward.

The following explanations are therefore intended to provide a very brief overview of some of the most commonly recurring themes, topics, biases, and controversies that are discussed in Critical Reading passages. There is, however, no guarantee that you will encounter any particular topic when you take the exam. Please note that while I have done my best to present these topics in straightforward terms, some of them are by nature quite esoteric and thus difficult to simplify beyond a certain point. If you would like to read further, I have also provided on p. 374 a list of suggested authors whose work has either appeared recently on the SAT, or who write about topics frequently discussed in Critical Reading passages.

The Arts: Visual Art, Music, Dance, Theater, Television

While arts passages discuss an exceedingly wide range of artistic personalities and genres, from Roman architecture to comic books to modern dance, they do nevertheless tend to contain similar themes and explore a limited number of central questions: what qualities make art "good" or "beautiful," and who is responsible for deciding what kind of art has value? What is the effect of social context (gender, time period, etc.) on art? Is the role of art merely to entertain, or does it serve a larger purpose?

Passages about forms of popular culture such as television or comic books often focus on the debate over whether they have any moral/educational value or whether they are simply junk. Some authors will vehemently insist that these types of entertainment have no redeeming qualities, whereas other authors may maintain that they are not nearly as harmful as their critics believe.

Sometimes, paired passage sets (Passage 1/Passage 2) will revolve around the subject of the arts in some form, with one passage arguing that art must serve a larger purpose in order to be considered worthy, while the other passage will argue that no larger purpose is necessary (or that "bad" art does in fact serve a purpose, just not the one that most people would expect). In addition, some arts passages will allude to the ancient Greek philosopher Plato, the first major thinker to argue that art was a corrupting force and that and that an ideal society should ban all of its poets – an idea that has been taken up by many thinkers throughout history, **and that SAT authors almost unanimously reject**.

The Effects of Technology on Reading and the Arts

A sub-category of arts passage – one that typically focuses on reading and literature, although it may occasionally also discuss another artistic genre – revolves around the increasing influence of technology and the Internet, and its impact on the book and the act of reading. Since the invention of moveable type and the printing of the Gutenberg Bible (the first book made with moveable type) in the mid-fifteenth century, reading has been associated with letters fixed to a page and viewed as an act involving large amounts of concentration and reflection. Over the last several decades, however, the rapidly increasing use of new technologies has fundamentally altered most people's experience of reading: text can be copied, pasted, and altered with remarkable rapidity, and myriad electronic devices compete for people's attention. Many SAT passages discuss the many forms of text, both old and new, that people regularly encounter: books, blogs, newspapers, etc., often from either the **negative** perspective that technology poses a serious danger to traditional reading, or from the **positive perspective** that new forms of reading can coexist with the old.

Minority Experience

Since coming under intense fire for elitism and discrimination against minorities during the 1970s and '80s, the College Board has gone out of its way to ensure that every SAT includes at least one passage that centers on a minority group (women, African-Americans, Hispanics, Native-Americans, Asian-Americans) and its experiences in American society, both present and past. Such passages come from a number of genres and cover a wide range of topics: history (historical passages may discuss how women's experiences of major events differed from men's experiences); art history; personal memoir; anthropology; science; and fiction.

The most important theme that runs through minority-themed passages is that of separation vs. assimilation: the desire to hold onto the culture of one's family or ancestors with the desire to blend into the "melting pot" of American society as a whole. While not every minority passage will explicitly discuss this theme, it is at least hinted at in the vast majority of such passages.

Important: Because the scores of African-American and Hispanic test-takers continue to lag behind those of Caucasian and Asian-Americans, the College Board is under intense political pressure to prove that the SAT is not unfairly biased against historically under-represented groups. As a result, Critical Reading passages will always portray minorities in a positive light, even if they discuss the difficulties or struggles faced by a particular figure. **Most tone and attitude questions that accompany minority-themed passages will therefore have positive answers**.

African-American

Although there are some exceptions, broadly speaking, African-American passages generally to fall into three broad categories: historical passages tend to focus on nineteenth century Black leaders such as Frederick Douglass and W.E.B. DuBois, particularly during the era after the Civil War; a second category deals with more recent events and focuses on the Civil Rights era (1950s and 1960s) and sometimes includes works of fiction as well as non-fiction; and the final type of passage revolves around the contemporary experience and African-Americans' attempts to create or maintain ties with Africa, and to understand the cultures from which they came. In general, these passages highlight African-Americans' ability to overcome adversity; they also emphasize the **difference** of the African-American experience and view total assimilation into white society or abandonment of one's heritage with suspicion.

Women

Passages that discuss women cover a wide range of genres, including history, science, fiction, and the arts, and they often focus on prominent women who defied conventional gender roles and stereotypes: the short passage describing Augusta Ada King, a mathematician and one of the pioneers of computer science (p. 391 in the Official Guide, 2nd Edition), is an excellent example of this type of passage. Historical passages also often focus on nineteenth-century figure such as first lady Abigail Adams and suffragist Susan B. Anthony, and they sometimes also discuss the relationship between women's and African-Americans' struggles for equal rights. Other passages describe more recent well-known women (e.g. Martha Graham), although in such cases the individual's accomplishments, beliefs, influences on her field, etc. rather than her gender are typically the focus of the passage. In such cases, however, the tone will generally be very positive. When women's lack of achievement in a traditionally male-dominated area is discussed (e.g. in Linda Nochlin's seminal essay "Why Have There Been No Great Women Artists?," a portion of which appeared on the October 2009 exam), it is attributed to **social and cultural factors** rather than to an innate lack of ability.

Immigrant/First-Generation American Experience

These passages typically focus on the benefits and difficulties involved in coming to the United States. On one hand, new immigrants and the children of immigrants often feel torn between their attachment to and pride in their original culture, language, food, etc., and their desire to assimilate into American society, learn English, and adopt American ways. Many passages that discuss **Asian-Americans** deal with the struggle between generations that develops when American-born children find themselves unable to relate to their parents' culture. Passages that discuss the **Hispanic** experience in the United States often focus on the challenges of bilingualism and the difficulties involved in transitioning from Spanish to English.

Native American

These passages often focus on Native Americans' traditional beliefs and stories, and on their connection to the natural world. They also sometimes discuss Europeans' historical exploitation of Native Americans and destruction of Native American culture. As a result, Native American passages will often be **negative** toward Europeans/European-Americans, who are portrayed as corrupting and misunderstanding of Native American society, and **positive** toward Native Americans.

Lost in Translation

Another common type of cross-culturally themed passage focuses on the difficulties of translation, often in relation to the immigrant experience. In such passages, the focus tends to be on the fact that words and ideas from one language cannot simply be translated word-for-word into another language. Something is always lost. From an immigrant standpoint, this means that it is often difficult to exist in two languages simultaneously when one language includes concepts that have no equivalent in the other language. Sometimes, however, such passages are more positive in tone, focusing on the need to **reconcile** (bring together) two identities: both American and foreign can co-exist in one person without either one being sacrificed. Identity is not simply a question of black and white, American and foreign (Latino, Asian, etc.), but rather of a combination of both.

Food

Over the last half-century, food-consumption habits in the United States have changed dramatically. Americans are increasingly cut off from the sources of the food they consume, and few people have any idea about how meals make their way from the farm to the plate. Food production has become increasingly industrialized, and new technologies such as genetic engineering have led to fears of "frankenfoods." At the same time, however, the American diet is remarkably varied, a hodgepodge of influences that reflects the United States' immigrant culture. What the American diet lacks in tradition, it often makes up for in diversity and openness to new influences.

Recommended author: Michael Pollan

Ancient Societies

These passages, which describe an aspect of an ancient culture or civilization, typically focus on a recently discovered piece of evidence that has overturned a longstanding theory about how people in that society, lived, traveled, grew crops, etc., and that may provide new insight into how those people lived or how their culture was organized. Such passages therefore almost inevitably follow the "they say/I say" structure, discussed on p. 107.

The Environment and Urban Planning

Since the Industrial Revolution in the nineteenth century and the invention of electricity and the automobile in the twentieth, the environments that people build and inhabit have undergone radical changes – SAT passages that discuss these themes often explore the consequences of those changes. Cars have changed the shape of cities and the ways in which people move within them, and the omnipresence of artificial lighting has fundamentally altered people's natural biorhythms (circadian rhythms), allowing them to remain awake and productive at virtually all hours of the day. Furthermore, the earth's population is growing at an increasingly rapid rate, leading to questions about just how many people the planet can sustain. Can the "green revolution" save the environment? Finally, some SAT passages explore the controversy over interfering with or even destroying various types of natural habitats in the name of scientific progress.

Henry David Thoreau: The Original Environmentalist

One of the SAT's favorite subjects is Henry David Thoreau. A leading figure in the transcendentalist movement, which flourished in New England in the mid-19th century and which stressed direct contact with nature as a means of enlightenment, Thoreau was the original American anti-industrialist who famously retreated from civilization to live alone in a cabin by Walden Pond in Concord, Massachusetts. (In reality, he made regular trips home to have his mother wash his laundry, but that part usually gets left out of the history books.) Passages about Thoreau focus on the ways that his works and attitudes toward nature and civilization have been interpreted and misinterpreted.

Perception: How do we know what we know? How do the body and the mind interact with one another?

The Mind-Body Problem

The contemporary **mind-body problem** has its roots in the seventeenth century, when the French philosopher Rene Descartes made his famous assertion, *Cogito ergo sum* ("I think, therefore I am"). Descartes believed that the mind and the body were separate substances – a belief known as **Cartesian dualism** – and that the mind alone was capable of perceiving truth through reason (**rationalism**). Direct observation based on the senses (e.g. seeing, hearing, feeling) was not to be trusted because the senses were not always reliable and could be misleading. Proponents of **empiricism**, on the other hand, believed that truth could be determined through direct (or empirical) observation. While scientists and philosophers have debated this theory for hundreds of years, recent breakthroughs in brain research have begun to shed more light on the relationship between the body and the mind and on the ways in which they interact – for example, neuroimaging technology has allowed scientists to observe the regions of the brain that light up when people feel a particular emotion or formulate an intention. While Cartesian dualism has largely been rejected, scientists still struggle to define just how consciousness is produced as well as the extent to which perception is influenced by outside forces. Many SAT passages discuss the mind-body problem in light of recent scientific research, focusing on the ways in which thoughts and emotions – both conscious and unconscious – can produce physical effects.

Brain Plasticity

Another focus of many cognitive science passages is the concept of **brain plasticity,** or the extent to which the brain is capable of rewiring itself to adapt to new circumstances, including accidents and illness. Such passages tend to be positive in tone and focus on the brain's remarkable ability to adapt to new and challenging situations.

Animal Cognition

Cognitive science passages are not just restricted to humans, however. Many passages also deal with the question of how intelligent animals (including dogs, dolphins, and parrots) perceive the world, and how their perception differs from human perception. Themes include the dangers of **anthropomorphism**, or judging animals according to human standards (e.g. assuming that dogs can feel guilty in the same way that humans do); the notion that certain behaviors evolve out of animals' need to adapt to their environments; and humans' inability to ever determine conclusively how animals see the world. Different passages focus on different aspects of animal behavior: some focus on play, especially among young animals, and its practical or evolutionary purposes. Others focus on communication among animals and how it differs from human speech. Still others focus on the senses (sight, hearing, smell) and how they allow animals to navigate and adapt to their environments.

Researchers whose work may be alluded to in these passages include I.P. Pavlov, who, in the early twentieth century, discovered the "conditioned reflex" when he observed that a dog who heard a bell rung before being given its food would eventually begin to salivate simply at the sound of the bell; B.F. Skinner, who pioneered the concept "behaviorism" – the belief that behaviors could be taught and reinforced through their consequences (Skinner discovered that a rat who obtained food by pressing on a lever would learn to press the lever more frequently in order to obtain more food); Irene Pepperberg, whose work with an African Gray Parrot named Alex suggested that parrots could develop mental capacities equivalent to those of a two year-old child (Alex eventually learned to recognize more than 150 words and 50 objects); Louis Herman, who has studied sensory perception and communication in dolphins; and Temple Grandin (whose work has appeared on the SAT), a high-functioning autistic and renowned animal researcher whose condition has given her unusual insight into the ways in which animal perception differs from human perception.

Astronomy: is there life out there in the universe?

Passages that discuss this topic typically focus on the question of whether we are truly alone in the universe, and if not, what else might be out there. Such passages frequently discuss why the Earth alone is physically capable of supporting life, and what distinguishes it in terms of temperature, atmosphere, etc. from other planets in the solar system – planets that may either contain or have contained some earth-like features (Venus), or that may have supported some form of life in the past (Mars).

Physics: String Theory

(Super)string theory is one of the SAT's favorite subjects. While it involves some exceedingly high-level mathematics, you are only responsible for understanding it at the most basic, non-mathematical level. String theory (of which there are actually many versions) represents physicists' attempts to bring together Einstein's theory of general relativity and quantum mechanics to come up with a unified theory of everything, and to explain once and for all how the universe works. It asserts that subatomic particles such as electrons are actually one-dimensional strings that vibrate at various frequencies, like the strings of a guitar. Those different frequencies correspond to different properties, such as mass. The theory also implies the existence of additional dimensions (dimensions beyond the three dimensions in which people exist) as well as the possibility of multiple universes or parallel worlds.

One important idea that the multiple universes theory suggests is that perception of the world depends on who is doing the perceiving – that is, there is no single, objective form of reality but rather many forms of reality that can change depending upon a given set of circumstances. In this sense, string theory seems to confirm the idea that the only thing people can know with certainty is their own thoughts; our experience of the external world is always shaped by the particularities of our individual perception.

If you think this sounds a lot like science fiction, you're not alone: string theory is **one of the most important scientific controversies today**, and many physicists, including Richard Feynman (one of the original developers of the atomic bomb), have criticized it for being **too difficult to test out empirically**. Because strings are so small, they cannot be observed directly but only understood through mathematical models. String theory has, however, been repeatedly shown to work mathematically, and many scientists believe that it will ultimately explain the Big Bang and the fate of the universe. They also believe that it can account for the existence of dark matter, an unproven form of matter believed to make up more than three-quarters of the matter in the universe.

Scientific Neutrality

One additional theme that some science passages discuss is the relationship between scientific research and the people who produce it. Although scientists typically consider their work purely objective – that is, entirely neutral and free from bias – in reality it can sometimes be subtly influenced by personal beliefs or interests. For example, a scientist who personally doubts the existence of global warming might focus on data indicating that extreme weather patterns are part of a normal cycle, while one who does believe in global warming might focus on data indicating that extreme weather patterns are highly abnormal. Passages that explore this theme focus on the extent to which science can truly be considered objective given that scientists are people with interests and biases that may unconsciously play a role in the conclusions they draw.

4. The Main Point

I spend a lot of time teaching people to stop looking so hard at the details. It's not that there's anything wrong with details – it's just that they're not always terribly relevant, or even relevant at all. There's actually a Critical Reading passage that discusses the qualities that make for a good physicist, and since most high school students don't have particularly positive associations with that subject, most of them tend to dislike the passage. The remarkable thing is, though, that the point of the passage is the point of the SAT: the mark of a good physicist is the ability to "abstract out" all irrelevant information. Likewise, the mark of a good SAT-taker is the ability to abstract out all irrelevant information and focus on what's actually being asked.

One of the things that people tend to forget is that the SAT is an exam about the big picture, and for the most part, the details only count insofar as they fit into that picture. Very often, smart, detail-oriented students have a tendency to worry about every single thing that sounds even remotely odd or incomprehensible, all the while missing something major that's staring them in the face. Frequently, they blame this on the fact that they've been taught in English class to read closely and pay attention to all the details.

Well, I have some news: when you're in college with a 500 page reading assignment that you have two days to get through, you won't have time to annotate every last detail – nor will your professors expect you to do so. Whether or not you're truly interested in what you're reading, your job will be to get the gist of the author's argument and then focus on a few key areas. And if you can't recognize those key areas, college reading will be, shall we say, a struggle; unlike the books you read in English class, most of what you read in college will not have easily-digestible summaries available courtesy of sparknotes.com. So while your college assignments will hopefully not consist of multiple-choice tests, they will require you to use the same skills as those tested on the SAT. But back to the test itself.

It's fairly common for people to simply grind to a halt when they encounter an unfamiliar turn of phrase. For example, you're probably not accustomed to hearing the word "abstract" used as a verb. If you can ignore that fact and draw a logical conclusion about its meaning from the context, you'll be ok. If you cannot, however, get past the fact that "abstract" is being used in a way you haven't seen before, you'll run into trouble. You'll probably read it and realize you haven't quite understood it. So you'll go back and read it again. If you still don't quite get it, you'll reread it yet again. And before you know it, you'll have wasted two or three minutes just reading the same five lines over and over again. Then you'll run out of time before you can answer all of the questions.

The problem is that ETS will always deliberately choose passages containing bits whose meaning isn't completely clear – that's part of the test. The goal is to see whether you can figure out their meaning from the general context; you're not expected to get every word, especially not the first time around. Your job is to ignore things that are initially confusing and move on to parts that you do understand. If you get a question about something you're not sure of, you can always skip it, but you should never get hung up on something you don't understand at the expense of something you do. If you get the gist, you can figure a lot of other things out, whereas if you focus on one little detail, you'll get . . . one little detail.

Important: always read the italicized blurb above the passage because it often provides an overview of the content as well as important contextual information.

What's the Point?

The point of a passage is the **primary idea** that the author wants to convey, and it, along with the **tone** (more about that later), should be the first thing you look for when you read a passage. Once you have identified it and underlined it or written it down, you can often skim through the rest of the passage – but before that, it needs to be your primary focus.

I cannot state this strongly enough: assuming that timing is not such a major problem for you that you need to answer the questions as you read the passage, it is crucial that you identify the main point upfront because most of the questions will relate to it, either directly or indirectly. If you keep it in mind, you can often either eliminate several answer choices simply because they do not fit or make sense in context, OR, better yet, identify the correct answer right away because it is the only option that corresponds directly to the main point.

Focusing on finding the point means you don't have a chance to get bored. It reduces the chance that you'll spend five minutes trying to absorb three lines while losing sight of the big idea that really counts. And it stops you from wasting time and energy trying to convince yourself that the passage is interesting when you're actually bored out of your mind.

But let me begin by saying what a main point is **not**:

-It is not a **topic** such as "bats" or "relationship between Africans and African Americans" or "importance of art."

-It is not a **theme** such as "oppression" or "overcoming."

Topics and themes will get you virtually nowhere – you need to know what the author *thinks*.

A main point is an **argument** that answers the question "so what?" – it tells us *why* the author thinks the topic is important or what essential information he or she wants to convey. The main point can be thought of as the following formula:

Topic + So What (why does the author care?) = Main Point

Sometimes the author will directly state the main point in the passage itself. If this is the case, you should **underline it immediately**; if not, you need to **write it yourself**.

How to Write an Effective Main Point

It isn't terribly effective to discuss writing a main point in the abstract, so let's start by taking a look at the following passage:

> Sometime near the end of the Pleistocene, a band of people left northeastern Asia, crossed the Bering land bridge when the sea level was low, entered Alaska and became the first Americans. Since the 1930s, archaeologists have thought
> 5 these people were members of the Clovis culture. First discovered in New Mexico in the 1930s, the Clovis culture is known for its distinct stone tools, primarily fluted projectile points. For decades, Clovis artifacts were the oldest known in the New World, dating to 13,000 years ago. But in recent years, researchers have found more and more evidence that
> 10 people were living in North and South America before the Clovis.
> The most recently confirmed evidence comes from Washington. During a dig conducted from 1977 to 1979, researchers uncovered a bone projectile point stuck in a
> 15 mastodon rib. Since then, the age of the find has been debated, but recently anthropologist Michael Waters and his colleagues announced a new radiocarbon date for the rib: 13,800 years ago, making it 800 years older than the oldest Clovis artifact. Other pre-Clovis evidence comes from
> 20 a variety of locations across the New World.

When they first start working with me, a lot of my students aren't quite clear on the difference between describing the content of a passage and summarizing its argument. Since the ability to summarize arguments quickly and accurately is perhaps the skill that is most crucial for success on the Critical Reading portion of the SAT, this is a serious problem.

There is a very important distinction between describing content and summarizing an argument, and not knowing the difference can cost you literally hundreds of points.

Describing Content = recounting the information presented in the text without necessarily distinguishing between main points and supporting evidence and/or counter-arguments. The goal is simply to relate what is being said, often in sequential "first x, then y, and finally z" form.

Summarizing an Argument = identifying the essential point that the author wants to convey and eliminating any unnecessary detail. The goal is not to cover all of the information presented or to relate it in the sequence it appears in the passage, but rather to pinpoint the overarching idea that determines the content of the passage.

Summarizing an argument requires you to make a leap from concrete to abstract because you must move beyond simply recounting the information presented to recognizing which parts of it are most important and relating them to other, more general ideas.

While some Critical Reading questions directly ask you to identify the point of a passage or paragraph, others will do so more subtly, asking which idea a particular example illustrates. Either way, you must be able to separate the details from the more general point.

When I first ask someone to summarize the main point of a passage, however, they generally respond in one of two ways:

1) They state the topic

The Clovis People

2) They summarize the content

Uh… so the guy basically talks about how these people, I think they were called the Clovis people, right? They were like the first people who came across the Bering Strait to America… Oh no, wait, they weren't actually the first people to come across, it's just that they thought that those people were first. But so anyway those people settled in New Mexico, I think it said like 13,000 years ago? Only now he's saying that there were other people who were actually there before the Clovis, and then he says something about a mastodon rib and then something about radiocarbon dating (I remember 'cuz we learned about it in Chem this year). Oh yeah, and then he mentions the New World.

Notice how long, not to mention how vague, this version is. It doesn't really distinguish between primary and secondary information; everything gets mushed in together, and frankly it doesn't make a lot of sense. That summary gives us exactly zero help in terms of figuring out the main point. It would also waste *colossal* amounts of time.

This is not what you want to do.

Argument Summary:

New evidence shows the first inhabitants of the Americas were NOT Clovis people.

Notice how this version just hits the big idea and omits the details. All the details.

Argument Summary in super-condensed SAT terms:

New: $CP \neq 1^{st}/$ Am.

Now notice how this version cuts out absolutely everything in order to focus on the absolute total utter bare essentials. It doesn't even attempt to incorporate any sort of detail beyond the subject of the passage (the first inhabitants of the Americas) and its result, the "so what?" – the part that tells us **why** the main focus of the passage is important (it's new evidence, which means that an old theory has been overturned).

So in four words and a number, we've managed to capture the essential information *without wasting any time*. It doesn't matter if anyone else would understand it as long as we know what it's saying.

Finding the Point

Regardless of length or type, most SAT passages have certain common features in terms of where important information is likely to be located. (Note: for a discussion of main point and fiction passages, please see p. 326.)

Short Passages

Short passages typically have their main points in one of two places:

1) The first sentence
2) The last sentence

Sometime, these two sentences will complement one another: the first will present the main point, and the last will reinforce it. Other times, the main point will appear in either sentence alone. While the passage may also include secondary information, those sentences are typically the ones that provide the information necessary to answer most of the questions.

In addition, you should circle any words or phrases that indicate the author is making a point: "the point is" (or: "the point is <u>not</u>"), "key," "goal," etc., along with words such as "important," "significant," and "central," and any italicized words.

If you have already accurately identified the point, questions that explicitly ask about it will require considerably reduced effort on your part.

Let's look at some examples on the next page.

Example #1

    <u>**Make no mistake—Dolley Madison was as fiercely**</u>
<u>**partisan as any male politician.**</u> Her declaration, "I confess
I do not admire contention in any form, either political or civil"
is often cited by historians as proof of her pacific nature.

5   The second half of the statement reveals more—"I would
rather fight with my hands than my tongue." And fight she did,
though hers was the arena of action, not words. Though Dolley
strove for discretion in her letters, anger at her husband's
enemies sometimes broke through. During his presidency, James

10 Madison was hampered by what Dolley called "a Capricious
Senate," whose objections she characterized as "allmost treason."
<u>***Still***</u><u>**, she subsumed her feelings, so that one guest declared,**</u>
<u>**"By her deportment in her own house you cannot discover**</u>
<u>**who is her husband's friends or foes."**</u>

The absolute main point of the passage is in the first sentence: by starting off with a statement as strong as, "Make no mistake," the author goes out of his way to tell us that this information is important. There's also a dash, which signals an explanation and is pretty much always important, and the word *fiercely*, which is pretty strong.

If we simply underlined that sentence, we'd probably have enough information to help us figure out the questions. For example:

> The author cites the declaration in lines 5-6 ("I would…my tongue") in order to support the point that Dolley Madison
>
> (A) had an unusually pacific nature
> (B) behaved aggressively toward her enemies
> (C) was accused of treason
> (D) did not admire contention in any form
> (E) held very strong convictions

(E) essentially rephrases the main point (fiercely partisan = holding strong convictions), and thus it is correct.

Notice, however, that the line reference provided does not match the place in the passage where the answer is actually located. The actual information you need is in the first line.

Example #2

Ideas matter. A relatively small number can be
classed as major historical events. And many times, their
best, most eloquent expression has been on paper, stamped
in ink, sewn on one side, and bound between hard covers.
5   In the beginning was the word, sure, but there's also a lot to
be said for the book. Think of Abraham Lincoln's comment,
one hundred and fifty years ago, upon meeting the creator
of a book, "So, this is the little lady who made this big war."
He was speaking to Harriet Beecher Stowe, the author of
10 Uncle Tom's Cabin. As we are asked to contemplate the
disappearance of books as such, it's worth pausing over the
astonishing range of personal, social, and political purposes
that have been served by books: the liberation of individuals,
the reinforcement of community, the expansion of self-
15 knowledge, the publication of scientific findings, the spread
of lies and promulgation of facts. **Vast are the aims served
by books.**

While the first sentence of this passage does provide important information, that information isn't quite specific enough – the focus of the passage is on *books*, not simply on ideas. In order to get a more precise idea of the essential point the author wants to convey, we must read until the end.

Notice, however, that we do get a hint of the main idea earlier in the passage: the phrase *astonishing range* previews that idea. That is why you always need to pay attention to **strong** or **extreme** language, such as *astonishing*: such words and phrases will often reinforce or indicate the author's point.

The basic structure of this passage is essentially the opposite of the structure of the previous passage: the beginning and middle of the passage provide support for the main idea (the effect of books on the Civil War, a list of all of the purposes that books have served), and the last sentence sums it all up in one big idea.

The author most likely includes the list in lines 12-16
("the liberation…satisfaction") in order to

(A) downplay the seriousness of a claim
(B) underscore the gravity of a situation
(C) emphasize the magnitude of an effect
(D) imply skepticism about an influence
(E) call attention to a pressing concern

In this case, (C) rephrases the main point – although perhaps not in quite the way you were expecting. Vast, astonishing range = Magnitude. Same idea, different words. Remember? The correct answer will usually contain a synonym for a key word in the passage.

They Say/I Say: A Passage is a Conversation

The "they say/I say" model is one of the most important concepts – if not the single most important concept – necessary for making sense out of Critical Reading passages, simply because so many passages make use of it in one way or another. It's also the name of a book written by Gerald Graff and Cathy Birkenstein, professors at the University of Illinois, Chicago, and if you have time (even if you don't have time), you need to run out and buy yourself a copy because it's very possibly the best work ever written to bridge the gap between high school and college learning. Although the book focuses on writing rather than reading, it covers many of the core "formulas" that appear in SAT passages and demystifies academic writing like nothing else.

So what is the "they say/I say" model? Well, let me start by saying this: most of the writing that you do in high school tends to be fairly one-sided. Unless you're explicitly asked to agree or disagree with someone else's opinion, most of your writing for school probably involves coming up with an original thesis and "proving" it by supporting it with various pieces of evidence that you've come up with on your own. Throughout the process, the focus is relentlessly on *your* thoughts, *your* ideas, *your* evidence. Potential objections to your argument? You probably don't spend two or three paragraphs describing them, let alone explaining their weaknesses. If you mention them at all, you probably discuss them pretty superficially. And if you are disagreeing with someone else's idea, you probably don't spend much time talking about the parts of their argument that you *do* agree with.

The writing that professional authors do is different. They're not writing for a grade, or to please their teacher, or to show that they've mastered the five-paragraph essay. They're not writing in a box. **On the contrary, they see themselves as part of a conversation.** They're always writing in response to what "other people" have said – usually because they don't agree with those other people's ideas, although they may agree with certain aspects of them. (If they agreed completely, they would have no reason to write!) So either directly or indirectly, they will often refer back to the people they are "conversing" with. They examine the history of the idea they are discussing, consider common interpretations and beliefs, and weigh the merits and shortcomings of those beliefs.

As a result, authors will sometimes spend a significant portion of a passage discussing ideas with which they *do not* agree. **In fact, the author's opinion may not emerge until halfway through the passage or later – occasionally not until the conclusion.** Although authors will sometimes state flat-out that a particular idea is wrong, just as often they will be far less direct. They'll "imply skepticism" by putting particular words or phrases in quotation marks or ask rhetorical questions such as "But is this really the case?" They'll use words like "imply" and "suggest" and "support," not "prove."

Just because they don't frame things in terms of absolute right or wrong does not, however, mean that they lack clear opinions. Regardless of how much time they spend discussing other people's ideas, sooner or later they'll tell you what they think – and that's something you need to pay very close attention to because that will be the point of the passage. While the "they say/I say" model can be found in passages covering virtually every topic and length, it is particularly common in science/natural history passages, many of which are organized in terms of the "people used to believe x, but now they believe y." In this structure, the author typically begins by discussing an accepted idea or theory, then, at a certain point, explains why that theory is wrong, and why a new or recent theory – the theory that the author believes – is actually correct.

The following list provides some common phrases that indicate when the author is talking about other peoples' ideas versus their own ideas.*

They Say

-Some people (scientists, readers, critics, etc.) believe…
-Many people think that…
-Most people think that…
-It is commonly thought that…
-Accepted/conventional wisdom holds that…
-In the past…
-For a long time/decades/hundreds of years…
-Traditionally, people have believed that…

I Say

-However, But in fact, In reality…
-But is it really true/the case that…?
-It seems to me that…
-It now seems (clear) that…
-Recently, it has been found that…
-People now think…
-New research/evidence shows/suggests that
-Another possibility is that…

A single passage will often contain two and occasionally three different points of view, and a Passage 1/Passage 2 pair can contain even more, but it's up to you to keep track of what the author thinks and what other people think. **Don't try to remember: write it down quickly or underline it and draw an arrow or a star next to it. Make your mark huge and obvious so that you don't forget to keep referring back to it.**

I cannot stress how important this is: when you are asked to juggle multiple points of view, relying on your memory is a recipe for disaster. If you're already scoring well, you may be able to do it up to a point, but chances are you're not always double-checking yourself. Having an approximate understanding isn't good enough – you have to be precise (not the same thing as being detailed or complicated). If you don't know which idea(s) the author supports/disagrees with and are unable to summarize those ideas simply and accurately, you risk choosing answers that are exactly the opposite of the ones you should be choosing.

*For an index of rhetorical templates, please see *They Say/I Say: The Moves that Matter in Academic Writing* by Gerald Graff and Cathy Birkenstein.

Using What "They Say" to Predict Main Point and Attitude

One of the reasons that it is so crucial you be able to recognize the types of the phrases that signal "they say/I say" is that those phrases often allow you to identify the point of the passage *before the author even states it*. Think of it this way: if the introduction of a passage includes a sentence with the words "many people think...," that's an absolute giveaway that the idea that follows is what "they say," and that the author's attitude toward that idea will be negative. The main point of the passage (positive attitude) is therefore virtually guaranteed to be the **opposite** of "their" idea. So from a single sentence, it is possible to predict the main point AND the author's likely attitude in various parts of the passage. You should always keep reading just to make sure, but once you've confirmed that the author does in fact hold the view that the introduction suggests, you can often skim through much of the body of the passage. For example, consider a passage that begins with the following sentence:

> Hoarder, moneylender, tax dodger — it's not how we
> **usually** think of William Shakespeare.

The word "usually" is a tip-off that the author is presenting the conventional wisdom – what "they" say. We can infer that his response is something along the lines of, "but Shakespeare actually *was* those things," and that the passage will present evidence in support of that view.

Let's look at another example – it's a classic beginning of a science passage:

> **Some scientists conclude** that music's influence may be
> a chance event, arising from its ability to hijack brain systems
> built for other purposes such as language, emotion and movement.

The phrase "some scientists conclude" is the equivalent of a flashing red signal that the author disagrees with the idea that music's influence is a "chance event." We can very reasonably assume that the author believes music's influence is **not** a chance event, and the remainder of the passage will explain why.

Some passages will also present what "they say" a bit more subtly. For example:

> The Amazon Kindle—a "new and improved" version of
> which has just been released—comes on like a technology for
> our times: crisp, affordable, hugely capacious, capable of
> connecting to the Internet, and green. How could one argue with
> 5 any of that? Or with the idea, which I've heard voiced over and
> over, that it will make the reading of texts once again seductive,
> using the same technology that has drawn people away from the
> page back to it.

Although it isn't quite as obvious that the author is introducing what "they say" as it is in the previous example, there are a number of clues. First, the quotation marks in the first line suggests **skepticism** (the author does not actually believe that the Kindle is really "new and improved"). Second, the phrase "how could one argue" in the rhetorical question in lines 4-5 implies that author's answer is "well actually, *I* can argue." And finally, the phrase "over and over" in lines 5-6 is the clearest tip-off that the author is presenting conventional wisdom.

"They Say/I Say" and Short Passages

As a general rule, the presence of the word "however" or "but" halfway through a short passage signals the presence of the "they say/I say" model. Whenever one of those words appears, you need to pay special attention to it. Not only will it provide important information about how the passage is structured, but it will also tell you where in the passage to focus because the author's opinion will virtually always be stated **after** that transition.

Look at the passage below: it's a classic example of this kind of structure. We've looked at it before, but now we're going to look at it in a slightly different way.

If you simply scan the passage without really reading it, you should be able to spot the word "but" in line 8, the last sentence of the first paragraph. The presence of that single word at the particular point in the passage gives you quite a bit of information: even if you don't know (or care) what the passage is about, that "but" suggests that everything before it will have something to do with the old model, and that everything after it will have something to do with the new model. You also know that the author's attitude toward the information at the beginning of the passage will be somewhat negative (i.e. *skeptical, critical*), and that the author's attitude at the end of the passage will be somewhat positive (i.e. *appreciative*). I say "somewhat" because science passages in particular tend to be written in an even more neutral manner than other kinds of passages… But more about that in the "Tone and Attitude" chapter. For now, let's stick to finding the point.

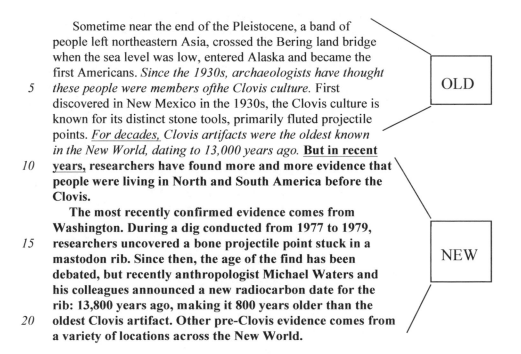

     Sometime near the end of the Pleistocene, a band of people left northeastern Asia, crossed the Bering land bridge when the sea level was low, entered Alaska and became the first Americans. *Since the 1930s, archaeologists have thought*
5 *these people were members ofthe Clovis culture.* First discovered in New Mexico in the 1930s, the Clovis culture is known for its distinct stone tools, primarily fluted projectile points. *For decades, Clovis artifacts were the oldest known in the New World, dating to 13,000 years ago.* **But in recent**
10 **years, researchers have found more and more evidence that people were living in North and South America before the Clovis.**
     The most recently confirmed evidence comes from Washington. During a dig conducted from 1977 to 1979,
15 **researchers uncovered a bone projectile point stuck in a mastodon rib. Since then, the age of the find has been debated, but recently anthropologist Michael Waters and his colleagues announced a new radiocarbon date for the rib: 13,800 years ago, making it 800 years older than the**
20 **oldest Clovis artifact. Other pre-Clovis evidence comes from a variety of locations across the New World.**

In order to keep yourself on track and avoid confusion, you should jot down for yourself the old idea and the new idea (what the author believes). And by "jot down," I mean scrawl in shorthand – you don't get points for neatness, and you're the only person who has to understand what you write. It should take you a few seconds at most.

$$O = CP\ 1^{st}\ NA \qquad\qquad \text{(Clovis people first in North America)}$$
$$N = Ppl\ in\ NA\ pre\text{-}CP \qquad \text{(People were in North America before Clovis)}$$

If you are truly concerned that writing these things down will take too much time, simply label them in the passage as is done above.

Whether you write the point yourself or simply underline it, you must remember to look back at your notes! Otherwise, they're useless. I've lost count of the number of times a student of mine has underlined the exact sentence where an answer was located but still gotten a question wrong just because they forgot to look back at what they'd written.

> The author mentions the "projectile point" (line 14)
> in order to
>
> (A) provide evidence in support of a claim
> (B) cast doubt on a controversial finding
> (C) shift the focus of the passage
> (D) introduce a digression
> (E) question the validity of a hypothesis

What's the author's point (i.e. claim)? That the Clovis People were NOT the first people to inhabit the Americas (OR: there were people in the Americas BEFORE the Clovis People).

We learn later in the passage the projectile point was dated at 13,800 years old but that the Clovis People only arrived 13,000 years ago. The author is therefore mentioning the projectile point as *evidence* that people inhabited the Americas before 13,000 years ago, i.e. before the Clovis People arrived. So the answer is (A).

Notice that the details of the line in question are borderline irrelevant: it doesn't matter if you know anything about projectile points and mastodons. All that counts is your ability to understand the importance of those details in context of the larger argument. If you understand the argument, you can see how the details fit; if you miss the argument, you'll have to start all over again with each new question. That's not to say you won't get plenty of answers right anyway, just that doing so will be a much more exhausting process.

How to Read Long Passages

As a rule, you should read the passage as quickly as you can while still absorbing the content, making sure to focus on the parts you do understand and not wasting time puzzling over confusing details. It is usually unnecessary to read every word in order to determine the point. Rather, a couple of a key places often provide sufficient information: **the main point itself is most often found at either the end of the first paragraph or the beginning of the second paragraph, and reiterated at the end of the conclusion.**

If you have excellent comprehension and are already strong at identifying and summarizing arguments, you should read the passage slowly until you figure out the point; then read the first (topic) and last sentence of each paragraph carefully, skimming through the body of each paragraph and circling major transitions/strong language; and read the conclusion carefully, focusing particularly on and underlining the last sentence or two because the main point will often be restated there. Reading this way will allow you to create a mental "map" of how the passage is structured: the introduction and conclusion will most likely give you the point of the passage, and each topic sentence will generally provide you with the point of the paragraph, allowing you to understand how it fits into the argument as a whole. Then when you're asked to think about the details, you'll already understand the ideas that they support and have a general sense of the roles that they play within the passage.

If you consistently run out of time reading long passages, you can try a version of the approach discussed above, reading the introduction slowly until you figure out the point, then reading the first and last sentence of each body paragraph carefully and skipping the information in between. Then read the conclusion slowly and underline the last sentence. That way, you'll get the major points without losing time. **If your comprehension is outstanding,** you should simply move on to the next section of the passage (the place where the idea clearly changes) once you've grasped the point of any particular section of the passage you happen to be reading – regardless of whether that section consists of one paragraph, two, or even three. You can worry about the details when you go back.

Alternately, if you feel that you simply can't read any portion of the passage upfront without running out of time, you can try reading short bits of the passage at a time and answering only the "detail" questions that ask about those lines. That way, you don't have to worry about trudging through the whole thing before you even get to the questions.

But a warning: while answering the questions as you read the passage can work well if you are a strong reader and timing is your *only* issue, it otherwise has some drawbacks. First, answers to some questions are **not** located in the immediate vicinity of their line references – if you don't read far enough ahead, you might not get all the information you need. Second, if you use this method as a way of getting around a weakness in understanding the big picture, it will be difficult to score above 700 unless you address the underlying issue. Reading passages bit by bit encourages you to see them as masses of details rather than arguments structured around a claim or idea; you never deal directly with what the test is actually testing. That's not to say that you can't still get lots – or all – of the questions right, just that the process will be much more tedious and open to far more possibility for error.

Skimming Effectively Means Knowing What to Focus On

One popular piece of Critical Reading wisdom holds that you should read the passage quickly and the questions slowly. For a strong reader, that can certainly be an effective strategy… but only if you're reading the passage quickly *the right way*. Effective skimming does not simply involve reading quickly, but rather knowing where to skip and where to slow down. As mentioned earlier, non-fiction authors tend to be pretty clear about the parts of their writing that they want you to pay attention to: if they're really generous, they'll even come right out and tell you what the point is. Even if they're not quite that blatant, however, they usually make a decent effort to tell you what's important.

So first, if the word "important" or any of its synonyms (*essential, crucial, central, key*) appears in the middle of a paragraph as you're racing through, you need to slow down, circle it, and read that part carefully. **If the author says it's important, it's important.** There's no trick.

Second, you need to learn to recognize when an argument changes or when new and important information is being introduced: transitions such as *however, therefore, in fact*; "unusual" punctuation such as dashes, italics, and colons; and strong language such as *only, never*, and *extremely* are all "clues" that tell you to pay attention. If one of these elements appears either **in or around** the lines you're given to read, **the answer will typically be located right around that spot.** As a general rule, you should avoid circling nouns (with the exception of words like *reason, explanation*, and *problem*) because they do not tell you *why* particular pieces of information are important.

If you are able to do so without disrupting your ability to absorb the content of the passage, you should also circle major transitions and "unusual" punctuation as you read. You don't have to worry about why they're there when you do an initial skim-through of the passage, but if you are able to do so without losing focus, you should mark them as you go so you'll know what to pay attention to when you go back to answer the questions.

If, on the other hand, you feel that looking for transitions will interfere with your comprehension, then you should not worry about them when you read through the passage initially. It is far more important that you gain a clear understanding of the passage. When you go back to answer the questions, however, you do need to take them into account because they will typically indicate where the answers are located.

To reiterate: the goal is not to look for transitions just for the sake of doing so. You don't need to circle every last "and" or "but" that appears, and in fact, you probably shouldn't. Rather, the goal is to use the "clues" that the passage provides as a means of identifying the *major* points of the argument – the places where you need to pay close attention.

For a complete list of key words and phrases, please see the chart on p. 179.

Let's look at an example.

The passage below is adapted from an article published in 2008. It discusses the effects of light pollution.

If humans were truly at home under the light of the moon and stars, we would go in darkness happily, the midnight world as visible to us as it is to the vast number of nocturnal species on this planet. Instead, we
5 are diurnal creatures, with eyes adapted to living in the sun's light. This is a basic evolutionary fact, even though most of us don't think of ourselves as diurnal beings any more than we think of ourselves as primates or mammals or Earthlings. **Yet** it's the only
10 way to explain what we've done to the night: We've engineered it to receive us by filling it with light. This kind of engineering is no different than damming a river. Its benefits come with consequences—**called light pollution**—whose effects scientists are only now
15 beginning to study. Light pollution is largely the result of bad lighting design, which allows artificial light to shine outward and upward into the sky, where it's not wanted, instead of focusing it downward, where it is.

Main Point

Ill-designed lighting washes out the darkness of night and radically alters the light levels—and rhythms—to which many forms of life, including ourselves have adapted.

For most of human history, the phrase "light
25 pollution" would have made no sense. Imagine walking toward London on a moonlit night around 1800, when it was Earth's most populous city. Nearly a million people lived there, making do, as they always had, with candles and lanterns. Only a few
30 houses were lit by gas, and there would be no public gaslights for another seven years. From a few miles away, you would have been as likely to smell London as to see its dim glow.

Now most of humanity lives under intersecting
35 domes of light, of scattering rays from overlit cities and suburbs, from light-flooded highways and factories. In most cities the sky looks as though it has been emptied of stars, leaving behind a vacant haze that mirrors our fear of the dark and resembles the
40 urban glow of dystopian science fiction. We've grown so used to this pervasive orange haze that the original glory of an unlit night—**dark enough for the planet Venus to throw shadows on Earth**—is wholly beyond our experience, beyond memory
45 almost.

We've lit up the night as if it were an unoccupied country, when **nothing could be further from the truth**. Light is a **powerful** biological force, and on many species it acts as a magnet. Migrating at
50 night, birds are apt to collide with brightly lit tall buildings; immature birds on their first journey suffer disproportionately. **And because** a longer day allows for longer feeding, it can also affect migration schedules. **The problem, of course,** is
55 that migration is a precisely timed biological behavior. Leaving early may mean arriving too soon for nesting conditions to be right.

It was **once thought** that light pollution only affected astronomers, who need to see the night sky
60 in all its glorious clarity. **And, in fact,** some of the earliest efforts to control light pollution were made to protect the view from Lowell Observatory. Unlike astronomers, most of us may not need an undiminished view of the night sky for our work,
65 but like most other creatures we do need darkness. Darkness is as **essential** to our internal clockwork, as light itself. The regular oscillation of waking and sleep in our lives is nothing less than a biological expression of the regular oscillation of light on
70 Earth. **So** fundamental are these rhythms to our being that altering them is like altering gravity.

For the past century or so, we've been performing an open-ended experiment on ourselves, extending the day, shortening the night,
75 and short-circuiting the human body's sensitive response to light. The **consequences** of our bright new world are more readily perceptible in less adaptable creatures living in the peripheral glow of our prosperity. **But** for humans, too, light pollution
80 may take a biological toll. **In a very real sense, light pollution causes us to lose sight of our true place in the universe, to forget the scale of our being, which is best measured against the dimensions of a deep night with the Milky Way**
85 **on the edge of our galaxy—arching overhead.**

Repetition of Main Point

We're going to look more closely at the purpose of all those transitions and punctuation in another chapter. For now, it's enough that you start to recognize the kind of information you need to pay attention to.

Recognizing "They Say/I Say" in Long Passages

"They say/I say" in long passages follows much the same principles as it does in short passages. The main difference is that because long passages are well, long, they tend to be less focused than short passages and contain more potentially confusing information to sift through. Rather than focusing on exclusively one idea at a time, an author may bounce back and forth between conflicting viewpoints. So while the presence of a transition such as "however" or "but" in a common key place (last sentence of the first paragraph, first sentence of the second paragraph), it may also appear in a somewhat less expected place (topic sentence of a body paragraph, last sentence of one of the first few paragraphs).

In addition, while the "they say/I say" structure may be conveyed directly through a transition such as "but" or "however," it may also be suggested in subtler ways. It is therefore extremely important that you be able to recognize the kinds of words and phrases that indicate the use of this structure, and you should make sure to familiarize yourself with the phrases on p. 186 so that you can recognize it when it occurs.

That said, however, recognizing when a passage is organized according to this model – particularly when it deals with an esoteric topic (e.g. quantum physics) that is extremely unfamiliar to most people – can make it much easier for you to grasp the basics of the author's argument. If you can understand the basic ideas that the author is "for" and "against" – or even the fact that the author is for something and against something period – the details won't matter so much, and the chances of your becoming confused are substantially reduced.

In the passage on the following page, references to the old model are italicized, and references to the new model are in bold. Key phrases are underlined.

The following passage is taken from a 2010 article written by a well-known theoretical physicist.

A few years ago the city council of Monza, Italy, barred pet owners from keeping goldfish in curved fishbowls. The sponsors of the measure explained that it is cruel to keep a fish in a bowl
5 because the curved sides give the fish a distorted view of reality. Aside from the measure's significance to the poor goldfish, the story raises an interesting philosophical question: How do we know that the reality we perceive is true? The goldfish is
10 seeing a version of reality that is different from ours, but can we be sure it is any less real? For all we know, we, too, may spend our entire lives staring out at the world through a distorting lens.

In physics, the question is not academic. Indeed,
15 physicists are finding themselves in a similar predicament to the goldfish's. *For decades we have strived to come up with an ultimate theory of everything—one complete and consistent set of fundamental laws of nature that explain every aspect*
20 *of reality.* **It now appears that this quest may yield not a single theory but a family of interconnected theories, each describing its own version of reality, as if it viewed the universe through its own fishbowl.**

25 This notion may be difficult for many people, including some working scientists, to accept. *Most people believe that there is an objective reality out there and that our senses and our science directly convey information about the material world.*
30 *Classical science is based on the belief that an external world exists whose properties are definite and independent of the observer who perceives them. In philosophy, that belief is called realism.*

Those who remember Timothy Leary and the
35 **1960s, however, know of another possibility: one's concept of reality can depend on the mind of the perceiver. That viewpoint, with various subtle differences, goes by names such as antirealism, instrumentalism or idealism. According to those**
40 **doctrines, the world we know is constructed by the human mind employing sensory data as its raw material and is shaped by the interpretive structure of our brains. This viewpoint may be hard to accept, but it is not difficult to understand. There is**
45 **no way to remove the observer— us—from our perception of the world.**

The way physics has been going, realism is becoming difficult to defend. In classical physics— the physics of Newton that so accurately describes our
50 *everyday experience—the interpretation of terms such as object and position is for the most part in harmony with our commonsense, "realistic" understanding of those concepts. As measuring devices, however, we are crude instruments. Physicists have found that*
55 *everyday objects and the light we see them by are made from objects that we do not perceive directly.*

These objects are governed not by classical physics but by the laws of quantum theory. The reality of quantum theory is a radical departure from that
60 **of classical physics. In the framework of quantum theory, particles have neither definite positions nor definite velocities unless and until an observer measures those quantities. Quantum physics also has important implications for our concept of the**
65 **past. In classical physics, the past is assumed to exist as a definite series of events, but according to quantum physics, the past, like the future, is indefinite and exists only as a spectrum of possibilities. Even the universe as a whole has no**
70 **single past or history. So quantum physics implies a different reality than that of classical physics— even though the latter still serves us well when we design things such as buildings and bridges.**

These examples bring us to a conclusion that
75 **provides an important framework with which to interpret modern science. In our view, there is no picture- or theory-independent concept of reality. Instead we adopt a view that we call model-dependent realism: the idea that a physical theory**
80 **or world picture is a model (generally of a mathematical nature) and a set of rules that connect the elements of the model to observations. According to model-dependent realism, it is pointless to ask whether a model is real,**
85 **only whether it agrees with observation. If two models agree with observation, neither one can be considered more real than the other. A person can use whichever model is more convenient in the situation under consideration.**

As you can see, references to the old and the new model are interwoven throughout the passage, although as the passage progresses, the new model (quantum theory) is discussed in more and more depth until the author focuses on it exclusively. Only at the very end, however, does the author say what he believes (a model only exists if it agrees with what people observe). We must therefore read until the very end of the passage to find the point.

If we were to summarize the two models, however, we could say something like this:

O = CP = world exists indep/observer
(Old Model = Classical Physics, says that the world exists independently of observer)

N= QT, existence depnds/obsrvtn
(New Model = Quantum Theory: model only exists if it agrees with observation)

And if we wanted to combine those ideas into a main point, we could say something like:

QT, not CP, describes reality

Or, if you want to forget about the "old model" and just focus on what the author thinks (which is fine if you're clear on what the author *doesn't* think), you could say something like:

QT right: reality varies w/observation

Again, it is crucial that you keep careful track of what each model says because otherwise, you risk misunderstanding the entire point of the passage. And if you were to encounter a question like the following, you might also run into some problems.

The author views the theory described in lines 27-29
("there is...world") as

(A) innovative
(B) perplexing
(C) destructive
(D) fallacious
(E) esoteric

One shortcut for answering this question is to back up to the start of the sentence, where the author states, "Most people think..." If a passage includes the phrase "most people think," then by definition, the author thinks that idea is **wrong**, i.e. *fallacious* (D).

It is especially crucial that you recognize this "clue" if you choose to answer the questions as you read the passage. In this case, the author does not directly indicate that the theory in question is wrong until the beginning of the next paragraph (line 34). If you haven't read that far yet, the phrase "most people think" is the only piece of information you have to go on. While the answer is usually located in the same paragraph as the lines referred to in the question, occasionally it will actually be somewhere else.

Now let's look at another one. As in the previous passage, references to what other people say are *italicized*, while references to what the author says are in **bold**.

The following passage was adapted from the introduction of a book of letters by the nineteenth century Impressionist* painter Berthe Morisot.

One of the first and most frequently repeated strategies used to cope with Berthe Morisot's position as a female member of a 'radical' art group participating in what is perceived as an exclusively
5 *man's world, has been to construct her as exceptional. Unlike other women artists, both before and during her time, she, it is claimed, does not fall into the inevitable traps which beset women artists. George Moore, writing in 1898, stated that Morisot's*
10 *pictures 'are the only pictures painted by a woman that could not be destroyed without creating a blank, a hiatus in the history of art.' In turn, her painting 'style,' Impressionism, is produced as a method which is suited to and the natural expression of an*
15 *appropriately feminine temperament. 'Impressionism' is offered as the answer to the problem of Morisot's 'femininity,' the problem posed by a skilled and prolific professional woman painter in a world which deemed such activities to be 'unfeminine.' From as*
20 *early as the 1870s Morisot's manner of working was seen to reflect a naturally feminine sensibility; it was repeatedly called 'charming,' 'feminine,' 'delicate' in a way which transposed onto the painting those characteristics most favored in the middle-class*
25 *women of the time.*

What representations of Morisot as the intuitive feminine painter do not take into account, however, is the fact that she was one of many women working as professional artists at the period and
30 **that these women represented in working methods the full range of artistic practices. Few used the painterly brushmarks and sketchy surfaces that are characteristic of much of Impressionist painting and most were unaware of Morisot's**
35 **existence, preferring to define their context as that of the Paris Salons or alternately the women's Salon which emerged in the early 1880s as a significant forum for the display of women's work. If Morisot shared any technical qualities**
40 **with her contemporaries, it was with male artists like Renoir and Monet. They, like her, were committed to an aesthetic of apparent spontaneity, using separated brushmarks, revealing the light ground of the canvas, eliminating the use of the art-**
45 **based pigment bitumen, and striving for the approximate effect of natural light. The resulting 'delicacy of touch' was part of a conscious strategy to free painting from the academic emphasis on finish, the highly polished surface with no traces of**
50 **individual brushmarks, and can in no way be attributed to the outpouring of an essential feminity.**

Accompanying the idea that Impressionism was a naturally feminine style of painting was the notion that Morisot's working methods flowed
55 *intuitively for her inner self without conscious*

*intervention or mediation. As Paul Valéry** was to put it: 'the peculiarity of Berthe Morisot...was to live her painting and to paint her life, as if the interchange between seeing and rendering, between*
60 *the light and her creative will, were to her a natural function, a necessary part of her daily life.'* **But her letters themselves do not allow this view to be sustained. If anything, they represent her often painful and intense involvement with**
65 **painting, described once as a 'pitched battle with her canvases.' Equally, they represent a woman who is absolutely aware of the ways in which she and her colleagues are received in the press, and is mindful of the reception of her own work and**
70 **that of her associates.**

But if the image of Morisot as an intuitive, unreflective artist living out her natural femininity through her painting cannot be sustained, neither can she be accommodated by today's
75 *feminist art historians in the role of the lofty female ancestor, politicized about her gender and the institutionalized sexism of her time. This does not mean that she was unaware of the debates around women's positions, or the restrictions, social and*
80 *psychic, which were placed on women's lives, but that her responses are not unified and worked out. They are often confused, ambiguous, and tellingly self-denigrating.*

The 'evidence' provided in her letters is
85 *fragmentary and suggestive. It presents a woman often confused, filled with self-doubt, frequently discontent, berated for her stubbornness and selfishness, envied and admired, a devoted friend, and above all, a committed artist. The texts of her*
90 *letters themselves, many of them by Morisot's family and friends, provide a telling contrast to the idealized mythic representation of the enigmatic, even muse-like figure, which so many accounts of Morisot construct.*

*Nineteenth century movement in French painting, which emphasized the accurate depiction of light as well as the portrayal of everyday scenes.

** French poet with a strong interest in painting and the visual arts.

The first thing to notice when you look at the passage is that it's literally arranged like a dialogue – that is, it alternates between what "other people" say and the author's response. If we were to make an outline of the argument, we could do the following:

1st Paragraph: They say

Morisot = exceptional b/c woman artist, Impressionism "natural" to women

Key phrases: *One of the most frequent strategies*

2nd Paragraph: I say

Morisot = one of many prof. female artists, technique reflective of Impressionist style, not inherently feminine

Key phrases: *What representations of Morisot as the intuitive feminine painter do not take into account, however, is the fact that she was one of many women working...*

3rd Pargaraph: They say/I say

They say: Morisot's art = intuitive (typically feminine)

I say: letters show Morisot struggled w/art, not easy at all

Key phrases: *Accompanying the idea that Impressionism was a naturally feminine style of painting... But her letters themselves do not allow this view to be sustained.*

4th & 5th Paragraphs: They say/I say

Morisot ≠ intuitive artist but ALSO ≠ feminist, letters = contradictory

Key phrases: *But if the image of Morisot as an intuitive, unreflective artist living out her natural femininity through her painting cannot be sustained, neither can she be accommodated by today's feminist art historians.*

Main point: Berthe Morisot was complex: her painting reflected neither a "natural" femininity nor a desire to fight for women's rights.

Or: BM = complex, art ≠ natural OR feminist

Notice that virtually all of the key transitions are in topic sentences – even if you don't read the interiors of the paragraphs, you can still get a pretty good idea of the argument. Even if you find parts of the passage confusing (and it's perfectly normal if you do), you can still figure out the basics of the argument just by looking at the key words.

As a matter of fact, even if you have no idea whatsoever what the passage is saying, the phrase *One of the most frequent strategies* is an immediate tip-off that the author is talking about a commonly-held belief, which virtually guarantees that she does not agree with it. In the second paragraph, the word *however* in the topic sentence indicates that she is shifting gears and talking about the idea that she *does* agree with. Those two "clues" are enough to tell you that the structure is "they say/I say;" that the attitude toward the ideas in the first paragraph is negative and that the attitude toward the ideas in the second paragraph is positive.

So if you were to see a question that looked like this:

The author's attitude toward the viewpoint described in lines 19-25 ("From as early...the time") can best be characterized as

(A) critical
(B) perplexed
(C) caustic
(D) appreciative
(E) indifferent

...you would know immediately that the answer had to be negative since lines 19-25 are in the first paragraph. That would eliminate (B), (D), and (E). (C) is too extreme, leaving (A).

So while it is most certainly NOT necessary that you outline the entire passage in your own words while you are actually taking the SAT, it can nevertheless be helpful to spend some time analyzing Critical Reading passages this way when you first begin to study. Although the process of breaking passages down this way may seem incredibly tedious and unnecessary, the ability to recognize the relationship between structure and meaning is actually the exact skill that the SAT tests, and you need to be able to call on it at will. When you really understand how an argument is put together, the answers start to leap out at you.

Explaining a Phenomenon

Another type of long passage – typically a science passage – has yet a third structure: the author begins by discussing a longstanding problem, then spends the remainder of the passage describing various potential solutions or explanations that have been proposed.

Sometimes these explanations will be discussed chronologically (in order of time), but sometimes they will not.

The passage will often conclude by returning to the original question and emphasizing that a conclusive answer has not yet been determined and perhaps may never be. Occasionally, however, such passages will not have a fully developed conclusion but will simply come to an end, as is the case for the passage on the following page. This is only logical: if scientists have been unable to reach a conclusion about why a particular phenomenon occurs, there is quite literally nothing to conclude!

Very often, these passages will also contain elements of "old model vs. new model" – in describing various explanations, the author will often discuss how certain theories have been discarded or overturned.

Let's look at an example on the following page: **references to the original problem are in bold, while discussions of the various explanations are underlined.**

Note that in this case, the explanations are presented chronologically and the author does discuss an explanation that was ultimately rejected (italicized).

In addition, note that there is no real conclusion: in this instance, the last sentence does not restate the main point; you must look at the beginning of the passage to find out its purpose.

The passage below originally appeared in a 2004 book about the origin of the universe.

In our attempts to uncover the history of the cosmos, we have continually discovered that the segments most deeply shrouded in mystery are those that deal with *origins* – of the universe itself, of its most massive structures (galaxies and galaxy clusters), and of the stars that provide most of the light in the cosmos. **These mysteries** arise in large part because during the cosmic "dark ages," when matter was just beginning to organize itself into self-contained units such as stars and galaxies, most of this matter generated little or no detectable radiation. **When we turn to the origin of planets, the mysteries deepen.** We lack not only *observations* of the crucial, initial stages of planetary formation but also successful *theories* of how the planets began to form.

Astrophysicists may now have more data but they have no better answers than before. The beginnings of planet building pose a remarkably intractable problem, to the point that one of the world's experts on the subject, Scott Tremaine, has elucidated (partly in jest) Tremaine's laws of planet formation. The first of these laws states that "all theoretical prediction about the properties of exosolar planets are wrong," and the second that "the most secure prediction about planet formation is that it can't happen." Tremaine's humor underscores the ineluctable fact that planets do exist, despite our inability to explain this astronomical enigma.

More than two centuries ago, attempting to explain the formation of the Sun and its planets, Immanuel Kant proposed a "nebular hypothesis," according to which a swirling mass of gas and dust that surrounded our star-in-formation condensed into clumps that became the planets. It its broad outlines, Kant's hypothesis remains the basis for modern astronomical approaches to planet formation, having triumphed over the concept, much in vogue **during the first half of the twentieth century,** that the Sun's planets arose from a close passage of another star by the Sun. In that scenario, the gravitational forces between the stars would have drawn masses of gas from each of them, and some of this gas could then have cooled and condensed to form the planets. This hypothesis, promoted by the famed British astrophysicist James Jeans, had the defect (or the appeal, for those inclined in that direction) of making planetary systems extremely rare, because sufficiently close encounters between stars probably occur only a few times during the lifetime of an entire galaxy. Once astronomers calculated that most of the gas pulled from the stars would evaporate rather than condense, ***they abandoned Jeans's hypothesis and returned to Kant's***, which implies that many, if not most, stars should have planets in orbit around them.

Astrophysicists **now** have good evidence that stars form, not one by one but by the thousands and tense of thousands, within giants clouds of gas and dust that may eventually give birth to about a million individual stars. One of these giant stellar nurseries has produced the Orion nebula, the closest large star-forming region to the solar system. Within a few million years, this region will have produced hundreds of thousands of new stars, which will blow most of the nebula's remaining gas and dust into space, so that astronomers a hundred thousand generations from now will observe the young stars unencumbered by the remnants of their starbirthing cocoons.

Astrophysicists **now** use radio telescopes to map the distribution of cool gas and dust in the immediate vicinities of young stars. Their maps typically show that young stars do not sail through space devoid of all surrounding matter; instead, the stars usually have orbiting disks of matter, similar in size to the solar system but made of hydrogen gas sprinkled throughout with dust particles. The term "dust" describes groups of particles that each contain several million atoms and have sizes much smaller than the period at the end of this sentence.

The formation of these particles in interstellar space has its own mysteries and detailed theories, which we may skip past with the happy thought that the cosmos *is* dusty. To make this dust, atoms have come together by the millions; in view of the extremely low densities between the stars, the likeliest sites for this process seem to be the extended outer atmospheres of cool stars, which gently blow material into space.

If you recognize the structure of the passage, then you can often jump immediately to the answer when you encounter a question that asks you about its primary purpose. If there's an answer choice that reads, "offer/propose explanations for phenomenon" or "discuss various explanations for a phenomenon," then you can pick it without hesitation.

What if the Main Point Isn't Obvious?

One factor that can make certain Critical Reading passages so challenging is that there is no main point – at least no obvious main point. Often, these passages take the form of memoir or first-person narrative. For example, consider the following:

The following passage was written by a well-known playwright and performer. In it, she discusses an experience from her first days of drama school.

Part I

We were 210 students, all there to study identity, change identities, to learn to "be." There are a variety of ways to describe what acting is. "Being," "Seeming," "Becoming," "Lying," "Truth Telling," "Magic,"
5   "Transforming." We were new. Some among us had known the building for an hour longer than the others of us. No one ever arrives at the same time as everybody else. We were going to learn how to talk to each other onstage, and through all of this how to take our own
10   special message to the *world*.
        On one of the first days I was coming into the building, a tall, thin aristocratic-looking white woman who appeared to be about my age, and whom we ultimately referred to as the Katherine Hepburn among
15   us, came breathlessly down a narrow hallway, saying to me (whom she had never seen except in that one instant), "Do you know where I can get a drink of water?"
        She said this as if she had known me all my life, as if I were a sister, a brother, a friend. She may have
20   even grabbed my hand. I wasn't put off by the fact that she was a stranger. Her presence in that question made me feel in an instant as if I had known her all my life. Having grown up in segregation, I found it odd that a white person would approach me without her own barriers up,
25   and without the expectation that I would have barriers. I was so stunned by her presence that I didn't speak. Besides, I didn't know where to get a drink of water. Just as rapidly and as urgently, she vanished down the hallway and out into the street. I thought that perhaps this was
30   what acting was. Because, as real as it was, realer than real, it also seemed like a moment out of a scene from Chekhov's *Uncle Vanya*,* or as if one of Tchaikovsky's* symphonies had burst into speech. *Urgency* is the word. And it's one of the top ten in the vocabulary of acting.

Part II

35   Acting is the furthest thing from lying that I have encountered. It is the furthest thing from make-believe. It is the furthest thing from pretending. It is the most unfake thing there is. Acting is a search for the authentic. It is a search for the authentic by using
40   the fictional as a frame, a house in which the authentic can live. For a moment. Because, yes indeed, real life inhibits the authentic.

*Checkhov was a nineteenth-century Russian playwright.
*Tchaikovsky was a nineteenth century Russian composer.

If you weren't sure what to make of the passage, don't worry – we're going to take it apart.

The first thing to understand is that this passage, like many other first-person passages, is divided into two basic parts.

I. Story (or **anecdote**) designed to introduce the topic and engage the reader

II. **Commentary** on the story, ending with the main point

The role of the commentary is to explain or reflect on why the story is important and to move it beyond the bounds of a single experience in order to make a general statement about the lesson or idea to draw from it.

Here, the fact that the author found the **specific** woman memorable because of her urgency and excessive "real-ness" leads her to the idea that urgency and authenticity (i.e. being real) are essential components of acting **in general**.

So the entire story is basically there in order to convey the idea that urgency is a key part of acting. That's the point. There are, of course, other pieces of information (the author was new to acting school, had grown up in segregation, was surprised that a white woman would speak to her with such a sense of intimacy), but they are **secondary**. How do we know that? Because the idea of urgency in acting comes in the conclusion, and **authors usually structure their writing so that the most important idea comes last**.

For a main point, we could put down something like:

acting = urgency + authenticity

Note that this is in no way a synopsis: it does not even try to cover the events that the author actually describes in the passage. It simply states the **idea** the story is there to convey. Note also that it uses the **exact same words** that are in the passage. It does not "interpret" anything – it simply condenses the information that is directly stated by the author. If we wanted to give a slightly more detailed main point, however, we could say:

Meet woman → acting = urgency + authenticity

That way we incorporate both parts of the passage into the point. But it's not necessary to write that much.

So to sum up, if you find yourself confused, focus on the **conclusion**. Don't waste time trying to figure out the relationship between the various parts of the passage if you're not sure upfront. If you understand the point of the conclusion, chances are that'll be the point of the beginning as well. And as a matter of fact:

**When in doubt, reread the end of the conclusion
(the last sentence or, if necessary, the last few sentences).**

Official Guide (Main) Point Questions*

Test 4	Section 5	Question 16	p. 591
Test 4	Section 5	Question 24	p. 592
Test 4	Section 8	Question 9	p. 607
Test 6	Section 3	Question 19	p. 710
Test 7	Section 2	Question 9	p. 763
Test 7	Section 2	Question 12	p. 764
Test 7	Section 2	Question 13	p. 765
Test 7	Section 5	Question 22	p. 784
Test 8	Section 2	Question 13	p. 827
Test 9	Section 4	Question 24	p. 902
Test 10	Section 4	Question 18	p. 963

*Main point exercises are included in the next chapter (see p. 138)

5. Same Idea, Different Words: Literal Comprehension

If you read my example in the previous chapter of the typical long-winded response I get when I ask someone to summarize the main point of a passage, you might have laughed (although more likely you stopped reading after the first sentence or two). Granted I might have exaggerated it just a bit for effect, but the truth is that the inability to summarize effectively – to pick out the most important ideas in a passage and condense them into a concise, direct statement – is one of the most important skills to have for the SAT. The most straightforward and common Critical Reading questions, the ones that directly test your comprehension of a given passage, essentially require you to understand ideas well enough to recognize accurate **summaries** of them.

Because this is the SAT, however, those summaries are rarely written using the same wording as that found in the passage – **the test is whether you understand the idea well enough to recognize it when it's stated using different, often more general, language.** Correct answers thus require you to recognize **paraphrased** versions of ideas, ones that only includes key points and omit all irrelevant details. If you understand the idea, there's a good chance you'll be fine; if you're too focused on the details, you might miss it completely.

To reiterate: the correct answer choice will almost always contain synonyms for key words in the passage but rarely the words themselves.

Questions testing your literal comprehension of words or ideas are often phrased in the following ways:

-In lines x-y, the author indicates that...

-This passage most extensively discusses...

-In line x, "this notion" refers to the idea that...

While these questions tend to be quite manageable, they can nevertheless pose difficulties, first because passages themselves can contain challenging syntax and vocabulary as well as highly unfamiliar content; and second because identifying the correct answer does in fact require you to recognize the relationship between the specific words used in the passage and the more general language used in the answer choices. So while these questions do directly test your comprehension, they do so in a way that isn't always 100% straightforward.

Let's look at some examples:

> Experimental scientists occupy themselves with observing and measuring the cosmos, finding out what stuff exists, no matter how strange that stuff may be. Theoretical physicists, on the other hand, are
> 5 not satisfied with observing the universe. They want to know why. They want to explain all the properties of the universe in terms of a few fundamental principles and parameters. These fundamental principles, in turn, lead to the "laws of nature," which govern the behavior
> 10 of all matter and energy.

This passage primarily discusses

(A) the influence of theoretical physicists on other kinds of scientists
(B) the fundamental principles of the universe
(C) the differences between two groups of scientists
(D) the limits of theoretical physics
(E) the conflict between experimental and theoretical approaches to physics

The first thing that you probably notice when you look at the answer choices is that pretty much all of them contain bits and pieces of ideas mentioned in the passage, and therefore it might seem like any one of them could be right.

But the question is asking what the passages **primarily** discusses – not what words or phrases happen to appear in the passage. It's asking you to make a leap from looking at the **specific words** of the passage to understanding the overall **goal** or **point** of the passage.

Let's look at how the passage is organized. That might not seem to have anything to do with this question, but in fact it's the simplest way to answer it.

First, the author describes what experimental scientists do.

Second, the author describes what theoretical physicists do. The phrase "on the other hand" (line 3) is key because it tells us that the author is setting up a **contrast** (=difference).

So the author is describing two groups of scientists and the differences between them. Which is exactly what (C) says.

It doesn't matter that the word "differences" does not appear in the passage – the **idea** of difference is indicated through the transition "on the other hand," and the correct answer conveys that idea. **Same idea, different words**.

Let's try another one.

For some activists, eating local foods is no
longer just a pleasure—it is a moral obligation. Why?
Because shipping foods over long distances results
in the unnecessary emission of the greenhouse gases
5   that are warming the planet. This concern has
given rise to the concept of "food miles," that is,
the distance food travels from farm to plate. Activists
particularly dislike air freighting foods because it uses
relatively more energy than other forms of trans-
10   portation. Food miles are supposed to be a simple way
to gauge food's impact on climate change.
      But food miles advocates fail to grasp the
simple idea that food should be grown where it is most
economically advantageous to do so. Relevant
15   advantages consist of various combinations of soil,
climate, labor, and other factors. It is possible to grow
bananas in Iceland, but Costa Rica really has the better
climate for that activity. Transporting food is just one
relatively small cost of providing modern consumers
20   with their daily bread, meat, cheese, and veggies.
Concentrating agricultural production in the most
favorable regions is the best way to minimize human
impacts on the environment.

In the second paragraph (lines 10-18) the author indicates
that food should be grown in regions where

(A) crops can be produced in a cost-effective manner
(B) temperatures remain warm throughout the year
(C) land is devoted primarily to agricultural use
(D) many crops varieties can be produced simultaneously
(E) agriculture plays a central role in the economy

Although the question appears to ask about the entire second paragraph, it's really only necessary to understand the point of that paragraph. Where is the point of the paragraph? Where it's usually located: in the topic sentence (*But food miles advocates fail to grasp the simple idea that food should be grown where it is most economically advantageous to do so*).

The "trick," of course, is that you need to understand the phrase "economically advantageous." But even if you're not 100% sure, you can probably figure it out. "Economically" means "having to do with the economy, or more generally, with money, and "advantageous" means that it provides an advantage. So it must mean something like "good for the economy." That's the **idea** that the correct answer choice must contain.

When you look at the answer choices, you're going to look specifically for words that have something to do with money or the economy. Right there, you're down to (A), which contains the word "cost-effective," and (E), which contains the word "economy." (A) seems to match the general idea – saying that something is produced in a "cost-effective manner" is essentially the same as saying it's produced in an "economically advantageous" one. (E), however, is too much of a stretch. The passage, and especially the topic sentence, says nothing about it being best to grow crops in places where agriculture plays a *central* role in the economy. It could be true, but we don't really have enough information. So it's (A).

One more:

> Even those who liked him conceded that Thoreau
> could be a cold fish. In a letter to his friend Daniel
> Ricketson in 1860, Thoreau addresses Ricketson's
> puzzlement over why he hasn't come to visit,
> 5   telling Ricketson, without much ceremony, that
> he's had much better things to do. But after explain-
> ing himself, Thoreau continued to correspond with
> Ricketson. Ralph Waldo Emerson, Thoreau's close
> friend and mentor, who came to grudgingly admire
> 10   Thoreau's argumentative streak, famously described
> him as "not to be subdued, always manly and able,
> but rarely tender, as if he did not feel himself except
> in opposition." In a remembrance of Thoreau, Emer-
> son offered this observation from one of Thoreau's
> 15   friends: "I love Henry, but I cannot like him; and as
> for taking his arm, I should as soon think of taking
> the arm of an elm-tree."

1. The passage focuses primarily on Thoreau's

   (A) philosophy
   (B) literary output
   (C) social conduct
   (D) personal eccentricities
   (E) generous nature

What's the **topic** of the passage? If we were to summarize it very, very briefly, we could say something like, "how Thoreau treated his friends (distant w/them)." In other words, it's about how he behaved toward other people. The answer that best **rephrases** that idea is "social conduct," because that phrase essentially means "how one behaves in society." So the answer is (C).

Making the Leap: Moving from Concrete to Abstract

One of the most common ways that both the authors of Critical Reading passages and the test-writers at ETS move between specific phrasings and more general language is by using **pronouns** (*this, that*) and **abstract nouns** (*notion, assertion, phenomenon*).

If you've already spent some time preparing for the Writing section of the SAT, you may be familiar with pronouns and antecedents (also known as referents), but even if you are, here's a refresher:

Pronoun = Word that replaces a noun (e.g *she, he, it, this, that*)

Antecedent = The specific noun(s) to which the pronoun refers

As a matter of fact, the testing of pronouns and antecedents is one of the places where the Critical Reading and Writing sections overlap. In the Writing section, the focus is primarily on spotting disagreement errors between pronouns and their antecedents. For example:

<u>Some</u> albino animals have difficulty <u>thriving in</u> the
　　A　　　　　　　　　　　　　　　　　B
wild because <u>its</u> skin is insufficiently dark to absorb
　　　　　　　C
sunlight during <u>harsh</u> winters. <u>No error</u>
　　　　　　　　D　　　　　　E

In the above sentence, the answer is (C) because the singular pronoun *it* refers to the plural noun *albino animals*, which is clearly stated at the beginning of the sentence.

The problem, however, is that pronouns and their antecedents are much less straightforward in Critical Reading than they are in Writing. In the above sentence, for example, the noun that *its* refers to is right there in the same sentence – *some albino animals* is really the only thing that *its* could logically refer to.

In Critical Reading, however, things get a bit more complicated. Nouns often do not appear in the same sentence as the pronouns that refer back to them. You will often have to back up and read a sentence or two **before** the pronoun appears in order to identify the specific noun to which it refers.

For example:

For as long as <u>writers</u> have written, they've tried to retract what they wrote. Hawthorne did it; Gogol and Auden, too. **They** rarely succeed.

The pronoun *they* in the second sentence is used to refer to the antecedent "writers," which appears in the first sentence.

Why Use Pronouns?

When people have difficulty recognizing the nouns or ideas that pronouns refer to, they often wonder why on earth an author would bother to use so many of them. After all, it's so much work to figure out what they refer to... and it's so easy to get confused. The reason is stylistic. Compare the following two versions of this passage. First without pronouns:

> Here in my house I am surrounded by books, books
> I have read and books I intend to read. Many of **the books**
> have been in the same spot on the shelf for years, my gaze
> sweeping over **the books** day after day until **the books** meta-
> morphose into a kind of protruding wallpaper. **The books**
> recede, becoming what **the books** were before **the books** were
> first singled out: possibilities. **The books** need to be singled
> out again in order to be seen. **The books** need to be stirred,
> **the books'** narrow profiles turned to full face.

Notice how incredibly awkward this version is. Now look at the version with pronouns.

> Here in my house I am surrounded by books, books
> I have read and books I intend to read, many of **which** have
> been in the same spot on the shelf for years, my gaze
> sweeping over **them** day after day until **they** metamorphose
> into a kind of protruding wallpaper. **They** recede, becoming
> what **they** were before they were first singled out: possibilities.
> **They** need to be singled out again in order to be seen. **They**
> need to be stirred, **their** narrow profiles turned to full face.

Notice how much smoother this version is. You don't get tangled up in the constant repetition of the same phrase, so it's much easier to read. The problem, however, is that authors don't always use pronouns to refer to a single word – they sometimes use pronouns to refer to entire *ideas*. For example, let's look back at our example from the previous page:

> For as long as writers have written, they've tried to retract what they wrote. Hawthorne did **it**;
> Gogol and Auden, too. They rarely succeed.

Here, the word "it" refers to authors' attempting to "retract what they wrote." It's questionable grammatically – if this were a Writing question, the second sentence would be incorrect because pronouns should refer to specific nouns, and here "it" fails to do so. In reality, however, authors write things like this all the time, and you are responsible for identifying the ideas that their pronouns refer to. While questions that ask about pronouns directly are extremely rare, many questions do address this skill indirectly by testing your literal comprehension. Without the ability to "track" an idea through a passage and recognize when it is being supported, challenged, etc. you can easily become confused about a passage's focus and purpose, as well as the argument it makes.

The topic of a passage is simply the person, object, or idea that appears most frequently. Sometimes the author will refer to the topic of the passage by name and sometimes with pronouns. To identify the topic, you must therefore recognize that pronouns and nouns refer to the same thing. For example, let's look at this passage again:

131

One of the first and most frequently repeated strategies used to cope with **Berthe Morisot's** position as a female member of a 'radical' art group participating in what is perceived as an exclusively

5 man's world, has been to construct **her** as exceptional. Unlike other women artists, both before and during her time, **she**, it is claimed, does not fall into the inevitable traps which beset women artists. George Moore, writing in 1898, stated that **Morisot's** pictures 'are the

10 only pictures painted by a woman that could not be destroyed without creating a blank, a hiatus in the history of art.' In turn, **her** painting 'style,' Impressionism, is produced as a method which is suited to and the natural expression of an appropriately

15 feminine temperament. 'Impressionism' is offered as the answer to the problem of **Morisot's** 'femininity,' the problem posed by a skilled and prolific professional woman painter in a world which deemed such activities to be 'unfeminine.' From as early as the 1870s

20 **Morisot's** manner of working was seen to reflect a naturally feminine sensibility; it was repeatedly called 'charming,' 'feminine,' 'delicate' in a way which transposed onto the painting those characteristics most favored in the middle-class women of the time.

25 What representations of **Morisot** as the intuitive feminine painter do not take into account, however, is the fact that **she** was one of many women working as professional artists in the period and that these women represented in working methods the full range of

30 artistic practices. Few used the painterly brushmarks and sketchy surfaces that are characteristic of much of Impressionist painting and most were unaware of **Morisot's** existence, preferring to define their context as that of the Paris Salons or alternately the Women's

35 Salon which emerged in the early 1880s as a significant forum for the display of women's work. If **Morisot** shared any technical qualities with **her** contemporaries, it was with male artists like Renoir and Monet. They, like **her**, were committed to an aesthetic of apparent

40 spontaneity, using separated brushmarks, revealing the light ground of the canvas, eliminating the use of the art-based pigment bitumen, and striving for the approximate effect of natural light. The resulting 'delicacy of touch' was part of a conscious strategy to

45 free painting from the academic emphasis on finish, the highly polished surface with no traces of individual brushmarks, and can in no way be attributed to the outpouring of an essential femininity.

Accompanying the idea that Impressionism
50 was a naturally feminine style of painting was the notion that **Morisot's** working methods flowed intuitively for **her** inner self without conscious intervention or mediation. As Paul Valéry was to put it: 'the peculiarity of **Berthe Morisot**…was to

55 live **her** painting and to paint **her** life, as if the inter-change between seeing and rendering, between the light and **her** creative will, were to **her** a natural function, a necessary part of her daily life.' But **her** letters themselves do not allow this view to be

60 sustained. If anything, they represent **her** often pain-ful and intense involvement with painting, described once as a 'pitched battle with her canvases.' Equally, they represent a woman who is absolutely aware of the ways in which **she** and her colleagues are

65 received in the press, and is mindful of the reception of **her** own work and that of **her** associates.

But if the image of **Morisot** as an intuitive, unreflective artist living out **her** natural femininity through her painting cannot be sustained, neither can

70 **she** be accommodated by today's feminist art historians in the role of the lofty female ancestor, politicized about **her** gender and the institutionalized sexism of **her** time. This does not mean that **she** was unaware of the debates around women's positions, or

75 the restrictions, social and psychic, which were placed on women's lives, but that **her** responses are not unified and worked out. They are often confused, ambiguous, and tellingly self-denigrating.

The 'evidence' provided in her letters is
80 fragmentary and suggestive. It presents a woman often confused, filled with self-doubt, frequently discontent, berated for **her** stubbornness and selfishness, envied and admired, a devoted friend, and above all, a committed artist. The texts of **her**

85 letters themselves, many of them by Morisot's family and friends, provide a telling contrast to the idealized mythic representation of the enigmatic, even muse-like figure, which so many accounts of **Morisot** construct.

Often, when I ask someone to tell me the topic of a passage such as this, I get a response along the lines of, "Umm… I *think* it's like talking about women artists, but honestly, I'm not totally sure." (Incidentally, I see this uncertainty even in some students scoring 700+ – they know the test well enough to spot wrong answers to detail questions, but when asked to state something as straightforward as the topic in their own words, they're suddenly lost.)

As a matter of fact, the topic is not in fact "women artists." It is actually one particular woman artist, namely Berthe Morisot. Its scope is specific, not general.

Ignoring, for a moment, that you've seen the passage before, you might respond to that assertion by thinking, "Ok, but the passage talks about a bunch of other stuff too. And some of it was really confusing. It, like, didn't make sense at all! OMG HOW AM I SUPPOSED TO KNOW IT'S REALLY ABOUT HER?!!!"

While it's true that the author does mention other people (Renoir, Paul Valéry), Berthe Morisot's name, as well as the pronouns *she* and *her*, which refer to Morisot, appear **repeatedly** throughout the passage. Those words appear more often than any other nouns or pronouns. In addition, the author introduces her in the first sentence of the entire passage, suggesting that she will be its focus.

To reiterate this for yourself, try an exercise: take a page from a book or piece of writing you're familiar with, one whose topic you know for sure. Now, as fast as you can, **count** how many times that topic – either the noun itself or a pronoun referring to it (*it, she/her, he/him, they/their*) – appears on the page. The number should be pretty high. Since you're already familiar with the subject, it should be easier for you to see the relationship between the subject and the pronoun. If you find that helpful, keep doing it, first with texts you know well and then with unfamiliar ones, until you can consistently identify topics, quickly spot the pronouns that refer to them, and restate them clearly and simply in your own words.

It is important that you be able to recognize the topics of passages because **the correct answer to primary purpose questions will often include the topic of the passage, albeit in a more general manner**. For example, Berthe Morisot would become "a particular artist" or "a female artist." If you cannot clearly identify the topic, you are likely to encounter considerable difficulty recognizing it in rephrased form.

Important: when defining a topic for yourself, try to use no more than a couple of words (e.g. Berthe Morisot, city ecosystems, importance of Venus) and avoid saying things like, "Well, so I think that basically the passage is like talking about xyz…" The former takes almost no time and gives you exactly the information you need; the latter is time-consuming, vague, and encourages you to view the topic as much more subjective than it actually is.

And one more point. The tendency to confuse general and specific (artists vs. one artist) is precisely the type of misunderstanding that many wrong answers to Critical Reading questions play on. For this reason, it is important to be precise when defining the *scope* of the topic. If you do not realize that a passage focuses on a single person rather than a group of people, you probably cannot make broad generalizations or assumptions about the group to which the person belongs, and answer choices that refer to that group as a whole (e.g. artists) are unlikely to be correct.

"Compression" Nouns

Pronouns won't always appear by themselves, though. More often, they'll appear in front of nouns. Sounds a lot more straightforward, right? Well…maybe yes, maybe no.

Sometime around third grade, you probably learned that a noun was a person, place, or thing. Pretty self-explanatory. When you learned that a noun was a "thing," however, you probably understood "thing" to mean an object like a bicycle or an apple or a house. That's certainly true. But words like *idea* or *assertion* or *concept* – words that don't refer to actual physical things – are also nouns. These nouns are sometimes referred to as **abstract nouns** or **compression nouns** because they compress lots of information into a single word.

On the SAT, these types of words appear constantly, and understanding what they refer to is often crucial to understanding a passage. **In fact, the ability to recognize the relationship between abstract nouns and the ideas that they refer to is absolutely central to making sense out of virtually every passage you will encounter on the SAT.** If you can't draw the relationship between the noun, say, *argument*, and the specific argument that it refers to, you probably can't answer a question that asks you to do exactly that. And you certainly can't answer a question that asks you what can be inferred from that argument or what sort of information would support or undermine it. Since many Critical Reading questions will only use abstract nouns such as "the description" or "the notion" or "the claim," the inability to understand the relationship between those nouns and their definitions within passages can lead to very big problems indeed.

What's more, these nouns, like pronouns, generally show up **after** the particular idea (argument, assertion, description, etc.) has been discussed, sometimes even in a different paragraph. If you encounter a question that asks you to identify what such a noun refers to, you need to back up and read **before** the place where the noun appeared. For example:

> Women's and African-American reading groups not
> only reinforced community bonds—and introduced countless
> readers to great works of literature—but indirectly and perhaps
> unwittingly cleared a path to suffrage and other civil rights.
> 5   In reading highbrow literature and discussing it in something
> like a classroom atmosphere, many women's reading groups
> created a rather formal semipublic arena for women to grow
> intellectually. No wonder that in Texas clubwomen led efforts
> to establish a women's dormitory at the University of Texas at
> 10 Austin, funded local and statewide scholarships for women, and
> were instrumental in founding what is today Texas Women's
> University. And though reading groups might host visiting
> suffragist speakers, in general the reading groups tended to be
> too conservative for **such reforms**, even as they trained their
> 15 members in many a fine point of civic virtue.

Contained in the phrase "such reforms" is the potential for trouble, especially since the author leaves the reader to infer the relationship between the phrase and what it actually refers to: suffragist speakers. Who were suffragists? Women who fought for the right to vote. So when the author uses the phrase "such reforms," he is indicating that women's and African-American reading groups were too conservative to fight for women's right to vote.

134

Now let's look at something a bit longer:

In our attempts to uncover the history of the cosmos, we have continually discovered that the segments most deeply shrouded in **mystery** are those that deal with origins – of the universe itself, of its most massive structures
5   (galaxies and galaxy clusters), and of the stars that provide most of the light in the cosmos. These mysteries arise in large part because during the cosmic "dark ages," when matter was just beginning to organize itself into self-contained units such as stars and galaxies, most of this matter generated
10 little or no detectable radiation. When we turn to the origin of planets, **the mysteries deepen**. We lack not only observations of the crucial, initial stages of planetary formation but also successful theories of how the planets began to form.
     Astrophysicists may now have more data but they have
15 no better answers than before. The beginnings of planet building pose a remarkably intractable **problem**, to the point that one of the world's experts on the subject, Scott Tremaine, has elucidated (partly in jest) Tremaine's laws of planet formation. The first of these laws states that "all theoretical
20 predictions about the properties of exosolar planets are wrong," and the second that "the most secure prediction about planet formation is that it can't happen." This underscores the ineluctable fact that planets do exist, despite our inability to explain **this astronomical enigma**.

In line 24, the "enigma" concerns

(A) the data collected by astrophysicists
(B) the creation and early existence of the planets
(C) the current properties of exosolar planets
(D) the amount of radiation emitted by stars and galaxies
(E) Tremaine's laws of planet formation

If you remember to read **before** the word *enigma* and to look for synonyms for it, this question is in fact very straightforward: *enigma* = *mystery*. What's the mystery? *The initial stages of planetary formation [and] how the planets began to form* – i.e. the creation and early existence of the planets. So the answer is (B).

Note that in the above question, **the word "enigma" is a compression noun because it refers not to a single word but to an entire idea**: the fact that astrophysicists do not know how or why the planets began to form because there was no way for them to view the planets forming.

"All of the Following EXCEPT"

Among literal comprehension questions, those that ask you to identify "all of the following EXCEPT" are some of the most resistant to shortcuts. Oftentimes, you will simply have to hunt back through the passage in order to see whether particular pieces of information are in fact mentioned. But that said, you can often eliminate several answer choices by using the main point or your overall knowledge of the passage, then go back and check the other two or three carefully. Sometimes you can even use the main point to identify the answer immediately. So while these questions may appear time-consuming, they do have the potential to be solved fairly quickly.

> Make no mistake—Dolley Madison was as fiercely
> partisan as any male politician. Her declaration, "I confess
> I do not admire contention in any form, either political or civil"
> is often cited by historians as proof of her pacific nature.
> 5 The second half of the statement reveals more—"I would
> rather fight with my hands than my tongue." And fight she did,
> though hers was the arena of action, not words. Though Dolley
> strove for discretion in her letters, anger at her husband's
> enemies sometimes broke through. During his presidency, James
> 10 Madison was hampered by what Dolley called "a Capricious
> Senate," whose objections she characterized as "allmost treason."
> **Still**, she subsumed her feelings, so that one guest declared,
> "By her deportment in her own house you cannot discover
> who is her husband's friends or foes."

As we saw earlier, the absolute main point of the passage is stated in the first sentence. We could, however, also go one step further and examine another key place: the last sentence.

The last sentence begins with the transition *still*, which signals a shift in the direction of the passage. And indeed, we do get some important new information that casts Dolley Madison in a somewhat different light. After focusing on the fact that Dolley Madison held very strong beliefs, the author now *qualifies* the original statement by introducing the idea that Dolley Madison hid those beliefs. And if we wanted to tweak our main point to include that information, we could write something like:

DM strong beliefs BUT hid

While that may seem like a small amount of information to add, it could become very important if a question like this were to appear:

> The author of the passage would most likely agree with all
> of the following statements about Dolley Madison EXCEPT
>
> (A) she treated her husband's friends and enemies alike
> (B) she viewed the Senate with disapproval during her
>   husband's presidency
> (C) she was unable to suppress a sense of irritation in
>   her letters
> (D) she was unsuccessful in hiding her emotions
> (E) she has frequently been misunderstood by historians

Remember, we're looking for a statement that the author of the passage would NOT agree with. At this point, it might be very tempting to start hunting back through the passage for the answers one by one. And that might be a perfectly effective strategy.

If you can think about the passage in terms of the main point, however, you can answer the question in a whole lot less time and, most likely, with a whole lot less chance of second-guessing yourself.

Again, what's the main point? That Dolley Madison *hid* her strong feelings.

So logically, what would the author NOT agree with? The opposite of that statement.

What's the opposite of that statement? Dolley Madison did *not* hide her strong feelings.

Which is exactly what choice (D) says.

While this is technically an inference question, it can also be considered a literal comprehension or "main point" question when viewed from this angle.

Granted such questions are not always quite this straightforward, but sometimes they truly are. If you'd like an example from the Official Guide, the logic behind #9 on p. 391 (from the October 2006 exam) is virtually identical to that in the example above. For an explanation of that question according to the strategy described above, please see p. 150.

Literal Comprehension Exercises

Directions: for the questions below, <u>underline</u> the word, phrase, or sentence(s) *within the passage* **that the question refers to.**

Example:

#4

#2

#1, #3

      Up close, amid the confusion of broken and standing stones, it still seems smaller than its reputation, notwithstanding the obvious feat represented by the erection of the
5 famous sarsen stones; the largest weighs as much as 50 tons. Indeed, **its massive lintels are bound to their supports by joints taken straight from carpentry**, an eloquent indication of just how radically new this hybrid monument must have been. But what in fact do they mean? Despite countless theories offered
10 over centuries, no one knows. **Stonehenge** is the most famous relic of prehistory in Europe and one of the best known, most contemplated monuments in the world—and we have no clear idea what the people who built it actually used it for.

1. In line 2, what does "it" refer to?

2. In line 7, what does "an eloquent indication" refer to?

3. In line 8, what does "this hybrid monument" refer to?

4. In line 9, what does "they" refer to?

1.   The book itself has not been surpassed by another technology. Like the piano it is perfect as it is. But we have also become very good at producing books and more books, to the point where libraries become overcrowded and
5 librarians overwhelmed. Thinkers looking at electronic networks' influence on societies globally are generally in agreement, then, that the ink-and-paper book may be in the first stages of losing its cultural centrality.

1. In line 2, what does "it" refer to?

2. In line 8, what does "its" refer to?

3. The passage indicates that the book may "lose its cultural centrality" (line 8) because of its excessive

  (A) fragility
  (B) irrelevance
  (C) abundance
  (D) profundity
  (E) frivolousness

2. Marie Curie was never easy to understand or categorize. That was because she was a pioneer, an outlier, unique for the newness and immensity of her achievements. But it was also because of her sex. Curie
5 worked during a great age of innovation, but proper women of her time were thought to be too sentimental to perform objective science. She would forever be considered a bit strange, not just a great scientist but a great woman scientist. You would not expect the
10 president of the United States to praise one of Curie's male contemporaries by calling attention to his manhood and his devotion as a father. Professional science until fairly recently was a man's world, and in Curie's time it was rare for a woman even to participate
15 in academic physics, never mind triumph over it.

1. In lines 1-7, the author indicates that Marie Curie was "an outlier" because of her

(A) excessive sentimentality
(B) devotion to her family as well as her work
(C) defiance of conventional gender roles
(D) revolutionary view of objective science
(E) personal eccentricities

2. In line 4, what does "it" refer to?

3. In line 15, what does "it" refer to?

3. In a speech given in 1963, the year after her World War I chronicle *The Guns of August* was published, Barbara Tuchman shared her research and writing process. When she started working on a book,
5 Tuchman surveyed secondary sources, which she considered "helpful but pernicious," then dived headfirst into primary sources. "Even an untrustworthy source is valuable for what it reveals about the personality of the author," she told the audience.
10 Published volumes of letters and telegrams were wonderful, but the real thing was better. "Nothing can compare with the fascination of examining material in the very paper and ink of its original."

1. In line 5, what does "which" refer to?

2. In line 8, what does "it" refer to?

3. In line 13, what does "its" refer to?

4. Which of the following statements best summarizes Barbara Tuchman's belief about primary sources?

(A) they lose most of their value when formally published
(B) they should be examined before secondary sources
(C) their existence is more important than their accuracy
(D) they are frequently untrustworthy
(E) they always reveal their author's personalities

4. Thoreau's literary output continues unabated, with new versions of his work still in progress. That work has shaped the career of Elizabeth Witherell, who joined the staff of the Thoreau Edition in 1974
5 and has served as its editor in chief since 1980. "Thoreau was not a person who revealed himself easily," says Witherell, offering a view shared by scholars and general readers for generations. Not that Thoreau's life lacked documentation. In addition to
10 Walden and a few celebrated travelogs, such as Cape Cod and A Week on the Concord and Merrimack Rivers, Thoreau (1817–1862) kept a copious journal that, in a previously published edition, stretched to fourteen volumes and some two million words. But the
15 sheer volume of Thoreau's prose has, paradoxically, complicated the task of gaining a complete understanding of his personality. The scale of Thoreau's work, not easily digested in its entirety, invites selective quotation, tempting readers to pick and
20 choose passages that support their pet theories about him

Which of the following statements best summarizes the paradox about Thoreau described in lines 13-15?

(A) Readers often misinterpret his work because they find his writing difficult to understand
(B) The quantity of his writing tends to obscure his individual identity
(C) Many popular theories about him are derived from works that he did not actually write
(D) His works reveal no information about his personality
(E) Readers find his work increasingly difficult to understand even as they become more familiar with it

5.   A quick glance through one of the many books that Herman Melville owned and studied—his copy of *The Poetical Works of William Wordsworth*, or *Don Quixote*, for example—reveals tangible evidence of his
5   creative approach to reading: the pages are covered with markings and annotations. There are vertical scores, underlines, brackets, checks, double- and triple-checks, x's, circles, as well as words, phrases, fragments of poetry, and even whole paragraphs of
10 prose. Despite his well-documented propensity for collecting fine editions of old books, Melville evidently had no qualms about picking up his pencil—or, in some rare instances, his crayon—and inscribing his thoughts in their margins.

1. In line 4, what does "tangible evidence" refer to?

2. In line 14, what does "their" refer to?

6.   In an essay in 1984—at the dawn of the personal computer era—the novelist Thomas Pynchon wondered if it was "O.K. to be a Luddite," meaning someone who opposes technological progress. A better question today
5   is whether it's even possible. Technology is everywhere, and a recent headline at an Internet humor site perfectly captured how difficult it is to resist: "Luddite invents machine to destroy technology quicker." Like all good satire, the mock headline comes perilously
10 close to the truth. Modern Luddites do indeed invent "machines"—in the form of computer viruses, cyberworms and other malware—to disrupt the technologies that trouble them.
      But despite their modern reputation, the original
15 Luddites were neither opposed to technology nor inept at using it. Many were highly skilled machine operators in the textile industry. Nor was the technology they attacked particularly new. Moreover, the idea of smashing machines as a form of industrial protest did
20 not begin or end with them. In truth, the secret of their enduring reputation depends less on what they did than on the name under which they did it.

1. In line 7, what does "it" refer to?

2. In line 10, what does "truth" refer to?

3. In lines 14 and 21, what does "reputation" refer to?

4. In line 16, what does "many" refer to?

5. In lines 20-22, the author makes which point about the Luddites?

(A) their modern reputation is entirely undeserved
(B) there was little justification for their protests
(C) they acquired their name by accident
(D) their fame is not only attributable to their actions
(E) their continued popularity is somewhat puzzling

7.   For some activists, eating local foods is no longer just a pleasure—it is a moral obligation. Why? Because shipping foods over long distances results in the unnecessary emission of the greenhouse
5   gases that are warming the planet. This concern has given rise to the concept of "food miles," that is, the distance food travels from farm to plate.
      But food miles advocates fail to grasp the simple idea that food should be grown where it is most
10 economically advantageous to do so. Relevant advantages consist of various combinations of soil, climate, labor, and other factors. It is possible to grow bananas in Iceland, but Costa Rica really has the better climate for that activity. Transporting food is just
15 one relatively small cost of providing modern consumers with their daily bread, meat, cheese, and veggies. Concentrating agricultural production in the most favorable regions is the best way to minimize human impacts on the environment.

1. In line 5, what does "this concern" refer to?

2. In line 14, what does "that activity" refer to?

8.   Sometime near the end of the Pleistocene, a band
of people left northeastern Asia, crossed the Bering
land bridge when the sea level was low, entered Alaska
and became the first Americans. Since the 1930s,
5   archaeologists have thought these people were
members of the Clovis culture. First discovered in New
Mexico in the 1930s, the Clovis culture is known for its
distinct stone tools, primarily fluted projectile points.
For decades, Clovis artifacts were the oldest known in
10 the New World, dating to 13,000 years ago. But in
recent years, researchers have found more and more
evidence that people were living in North and South
America before the Clovis.
       The most recently confirmed evidence comes
15 from Washington. During a dig conducted from 1977
to 1979, researchers uncovered a bone projectile point
stuck in a mastodon rib. Since then, the age of the find
has been debated, but recently anthropologist Michael
Waters and his colleagues announced a new
20 radiocarbon date for the rib: 13,800 years ago, making
it 800 years older than the oldest Clovis artifact. Other
pre-Clovis evidence comes from a variety of locations
across the New World.

1. In line 5, who does "these people" refer to?

2. In line 9, what does "artifacts" refer to?

3. What is the "evidence" (line 12)?

4. In line 17, what does the "find" refer to?

5. Lines 17-20 ("Since then...rib) indicate that
   researchers

   (A) have not reached a consensus about the age of
       the mastodon rib
   (B) believe that the oldest Clovis artifact is also the
       oldest human artifact in the New World
   (C) have based their conclusions on an unreliable
       form of technology
   (D) believe that the projectile point could be a fraud
   (E) believe that more projectile points will be
       discovered at the original site

6. In context of the passage, the author mentions the
   "rib" (line 17) in order to support which idea?

9.   We were 210 students, all there to study identities, change identities, to learn to "be." There are a variety of ways to describe what acting is. "Being," "Seeming," "Becoming," "Lying," "Truth Telling," "Magic,"

5 "Transforming." We were new. Some among us had known the building for an hour longer than the others of us. No one ever arrives at the same time as everybody else. We were going to learn how to talk to each other onstage, and through all of this how to take our own

10 special message to the *world*.

    On one of the first days I was coming into the building, a tall, thin aristocratic-looking white woman who appeared to be about my age, and whom we ultimately referred to as the Katherine Hepburn among

15 us, came breathlessly down a narrow hallway, saying to me (whom she had never seen except in that one instant), "Do you know where I can get a drink of water?"

    She said this as if she had known me all my life, as if I were a sister, a brother, a friend. She may have

20 even grabbed my hand. I wasn't put off by the fact that she was a stranger. Her presence in that question made me feel in an instant as if I had known her all my life. Having grown up in segregation, I found it odd that a white person would approach me without her own barriers up,

25 and without the expectation that I would have barriers. I was so stunned by her presence that I didn't speak. Besides, I didn't know where to get a drink of water. Just as rapidly and as urgently, she vanished down the hallway and out into the street. I thought that perhaps this was

30 what acting was. Because, as real as it was, realer than real, it also seemed like a moment out of a scene from Chekhov's *Uncle Vanya*, or as if one of Tchaikovsky's symphonies had burst into speech. *Urgency* is the word. And it's one of the top ten in the vocabulary of acting.

35 Acting is the furthest thing from lying that I have encountered. It is the furthest thing from make-believe. It is the furthest thing from pretending. It is the most unfake thing there is. Acting is a search for the authentic. It is a search for the authentic by using

40 the fictional as a frame, a house in which the authentic can live. For a moment, because, yes indeed, real life inhibits the authentic.

1. In lines 24 and 25, the author uses the word "barriers" as a metaphor for

(A) cultural divisions
(B) theatrical conventions
(C) physical impediments
(D) geographical differences
(E) psychological defenses

2. In line 40, the "frame" refers to

(A) an imaginary boundary
(B) a sacred space
(C) an uncomfortable situation
(D) a theatrical convention
(E) a memorable experience

3. When the author says that "real life inhibits the authentic" (line 42), she most nearly means that

(A) authenticity is only accessible to members of the theatrical community
(B) theater presents a fundamentally distorted view of human relationships
(C) societal pressures often dissuade people from pursuing artistic careers
(D) people are not encouraged to reveal their true selves in their daily existence
(E) people tend to be more comfortable expressing their emotions at home than in public

10.   I vacillate on Thoreau. I consider myself
fairly well read when it comes to the writers of
Concord…though certainly no expert. In my younger
days, I walked the same woods he walked and was
5   inspired by his love of simplicity and nature. Lately,
however, I have been reading a compilation of excerpts
from his journals, and what struck me most about
Thoreau's observations is his judgmental tone of
superiority. As a younger man, poring over Walden, I
10   believe I idealized Thoreau. Now I begin to wonder if
he was, in fact, a misanthrope.
        I'm certainly not the first person to ponder this
matter. Journalist Alex Beam wrote an interesting article
about Thoreau in the *New York Times* saying, "Over the
15   years I have called him a misanthrope, a slob, a loser, 'a
world-class mooch,' and a 'tree-hugging pyromaniac.'"
Other contemporaries noted this too. Perhaps no one more
than Ralph Waldo Emerson, one of Thoreau's dearest
friends and admirers, who writes frankly of Thoreau's
20   judgmental attitude, what I might call misanthropy.
        The prevailing theme of Thoreau's journal
entries is Thoreau's ability to find nobility, beauty, even
poetry in the lives of simple, virtuous men. That's fine, I
suppose. But, I can't help but fixate on his condemnations
25   of those he deemed to be worthless. What made Thoreau
so sure in his judgments? He seemed to believe that he
possessed the true compass as to what was good and
noble as he looked at other men, coldly assessing their
worth and disturbingly certain as to his judgment.
30   It would be unjust if I did not mention that
several scholars vehemently refute this image of Thoreau.
Sandra Harbert Petrulionis, in her book, *Thoreau in His
Own Time*, criticizes Emerson for flippantly immortalizing the term, "that terrible Thoreau." Instead of focusing
35   on "incidents of understandable local ire" against
Thoreau, Petrulionis argues we should focus on the fact
that "Thoreau engaged in a lifelong habit of serving and
educating his community". This is an important point.
Thoreau valued his community tremendously. And he
40   valued education and the dissemination of truth and
knowledge.
        But I, for one, will always have a greater respect for
Emerson, a man who worked within the difficult confines
of the real world. As it turns out, Thoreau had the longer-
45   lasting and more powerful influence. His iconoclastic

ideals influenced some of the greatest men of the
20th century. But which is better, really? To fire the
imaginations of men and women with inspiration
during your own life, as Emerson did, or to
50   retreat to the woods and influence men and women a
century after your death, doing comparatively little
for those of your own generation, as Thoreau did?
        I'm not sure I know the answer to that
question. But I do get the sense I would not have
55   liked Thoreau had I met him. And he certainly would
not have liked me.

1. In lines 12-13, what does "this matter" refer to?

2. In line 31, what does "this image" refer to?

3. The author mentions Sandra Harbert Petrulionis
   (line 32) in order to support the point that

   (A) accusations made against Thoreau during
        his lifetime were thoroughly baseless
   (B) Thoreau frequently behaved in an arrogant
        manner
   (C) Thoreau was not entirely devoid of
        redeeming qualities
   (D) Emerson was primarily responsible for
        immortalizing Thoreau
   (E) Thoreau was a consistent source of
        irritation for his neighbors

4. Throughout the passage, the author mentions all
   of the following about Thoreau EXCEPT

   (A) his appreciation of the natural world
   (B) his condescending attitude
   (C) his enduring influence
   (D) his lack of community involvement
   (E) his love of learning

11.   One of the first and most frequently repeated strategies used to cope with Berthe Morisot's position as a female member of a 'radical' art group participating in what is perceived as an exclusively
5   man's world, has been to construct her as exceptional. Unlike other women artists, both before and during her time, she, it is claimed, does not fall into the inevitable traps which beset women artists. George Moore, writing in 1898, stated that Morisot's pictures 'are the
10   only pictures painted by a woman that could not be destroyed without creating a blank, a hiatus in the history of art.' In turn, her painting 'style,' Impressionism, is produced as a method which is suited to and the natural expression of an appropriately
15   feminine temperament. 'Impressionism' is offered as the answer to the problem of Morisot's 'femininity,' the problem posed by a skilled and prolific professional woman painter in a world which deemed such activities to be 'unfeminine.' From as early as the 1870s
20   Morisot's manner of working was seen to reflect a naturally feminine sensibility; it was repeatedly called 'charming,' 'feminine,' 'delicate' in a way which transposed onto the painting those characteristics most favored in the middle-class women of the time.
25   What representations of Morisot as the intuitive feminine painter do not take into account, however, is the fact that she was one of many women working as professional artists in the period and that these women represented in working methods the full range of
30   artistic practices. Few used the painterly brushmarks and sketchy surfaces that are characteristic of much of Impressionist painting and most were unaware of Morisot's existence, preferring to define their context as that of the Paris Salons or alternately the Women's
35   Salon which emerged in the early 1880s as a significant forum for the display of women's work. If Morisot shared any technical qualities with her contemporaries, it was with male artists like Renoir and Monet. They, like her, were committed to an aesthetic of apparent
40   spontaneity, using separated brushmarks, revealing the light ground of the canvas, eliminating the use of the art-based pigment bitumen, and striving for the approximate effect of natural light. The resulting 'delicacy of touch' was part of a conscious strategy to
45   free painting from the academic emphasis on finish, the highly polished surface with no traces of individual brushmarks, and can in no way be attributed to the outpouring of an essential femininity.
    Accompanying the idea that Impressionism
50   was a naturally feminine style of painting was the notion that Morisot's working methods flowed intuitively for her inner self without conscious intervention or mediation. As Paul Valéry was to put it: 'the peculiarity of Berthe Morisot…was to
55   live her painting and to paint her life, as if the inter-

change between seeing and rendering, between the light and her creative will, were to her a natural function, a necessary part of her daily life.' But her letters themselves do not allow this view to be
60   sustained. If anything, they represent her often painful and intense involvement with painting, described once as a 'pitched battle with her canvases.' Equally, they represent a woman who is absolutely aware of the ways in which she and her colleagues are
65   received in the press, and is mindful of the reception of her own work and that of her associates.
    But if the image of Morisot as an intuitive, unreflective artist living out her natural femininity through her painting cannot be sustained, neither can
70   she be accommodated by today's feminist art historians in the role of the lofty female ancestor, politicized about her gender and the institutionalized sexism of her time. This does not mean that she was unaware of the debates around women's positions, or
75   the restrictions, social and psychic, which were placed on women's lives, but that her responses are not unified and worked out. They are often confused, ambiguous, and tellingly self-denigrating.
    The 'evidence' provided in her letters is
80   fragmentary and suggestive. It presents a woman often confused, filled with self-doubt, frequently discontent, berated for her stubbornness and selfishness, envied and admired, a devoted friend, and above all, a committed artist. The texts of her
85   letters themselves, many of them by Morisot's family and friends, provide a telling contrast to the idealized mythic representation of the enigmatic, even muse-like figure, which so many accounts of Morisot construct.

1. The "delicacy of touch" (line 44) can best be characterized as

    (A) an admirable trait
    (B) a deliberate aesthetic choice
    (C) an unintended consequence
    (D) a conventional technique
    (E) a hard-won achievement

2. In line 59, "this view" refers to

3. The author mentions the "pitched battle" (line 62) in order to support the idea that Berthe Morisot regarded painting as

    (A) a strenuous and difficult undertaking
    (B) an intuitive and natural endeavor
    (C) a form of political engagement
    (D) violent and dangerous activity
    (E) a means of self-promotion

12.   A few years ago the city council of Monza, Italy, barred pet owners from keeping goldfish in curved fishbowls. The sponsors of the measure explained that it is cruel to keep a fish in a bowl

5 because the curved sides give the fish a distorted view of reality. Aside from the measure's significance to the poor goldfish, the story raises an interesting philosophical question: How do we know that the reality we perceive is true? The goldfish is

10 seeing a version of reality that is different from ours, but can we be sure it is any less real? For all we know, we, too, may spend our entire lives staring out at the world through a distorting lens.

In physics, the question is not academic. Indeed,
15 physicists are finding themselves in a similar predicament to the goldfish's. For decades we have strived to come up with an ultimate theory of everything—one complete and consistent set of fundamental laws of nature that explain every aspect

20 of reality. It now appears that this quest may yield not a single theory but a family of interconnected theories, each describing its own version of reality, as if it viewed the universe through its own fishbowl.

This notion may be difficult for many people,
25 including some working scientists, to accept. Most people believe that there is an objective reality out there and that our senses and our science directly convey information about the material world. Classical science is based on the belief that an external world

30 exists whose properties are definite and independent of the observer who perceives them. In philosophy, that belief is called realism.

Those who remember Timothy Leary and the 1960s, however, know of another possibility: one's
35 concept of reality can depend on the mind of the perceiver. That viewpoint, with various subtle differences, goes by names such as antirealism, instrumentalism or idealism. According to those doctrines, the world we know is constructed by the

40 human mind employing sensory data as its raw material and is shaped by the interpretive structure of our brains. This viewpoint may be hard to accept, but it is not difficult to understand. There is no way to remove the observer—us—from our perception of the

45 world. The way physics has been going, realism is becoming difficult to defend. In classical physics—the physics of Newton that so accurately describes our everyday experience—the interpretation of terms such as object and position is for the most part in harmony

50 with our commonsense, "realistic" understanding of those concepts. As measuring devices, however, we are crude instruments. Physicists have found that everyday objects and the light we see them by are made from objects that we do not perceive directly. These

55 objects are governed not by classical physics but by the laws of quantum theory. The reality of quantum theory is a radical departure from that of classical physics. In the framework of quantum theory, particles have neither definite positions nor

60 definite velocities unless and until an observer measures those quantities. Quantum physics also has important implications for our concept of the past. In classical physics, the past is assumed to exist as a definite series of events, but according to quantum

65 physics, the past, like the future, is indefinite and exists only as a spectrum of possibilities. Even the universe as a whole has no single past or history. So quantum physics implies a different reality than that of classical physics—even though the latter still

70 serves us well when we design things such as buildings and bridges.

These examples bring us to a conclusion that provides an important framework with which to interpret modern science. In our view, there is no

75 picture- or theory-independent concept of reality. Instead we adopt a view that we call model-dependent realism: the idea that a physical theory or world picture is a model (generally of a mathematical nature) and a set of rules that connect the elements of the model to

80 observations. According to model-dependent realism, it is pointless to ask whether a model is real, only whether it agrees with observation. If two models agree with observation, neither one can be considered more real than the other. A person can use whichever model is

85 more convenient in the situation under consideration.

1. In line 20, what does "this quest" refer to?

2. In line 24, what does "this notion" refer to?

3. In line 32, what does "that belief" refer to?

4. In line 36, what does "that viewpoint" refer to?

5. Which of the following statements best summarizes "those doctrines" (lines 38-39)?

   (A) one complete and consistent set of fundamental laws of nature that explain every aspect of reality (lines 18-20)
   (B) an external world exists whose properties are definite and independent (lines 29-30)
   (C) one's concept of reality can depend on the mind of the perceiver (lines 34-36)
   (D) the physics of Newton that so accurately describes our everyday experience (46-48)
   (E) the past is assumed to exist as a definite series of events (lines 63-64)

6. In line 42, what does "this viewpoint" refer to?

7. The author states that "realism is becoming difficult to defend" (lines 45-46) because

   (A) physicists' measuring devices are crude and
       unreliable
   (B) Newtonian physics accurately describes the
       behavior of everyday objects
   (C) people no longer perceive the world in a manner
       consistent with the laws of classical physics
   (D) practical applications for classical physics
       have completely ceased to exist
   (E) quantum theory has been shown to underlie
       many common phenomena

8. In lines 54-55, what does "these objects" refer to?

9. In line 69, what does "the latter" refer to?

10. In line 72, what does "a conclusion" refer to?

11. Which of the following best summarizes the view
    presented in lines 76-82 ("Instead…observation")?

   (A) the universe contains no single past or future
   (B) the validity of a model depends on whether it
       can be perceived directly
   (C) quantum physics may eventually lead to an
       objective understanding of reality
   (D) a model does not have to be observable to
       be correct
   (E) the universe is fundamentally inexplicable

Official Guide
Literal Comprehension Questions

Test 1	Section 2	Question 11	p. 392	
Test 1	Section 2	Question 18	p. 395	
Test 1	Section 9	Question 7	p. 427	
Test 1	Section 9	Question 10	p. 427	
Test 1	Section 9	Question 11	p. 427	
Test 1	Section 9	Question 12	p. 427	
Test 1	Section 9	Question 14	p. 428	
Test 1	Section 9	Question 17	p. 428	
Test 1	Section 9	Question 18	p. 428	
Test 2	Section 4	Question 17	p. 461	
Test 2	Section 4	Question 20	p. 461	
Test 2	Section 7	Question 7	p. 476	
Test 2	Section 7	Question 20	p. 480	
Test 2	Section 7	Question 21	p. 480	
Test 2	Section 7	Question 23	p. 480	
Test 2	Section 9	Question 9	p. 489	
Test 2	Section 9	Question 16	p. 489	
Test 3	Section 4	Question 16	p. 523	
Test 3	Section 4	Question 17	p. 523	
Test 3	Section 4	Question 21	p. 523	
Test 3	Section 4	Question 23	p. 523	All EXCEPT
Test 3	Section 7	Question 7	p. 538	
Test 3	Section 7	Question 13	p. 540	
Test 3	Section 7	Question 22	p. 542	
Test 3	Section 9	Question 8	p. 551	
Test 3	Section 9	Question 11	p. 551	
Test 3	Section 9	Question 13	p. 551	
Test 4	Section 2	Question 12	p. 577	
Test 4	Section 2	Question 15	p. 577	
Test 4	Section 2	Question 16	p. 577	
Test 4	Section 5	Question 13	p. 589	
Test 4	Section 5	Question 15	p. 590	
Test 4	Section 5	Question 21	p. 592	
Test 4	Section 8	Question 7	p. 606	
Test 4	Section 8	Question 11	p. 607	
Test 4	Section 8	Question 14	p. 607	
Test 4	Section 8	Question 15	p. 607	
Test 4	Section 8	Question 18	p. 608	
Test 4	Section 8	Question 20	p. 608	
Test 5	Section 3	Question 9	p. 645	
Test 5	Section 3	Question 14	p. 647	All EXCEPT
Test 5	Section 3	Question 19	p. 648	
Test 5	Section 3	Question 20	p. 649	
Test 5	Section 7	Question 14	p. 665	
Test 5	Section 7	Question 20	p. 665	

Explanations: Literal Comprehension Exercises

"Augusta Ada King" Passage, Official Guide p. 391, #9

The passage is essentially divided into two parts, with the second part beginning with the word "however" in line 6.

Part 1: King = famous b/c pioneer in computer science

Part 2: King = famous b/c family ("father + lineage")

Main Point: King = famous b/c CS + family

The author would therefore disagree with the idea that King's family did NOT cause people to be interested in King. That idea directly contradicts the main point of the passage.

Passage #1

1. It = the book (line 1)

2. Its = the ink-and-paper book (line 7)

3. C: The passage states that "we have also become very good at producing books and more books, to the point where libraries become overcrowded and librarians overwhelmed." In other words, there are too many books, i.e. they are excessively *abundant*.

Passage #2

1. C: The passage states that Marie Curie was an outlier "because of her sex," which is simply another way of saying that she "defied conventional gender roles."

2. It = (The fact that) Marie Curie was never easy to understand or categorize (lines 1-2)

3. It = academic physics (line 15)

Passage #3

1. Which = secondary sources (line 5)

2. It = an untrustworthy source (lines 7-8)

3. Its = material (line 12)

4. C: The passage states that Barbara Tuchman was unconcerned about the trustworthiness of primary sources because the very act of examining those sources was revealing in and of itself (even an untrustworthy source is valuable for what it reveals about the personality of the author). In other words, their accuracy isn't terribly important – it's the fact that they exist that makes them interesting. Which is what (C) says. Careful not to get tricked by (E): just because *inaccurate* primary sources are useful for revealing their author's personalities, it does not follow that *all* primary sources reveal their authors' personalities because some accurate sources could reveal no information about their authors' personalities at all.

Passage #4

B: The "paradox" is that *the sheer volume of Thoreau's work has complicated the task of gaining a complete understanding of his personality. Sheer volume* = quantity. In other words, Thoreau wrote so much that it's hard to figure out who he actually was and what he actually believed. In other words it "obscures his individual identify." In order to recognize the correct answer, you must recognize that "obscure" is essentially being used as a synonym for the word "complicated," which appears in the passage.

Passage #5

1. Tangible evidence = vertical scores, underlines, brackets, checks, double- and triple-checks, x's, circles, as well as words, phrases, fragments of poetry, and even whole paragraphs of prose. (lines 6-10)

2. Their = fine editions of old books (line 11)

Passage #6

1. It = technology (line 5)

2. Truth = Modern Luddites do indeed invent "machines"—in the form of computer viruses, cyberworms and other malware—to disrupt the technologies that trouble them. (lines 10-13)

3. Reputation = Someone who opposes technological progress (line 4)

4. Many = The original Luddites (lines 14-15)

5. D: The last sentence indicates that the Luddites have remained famous (=their enduring reputation) more because they protested under the name "Luddite" than because they actually smashed machines (=their actions). In other words, their actions are not the only reason they've stayed famous. Which is what (D) says.

Passage #7

1. Concern = shipping foods over long distances results in the unnecessary emission of the greenhouse gases that are warming the planet. (lines 3-5)

2. That activity = growing bananas in Iceland (lines 12-13)

Passage #8

1. These people = a band of people [who] left northeastern Asia, crossed the Bering land bridge when the sea level was low, entered Alaska and became the first Americans. (lines 1-4)

2. Artifacts = distinct stone tools, primarily fluted projectile points (lines 8)

3. Evidence = a bone projectile point (line 16)

4. The find = a bone projectile point (line 16)

5. A: Lines 17-18 state that *since [the dig in 1977-1979], the age of the find has been debated* – in other words, researchers don't agree (=have not reached a consensus) about how old it actually is.

6. "People were living in North and South America before the Clovis" (lines 12-13)

Passage #9

1. E: The author discusses "barriers" in the context of her interaction with the woman, stating that she is surprised by the fact that the woman treats her like a friend or a member of her family. The author focuses on the deep sense of familiarity she felt (emphasis on her emotions), despite the fact that her experience with segregation had taught her that white people would be suspicious of her. Given this context, "barriers" is used as a metaphor for the emotional or psychological walls (i.e. defenses) that she and a white person would be expected to maintain when interacting with one another.

2. A: The author defines a "frame" as a "house in which the authentic can live." Clearly, since the "authentic" is not an physical object (like a painting) that can be put inside a frame, she's not talking about an actual frame (=imaginary). A frame, by definition, is a boundary – something that confines what's inside it – hence the answer is (A).

3. D: The author describes acting as something that is "realer than real" and that that quality makes acting "authentic." What does it mean to be "authentic?" To reveal one's true self. So when she asserts that "real life inhibits the authentic," she is simply saying that people are unable to be their true selves in daily life. (D) simply rephrases what the passage is saying.

Passage #10

1. This matter = Whether [Thoreau] was, in fact, a misanthrope. (line 11)

2. This image = [Thoreau seemed to believe that he possessed the true compass as to what was good and noble as he looked at other men, coldly assessing their worth and disturbingly certain as to his judgment.] (lines 26-29)

3. C: What does Sandra Petrulionis believe? That despite his shortcomings, Thoreau was basically a good guy and that people should focus on the positive things he did. Why does the author mention her? In order to indicate that he is aware Thoreau had some good points, i.e. that he was not all bad. Not all bad = not entirely devoid of redeeming qualities. (Note that the answer is relatively straightforward but somewhat difficult to recognize because of the double negative in the correct answer choice).

4. D: In lines 37-39, the author clearly acknowledges that Thoreau played an important role in his community. He did not at all "lack" community involvement.

Passage #11

1. B: In lines 44-47, the author states that Morisot's delicacy was "part of a conscious strategy to free painting from the academic emphasis on finish, the highly polished surface with no traces of individual brushmarks..." Deliberate = conscious strategy. Aesthetic = related to art.

2. This view = the notion that Morisot's working methods flowed intuitively for her inner self without conscious intervention or mediation. (lines 51-53)

3. A: The author uses the phrase "pitched battle" to illustrate the idea that Morisot's "involvement" with painting was "painful and intense" (line 60-61). (A) most closely rephrases that idea; (D) is too extreme – there is nothing in the passage that directly suggests that Morisot viewed painting as literally violent or dangerous.

Passage #12

1. This quest = For decades we have strived to come up with an ultimate theory of everything—one complete and consistent set of fundamental laws of nature that explain every aspect of reality. (lines 16-20)

2. This notion = a family of interconnected theories, each describing its own version of reality (lines 21-22).

3. That belief = the belief that an external world exists whose properties are definite and independent of the observer who perceives them. (lines 29-31)

4. That viewpoint = one's concept of reality can depend on the mind of the perceiver. (lines 34-36)

5. C: "Those doctrines" refers to the doctrines mentioned in the previous sentence: *antirealism, instrumentalism, or idealism*. What do those doctrines actually state? *One's concept of reality can depend on the mind of the perceiver.*

6. This viewpoint = the world we know is constructed by the human mind employing sensory data as its raw material and is shaped by the interpretive structure of our brains. (lines 39-42)

7. E: Careful here. Although the line reference points you towards lines 45-46, the answer itself is in lines 52-56: *Physicists have found that everyday objects and the light we see them by are governed...not by classical physics but by the law of quantum theory.* So basically, quantum theory is at the base of (=underlies) things that happen every day (=many common phenomena).

8. These objects = Everyday objects (line 53)

9. The latter = classical physics (line 69)

10. A conclusion = there is no picture- or theory-independent concept of reality. Instead we adopt a view that we call model-dependent realism: the idea that a physical theory or world picture is a model (generally of a mathematical nature) and a set of rules that connect the elements of the model to observations. (lines 74-80)

11. B: Lines 76-82 indicate that the only thing that determines whether a model holds up (=its validity) is whether it "agrees with observation" (=can be directly perceived).

6. Vocabulary in Context

Vocabulary-in-context questions are among the most common types of questions to appear in Critical Reading: nearly every long passage on every test will contain at least one, and, compared to other types of Critical Reading questions, they tend to be relatively straightforward. While keeping in mind the overall context of the passage can help you to answer them in some cases, just as often the correct response can be determined simply by looking at the sentence in which the word appears.

As discussed earlier, the SAT is in many ways the opposite of a traditional vocabulary test: while vocabulary tests given in school tend to focus on a word's first, most common meaning, the SAT often tests the second or third meanings of common words. Vocabulary-in-context questions extend this principle even further, and it can be summed up as follows:

Context determines meaning

In Critical Reading, words can be used to mean whatever an author happens to want them to mean, regardless of their dictionary definition(s). As a matter of fact, it doesn't necessarily matter if you know the definition of the word being tested, as long as you 1) can use context clues to understand the word in question, and 2) can figure out the definitions of the words in the answer choices. Sometimes the word being tested will in fact be used in a way that's fairly similar to its most common meaning – but then again, sometimes it won't.

The one thing you can be reasonably certain of, however, is that a *common* word will not be used to mean what it most commonly means (e.g. "spill" will not mean "knock over"). If it did, there would be no reason to test that word in the first place! As a general rule, if you see the usual definition of a word among the answer choices, you should start by assuming that it's wrong and only reevaluate that assumption if nothing else seems to work.

It also means that when you see a question that says, "In line 14, *fraught* most nearly means…," you can think of the question as saying, "In line 14, ------- most nearly means." The fact that the word *fraught*, as opposed to some other word, happens to be used in the original text is almost entirely irrelevant. Yes, knowing that *fraught* has a negative connotation *might* help you eliminate answers, but that knowledge might also drag you in the wrong direction. Words that are normally positive can sometimes be given negative connotation, and vice-versa. Better to start by looking at the context and forgetting about the word itself.

Strategies:

1) Plug in your own word and find the answer choice that matches

The only potential difficulty involved in this approach is that sometimes, even if you supply a perfectly adequate synonym for the word in question, the correct answer will be a less common word, or the second meaning of a common word – one that you may not recognize as having the same meaning as the word you supplied.

2) Plug each answer choice into the sentence

Frequently, you'll be able to hear that a particular choice does not sound correct or have the right meaning within the context of a sentence. The only potential downside is that sometimes, as is true for #1, the correct word is not a word you would think to use. As a result, you might talk yourself out of choosing that answer (or eliminate it immediately) because you think it sounds funny.

3) Play positive/negative, then plug in

If you can determine from context whether the word is positive or negative, you can often eliminate at least two or three of the answer choices. You can then plug the remaining answers back into the sentence and see which one works best.

While some people feel most comfortable using a single approach for all vocabulary-in-context questions, it is also true that certain questions lend themselves better to certain approaches. On some straightforward questions you may find it easiest to plug in your own word, while on other, less clear-cut questions, a combination of positive/negative and process of elimination might be the most effective way of working toward the answer.

Important: sometimes you will not be able to determine the meaning of a word from the sentence in which it appears. In such cases, you need to establish a slightly larger context. Read from the sentence above to the sentence below – one of those sentences will very likely contain a synonym for the word in question and thus for one of the answer choices.

Let's look at a couple of examples:

The black Africans who survived the dreaded "Middle Passage" from the west coast of Africa to the New World did not sail alone. Violently and radically abstracted from their civilizations, these Africans none-
5 theless carried within them to the Western hemisphere aspects of their cultures that were meaningful, that could not be obliterated, and that they chose, by acts of will, not to forget: their music, their myths, their systems of order, and their forms of performance.

In line 3, *abstracted* most nearly means

(A) pondered
(B) uprooted
(C) reproached
(D) minimized
(E) deterred

Solution:

The first thing we need to do is forget about the word "abstracted." Normally, *abstract* is the opposite of *concrete* and, on the SAT, a synonym for *abstruse* and sometimes *esoteric*. But here we're talking about slavery and the journey from Africa to the New World – things that have nothing whatsoever to do with the usual meaning of abstraction.

If we wanted to start by attempting to plug in our own word, we could go back and consider the context: the passage is talking about how Africans were taken forcibly from their civilizations and sent to the New World, so in place of "abstracted," we could stick in a word like "removed" or "stolen" or, if we felt like being a bit more dramatic, "ripped away."

If we then consider the answer choices, we see that (B), uprooted, comes closest in meaning to the idea of being stolen (it literally means "to remove violently"). It doesn't matter whether "uprooted" is a word that you would think to use – the definition matches perfectly, so it's right.

Alternately, you can start by playing positive/negative and then plug in: the topic, the Middle Passage, is clearly negative, so you can assume that anything positive or neutral is wrong. There aren't any really positive words, but (A) *ponder* (think about, mull over) is pretty neutral, so that at least can be eliminated.

Now we look at the rest of the choices in order:

(B) If you know that "uprooted" means "violently removed," you can probably see pretty quickly that it fits. But even if you're not 100% sure, you can probably make a semi-educated guess that it involves yanking something out by its roots. Still, if you're not sure, you can check the other answers.

(C) "Reproached" means "scolded." If you know what it means, you can eliminate it easily since the passage is not talking about scolding. If you don't… you can guess that "uprooted" sounds more like what's being described.

(D) "Minimized" means "made smaller" or "not taken seriously," neither of which has anything to do with the situation described.

(E) "Deterred" means "discouraged from," which also doesn't fit the context.

So once again, we've arrived at (B) as the answer.

One more:

> Make no mistake—Dolley Madison was as fiercely partisan as any male politician. Her declaration, "I confess I do not admire contention in any form, either political or civil" is often cited by historians as proof of her pacific
> 5   nature. The second half of the statement reveals more—"I would rather fight with my hands than my tongue." And fight she did, though hers was the arena of action, not words. Though Dolley strove for discretion in her letters, anger at her husband's enemies sometimes broke through. During
> 10   his presidency, James Madison was hampered by what Dolley called "a Capricious Senate," whose objections she characterized as "almost treason." Still, she subsumed her feelings, so that one guest declared, "By her deportment in her own house you cannot discover who is her husband's
> 15   friends or foes."

In line 10, *hampered* most nearly means

(A) captivated
(B) mollified
(C) legislated
(D) endorsed
(E) constrained

Solution:

Even if you have no idea what "hampered" means, you can determine that it has a pretty negative connotation by looking at the sentence in which it appears, as well as the surrounding sentences. Since "objections" (line 11) and "treason" (line 12) are bad, it stands to reason that they would have a negative effect, and that means you can eliminate any answer that is either positive or neutral.

"Captivated" and "endorsed," which are both positive, are out, and if you know that "mollified" is positive as well, you can get rid of it also. "Legislated" is neutral, so that leaves "constrained" the only negative word, so the answer is (E).

Note that in some ways this question really is a pretty straightforward test of vocabulary, as is sometimes the case when harder words appear both in the passage and among the answer choices. "Constrained" is in fact reasonably close in meaning to "hampered;" both essentially mean "limited." The question is only difficult because many test-takers will not be certain of the definition of either word. In addition, "mollified" is among the hard words regularly tested on sentence completions – if you don't know what it means, or, at the very least, whether it's positive or negative, the question has the potential to become a little more confusing.

"Legislated," by the way, is the trick answer because it plays on associative interference: if the only thing you understand about the passage is that it's talking about politics you could leap to the conclusion that since "legislated" has something to do with politics, it must be the answer.

Now try one on your own: if you don't see the answer immediately, try to figure it out.

In line 12, *subsumed* most nearly means

Context clues: _____

Your word OR positive/negative: _____

Now look at the choices

    (A) denied
    (B) fostered
    (C) suppressed
    (D) assumed
    (E) analyzed

Solution: The passage quotes a guest of Dolley Madison stating that, "By her deportment in her own house you cannot discover who is her husband's friends or foes." In other words, you can't tell whom she likes or dislikes from the way she acts. It is therefore logical that she would be *suppressing* (hiding) her feelings. The answer must therefore be (C).

Recognizing Definitions

A second kind of vocabulary question tests your ability to recognize definitions or descriptions of words in the context of a passage. Instead of recognizing what a particular word means in context of the passage, you must recognize the definition that the passage provides and relate it to the word or phrase that matches the definition. Very often, one or more answer choices include high-frequency words such as *unsubstantiated* or *perplexing*.

These questions also indirectly test your understanding of other words contained within the passage itself – in order to recognize the correct answer, you must understand how the specific words used by the author work together to indicate a particular definition.

For example:

> Marie Curie was never easy to understand or categorize. That was because she was a pioneer, an outlier, unique for the newness and immensity of her achievements. But it was also because of her sex. Curie worked during a great age of innovation,
> 5 but proper women of her time were thought to be too sentimental to perform objective science. She would forever be considered a bit strange, not just a great scientist but a great woman scientist. You would not expect the president of the United States to praise one of Curie's male contemporaries by calling attention to his
> 10 manhood and his devotion as a father. Professional science until fairly recently was a man's world, and in Curie's time it was rare for a woman even to participate in academic physics, never mind triumph over it.

According to the first sentence (line 1), Marie Curie could best be described as

(A) an autocrat
(B) an enigma
(C) a maverick
(D) a charlatan
(E) an equivocator

An **enigma** is a puzzle or something perplexing, and the passage states that, "Marie Curie was never easy to understand." So the answer is (B).

Based on the description in the last sentence (lines 10-14) Marie Curie could best be characterized as

(A) a polemicist
(B) a skeptic
(C) an anomaly
(D) a prodigy
(E) a misanthrope

An **anomaly** is something or someone out of the ordinary, and the passage states that, "in Curie's time it was rare for a woman even to participate in academic physics, never mind triumph over it." So the answer is (C).

Understanding Connotation

Yet a third kind of vocabulary question tests your understanding of **connotation**, or of the implications that particular words carry and of the ways in which they influence the meaning of a piece of writing. While these types of questions could also be considered inference questions, I am discussing them here because they do test vocabulary directly, though at a somewhat subtler level than the other kinds of vocabulary questions covered in this chapter. Sometimes these questions explicitly target your understanding of relatively difficult words, although they do ask about somewhat more common words as well. In either case, you must understand how the choice of the particular word in question serves to convey a point or attitude.

Let's look at an example:

> Women's and African-American reading groups not
> only reinforced community bonds—and introduced countless
> readers to great works of literature—but indirectly and perhaps
> unwittingly cleared a path to suffrage and other civil rights.
> 5   In reading highbrow literature and discussing it in something
> like a classroom atmosphere, many women's reading groups
> created a rather formal semipublic arena for women to grow
> intellectually. No wonder that in Texas clubwomen led efforts
> to establish a women's dormitory at the University of Texas at
> 10   Austin, funded local and statewide scholarships for women, and
> were instrumental in founding what is today Texas Women's
> University. And though reading groups might host visiting
> suffragist speakers, in general the reading groups tended to be
> too conservative for such reforms, even as they trained their
> 15   members in many a fine point of civic virtue.

In line 4, the use of the word "unwittingly" suggests that women's and African-American reading groups

(A) played an important role women's intellectual development
(B) did not actively attempt to bring about social change
(C) strengthened ties between their members
(D) fought passionately for civil rights
(E) allowed women to express their ideas publicly

"Unwittingly" means "unintentionally," so the sentence is saying that if these groups made it easier for women and African-Americans to acquire civil rights, they did not go out of their way to fight for those rights. Unwittingly = did not actively attempt, civil rights = social change, hence (B).

If you didn't know what "unwittingly" meant, you'd be just as likely to pick (D) since that answer repeats almost word-for-word the information in the passage. The problem is that (D) says the exact *opposite* of what the passage says. That said, in the passage, "unwittingly" is linked to "indirectly" by the word "and," indicating that the two words must have approximately the same meaning. So even if you don't know what "unwittingly" means, the passage is still set up so that you can figure it out.

Vocabulary in Context Exercises

1.   Math poses difficulties. There's little room for eyewitness testimony, seasoned judgment, a skeptical eye or transcendental rhetoric.

In line 2, "seasoned" most nearly means

(A) determined
(B) innate
(C) tasteful
(D) experienced
(E) objective

2.   To the degree that Audubon's prose has the shapely feel of a novel, it's because he was deft at crafting his observations into the stuff of story; the birds that he chronicles became not merely objects of scientific data,
5   but characters in a dramatic narrative.

1. In line 2, "feel" most nearly means

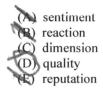

(A) sentiment
(B) reaction
(C) dimension
(D) quality
(E) reputation

3.   It is a powerful image: desperate refugees fleeing environmental apocalypse, crossing boundaries to save their very lives. But this notion is flawed. Rather than seeing environmental migration as bad, we need
5 to see it as part of the solution to environmental change.

1. The author views the "image" mentioned in line 1 as

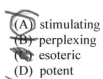

(A) stimulating
(B) perplexing
(C) esoteric
(D) potent
(E) elusive

4.   Neuroscientists and humanists are tackling similar questions—by joining forces, they might vastly refine our understanding of the role that narrative plays in human cognition, for example, or
5 explore with empirical precision the power of literature to represent consciousness.

In line 3, "refine" most nearly means

(A) purify
(B) ameliorate
(C) define
(D) capture
(E) reprimand

5.   Most people have so-called flashbulb memories of where they were and what they were doing when something momentous happened. (Unfortunately, staggeringly terrible news seems to come out of the
5 blue more often than staggeringly good news.) But as clear and detailed as these memories feel, psychologists have discovered they are surprisingly inaccurate.

The author indicates that "flashbulb memories" (line 1) are

(A) muddled and obscure
(B) utterly perplexing
(C) controversial yet intriguing
(D) lucid yet unreliable
(E) universal yet poorly understood

6.   Quantum mechanics is more than a hundred years old, but we still don't understand it. In recent years, however, physicists have found a fresh enthusiasm for exploring the questions about quantum theory that were
5   swept under the rug by its founders. Advances in experimental methods make it possible to test ideas about why objects on the scale of atoms follow different rules from those that govern objects on the everyday scale. In effect, this becomes an enquiry into the sense in
10 which things exist at all.

In line 3, "fresh" most nearly means

(A) novel
(B) renewed
(C) preserved
(D) profound
(E) inexplicable

7.   Shakespeare in the world of ants, untroubled by any such war between honor and treachery, and chained by the rigid commands of instinct to a tiny repertory of feeling, would be able to write only one drama of
5   triumph and one of tragedy. Ordinary people, on the other hand, can invent an endless variety of such stories, and compose an infinite symphony of ambience and mood.

1. In line 2, "chained" most nearly means

(A) riveted
(B) influenced
(C) struggled
(D) reversed
(E) bound

2. In line 7, the word "infinite" is used to suggest

(A) the diversity of the natural world
(B) the range of human creativity
(C) the fundamental limitations of insect behavior
(D) the genius of Shakespearean drama
(E) the inherent power of music

8.   Until the past few years, physicists agreed that the entire universe is generated from a few mathematical truths and principles of symmetry, perhaps throwing in a handful of parameters like
5   the mass of the electron. It seemed that we were closing in on a vision of our universe in which everything could be calculated, predicted, and understood. However, two theories, eternal inflation and string theory, now suggest that the same
10 fundamental principles from which the laws of nature derive may lead to many different self-consistent universes, with many different properties.

In line 6, "closing in" most nearly means

(A) shutting down
(B) trapping
(C) calculating
(D) approaching
(E) simulating

9.   There's a certain way jazz musicians from the 1930s pose for photographs, half-turned to face the camera, symmetrically arrayed around the bandleader, who can be identified by his regal
5   smile and proximity to the microphone. Publicity stills of the period were the equivalent of English court paintings, hackwork intended to exalt their subjects and attract admiration to their finery. Bandleaders even took titles borrowed from the
10 aristocracy: Duke Ellington, Count Basie, Earl Hines... well, Earl was actually the man's given name, but he lived up to it in a way no tracksuited rap star could approach, no matter how big the diamond in his earlobe.

In line 6, "stills" most nearly means

(A) masterpieces
(B) statues
(C) photographs
(D) constructions
(E) developments

10. The book is a self-contained utterance. It is finished, the very opposite of a "slug" you encounter on a website casting about for visitors to contribute writing and research. It is much more than a slug, much more than
5 the most basic information readily available. The discrete physical embodiment of text, it makes the perfect gift, the perfect giveaway, the perfect method of saying, "Consider the following . . ." We often think of imaginative literature when we think of book-reading,
10 along with notional scenes of people entering other worlds through books, but the world we know, the communities to which we already belong, are reified and reinforced by books. Such is the incredible and incredibly flexible power of this primitive technology.

The author characterizes a "slug" (line 2) as something

(A) puzzling
(B) incomplete
(C) secretive
(D) illusory
(E) eclectic

11. A century and a half after his death, Henry David Thoreau's literary output continues unabated, with new versions of his work still in progress. That work has shaped the career of Elizabeth Witherell, who joined the
5 staff of the Thoreau Edition in 1974 and has served as its editor in chief since 1980. "Thoreau was not a person who revealed himself easily," says Witherell, offering a view shared by scholars and general readers for generations. Not that Thoreau's life lacked document-
10 ation. In addition to Walden and a few celebrated travelogs, such as Cape Cod and A Week on the Concord and Merrimack Rivers, Thoreau (1817–1862) kept a copious journal that, in a previously published edition, stretched to fourteen volumes and some two
15 million words. But the sheer volume of Thoreau's prose has, paradoxically, complicated the task of gaining a complete understanding of his personality. The scale of Thoreau's work, not easily digested in its entirety, invites selective quotation, tempting readers to pick and
20 choose passages that support their pet theories about him.

1. In lines 6-9 ("Thoreau was not...generations"), Thoreau is portrayed as

(A) diffident
(B) erudite
(C) didactic
(D) reclusive
(E) candid

2. In line 18, "digested" most nearly means

(A) compressed
(B) comprehended
(C) endured
(D) swallowed
(E) abridged

3. In line 19, "invites" most nearly means

(A) offers
(B) precludes
(C) simplifies
(D) encourages
(E) activates

4. In line 20, "pet" most nearly means

(A) tame
(B) outrageous
(C) favored
(D) indisputable
(E) popular

12. With its collection of temples, stone kiosks, obelisks, a sacred lake, walls, and pylons built over fifteen hundred years and spread over more than six hundred acres—nearly twice the size of the National Mall in Washington— Karnak is mind-bogglingly
5 vast in both space and time. Even in partial ruin, Karnak provides a window into the formidable engineering and artistic abilities of ancient Egypt.
   The pyramids may be more stupendous and the Parthenon more beautiful, wrote British adventurer
10 Amelia Edwards in 1877 after wandering through the famous Hypostyle Hall which alone covers nearly 1.5 acres. "Yet in nobility of conception, in vastness of detail, in mystery of the highest order," she wrote, the pillared space of Karnak at the heart of the complex
15 surpasses them all. It was, she insisted without reservation, "the noblest architectural work ever designed and executed by human hands."

1. In line 16, "reservation" most nearly means

(A) hesitation
(B) appointment
(C) comprehension
(D) imagination
(E) investigation

2. In line 17, "executed" most nearly means

(A) destroyed
(B) undermined
(C) decorated
(D) demonstrated
(E) constructed

13.　　In our attempts to uncover the history of the
cosmos, we have continually discovered that the
segments most deeply shrouded in mystery are those
that deal with origins – of the universe itself, of its
5　most massive structures (galaxies and galaxy clusters),
and of the stars that provide most of the light in the
cosmos. These mysteries arise in large part because
during the cosmic "dark ages," when matter was just
beginning to organize itself into self-contained units
10　such as stars and galaxies, most of this matter generated little or no detectable radiation. When we turn
to the origin of planets, the mysteries deepen. We lack
not only observations of the crucial, initial stages of
planetary formation but also successful theories of
15　how the planets began to form. Astrophysicists may
now have more data but they have no better answers
than before. The beginnings of planet building pose a
remarkably intractable problem, to the point that one
of the world's experts on the subject, Scott Tremaine,
20　has elucidated (partly in jest) Tremaine's laws of planet
formation. The first of these laws states that "all
theoretical predictions about the properties of exosolar
planets are wrong," and the second that "the most
secure prediction about planet formation is that it can't
25　happen." Tremaine's humor underscores the
ineluctable fact that planets do exist, despite our
inability to explain this astronomical enigma.

In line 18, the word "intractable" is used to emphasize

(A) the practical challenges of astrophysical research
(B) the random nature of the universe
(C) the difficulty of a predicament
(D) the mystery of the sun's origin
(E) the challenges of scientific collaboration

14.　　In an essay in 1984—at the dawn of the
personal computer era—the novelist Thomas
Pynchon wondered if it was "O.K. to be a Luddite,"
meaning someone who opposes technological
5　progress. A better question today is whether it's
even possible. Technology is everywhere, and a
recent headline at an Internet humor site perfectly
captured how difficult it is to resist: "Luddite
invents machine to destroy technology quicker."
10　Like all good satire, the mock headline comes
perilously close to the truth. Modern Luddites do
indeed invent "machines"—in the form of computer viruses, cyberworms and other malware—
to disrupt the technologies that trouble them.
15　　But despite their modern reputation, the original
Luddites were neither opposed to technology nor
inept at using it. Many were highly skilled machine
operators in the textile industry. Nor was the
technology they attacked particularly new. Moreover,
20　the idea of smashing machines as a form of industrial
protest did not begin or end with them. In truth, the
secret of their enduring reputation depends less on
what they did than on the name under which they did
it.

1. In lines 6-8 ("Technology…resist"), the author
describes technology as

(A) costly
(B) impractical
(C) devastating
(D) ubiquitous
(E) revolutionary

2. The information in the second paragraph
(lines 15- 24) indicates that the Luddites'
"modern reputation" is

(A) admirable
(B) mundane
(C) indefensible
(D) elusive
(E) unsubstantiated

15.   By the middle of his life, Edmund Wilson was
a fat, ferocious man: petty, pretentious, and petulant, a
failure at many of the most ordinary tasks of life. But he
could dance: through a poem, through a book, through a
5   library. He was the Nureyev, at what he did—a genius,
really: probably the greatest reader the United States has
ever known.

   That's not to say he was the most influential
figure of his time. Sometimes he got it wrong. His prose
10   was merely good enough—not sparkling; only clear and
well organized—and he got nosebleeds whenever he
tried to follow philosophy up into the stratosphere of
metaphysics. For that matter, he never understood
escapism, and so, in a golden age of Hollywood
15   screwball fluff, he condemned American movies as
inferior to European—to say nothing of his famous essay
that thundered against mystery novels.

   Mostly, though, he got it right. And if he seems
lost to us now, that's not just because we have no similar
20   genius to occupy the space that he filled. It's also
because that space has nearly disappeared. The
magisterial critic has no role left in the United States,
really. We appreciate, we enjoy, we peruse, we watch.
But we don't define ourselves by reading anymore. The
25   novel, the premier art form of western civilization over
the last two hundred years, has ceased to be the mark of
civilization. And so what need have we of Edmund
Wilson—that fat, ferocious man, so nimble on his feet?

1. In line 17, "thundered" most nearly means

   (A) defended
   (B) railed
   (C) cautioned
   (D) exclaimed
   (E) weathered

2. In line 22, the word "magisterial" suggests that

   (A) the novel has undergone a rapid decline over the
       last two centuries
   (B) television has supplanted novels the novel as the
       most popular form of entertainment
   (C) literary critics once occupied a privileged position
       in the United States
   (D) the nature of Edmund Wilson's genius was
       misunderstood during his lifetime
   (E) many of Edmund Wilson's writings have become
       accessible to the general public

3. In line 25, "premier" most nearly means

   (A) preeminent
   (B) original
   (C) unique
   (D) profound
   (E) principal

16.　　　Many readers, faced with Thoreau's enigmatic Yankee persona, have resorted to a kind of pop-culture shorthand for describing his life. As the capsule summary goes, Thoreau was an oddball loner who lived by a lake, writing
5　in praise of nature and against modern progress.

　　　But the full story of Thoreau's life involves subtleties and contradictions that call his popular image into question. One idea that has persisted is that he was a hermit who cared little for others, yet he was active in his
10　community and responsible for circulating petitions for neighbors in need. In yet another way Thoreau was politically active, penning an essay, "Civil Disobedience," that would later inform the thinking of Mohandas Gandhi and the Rev. Martin Luther King Jr.

15　　　Despite his fame as a champion of solitude—a practice that he chronicled with wisdom and wit—Thoreau made no secret of the social life he indulged during his stay at Walden Pond from 1845 to 1847. In fact, one of the chapters of Walden, titled "Visitors," offers an extended
20　account of Thoreau's dealings with others. In it, the lifelong bachelor Thoreau lays out his rules for entertaining:

I had three chairs in my house; one for solitude, two for friendship, three for society. When visitors came in
25　*larger and unexpected numbers there was but the third chair for them all, but they generally economized the room by standing up... I have had twenty-five or thirty souls, with their bodies, at once under my roof, and yet we often parted without being aware that we had come very*
30　*near to one another.*

　　　But even if Thoreau wasn't always averse to human company, the idea that he was a loner might stem from the assumption that he was the kind of person who should have been alone. Thoreau was capable of friendship,
35　but on his own terms. He could be prickly to a fault. "I sometimes hear my Friends complain finely that I do not appreciate their fineness," he once wrote. "I shall not tell them whether I do or not. As if they expected a vote of thanks for every fine thing which they uttered or
40　did."

　　　Even those who liked him conceded that Thoreau could be a cold fish. In a letter to his friend Daniel Ricketson in 1860, Thoreau addresses Ricketson's puzzlement over why he hasn't come to visit, telling Ricketson, without much
45　ceremony, that he's had much better things to do. But after explaining himself, Thoreau continued to correspond with Ricketson. Ralph Waldo Emerson, Thoreau's close friend and mentor, who came to grudgingly admire Thoreau's argumentative streak, famously described him as "not to be
50　subdued, always manly and able, but rarely tender, as if he did not feel himself except in opposition." In remembrance of Thoreau, Emerson offered this observation from one of Thoreau's friends: "I love Henry, but I cannot like him; and as for taking his
55　arm, I should as soon think of taking the arm of an elm-tree."

1. In line 12, "penning" most nearly means

　(A) inscribing
　(B) deploying
　(C) recounting
　(D) marking
　(E) composing

2. In line 17, "indulged" most nearly means

　(A) nourished
　(B) sustained
　(C) tolerated
　(D) associated with
　(E) engaged in

3. In line 32, "stem" most nearly means

　(A) evoke
　(B) imply
　(C) result
　(D) enlarge
　(E) plant

4. Lines 41-45 ("Even those...to do") portray Thoreau as

　(A) amicable
　(B) timorous
　(C) impatient
　(D) aloof
　(E) enigmatic

5. In line 43, "addresses" most nearly means

　(A) explains
　(B) responds to
　(C) implicates
　(D) decries
　(E) puzzles over

6. In line 52, "offered" most nearly means

　(A) cited
　(B) reconstructed
　(C) endowed
　(D) sought
　(E) defined

17.   We were 210 students, all there to study identities, change identities, to learn to "be." There are a variety of ways to describe what acting is. "Being," "Seeming," "Becoming," "Lying," "Truth Telling," "Magic,"
5 "Transforming." We were new. Some among us had known the building for an hour longer than the others of us. No one ever arrives at the same time as everybody else. We were going to learn how to talk to each other onstage, and through all of this how to take our own
10 special message to the *world*.
    On one of the first days I was coming into the building, a tall, thin aristocratic-looking white woman who appeared to be about my age, and whom we ultimately referred to as the Katherine Hepburn among
15 us, came breathlessly down a narrow hallway, saying to me (whom she had never seen except in that one instant), "Do you know where I can get a drink of water?"
    She said this as if she had known me all my life, as if I were a sister, a brother, a friend. She may have
20 even grabbed my hand. I wasn't put off by the fact that she was a stranger. Her presence in that question made me feel in an instant as if I had known her all my life. Having grown up in segregation, I found it odd that a white person would approach me without her own barriers up,
25 and without the expectation that I would have barriers. I was so stunned by her presence that I didn't speak. Besides, I didn't know where to get a drink of water. Just as rapidly and as urgently, she vanished down the hallway and out into the street. I thought that perhaps this was
30 what acting was. Because, as real as it was, realer than real, it also seemed like a moment out of a scene from Chekhov's *Uncle Vanya*, or as if one of Tchaikovsky's symphonies had burst into speech. *Urgency* is the word. And it's one of the top ten in the vocabulary of acting.
35   Acting is the furthest thing from lying that I have encountered. It is the furthest thing from make-believe. It is the furthest thing from pretending. It is the most unfake thing there is. Acting is a search for the authentic. It is a search for the authentic by using
40 the fictional as a frame, a house in which the authentic can live. For a moment, because, yes indeed, real life inhibits the authentic.

1. The author uses the word "breathlessly" (line 15) to convey the woman's sense of

(A) elation
(B) fascination
(C) bewilderment
(D) urgency
(E) shock

2. In line 20, "put off" most nearly means

(A) delayed
(B) immobilized
(C) bothered
(D) mystified
(E) evaded

18.   One of the first and most frequently repeated strategies used to cope with Berthe Morisot's position as a female member of a 'radical' art group participating in what is perceived as an exclusively man's world, has

5   been to construct her as exceptional. Unlike other women artists, both before and during her time, she, it is claimed, does not fall into the inevitable traps which beset women artists. George Moore, writing in 1898, stated that Morisot's pictures "are the only pictures painted by

10   a woman that could not be destroyed without creating a blank, a hiatus in the history of art." In turn, her painting "style," Impressionism, is produced as a method which is suited to and the natural expression of an appropriately feminine temperament. 'Impressionism' is offered

15   as the answer to the problem of Morisot's 'femininity,' the problem posed by a skilled and prolific professional woman painter in a world which deemed such activities to be "unfeminine." From as early as the 1870s Morisot's manner of working was seen to reflect a naturally

20   feminine sensibility; it was repeatedly called "charming," "feminine," "delicate" in a way which transposed onto the painting those characteristics most favored in the middle-class women of the time.

        What representations of Morisot as the intuitive

25   feminine painter do not take into account, however, is the fact that she was one of many women working as professional artists at the period and that these women represented in working methods the full range of artistic practices. Few used the painterly brushmarks and

30   sketchy surfaces that are characteristic of much of Impressionist painting and most were unaware of Morisot's existence, preferring to define their context as that of the Paris Salons or alternately the women's Salon which emerged in the early 1880s as a significant forum

35   for the display of women's work. If Morisot shared any technical qualities with her contemporaries, it was with male artists like Renoir and Monet. They, like her, were committed to an aesthetic of apparent spontaneity, using separated brushmarks, revealing the light ground of the

40   canvas, eliminating the use of the art-based pigment bitumen, and striving for the approximate effect of natural light. The resulting "delicacy of touch" was part of a conscious strategy to free painting from the academic emphasis on finish, the highly polished surface

45   with no traces of individual brushmarks, and can in no way be attributed to the outpouring of an essential femininity.

        Accompanying the idea that Impressionism was a naturally feminine style of painting was the

50   notion that Morisot's working methods flowed intuitively for her inner self without conscious intervention or mediation. As Paul Valéry was to put it: "the peculiarity of Berthe Morisot…was to live her painting and to paint her life, as if the interchange

55   between seeing and rendering, between the light and her creative will, were to her a natural function, a

necessary part of her daily life." But her letters themselves do not allow this view to be sustained. If anything, they represent her often painful and

60   intense involvement with painting, described once as a 'pitched battle with her canvases.' Equally, they represent a woman who is absolutely aware of the ways in which she and her colleagues are received in the press, and is mindful of the recep-

65   tion of her own work and that of her associates.

        But if the image of Morisot as an intuitive, unreflective artist living out her natural femininity through her painting cannot be sustained, neither can she be accommodated by today's feminist art

70   historians in the role of the lofty female ancestor, politicized about her gender and the institution- alized sexism of her time. This does not mean that she was unaware of the debates around women's positions, or the restrictions, social and psychic,

75   which were placed on women's lives, but that her responses are not unified and worked out. They are often confused, ambiguous, and tellingly self- denigrating.

        The "evidence" provided in her letters is

80   fragmentary and suggestive. It presents a woman, often confused, filled with self-doubt, frequently discontent, berated for her stubbornness and selfishness, envied and admired, a devoted friend and above all, a committed artist. The texts of her

85   letters themselves, many of them by Morisot's family and friends, provide a telling contrast to the idealized mythic representation of the enigmatic, even muse-like figure, which so many accounts of Morisot construct.

1. In line 22, "transposed" most nearly means

    (A) projected
    (B) demonstrated
    (C) modified
    (D) composed
    (E) filtered

2. In line 68, "sustained" most nearly means

    (A) withstood
    (B) upheld
    (C) prolonged
    (D) persevered
    (E) extended

3. In line 76, "worked out" most nearly means

    (A) solitary
    (B) elaborate
    (C) cohesive
    (D) clear
    (E) fortuitous

Official Guide Vocabulary in Context Questions

Test 1	Section 2	Question 13	p. 392
Test 1	Section 2	Question 21	p. 395
Test 1	Section 5	Question 13	p. 404
Test 1	Section 5	Question 20	p. 405
Test 2	Section 4	Question 13	p. 460
Test 2	Section 4	Question 15	p. 461
Test 2	Section 4	Question 16	p. 461
Test 2	Section 4	Question 17	p. 461
Test 2	Section 4	Question 23	p. 461
Test 2	Section 7	Question 8	p. 476
Test 2	Section 7	Question 9	p. 476
Test 2	Section 7	Question 16	p. 479
Test 2	Section 9	Question 8	p. 489
Test 2	Section 9	Question 15	p. 489
Test 3	Section 4	Question 20	p. 523
Test 3	Section 7	Question 10	p. 539
Test 3	Section 7	Question 16	p. 541
Test 3	Section 9	Question 17	p. 552
Test 4	Section 2	Question 14	p. 577
Test 4	Section 2	Question 18	p. 577
Test 4	Section 2	Question 20	p. 577
Test 4	Section 5	Question 17	p. 591
Test 4	Section 8	Question 8	p. 607
Test 4	Section 8	Question 17	p. 607
Test 5	Section 3	Question 6	p. 645
Test 5	Section 3	Question 20	p. 649
Test 5	Section 7	Question 17	p. 665
Test 5	Section 9	Question 11	p. 674
Test 5	Section 9	Question 12	p. 674
Test 6	Section 3	Question 10	p. 708
Test 6	Section 3	Question 22	p. 711
Test 6	Section 3	Question 23	p. 711
Test 6	Section 7	Question 13	p. 726
Test 6	Section 7	Question 15	p. 727
Test 6	Section 9	Question 8	p. 736
Test 6	Section 9	Question 12	p. 736
Test 7	Section 2	Question 14	p. 765
Test 7	Section 2	Question 17	p. 766
Test 7	Section 5	Question 21	p. 784
Test 7	Section 8	Question 13	p. 793
Test 7	Section 8	Question 16	p. 793
Test 7	Section 8	Question 17	p. 793
Test 7	Section 8	Question 19	p. 793
Test 8	Section 2	Question 21	p. 829
Test 8	Section 5	Question 10	p. 843
Test 8	Section 5	Question 12	p. 843

Explanations: Vocabulary in Context Exercises

1. D

This is essentially a straightforward second meanings question since the passage gives very little context – the second meaning of "seasoned" is in fact "experienced," which fits with what the passage's meaning: judgment, even experienced judgment, plays no role in math because an answer is always right or wrong, and opinion plays no role.

2. D

The passage describes just what made Audubon so good at writing about birds – in other words, the *qualities* that made his writing so engaging.

3. D

3.1 In line 1, the author states that the image is *potent*, which is a synonym for *powerful*.

4. B

The passage indicates that the neuroscientists and humanists might have an enormously positive impact on the knowledge in their relative fields. "Refine" must therefore mean something like "improve" or "make better," which is the definition of "ameliorate."

5. D

The passage states that flashbulb memories are "clear and detailed" as well as "inaccurate." *Lucid* is a synonym for "clear," and *unreliable* is a synonym for "inaccurate."

6. B

The opposition between "more than a hundred years ago" and "in recent years" suggests that physicists have found a *new* enthusiasm for exploring questions about quantum physics. (B) is therefore the correct answer.

7. 1E, 2B

7.1 The passage indicates that ants, unlike humans, are essentially slaves to their instincts – the word "chained" is used to convey the idea that they are unable to escape, and so the correct answer must carry that connotation as well. (E) is the correct answer because "bound," the past participle of the verb "to bind," literally means "tied up."

7.2 What's the point? That people, unlike ants, possess incredible powers of creativity. What does the word "infinite" mean? Endless. So in this context, "infinite" is used to suggest how immense people's creativity is, i.e. its range.

8. D

The beginning of the passage describes how physicists believed they were beginning to understand how to describe the universe mathematically. "Closing in" must therefore mean something like "coming close to." That is the definition of "approaching," so (D) is correct.

9. C

The passage is devoted to describing *photographs* of jazz musicians, as indicated in the first sentence, and "still" (i.e. "still picture," the opposite of "motion picture") is simply another word for "photograph." Although the answer is directly stated in line 2, it is up to the reader to understand that the author is continuing the idea begun in the first sentence, just using different words.

10. B

The author states that the book is *the very opposite of a slug*, and since a book is defined as something that is finished, a slug must be something unfinished, i.e. incomplete.

11. 1A, 2B, 3D, 4C

11.1 Lines 6-7 state that Thoreau *was not a person who revealed himself easily*. In other words, he was distant, not open. That is essentially the meaning of "diffident," so (A) is correct.

11.2 In the last sentence of the passage, which includes line 18, the author indicates that it is easy for readers to select only the parts of Thoreau's work that support their ideas about him – in other words, they don't *[gain] a complete understanding of his personality*. "Digest" must therefore mean something like "understand," and since "comprehend" is a synonym for "understand," it is the answer.

11.3 If the scale of Thoreau's work "tempts" readers to pick and choose passages that support their theories about him, then "invites" must mean something relatively close to "tempts." "Encourages" is closest in meaning, so the answer is (D).

11.4 Since the readers are looking for passages that *support* their "pet theories," the phrase "pet theories" must mean something like "theories they like." Since "favor" is a general synonym for "like," (C) is correct.

12. 1A, 2E

12.1 The passage indicates that Amelia Edwards was in awe of Karnak and that she praised it in the strongest terms possible. "Without reservation" must therefore mean something "without any doubt." "Without hesitation" is the closest in meaning to that phrase.

12.2 In context of the passage, "executed" must mean something like "built," since logically Karnak was built after it was designed. "Constructed" is a synonym for "built," hence it is correct.

13. C

"Intractable" means "stubborn" or "unmovable." What's the context? That scientist just cannot solve the mystery of planet formation. So logically, "intractable" must be used to emphasize how difficult that problem (i.e. predicament) is. So the answer is (C).

14. 1D, 2E

14.1 Line 6 states that "technology is everywhere," and "ubiquitous" means "everywhere."

14.2 The second paragraph indicates that the historical Luddites were not particularly opposed to technology, whereas the term "Luddite" is now associated with someone vehemently opposed to technology. Because the Luddites' modern reputation is not supported by historical fact, it is *unsubstantiated* (unsupported).

15. 1B, 2C, 3A

15.1 The word "condemned" in line 15 indicates that Wilson's attitude toward mystery novels was extremely negative, so "thundered" must mean something like "denounced." In this case, the correct answer involves a second meaning of its own – to "rail" against something means to denounce it loudly and dramatically.

15.2 Even if you do not know what the word "magisterial" means, you can probably figure out that it's something pretty good. You might be able to relate it to a word such as "majesty," which would suggest that it's something pretty important. In fact, "magisterial" means "authoritative" or "having great importance," which goes along with the author's idea that critics like Wilson used to be pretty important in the United States. To say that someone "occupies a privileged place" is simply a fancier way of saying they're important. Hence (C).

15.3 The passage indicates that literary critics once occupied a place of great importance in the United States. "Premier" must therefore mean something like "extremely important" (or "most important," since the word "premier" carries a connotation of "first"). Since that is the definition of "preeminent," (A) is correct.

16. 1E, 2E, 3C, 4D, 5B, 6A

16.1 Because the word "penning" is used to describe what Thoreau did as an author, it must mean something like "writing." "Composing" is closest in meaning to that word. Although it is more often used in a musical context, it can refer to writing words as well.

16.2 A social life is typically something one participates in, and so the correct word must mean something like "participate." Since "engage in" is a synonym for "participate," it is correct.

16.3 The passages indicates that people might think Thoreau was a loner because he was the kind of person *who should have been alone.* In other words, it's giving an explanation: one belief came about because of another. "Stem" must therefore mean something like "come from" or "result from." Hence (C).

16.4 Lines 44-48 indicate that Thoreau was *a cold fish,* someone who brushed off his friend, i.e. standoffish or antisocial. That is the definition of "aloof," so (D) is correct.

16.5 Since the passage is describing what Thoreau wrote in his letter to his friend Ricketson, it is logical that he would be responding to him.

16.6 The word "offered" is being used in the context of introducing a quotation – another word for a quotation is "citation," making "cited" the correct answer.

17. 1D, 2C

17.1 Why use the word "breathlessly?" The point that the author wants to convey is that the woman's actions were performed with great *urgency,* and "breathlessly" (which implies doing something in a hurry or very intensely) is used to emphasize that idea. This is a question whose answer is literally in the passage – it's just mentioned later on. While the correct answer will typically contain a synonym for a key word in the passage, occasionally, ETS will in fact provide an answer stated verbatim in the passage, just not in the lines given.

17.2 The author states that the woman treated her like a "sister" or a "friend," and that she felt as if she had known the woman "all her life." In other words, she felt pretty good about her, even if she found her behavior odd. So in this context, "put off" must be negative. If you want to plug in your own word, you could fill in something like "annoyed," which would give you (C).

(A) doesn't make sense because woman didn't make the author *late* (even though "delay" is another meaning of "put off"), and (B) doesn't work either because there's nothing to suggest the author couldn't move. (D) is wrong because the author clearly indicates that she *was* puzzled by the woman's behavior, and she was *not* "put off." (E) is wrong because "evaded" ("avoided") simply makes no sense in context.

18. 1A, 2B, 3C

18.1 The passage states that "the characteristics most favored in the middle class women of the time were transposed" onto Morisot, so "transposed" must mean something like "moved onto." (B), (C), and (D) clearly do not fit that definition. "Filtered" has a connotation of removing impurities, and that doesn't fit either. So (A) is correct because "projected" does in fact mean to attribute the characteristics associated with one person of thing to another person or thing.

18.2 What's the context for "sustained?" We're talking about a point of view, one that the author is clearly rejecting. So in this context, "sustained" must mean something like "supported." (B) comes closest to that meaning since "uphold" literally means "hold up," which is the definition of support.

18.3 The passage pairs the phrase "worked out" with "unified," and opposes it to "fragmentary." "Worked out" must therefore mean something similar to "unified" and the opposite of "fragmentary." Only "cohesive" fits that definition.

7. Reading for Function

If you've already spent some time studying for the SAT, you've most likely had the following experience: you see a question that asks you the primary purpose of a few lines or a paragraph. You go back, read the lines, and feel pretty confident that you understand what they're saying. When you look at the answers, however, they don't seem to have anything to do with what you've just read. You go back to the passage, frantically re-reading, trying to figure out what you've missed, then look back at the answers. Clear as mud. You get rid of a couple that are obviously wrong but find yourself stuck between (B) and (C), which both seem equally plausible. You remember hearing that (C) is the most common answer, so you decide to just pick it and hope for the best.

This scenario typically stems from the fact that most people don't truly understand that "function" questions are not asking *what* the lines say but rather *why* they say it. One of the things that people often find very foreign is the fact that the SAT not only tests the ability to comprehend *what* is written in a passage but also *how* it's written. Unlike literal comprehension questions, which require you to identify a paraphrased version of an idea contained in the passage, function questions ask you to move beyond understanding the literal meaning of an idea contained in the passage to understanding the **role** of that content within the larger context of the passage or paragraph.

Frequently, I'll ask someone what role a particular piece of information is playing, only to be given either a play-by-play account of the content or a student's interpretation of the passage instead. Let me be absolutely clear: content, interpretation, and function are completely different things, and you need to understand the distinction between them.

Content = literal meaning

Function = the *relationship* of a one idea to another, or the **rhetorical purpose** (e.g. support, refute, question) of a given word, phrase, section, or entire passage

Interpretation = explaining the meaning or significance of a piece of information

In short, you cannot understand function without understanding content, but understanding content alone is not enough to understand function.

Furthermore, you will never be asked to interpret a passage beyond what is directly *stated* or *implied* in the text itself. Anything beyond that falls into the realm of **speculation**, and SAT answers that involve speculation will always be incorrect.

Types of Function Questions

Function questions can ask about the role of virtually any aspect of a passage, including:

-Single words
-Punctuation marks (e.g. quotation marks)
-Phrases
-Sentences or groups of several sentences
-Paragraphs
-Entire passage

They are typically phrased in the following ways:

- The primary purpose of this passage is to/This passage primarily concerns…

- The quotation/phrase, etc. in lines x-y primarily serves to…

- The quotation/phrase, etc. in lines x-y primarily is used to…

- The author makes the comparison in lines x-y in order to…

- The function of lines x-y is to…

….and their answers fall into two groups:

1) Those that can **only** be answered by looking at the specific wording in the lines provided in the question. In such cases, the lines will typically contain punctuation, phrasing, or an important transition that points to a particular answer.

2) Those that **cannot** be obtained by looking at the lines provided in the question but that instead depend on contextual information.

For these questions especially, line references simply tell you where the word(s) or sentence(s) in question are located – they do *not* tell you their relationship to anything else in the passage. **The information necessary to obtain the answer will often be either before the line(s) referred to in the question, or, less frequently, after.**

There is no way to tell upfront which category a particular question will fall into, and sometimes determining the answer will require elements of both. Consequently, when you encounter a function question, you should generally be prepared to read a sentence or two both before and after the lines provided, then go back and focus on the appropriate section more closely if necessary.

Important: if the lines given in the question are relatively close to the beginning of a paragraph, you should begin reading from there – topic sentences will nearly always give you the point of a paragraph, making it much easier for you to understand the role of a particular word or sentence within it.

Understanding "Function" Answer Choices

Function questions comprise a significant number of the questions in the passage-based portion of the Critical Reading section, and they are at the heart of what the SAT tests – namely the ability to understand how arguments are organized and why authors choose to include particular words, phrases, information, and rhetorical strategies.

These questions almost always require you to make a cognitive leap from concrete to abstract – you are expected to understand not only the literal meaning of a passage or portion of a passage but also to understand its more general *relationship* (supporting, refuting, illustrating, emphasizing, comparing, questioning) to the argument as a whole or to another idea presented in the passage.

While answers to "function" questions are based on the specific wording in the passage, the answer itself is not stated directly in the passage. In fact, the wording of the answer choices to function questions will often be entirely unrelated to the wording of the passage itself; a literal answer that simply rephrases the information presented in the passage – the answer that most people are expecting – will not appear at all.

Instead, you'll generally see something like:

(A) justify an approach
(B) qualify a statement
(C) criticize a response
(D) promote a theory
(E) refute a claim

You are responsible for drawing a connection between a specific person or idea discussed in the passage and its more general counterpart in the answer choice.

Sometimes, however, certain answer choices will contain slightly more information. In such cases, in addition to including a function word such as "argue" or "criticize," the **correct** answer will also typically refer to the general *topic* of a passage in a more general manner. If a passage discusses Frederick Douglass in detail, you should therefore look closely at an answer choice that simply refers to "an individual."

Likewise, you should never assume that an answer is more likely to be correct simply because it *does* mention the subject of the passage by name – if anything, an answer that refers to the subject of the passage by name is more likely to be **wrong**. Remember: the SAT is set up to test your ability to move from specific to general – it is *not* designed to test whether you can spot familiar words from the passage.

In short, do not ever be afraid to pick an answer simply because it does not mention by name the person or event discussed in the passage.

For example, a question accompanying a hypothetical passage about the friendship between American painter Mary Cassatt and French impressionist Edgar Degas might contain the following set of answer choices:

(A) promote the work of an overlooked artist
(B) analyze the influence of Edgar Degas' later works
(C) explore the influence of the Impressionists on United States artists
(D) describe the significance of a relationship
(E) compare and contrast the careers of Mary Cassatt and Berthe Morisot

Choices (B), (C), and (E) all contain references to specific figures presumably mentioned in the passage (Edgar Degas, Mary Cassatt, Berthe Morisot), while (A) and (D) are phrased much more generally – (A) refers to "an overlooked artist," while (D) simply mentions "a relationship." Those phrasings immediately suggest that the correct answer is either (A) or (D), and since the inclusion of the word "promote" in an answer choices almost invariably indicates an incorrect answer, the most likely answer would be (D).

Important: approaching answer choices this way is not a surefire "trick" for getting you to the right answer; rather, it's a tool that allows you to quickly identify answer that are *likely* to be correct and minimize second-guessing. **Even if you are reasonably certain, you should still go back to the passage and make sure that the answer choice in question truly does fit the passage.** Certain does not equal right.

If you can keep these things in mind from the moment you encounter a function question, you'll already be a step ahead.

Transitions, Punctuation & Key Words and Phrases

Since the SAT is largely a test that deals with the relationships between ideas, it follows that the majority of the questions tend to be based on the places in the passage where the ideas come into contact into with one another – that is, where new information is introduced, or where there is a change in focus, point of view, or tone.

The relationships between these ideas are sometimes indicated through the use of specific words and phrases – particularly transitions – as well as specific kinds of punctuation. These words/phrases and punctuation marks correlate in turn with particular function words.

Not every function word corresponds to specific textual "clues," but a number of them do; the chart on the next page lists some of the more common key words, phrases, and types of punctuation, along with the functions to which they correspond.

Functions of Key Words and Punctuation

Continuers

Support, Illustrate, Bolster, Provide Evidence

And
Furthermore
Moreover
In addition
Also
As well as
First
In the first place
Second
Next
Then
Finally
For example
For instance
One reason/another reason

Explain, Clarify

Because
The reason is
The answer is
That is, That is why
Colon
Dash

Draw a conclusion

So
Therefore
Thus
Thereby
As a result

Compare, Draw an Analogy

Similarly
Like/likewise
As
Just as
Much as/like

Define

That is/That is to say
Properly speaking
Colon
Dash
Parentheses

Hypothesize, Speculate

If
May
Maybe
Might
Could
Perhaps
It is possible

Emphasize, Highlight, Call attention to, Underscore

Indeed
In fact
Let me be clear
Italics
Capital letters
Exclamation point
Repetition (of a word, phrase)

Indicate Importance

Important
Significant
Essential
Fundamental
Central
Key
The point is

Contradictors

Refute, Criticize, Challenge, Dispute, Contrast

But
However
Yet
(Al)though
On the contrary
On one hand/on the other hand
In contrast
Whereas
While
Despite
In spite of
Nevertheless
Meanwhile
Instead
Still
Rather than
Misguided
False

Question, Imply skepticism

But is it really true…?
Question mark
Quotation marks

Qualify

Dashes
Parentheses

Main Point vs. Primary Purpose

Very often, when one of my students encounters a question asking about the **overall purpose** of a passage, he or she will reiterate the main point, then become confused when a version of it does not appear among the answer choices. While it is important to determine the main point, knowing the point alone will not necessarily give you sufficient information to answer primary purpose questions.

The purpose and point of the passage are related, sometimes directly and sometimes in ways that are less obvious. They are not, however, the same thing, and it is important to understand the distinction between them because some questions ask you to identify one, and some questions ask you to identify the other.

> **Main Point** - the primary **argument** the author is making. It is usually stated more or less directly in the passage, in the introduction, the conclusion, or all three.

> **Primary Purpose** - the **rhetorical function** of the passage as a whole (e.g. assert, refute, propose). While the primary purpose is based on the overall passage, there is often a key sentence that will point to a particular answer.

For example, consider the following passage:

> In an era when few men and no women received such international renown, Dolley Madison's stature has perplexed historians and modern Americans (who associate her name with ice cream and a line of packaged pastries). In
> 5 our time, reality stars can become "fame-ish" overnight; but the people of the nineteenth century bestowed fame on individuals—mostly male—who they felt had made significant contributions to history. Why did the residents of Washington City, the members of government and their families, and,
> 10 indeed, all of America declare Dolley the nation's "Queen"? What did they understand about Dolley Madison that we don't?

The primary purpose of the passage is to

(A) contrast fame in the nineteenth century with fame today
(B) describe a puzzling situation
(C) explain the significance of a historical figure
(D) condemn the superficiality of reality television
(E) mock nineteenth century Americans' preoccupation with Dolley Madison

Main Point: Why DM so famous 19C? **Or:** No one knows why DM famous 19C

When we look at the answer choices, there is in fact no answer choice that rephrases the main point exactly. But there is one choice that is generally related to that concept: (B). The entire passage revolves around the fact that no one today understands why Dolley Madison was so famous – in other words, they're *puzzled*.

The relationship becomes even clearer when we look at the first sentence of the passage (one of the places the point is most likely to be located), which states that "Dolley Madison's stature has *perplexed* historians and modern Americans." Perplexed = puzzled.

We can also focus on the rhetorical questions in the other significant part of the passage – the end: "*Why* did the residents of Washington City, the members of government and their families, and, indeed, all of America declare Dolley the nation's "Queen"? *What* did they understand about Dolley Madison that we don't?"

The presence of questions directly indicates uncertainty, skepticism, or here, *puzzlement*.

"Main Point" Questions and Other Kinds of Function Questions

For questions that ask only about **smaller sections** of a passage, however, it is frequently helpful to keep the main point – or at the least the point of the paragraph – in mind in order to determine how the word or phrase you're being about asked relates to it. Let's take a look at the same passage from a slightly different angle:

> In an era when few men and no women received such international renown, Dolley Madison's stature has perplexed historians and modern Americans (who associate her name with ice cream and a line of packaged pastries). In
> 5 our time, reality stars can become "fame-ish" overnight; but the people of the nineteenth century bestowed fame on individuals—mostly male—who they felt had made significant contributions to history. Why did the residents of Washington City, the members of government and their families, and,
> 10 indeed, all of America declare Dolley the nation's "Queen"? What did they understand about Dolley Madison that we don't?

The author mentions "ice cream" and "packaged pastries" (line 4) in order to

(A) criticize a harmful development
(B) provide a historical perspective
(C) describe an unexpected consequence
(D) downplay an important distinction
(E) indicate the magnitude of a shift

Knowing the main point of the passage won't directly get you the answer here, but it can help. Again, what's the point? That DM was a "Queen" in the 19th century but today no one understands just why.

Now we have to figure out the relationship between the lines in question and that fact. The first thing we're going to do is re-read the *entire sentence* in which those words appear:

> *In an era when few men and no women received such international renown, Dolley Madison's stature has perplexed historians and modern Americans (who associate her name with ice cream and a line of packaged pastries).*

So the author mentions "ice cream" and "pastries" in order to show how Americans view her today – they associate her with junk food.

Why is that important?

Well, in the nineteenth century people thought she was a pretty big deal.

That's a pretty huge change, from being internationally renowned, the nation's "Queen," to showing up on a junk food box.

A big change = *magnitude* of a shift. Again: same idea, different words. Hence (E).

Admittedly, the relationship between the main point and the answer to the question isn't 100% straightforward; if you have trouble understanding the language of the passage or in identifying the point, this strategy will be of minimal help. But the relationship is there, and if you can identify it, questions such as these become much more straightforward. You'll still have to put in some thought in order to make the leap – the answer probably won't leap off the page, which is to be expected since the test is often designed to *obscure* the correct answer – but at least you'll have a way of approaching things in a more logical manner.

Playing Positive and Negative with Function Questions

One of the simplest ways to approach function questions and eliminate answer choices quickly is to play positive/negative with them. Positive passages or portions of passages tend to have positive answers (*explain, clarify, highlight*), while negative passages and portions of passages tend to have negative answers (*imply skepticism, question, criticize*).

Keep in mind, however, that correct answers often contain "function verbs" far more neutral than the words in the passage itself. This is particularly true for passages that are positive in tone – negative passages are much more likely to have questions whose answers are clearly negative.

On the other hand, a passage that is clearly negative toward the shift from paper to electronic books might contain a primary purpose question whose correct answer reads, "criticize a development."

Very Important: as is true for Critical Reading answers in general, function answers that contain extreme language, either positive or negative (e.g. "condemn," "attack," "prove"), are usually incorrect.

While this strategy will not work for every single function question – some passages will simply be too neutral and some questions will contain all positive or all negative answers – it does work for many questions, and employing it when you are able to do so can help you to very quickly narrow down your choices.

Let's look at an example:

> For Egyptologists, the temple at Karnak offers a treasure trove of data on Egypt's evolution into an inter-national power with great wealth, a unique and mysterious religion, and a way of life centered on the ebb and flow
> 5 of the Nile, which coursed through the country's heart. One relief, for example, which lists pharaohs stretching back to the Old Kingdom, provides scholars with important inform-ation on the ruling class. Even destruction tells a tale: Some pharaohs chiseled away their predecessors' names in
> 10 an attempt to wipe out any memory of their existence and accomplishments.

The primary purpose of the passage is to:

(A) explain the significance of a place
(B) criticize the pharaohs for removing their
      ancestors' names
(C) describe ancient Egypt's ruling class
(D) explore how the Nile shaped life in the Old
      Kingdom
(E) lament the destruction of a portion of Karnak

The first sentence tells us that Karnak "offers a treasure trove," indicating that the passage is positive, and there is nothing in the remainder of the passage to contradict that first impression. Keeping that in mind, you can eliminate (B) and (E) automatically – don't read, just look at the first word, see that it's negative, and cross out. Worst comes to worst, if nothing else seems to fit, you can go back and reassess those answers. That's why you work in pencil.

That leaves us with (A), (C), and (D), all of which are fairly neutral. The only semi-positive "clue" we have in any of those answer is the word "significant" in (A). Significant = important, and the passage is in fact telling us why (i.e. *explaining*) Karnak is important. The answer is in fact (A).

If you weren't sure, however, you could check (C) and (D) out individually.

(C) The passage only tells us that Karnak provides information about the ruling class – it doesn't actually *describe* that class.

(D) Again, the passage only tells us the fact that life in ancient Egypt centered on the Nile – it never says how it shaped life or provides any details.

The following page provides a chart of common answers to function questions, divided into positive, negative, and neutral.

A note about "proving" and "disproving": One common point of confusion concerns the terms "prove" and "disprove." Most high school students are accustomed to hearing teachers tell them to "prove their thesis," and so it seems logical that SAT authors would do the same. This, alas, is one of the major differences between high school and college-level work: while high school assignments tend to be framed in terms of black-and-white ("Prove your thesis!" "Knock down the opposition!"), the reality is that authors who write for adult readers are far more **nuanced** – that is, that they discuss *theories* that can be supported, illustrated, challenged, etc., but that cannot be definitively proved or disproved. Remember that in science, even phenomena like gravity and evolution are technically considered theories, albeit ones for which there is very strong evidence. "Proving and "disproving" are therefore far outside the bounds of what any author could accomplish in 85 lines or less.

* signals an answer that is typically incorrect

Positive	Negative	Neutral
Support	**Refute**	**Describe**
Illustrate	Criticize	Discuss
Provide/offer an example	Question	Present
Provide/offer evidence	Challenge	Characterize
Exemplify	Dismiss	Portray
Bolster	Disparage	Depict
Substantiate	Decry	Represent
Advance (a claim)	Contradict	Evoke
Affirm	Deny	Trace
Defend	Imply skepticism	Dramatize
Claim	Debate	Show
Prove*	Dispel	
	Undermine*	**Indicate**
Praise	Discredit*	Point out
	Attack*	Identify
Acknowledge	Condemn*	
Concede	Disprove*	**Introduce**
Propose	**Warn**	**Shift**
Offer	Raise concern	Change
Suggest		Digress*
	Make fun of	
Emphasize	Satirize	**Restate**
Highlight	Mock	Summarize
Call attention to	Scoff at*	Paraphrase
Stress	Jeer at*	
Focus on		**Hypothesize**
Underscore	**Exaggerate**	Speculate
Reinforce		
Reiterate	**Downplay**	**Analyze**
	Minimize*	Examine
Explain	Trivialize*	Explore
Account for		Develop
Qualify	**Lament**	Explicate
Clarify	Bemoan*	Consider
Articulate		Reflect on
Specify		
Define		**Attribute**
Justify*		Cite
		Allude
Promote*		
Encourage*		**Simulate***
Advocate*		
Persuade		

For a glossary of selected terms, please see p. 213

Examples and Explanations

Passage #1

      Real objects cannot have infinite charge or mass.
But when scientists in the 1950s started calculating those
quantities with their latest and fanciest theories, infinities
kept sprouting up and ruining things. Rather than abandon
5   the theories, though, a few persistent scientists realized
that they could do away with the infinities through mathematical wrangling.
      No one liked this fudging, but because it led to such
stunningly accurate answers, scientists couldn't dismiss it.
10 In the reigning paradigm in physics today—which
describes the workings of invisible "fields" (similar to
magnetic fields) — would not exist without this hand
waving. And now physics is stuck with fields: they've
become more fundamental to understanding the universe
15 than mass or charge. Fields have become the very fabric
of reality—even if our understanding of them relies on
some unrealistic assumptions.

Purpose of punctuation:

The author uses quotation marks around the word "fields"
(line 11) in order to

(A) defend a controversial notion
(B) present a novel approach
(C) offer a hypothesis
(D) imply skepticism about a concept
(E) cite an expert opinion

Solution:

Aside from the fact that "implying skepticism" (or "questioning") is the function most commonly indicated by quotation marks, the question can also be thought of in terms of the main point.

MP: Fields = questionable science

What exactly does the author think about "fields"? That "no one liked the fudging" they involved, and that our understanding of them "relies on some unrealistic assumptions." In other words, he's pretty suspicious. So he's using those quotes to convey that suspicion.

Suspicious, questionable = skeptical, "fields" = a concept. Hence (D). Alternately, if you knew that the author's attitude was negative, you could immediately eliminate (A), (B), and (E), then get rid of (C) because "fields" are described as an accepted fact ("the very fabric of reality"), not a hypothesis that the author is offering.

Passage #2

Like La Fontaine, Audubon was a quaint moralist
about the natural world, assigning human strengths and weaknesses to the creatures he chronicled in his writings. The
result is dubious science, but lively reading. Audubon's
5   anthropomorphic view of the birds he encountered might
sound archaic by the yardstick of modern ornithology,
but on at least one level, the morality plays of his expansive
aviary seem thoroughly modern. Read Audubon for any length
of time, and you realize that his careful distillation of nature
10   into narratives of good versus evil anticipated the age of
television wildlife documentary. When we watch TV shows
that are carefully constructed to make us root for the terrified
antelope as it runs from the hungry lion, we're indulging a
tradition that Audubon, America's abiding dramatist of the
15   great outdoors, helped to popularize.

Purpose of an example:

The example in lines 11-15 serves to

(A) criticize a development
(B) illustrate a claim
(C) highlight a paradox
(D) celebrate a tradition
(E) characterize an impulse

Solution:

Don't be fooled by the relatively complex language of the passage – when you consider the question in terms of the main point, it becomes remarkably straightforward.

What do lines 11-15 say?

> *When we watch TV shows that are carefully constructed to make us
> root for the terrified antelope as it runs from the hungry lion, we're indulging a
> tradition that Audubon, America's abiding dramatist of the great outdoors, helped
> to popularize.*

Now let's consider the main point:

TV portrays animals with human qualities because of Audubon.

What's the relationship? Well, the example describes how television *constructs* its depictions of animals so that they have human qualities. In other words, it is simply designed to support, i.e. *illustrate*, the main point, i.e. *a claim*. So the answer is (B).

Alternately, the question could have been asked this way:

The author mentions the "terrified antelope" and the "hungry lion" in order to:

(A) criticize a development
(B) dramatize an interaction
(C) highlight a paradox
(D) celebrate a tradition
(E) characterize an impulse

Solution:

Even though this looks like basically the same question, it's actually asking you to approach the passage from a different angle – that of the *language* itself rather than the main point.

What do the words *terrified* and *hungry* do? They're adjectives: they describe just how documentaries construct the *interactions* between animals, and they create a sense of *drama* – they allow the reader to form an image of the typical wildlife documentary scene flipping between the wide-eyed, frightened prey and the slinking predator about to pounce, with the viewer cheering the former on. So the answer is (B).

Passage #3

In an essay in 1984—at the dawn of the personal
computer era—the novelist Thomas Pynchon wondered if
it was "O.K. to be a Luddite," meaning someone who opposes technological progress. A better question today is whether
5   it's even possible. Technology is everywhere, and a recent
headline at an Internet humor site perfectly captured how
difficult it is to resist: "Luddite invents machine to destroy
technology quicker." Like all good satire, the mock headline
comes perilously close to the truth. Modern Luddites do
10 indeed invent "machines"—in the form of computer viruses,
cyberworms and other malware—to disrupt the technologies
that trouble them.
   But despite their modern reputation, the original
Luddites were neither opposed to technology nor inept at us-
15 ing it. Many were highly skilled machine operators in the
textile industry. Nor was the technology they attacked
particularly new. Moreover, the idea of smashing machines as
a form of industrial protest did not begin or end with them.
In truth, the secret of their enduring reputation depends less on
20 what they did than on the name under which they did it.

Purpose of a paragraph:

In context of the passage as a whole, the purpose of the
second paragraph (lines 13-20) is to

(A) acknowledge a point
(B) refute a misconception
(C) criticize a tradition
(D) dispute an influence
(E) praise an invention

Solution:

Before we look at how to solve the question for real, let's look at a common mistake:
considering the paragraph only from the standpoint of its content.

Content Summary (what not to do)

If you summarized the *content* of the second paragraph, you might say that it describes how
the Luddites were skilled machine operators, that they didn't attack new technology, and that
they weren't the only people to protest by destroying machines.

When looking at the answer choices, you might seize on the lines, "…the original Luddites
were neither opposed to technology nor inept at using it. Many were highly skilled machine
operators in the textile industry" and conclude that since the author seems to like the
Luddites in those lines, then (E) would make sense. You might not be sure about the
invention part, but hey, the passage talks about machines, and machines are inventions, so it
must be the answer, right? (It's not.)

As discussed earlier, the problem with this approach is that it relies on a fundamental misconception of what the question is asking. The question is not asking what the second paragraph says. Rather, it is asking about second paragraph's function within the passage and its relationship to the first paragraph.

Function

To figure out the second paragraph's function, you must back up and figure out its relationship to the first paragraph. There are only two paragraphs in the passage, so it is unnecessary to take anything else into consideration.

1) Use transitions to narrow it down

Since the question is asking about the function of the second paragraph, you can also look at the first (topic) sentence of that paragraph for clues.

Sure enough, it starts with "But despite…" which tells us immediately that its function is to contradict. (B), (C), and (D) all generally go along with that idea, but (A) and (E) do not, so they can be eliminated.

This is where things get tricky – you might be able to get rid of (C) based on the fact that the passage isn't really talking about a tradition, but if you don't know how to figure it out for real, you're reduced to guessing.

2) Identify the idea that the second paragraph is contradicting

The topic sentence of the second paragraph states, "But despite their modern reputation, the original Luddites were neither opposed to technology nor inept at using it."

So the question now becomes, "what is the Luddites' modern reputation?"

The first paragraph states that in 1984, Thomas Pynchon used the term "Luddite" to mean "someone who opposes technological progress" – so that's the modern definition.

The second paragraph, however, states that the *original* Luddites were pretty good with machines and not all that opposed to them.

What's the relationship? Well, the second paragraph indicates that the first paragraph's definition of a Luddite as someone opposed to new technology is actually wrong – in other words, the accepted notion of a Luddite is wrong, i.e. *a misconception* to which the author is opposed, i.e. *refuting*. Which gives us (B).

Passage #4

Edgar Allan Poe should have become a lawyer. A brilliant, inventive mind with an eye for detail, Poe could have spotted the need for copyright protections, the absence of which made it difficult for him to prosper as a writer. The
5 alternative would have had other benefits as well. It would have been acceptable to his foster father, as law was an appropriate profession for a Virginia gentleman, and it would have allowed Poe to manage the family import-export business in his spare time. Perhaps, also, the city of Rich-
10 mond would today be honoring a favorite son with a statue with the inscription "Edgar Allan Poe, fortunate son of Virginia, graduate of the University, and creator of the international legal system that endures to this day." Edgar Allan Poe, Esq. probably would thus be memorialized in
15 stone, just as the actual Mr. Edgar Allan Poe, writer, is not.

Primary purpose of a passage:

The primary purpose of the passage is to

(A) advocate a controversial interpretation
(B) speculate about an outcome
(C) offer an analysis of an author's work
(D) highlight an achievement
(E) explain why Edgar Allan Poe failed to
     prosper as a writer

Solution:

1) Use the main point

This is a short passage, so its main point is likely to be located in either the first or last sentence. In this case, it's the first sentence because it sets up the information in the rest of the passage by making a claim ("Edgar Allan Poe should have become a lawyer") that is supported by specific reasons throughout the remainder of the passage.

Main Point:

If EAP lawyer = more successful/writer (if Edgar Allan Poe had become a lawyer, he would have become more successful than he was as a writer).

We still have to determine the *function* of that point, though, and here "if" is the operative word. It tells us that the passage is describing a situation that did not actually occur – in other words, it's *hypothetical* or *speculative*, and (B) is the answer that indicates that the passage's function is to speculate.

If you're not sure, look at the rest of the passage: the words *would have*, *might*, and *probably*, which also indicate speculation, appear throughout.

If that seems like too much of a jump to make, you could also approach it this way:

2) Narrow it down by looking at the wording of the answer choices

The word "advocate" typically signals an incorrect answer, so you can get rid of (A). In addition, (B) and (D) are phrased most generally, so you might want to pay particular attention to them and start by checking them out first, but if you're not really sure:

3) Check out the answers one by one

(A) advocate a controversial interpretation

There is absolutely nothing in the passage to directly indicate that the author's idea of what Poe could have accomplished as a lawyer is controversial. In addition, the author isn't really "interpreting" anything – he's merely describing what Poe might have done under alternate circumstances.

(B) See above

(C) offer an analysis of an author's work

The author never discusses any of Poe's work directly, only the fact that he was an author.

(D) highlight an achievement

The author talks about what Poe *could have achieved*, not what he *actually* achieved. And no, you can't stretch the answer and assume that it could apply to things that didn't actually happen. Besides, it's just not the author's goal here.

(E) explain why Edgar Allan Poe failed to prosper as a writer

Careful. The passage does in fact tell us why Poe failed to prosper as a writer (because his work wasn't protected by copyright), but that's a detail, not the point of the entire passage. Besides, the wording of the answer choice is too close to that of the passage (the phrase "prosper as a writer" appears in both), which immediately suggests that it is wrong.

Passage #5

Up close, amid the confusion of broken and standing stones, it still seems smaller than its reputation, notwithstanding the obvious feat represented by the erection of the

5 famous sarsen stones; the largest weighs as much as 50 tons. Indeed, its massive lintels are bound to their supports by joints taken straight from carpentry, an eloquent indication of just how radically new this hybrid monument must have been. **But what in fact do they mean?** Despite countless theories offered

10 over centuries, no one knows. Stonehenge is the most famous relic of prehistory in Europe and one of the best known, most contemplated monuments in the world—and we have **no clear idea** what the people who built it actually used it for.

Part 1

Part 2

Primary purpose of a passage:

This passage is primarily concerned with

(A) explaining how and why Stonehenge was built
(B) describing a longstanding puzzle
(C) criticizing a theory about European prehistory
(D) advocating a solution to a problem
(E) praising the eloquence of writers who have
  described Stonehenge

The easiest way to answer this question is to use the last couple of sentences, where important information is usually located. Those sentences indicate that despite centuries of speculation (=longstanding), no one still has a clear idea why Stonehenge exists (=a puzzle), which points you directly to the answer, (B).

If you weren't sure where to focus, however, consider the structure of the passage: the presence of a rhetorical question introduced by the transition "but" halfway through the passage suggests that the important information is going to be located close to the end.

The first half of the passage indicates that although the construction of Stonehenge represented a massive feat, Stonehenge is smaller than its reputation would suggest. At this point, though, the author is primarily describing how immense Stonehenge is – he is not really telling us the *significance* of that description.

The second half of the passage shifts direction and introduces the idea that Stonehenge has been a **mystery** (=puzzle) for centuries because no one knows what it means. That section of the passage **comments on** the first section, explaining why Stonehenge is being discussed – so while the author does include other information in the passage, the information in the second part is *more important* because it explains why the author is bothering to discuss Stonehenge in the first place.

Now let's look at something a bit longer:

The passage below is adapted from an article published in 2008. It discusses the effects of light pollution.

If humans were truly at home under the light of the moon and stars, we would go in darkness happily, the midnight world as visible to us as it is to the vast number of nocturnal species on this planet. Instead, we
5 are diurnal creatures, with eyes adapted to living in the sun's light. This is a basic evolutionary fact, even though most of us don't think of ourselves as diurnal beings any more than we think of ourselves as primates or mammals or Earthlings. Yet it's the only way to
10 explain what we've done to the night: We've engineered it to receive us by filling it with light. This kind of engineering is no different than damming a river. Its benefits come with consequences—called light pollution—whose effects scientists are only now
15 beginning to study. Light pollution is largely the result of bad lighting design, which allows artificial light to shine outward and upward into the sky, where it's not wanted, instead of focusing it downward, where it is. Ill-designed lighting washes out the darkness of night
20 and radically alters the light levels—and rhythms—to which many forms of life, including ourselves, have adapted.

For most of human history, the phrase "light pollution" would have made no sense. Imagine
25 walking toward London on a moonlit night around 1800, when it was Earth's most populous city. Nearly a million people lived there, making do, as they always had, with candles and lanterns. Only a few houses were lit by gas, and there would be no public gaslights
30 for another seven years. From a few mile away, you would have been as likely to smell London as to see its dim glow.

Now most of humanity lives under intersecting domes of light, of scattering rays from overlit cities
35 and suburbs, from light-flooded highways and factories. In most cities the sky looks as though it has been emptied of stars, leaving behind a vacant haze that mirrors our fear of the dark and resembles the urban glow of dystopian science fiction. We've grown
40 so used to this pervasive orange haze that the original glory of an unlit night—dark enough for the planet Venus to throw shadows on Earth—is wholly beyond our experience, beyond memory almost.

We've lit up the night as if it were an unoccupied
45 country, when nothing could be further from the truth. Light is a powerful biological force, and on many species it acts as a magnet. Migrating at night, birds are apt to collide with brightly lit tall buildings; immature birds on their first journey suffer
50 disproportionately.

And because a longer day allows for longer feeding, it can also affect migration schedules. The problem, of course, is that migration is a precisely timed biological behavior. Leaving early may mean arriving
55 too soon for nesting conditions to be right.

It was once thought that light pollution only affected astronomers, who need to see the night sky in all its glorious clarity. And, in fact, some of the earliest efforts to control light pollution were made to
60 protect the view from Lowell Observatory. Unlike astronomers, most of us may not need an undiminished view of the night sky for our work, but like most other creatures we do need darkness. Darkness is as essential to our internal clockwork as
65 light itself. The regular oscillation of waking and sleep in our lives is nothing less than a biological expression of the regular oscillation of light on Earth. So fundamental are these rhythms to our being that altering them is like altering gravity.

70 For the past century or so, we've been performing an open-ended experiment on ourselves, extending the day, shortening the night, and short-circuiting the human body's sensitive response to light. The consequences of our bright new world are more
75 readily perceptible in less adaptable creatures living in the peripheral glow of our prosperity. But for humans, too, light pollution may take a biological toll. In a very real sense, light pollution causes us to lose sight of our true place in the universe, to forget
80 the scale of our being, which is best measured against the dimensions of a deep night with the Milky Way— the edge of our galaxy—arching overhead.

Primary purpose of a long passage:

The primary purpose of the passage is to

(A) describe the results of a harmful development
(B) defend a controversial theory
(C) compare possible explanations for a phenomenon
(D) promote a particular course of action
(E) trace the evolution of a phenomenon

Solutions:

1) Focus on the blurb before the passage and the introduction

One common misconception about "big picture" questions is that it's always necessary to read the entire passage to answer them. By definition, however, **the purpose of the introduction is to define the topic as well as the central idea or question that the passage will discuss**. Remember that questions are listed chronologically in order of the passage, so if a "primary purpose" question appears first, the information necessary to answer the question will almost certainly be provided at the beginning. And sure enough, that's where the author introduces the topic: light pollution (i.e. a *harmful* development – on the SAT, you can assume that pollution is not a good thing!), and its consequences (it alters natural rhythms).

When it provides information beyond the passage's publication date, the blurb can also be an incredibly useful source of information for "big picture" questions when it gives an overview of passage content. Here, the blurb tells us that the passage will "discuss the effects of light pollution," so the correct answer is probably going to rephrase that statement in some general way – and indeed "describe" is the closest synonym for "discuss." Again, the word "pollution" is a pretty big immediate tip-off that the author isn't going to have a particularly positive attitude toward the topic.

2) Play positive/negative with the passage itself

The simplest and most straightforward way to solve this question is to use the tone: the passage is negative – the author is clearly against light pollution and spends most of the passage explaining its detrimental effects – so it makes sense to look for a negative answer. Even though all of the answers begin with neutral verbs, (A) is the only choice that contains a clearly negative word ("harmful"). So (A) is the answer.

3) Use the main point

Although the passage is long and relatively dense, the main point is located exactly where it is most often located: it is introduced in the last sentence of the first paragraph and reiterated in the last sentence of the passage. **Main Point:** Light poll. destroys natural rhythms/life.

In other words, the passage describes how light pollution, i.e. *a development* (something that was created or developed) is *harmful*. Which again gives us (A).

Reading for Function Exercises

1.   Math poses difficulties. There's little room for eyewitness testimony, seasoned judgment, a skeptical eye or transcendental rhetoric.

The function of the second sentence is to

(A) criticize an approach
(B) qualify a an assertion
(C) refute a controversial theory
(D) offer a solution to a problem
(E) introduce a digression

2.   Around the middle of the 20th century, science dispensed with the fantasy that we could easily colonize the other planets in our solar system. Science fiction writers absorbed the new reality: soon, moon
5   and asteroid settings replaced Mars and Venus.

The reference to "moon and asteroid settings" (lines 4-5) primarily serves to

(A) exemplify a change
(B) highlight an inconsistency
(C) advocate an action
(D) undermine an assertion
(E) simulate an approach

3.   When Library of America published a collection of Pauline Kael's film, many of Kael's admirers fondly recalled her as the first writer to elevate film criticism to literature. But that distinction actually belongs to an
5   earlier author, James Agee.

The author mentions "that distinction" (line 4) in order to

(A) analyze a phenomenon
(B) bolster a claim
(C) condemn a theory
(D) point out a misconception
(E) justify an assertion

4.   To the degree that Audubon's prose has the shapely feel of a novel, it's because he was deft at crafting his observations into the stuff of story; the birds that he chronicles became not merely objects
5   of scientific data, but characters in a dramatic narrative.

Lines 2-3 ("it's...story") primarily serve to

(A) explain an impression
(B) minimize an effect
(C) condemn an approach
(D) question a theory
(E) propose an alternative

5.   Why is the connection between smells and memories so strong? The reason for these associations is that the brain's olfactory bulb is connected to both the amygdala (an emotion center) and to the hippocampus, which is involved
5   in memory. And, because smells serve a survival function (odors can keep us from eating spoiled or poisonous foods), some of these associations are made very quickly, and may even involve a one-time association.

The primary purpose of the passage is to

(A) imply skepticism about a controversial theory
(B) dispute a popular misconception about the amygdala
(C) provide an explanation for a phenomenon
(D) praise a groundbreaking type of research
(E) explore the role of the hippocampus in forming associations

6.   It may be small and hard to find, but Eatonville is important for two reasons: It was the first all-black incorporated town in the United States, and it was the childhood home of Zora Neale Hurston. Much of
5 Hurston's writing is set here, and many of her characters are thinly disguised versions of actual residents.

The primary purpose of the passage is to

(A) evoke the people on whom Zora Neale Hurston's characters were based
(B) explain the exceptional role that Eatonville played in United States history
(C) question a common assumption about a well-known author
(D) trace the evolution of Zora Neale Hurston's literary career
(E) discuss the significance of a location

7.   Most people have so-called flashbulb memories of where they were and what they were doing when something momentous happened. (Unfortunately, staggeringly terrible news seems to come out of the
5 blue more often than staggeringly good news.) But as clear and detailed as these memories feel, psychologists have discovered they are surprisingly inaccurate.

The function of the last sentence is to

(A) downplay the significance of a theory
(B) point out an unexpected finding
(C) criticize an opposing viewpoint
(D) propose an alternate hypothesis
(E) attack a harmful misconception

8.   Neuroscientists and humanists are tackling similar questions—by joining forces, they might vastly refine our understanding of the role that narrative plays in human cognition, for example, or explore with empirical
5 precision the power of literature to represent consciousness.

Lines 2-5 ("by joining forces...consciousness") primarily serve to

(A) highlight the importance of a discovery
(B) speculate about the outcome of a collaboration
(C) denounce a popular misconception
(D) describe the relationship between literature and science
(E) explain the role of narrative in human cognition

9.   Shakespeare in the world of ants, untroubled by any such war between honor and treachery, and chained by the rigid commands of instinct to a tiny repertory of feeling, would be able to write only one
5 drama of triumph and one of tragedy. Ordinary people, on the other hand, can invent an endless variety of such stories, and compose an infinite symphony of ambience and mood.

The function of the second sentence (lines 5-8) is to

(A) offer a solution
(B) concede a point
(C) highlight a contrast
(D) bolster a claim
(E) qualify an assertion

10.   The Romans started making concrete more than 2,000 years ago, but it wasn't quite like today's concrete. They had a different formula, which resulted in a substance that was not as strong
5 as the modern product. Yet structures like the Pantheon and the Colosseum have survived for centuries, often with little to no maintenance. That resistance, or durability against the elements, may be due to one of the concrete's key ingredients:
10 volcanic ash.

1. Lines 5-7 ("Yet...maintenance") primarily serve to

(A) note a paradox
(B) refute a popular misconception
(C) trivialize an assertion
(D) propose a solution
(E) acknowledge a shortcoming

2. The function of the last sentence is to

(A) analyze a claim
(B) offer a hypothesis
(C) advocate an action
(D) justify an approach
(E) concede a point

11. To be a woman in the Victorian age was to be weak: the connection was that definite. To be female was also to be fragile, dependent, prone to nerves and—not least—possessed of a mind that was several

5 degrees inferior to a man's. For much of the 19th century, women were not expected to shine either academically or athletically, and those who attempted to do so were cautioned that they were taking an appalling risk. Mainstream medicine was clear on this

10 point: to dream of studying at the university level was to chance madness or sterility, if not both. It took generations to transform this received opinion; that, a long series of scientific studies, and the determination and hard work of many thousands of women. For all

15 that, though, it is still possible to point to one single achievement, and one single day, and say: this is when everything began to change.

The author mentions "one single day" (line 16) in order to

(A) lament an unfortunate development
(B) criticize a discriminatory situation
(C) analyze an influential study
(D) emphasize the abruptness of a shift
(E) underscore the difficulty of an achievement

12. Our psychological habitat is shaped by what you might call the magnetic property of home, the way it aligns everything around us. Perhaps you remember a moment, coming home from a trip, when the house you

5 call home looked, for a moment, like just another house on a street full of houses. But then the illusion faded and your house became home again. That, I think, is one of the most basic meanings of home—a place we can never see with a stranger's eyes for more than a moment.

The primary purpose of the last sentence is to

(A) explicate a claim
(B) speculate about a result
(C) define a term
(D) refute a popular misconception
(E) advocate an approach

13. Are we overwhelmed by the new or trapped in the old? The digital age bombards us with technological wonders. And yet, our attachment to the past leads us to consume pop culture well past its shelf life. The iPod

5 may have revolutionized how we listen to music, but many people are using it to listen to tunes that hit the big time half a century ago—or using their iPads to book tickets for a revived 1950s Broadway musical or for the latest movie based on a comic book from the 1940s.

The function of the last sentence is to

(A) analyze an approach
(B) criticize a development
(C) downplay a phenomenon
(D) illustrate a claim
(E) highlight a misconception

14. Frederick Law Olmsted's *Walks and Talks* has all the wide-eyed quality of an American in England for the first time: Ah, homely cottages! Ooh, blooming hawthorn! He even marvels at the

5 sight of a "real (unimported) Hereford cow over the hedge," though he had surely seen a cow before. But tucked into the breathless prose is naturalist poetry. His observation, for instance, of "mild sun beaming through the watery atmosphere, and all so

10 quiet" captures how achingly beautiful the softly lit English countryside is. This emotional affinity for the pastoral shaped Olmsted's vision for Central Park and many future works.

1. The purpose of the passage is to

(A) dispute a claim
(B) describe an influence
(C) anticipate an objection
(D) justify a response
(E) reflect on a conflict

2. Lines 3-6 ("Ah, homely…hedge") serve to

(A) analyze an attitude
(B) simulate an experience
(C) undermine a claim
(D) emphasize a reaction
(E) advocate an action

3. The purpose of lines 8-10 is to

(A) articulate an approach
(B) highlight a contrast
(C) downplay an influence
(D) note an impression
(E) mock a perception

15. Until the past few years, physicists agreed that the entire universe is generated from a few mathematical truths and principles of symmetry, perhaps throwing in a handful of parameters like the mass of the electron. It

5   seemed that we were closing in on a vision of our universe in which everything could be calculated, predicted, and understood. However, two theories, eternal inflation and string theory, now suggest that the same fundamental principles from which the laws of

10 nature derive may lead to many different self-consistent universes, with many different properties.

The primary purpose of lines 7-11 ("However... properties") is to

(A) challenge a novel theory
(B) question a controversial hypothesis
(C) substantiate a claim
(D) undermine an interpretation
(E) highlight an unexpected finding

16. Eating should be seen as pleasure and not penance; something that brings happiness and joy rather than anxiety. By viewing the acquisition and consumption of food as an ethical and moral act, we diminish the

5   fundamental pleasure that eating food provides us. By attaching social worth and political meaning to what we eat, and hoping that consumption can make the world a better place, we will not only fail to improve the world, but in the process lose the essential fact that eating

10 should be about enjoyment.

Lines 3-5 ("By viewing...us") primarily serve to

(A) criticize an attitude
(B) provide an alternative
(C) highlight an inconsistency
(D) trivialize a problem
(E) concede a point

17. The book is a self-contained utterance. It is finished, the very opposite of a "slug" you encounter on a website casting about for visitors to contribute writing and research. It is much more than

5   a slug, much more than the most basic information readily available. The discrete physical embodiment of text, it makes the perfect gift, the perfect giveaway, the perfect method of saying, "Consider the following . . ." We often think of imaginative

10 literature when we think of book-reading, along with notional scenes of people entering other worlds through books, but the world we know, the communities to which we already belong, are reinforced by books. Such is the incredible and

15 incredibly flexible power of this primitive technology.

The repetition in lines 7-9 primarily serves to

(A) attack a particular form of technology
(B) advocate a novel approach to literature
(C) simulate the imaginative process
(D) argue for a reinforcement of communities
(E) underscore the intensity of a conviction

18. Experimental scientists occupy themselves with observing and measuring the cosmos, finding out what stuff exists, no matter how strange that stuff may be. Theoretical physicists, on the other hand, are

5   not satisfied with observing the universe. They want to know why. They want to explain all the properties of the universe in terms of a few fundamental principles and parameters. These fundamental principles, in turn, lead to the "laws of nature," which

10 govern the behavior of all matter and energy.

The primary purpose of the passage is to

(A) explain the fundamental limitations of scientific investigation
(B) criticize experimental scientists for their lack of theoretical interest
(C) describe contrasting approaches to a subject
(D) reflect on the principles governing matter and energy
(E) advance a hypothesis about the laws of nature

19.   Dwight Macdonald, the greatest American hatchet man, applied his merciless craft also to himself. When he collected his essays, he added footnotes, appendices, and other forms of addenda taking issue with his own writings.
5 "This paragraph much too dismissive." "Why I wrote such a false statement, I don't know."… In the right mood, he could muster sufficient detachment to view himself with complete clarity: "My greatest vice is my easily aroused indignation—also, I suppose, one of my great strengths,"
10 he confided in a letter to a boarding school chum. "I can work up a moral indignation quicker than a fat tennis player can work up a sweat." His self-criticisms were paralyzing, so much so that he never could sustain faith in any of his big ideas long enough to unfurl them across a
15 whole book.

The last sentence primarily serves to

(A) describe the consequences of a particular trait
(B) offer an analysis of Dwight Macdonald's work
(C) emphasize the importance of self-criticism in the artistic process
(D) argue that Dwight Macdonald's essays have been unfairly overlooked
(E) promote the writings of an obscure author

20.   For some activists, eating local foods is no longer just a pleasure—it is a moral obligation. Why? Because shipping foods over long distances results in the unnecessary emission of the green-
5 house gases that are warming the planet. This concern has given rise to the concept of "food miles," that is, the distance food travels from farm to plate.
        But food miles advocates fail to grasp the
10 simple idea that food should be grown where it is most economically advantageous to do so. Relevant advantages consist of various combinations of soil, climate, labor, and other factors. It is possible to grow bananas in Iceland, but Costa
15 Rica really has the better climate for that activity. Transporting food is just one relatively small cost of providing modern consumers with their daily bread, meat, cheese, and veggies. Concentrating agricultural production in the most favorable
20 regions is the best way to minimize human impacts on the environment.

1. In context of the passage, lines 7-8 ("that is…plate") primarily serve to

(A) define a term
(B) encourage an approach
(C) shift the focus of a discussion
(D) qualify an assertion
(E) offer evidence for a claim

2. The author mentions "Costa Rica" (lines 14-15) in order to

(A) advance a controversial hypothesis
(B) cite an authority
(C) refute a claim
(D) suggest an alternative
(E) speculate about a possibility

3. The function of the last sentence is to

(A) analyze an assertion
(B) criticize an attitude
(C) minimize an objection
(D) highlight a development
(E) propose a solution

21.   In our attempts to uncover the history of the cosmos, we have continually discovered that the segments most deeply shrouded in mystery are those that deal with origins – of the universe itself, of its

5   most massive structures (galaxies and galaxy clusters), and of the stars that provide most of the light in the cosmos. These mysteries arise in large part because during the cosmic "dark ages," when matter was just beginning to organize itself into self-contained units

10   such as stars and galaxies, most of this matter generated little or no detectable radiation. When we turn to the origin of planets, the mysteries deepen. We lack not only observations of the crucial, initial stages of planetary formation but also successful theories of

15   how the planets began to form. Astrophysicists may now have more data but they have no better answers than before. The beginnings of planet building pose a remarkably intractable problem, to the point that one of the world's experts on the subject, Scott Tremaine,

20   has elucidated (partly in jest) Tremaine's laws of planet formation. The first of these laws states that "all theoretical predictions about the properties of exosolar planets are wrong," and the second that "the most secure prediction about planet formation is that it

25   can't happen." Tremaine's humor underscores the ineluctable fact that planets do exist, despite our inability to explain this astronomical enigma.

In 27, the author uses the word "astronomical" in order to

(A) criticize scientists for their flawed methodology
(B) call attention to the double meaning of a term
(C) prove a novel claim about the formation of exosolar planets
(D) praise Scott Tremaine for his insight
(E) resolve a longstanding paradox

22.   In an essay in 1984—at the dawn of the personal computer era—the novelist Thomas Pynchon wondered if it was "O.K. to be a Luddite," meaning someone who opposes technological progress. A

5   better question today is whether it's even possible. Technology is everywhere, and a recent headline at an Internet humor site perfectly captured how difficult it is to resist: "Luddite invents machine to destroy technology quicker." Like all good satire, the

10   mock headline comes perilously close to the truth. Modern Luddites do indeed invent "machines"— in the form of computer viruses, cyberworms and other malware—to disrupt the technologies that trouble them.

15   But despite their modern reputation, the original Luddites were neither opposed to technology nor inept at using it. Many were highly skilled machine operators in the textile industry. Nor was the technology they attacked particularly new. Moreover,

20   the idea of smashing machines as a form of industrial protest did not begin or end with them. In truth, the secret of their enduring reputation depends less on what they did than on the name under which they did it.

In line 11, the quotation marks primarily serve to

(A) cast doubt on a theory
(B) defend an unpopular notion
(C) emphasize a contrast
(D) indicate a specialized definition of a term
(E) condemn a behavior

23.   We were 210 students, all there to study identities, change identities, to learn to "be." There are a variety of ways to describe what acting is. "Being," "Seeming," "Becoming," "Lying," "Truth Telling," "Magic,"
5   "Transforming." We were new. Some among us had known the building for an hour longer than the others of us. No one ever arrives at the same time as everybody else. We were going to learn how to talk to each other onstage, and through all of this how to take our own special
10   message to the *world*.

     On one of the first days I was coming into the building, a tall, thin aristocratic-looking white woman who appeared to be about my age, and whom we ultimately referred to as the Katherine Hepburn among us, came breathlessly down
15   a narrow hallway, saying to me (whom she had never seen except in that one instant,) "Do you know where I can get a drink of water?"

     She said this as if she had known me all my life, as if I were a sister, a brother, a friend. She may have
20   even grabbed my hand. I wasn't put off by the fact that she was a stranger. Her presence in that question made me feel in an instant as if I had known her all my life. Having grown up in segregation, I found it odd that a white person would approach me without her own barriers up,
25   and without the expectation that I would have barriers. I was so stunned by her presence that I didn't speak. Besides, I didn't know where to get a drink of water. Just as rapidly and as urgently, she vanished down the hallway and out into the street. I thought that perhaps this was
30   what acting was. Because, as real as it was, realer than real, it also seemed like a moment out of a scene from Chekhov's *Uncle Vanya*, or as if one of Tchaikovsky's symphonies had burst into speech. *Urgency* is the word. And it's one of the top ten in the vocabulary of acting.
35   Acting is the furthest thing from lying that I have encountered. It is the furthest thing from make-believe. It is the furthest thing from pretending. It is the most unfake thing there is. Acting is a search for the authentic. It is a search for the authentic by using
40   the fictional as a frame, a house in which the authentic can live. For a moment, because, yes indeed, real life inhibits the authentic.

1. The primary purpose of the passage is to

(A) explain people's inherent desire for authenticity
(B) encourage young performers to pursue theatrical careers
(C) describe the origins of a popular art form
(D) explore the psychological consequences of segregation
(E) discuss the significance of an encounter

2. The author mentions "segregation" (line 23) in order to

(A) condemn an injustice
(B) convey her sense of isolation
(C) explain a reaction
(D) draw attention to the political nature of acting
(E) justify her suspicion of strangers

24.   Many readers, faced with Thoreau's enigmatic Yankee persona, have resorted to a kind of pop-culture shorthand for describing his life. As the capsule summary goes, Thoreau was an oddball loner who lived by a lake, writing
5   in praise of nature and against modern progress.

    But the full story of Thoreau's life involves subtleties and contradictions that call his popular image into question. One idea that has persisted is that he was a hermit who cared little for others, yet he was active in his
10 community and responsible for circulating petitions for neighbors in need. In yet another way Thoreau was politically active, penning an essay, "Civil Disobedience," that would later inform the thinking of Mohandas Gandhi and the Rev. Martin Luther King Jr.

15 Despite his fame as a champion of solitude—a practice that he chronicled with wisdom and wit—Thoreau made no secret of the social life he indulged during his stay at Walden Pond from 1845 to 1847. In fact, one of the chapters of Walden, titled "Visitors," offers an extended
20 account of Thoreau's dealings with others. In it, the lifelong bachelor Thoreau lays out his rules for entertaining:

    I had three chairs in my house; one for solitude, two for friendship, three for society. When visitors came in
25 *larger and unexpected numbers there was but the third chair for them all, but they generally economized the room by standing up... I have had twenty-five or thirty souls, with their bodies, at once under my roof, and yet we often parted without being aware that we had come*
30 *very near to one another.*

    But even if Thoreau wasn't always averse to human company, the idea that he was a loner might stem from the assumption that he was the kind of person who should have been alone. Thoreau was capable of
35 friendship, but on his own terms. He could be prickly to a fault. "I sometimes hear my Friends complain finely that I do not appreciate their fineness," he once wrote. "I shall not tell them whether I do or not. As if they expected a vote of thanks for every fine thing which they uttered or
40 did."

    Even those who liked him conceded that Thoreau could be a cold fish. In a letter to his friend Daniel Ricketson in 1860, Thoreau addresses Ricketson's puzzlement over why he hasn't come to visit, telling Ricketson, without much
45 ceremony, that he's had much better things to do. But after explaining himself, Thoreau continued to correspond with Ricketson. Ralph Waldo Emerson, Thoreau's close friend and mentor, who came to grudgingly admire Thoreau's argumentative streak, famously described him as "not to be
50 subdued, always manly and able, but rarely tender,

as if he did not feel himself except in opposition." In remembrance of Thoreau, Emerson offered this observation from one of Thoreau's friends: "I love Henry, but I cannot like him; and as for taking his
55 arm, I should as soon think of taking the arm of an elm-tree."

1. In lines 6-7, the author mentions "subtleties and contradictions" in order to

(A) criticize a popular work
(B) refute a common misconception
(C) exemplify a claim
(D) praise a unique individual
(E) undermine a novel theory

2. The author mentions the "assumption" in line 33 primarily in order to

(A) describe how Thoreau entertained company when he was living at Walden Pond
(B) analyze the origin of Thoreau's solitary tendencies
(C) indicate a significant difference between Thoreau and his contemporaries
(D) illustrate the contradictory nature of artistic personalities
(E) point out an explanation for a particular belief

3. The quotation in lines 36-40 ("I sometimes... did") serves to

(A) justify a response
(B) criticize a behavior
(C) defend a response
(D) illustrate a claim
(E) condemn an attitude

25.   A few years ago the city council of Monza, Italy, barred pet owners from keeping goldfish in curved fishbowls. The sponsors of the measure explained that it is cruel to keep a fish in a bowl because the curved sides

5   give the fish a distorted view of reality. Aside from the measure's significance to the poor goldfish, the story raises an interesting philosophical question: How do we know that the reality we perceive is true? The goldfish is seeing a version of reality that is different from ours,

10   but can we be sure it is any less real? For all we know, we, too, may spend our entire lives staring out at the world through a distorting lens.

   In physics, the question is not academic. Indeed, physicists are finding themselves in a similar

15   predicament to the goldfish's. For decades we have strived to come up with an ultimate theory of everything—one complete and consistent set of fundamental laws of nature that explain every aspect of reality. It now appears that this quest may yield not

20   a single theory but a family of interconnected theories, each describing its own version of reality, as if it viewed the universe through its own fishbowl.

   This notion may be difficult for many people, including some working scientists, to accept. Most

25   people believe that there is an objective reality out there and that our senses and our science directly convey information about the material world. Classical science is based on the belief that an external world exists whose properties are definite and independent of the observer

30   who perceives them. In philosophy, that belief is called realism.

   Those who remember Timothy Leary and the 1960s, however, know of another possibility: one's concept of reality can depend on the mind of the perceiver. That

35   viewpoint, with various subtle differences, goes by names such as antirealism, instrumentalism or idealism. According to those doctrines, the world we know is constructed by the human mind employing sensory data as its raw material and is shaped by the interpretive structure

40   of our brains. This viewpoint may be hard to accept, but it is not difficult to understand. There is no way to remove the observer— us—from our perception of the world. The way physics has been going, realism is becoming difficult to defend. In classical physics—the physics of Newton

45   that so accurately describes our everyday experience—the interpretation of terms such as object and position is for the most part in harmony with our commonsense, "realistic" understanding of those concepts. As measuring devices, however, we are crude instruments. Physicists have found

50   that everyday objects and the light we see them by are made from objects that we do not perceive directly. These objects are governed not by classical physics but by the laws of quantum theory. The reality of quantum theory is a rad-

55   ical departure from that of classical physics. In the framework of quantum theory, particles have neither definite positions nor definite velocities unless and until an observer measures those quantities. Quantum physics also has

60   important implications for our concept of the past. In classical physics, the past is assumed to exist as a definite series of events, but according to quantum physics, the past, like the future, is indefinite and exists only as a spectrum of poss-

65   ibilities. Even the universe as a whole has no single past or history. So quantum physics implies a different reality than that of classical physics—even though the latter still serves us well when we design things such as buildings and

70   bridges.

   These examples bring us to a conclusion that provides an important framework with which to interpret modern science. In our view, there is no picture- or theory-independent concept of reality.

75   Instead we adopt a view that we call model-dependent realism: the idea that a physical theory or world picture is a model (generally of a mathematical nature) and a set of rules that connect the elements of the model to observations.

80   According to model dependent realism, it is pointless to ask whether a model is real, only whether it agrees with observation. If two models agree with observation, neither one can be considered more real than the other. A person can

85   use whichever model is more convenient in the situation under consideration.

1. The primary purpose of the passage is to

(A) compare and contrast several explanations for a phenomenon
(B) discuss a potentially controversial hypothesis
(C) question the validity of model-dependent realism
(D) describe several of Timothy Leary's experiments
(E) thoroughly disprove the underpinnings of classical realism

2. In line 13, the author uses the phrase "not academic in order to

   (A) indicate the difference between human and animal perception
   (B) criticize the Monza city council members
   (C) highlight a common perceptual difficulty
   (D) emphasize the practical nature of problem
   (E) trivialize a dubious theory

3. The author mentions Timothy Leary (line 32) in order to

   (A) emphasize the novelty of a theory
   (B) propose a solution to a pressing problem
   (C) offer an alternative to a commonly accepted point of view
   (D) explain how the brain interprets sensory data
   (E) refute a claim about the importance of instrumentalism

4. The purpose of the quotation marks in line 47 is to

   (A) imply skepticism about a notion
   (B) hypothesize about an outcome
   (C) define an unfamiliar term
   (D) highlight a startling discovery
   (E) defend an unlikely theory

5. Lines 66-70 ("So quantum…and bridges") primarily serve to

   (A) discredit a theory
   (B) advocate an action
   (C) explain a term
   (D) qualify an assertion
   (E) simulate an experience

Official Guide Function Questions

Test 1	Section 2	Question 8	p. 391	Primary Purpose
Test 1	Section 2	Question 10	p. 392	Primary Purpose
Test 1	Section 2	Question 12	p. 392	
Test 1	Section 2	Question 19	p. 395	
Test 1	Section 5	Question 17	p. 405	
Test 1	Section 5	Question 19	p. 405	
Test 1	Section 5	Question 24	p. 406	Paragraph Purpose
Test 2	Section 4	Question 14	p. 460	
Test 2	Section 4	Question 21	p. 461	
Test 2	Section 7	Question 6	p. 476	
Test 2	Section 7	Question 8	p. 476	Primary Purpose
Test 2	Section 7	Question 10	p. 477	Primary Purpose
Test 2	Section 7	Question 11	p. 477	
Test 2	Section 7	Question 12	p. 477	
Test 2	Section 9	Question 10	p. 489	
Test 2	Section 9	Question 13	p. 489	
Test 3	Section 4	Question 12	p. 521	
Test 3	Section 4	Question 14	p. 522	
Test 3	Section 4	Question 19	p. 523	
Test 3	Section 4	Question 24	p. 523	
Test 3	Section 7	Question 8	p. 538	Primary Purpose
Test 3	Section 7	Question 12	p. 540	
Test 3	Section 7	Question 17	p. 541	
Test 3	Section 7	Question 18	p. 542	
Test 3	Section 9	Question 14	p. 551	Primary Purpose
Test 3	Section 9	Question 16	p. 551	
Test 3	Section 9	Question 19	p. 552	
Test 4	Section 2	Question 10	p. 577	
Test 4	Section 5	Question 19	p. 592	
Test 4	Section 8	Question 10	p. 607	
Test 5	Section 3	Question 10	p. 646	
Test 5	Section 3	Question 12	p. 646	
Test 5	Section 3	Question 13	p. 647	
Test 5	Section 3	Question 16	p. 647	
Test 5	Section 7	Question 15	p. 665	
Test 5	Section 7	Question 18	p. 665	
Test 5	Section 9	Question 10	p. 674	
Test 6	Section 3	Question 15	p. 709	Primary Purpose
Test 6	Section 7	Question 16	p. 727	
Test 6	Section 7	Question 19	p. 727	
Test 7	Section 2	Question 6	p. 763	
Test 7	Section 2	Question 10	p. 764	
Test 7	Section 2	Question 11	p. 764	
Test 7	Section 2	Question 15	p. 765	
Test 7	Section 2	Question 16	p. 765	
Test 7	Section 2	Question 18	p. 766	

Explanations: Reading for Function Exercises

1. B

The second sentence expands on the general claim or **assertion** made in the first sentence by explaining why math poses difficulties. In other words, it takes an extremely broad statement and provides **qualifying** information to give the reader more information about why that statement is true.

2. A

The passage states that in the mid-20th century, science fiction accepted the reality that other planets could not be colonized. The author uses the Moon and asteroids as **examples** of settings that science fiction writers used to replace other planets (replacing = a change).

3. D

What's "that distinction?" Being the first writer to elevate film criticism to literature. Why mention it? To point out that Pauline Kael was not in fact the first person to accomplish that – James Agee did it first. The author is thus indicating that "many of Kael's admirers" were in fact wrong, i.e. *refuting a misconception*.

4. A

The key word is "because" (*because he was deft at crafting*, lines 2-3) which indicates that the author is providing an explanation. *Shapely feel* = impression. Hence, explain an impression.

5. C

The key word is "reason" (line 2), which indicates that the author is providing an explanation for the question that has just been posed. The purpose of the passage is thus to explain the **phenomenon** of the strong link between smells and memories.

6. E

The key word is "important" (*Eatonville is important for two reasons*, lines 1-2), which indicates that the passage will be about why Eatonville (a location) will be important (=significant). Although *explain* in (B) could also work as a function word, the passage only explains the role that Eatonville played in Zora Neale Hurston's works, not in United States history.

7. B

The key word is "surprisingly" because it indicates that psychologists were unprepared to discover that "flashbulb memories" were inaccurate. In other words, they found something unexpected.

8. B

The key word is "might" because it indicates speculation – it tells us that the author is discussing things that *could* potentially happen (=outcomes) because of humanists and neuroscientists' partnership (=collaboration).

9. C

The key phrase is "on the other hand" because it indicates that the author is introducing a contrast between the idea that has just been presented (ants could not write great drama because their lives are dictated by instinct) and the one that follows (humans can produce great drama because they can experience such a wide range of emotions). The phrase "on the other hand" calls attention to (=highlights) that contrast.

10. 1A, 2B

10.1 In order to understand the role that lines 5-7 play in the passage, it is necessary to back up to the beginning and consider them in context. When we read from the beginning of the passage, what do we learn? Roman concrete was not as strong as modern concrete, BUT structures containing it have lasted for centuries – a situation that would seem to be contradictory. In other words, a **paradox**.

10.2. The key word is "may," which indicates that the author is discussing something that *could* happen but that has not actually happened. Indeed, this sentence offers a potential explanation or **a hypothesis** (volcanic ash makes concrete durable) for the situation described in the previous sentence (structures made of Roman concrete, which is less strong than modern concrete, have nevertheless survived for a very long time).

11. D

What piece of information do we get in the sentence in which "one single day" appears? That in one regard, the way in which women were viewed academically changed (=shifted) very quickly (=abruptly) despite the fact that the change also happened across generations. The words "one day" stand in direct contrast to "generations," "long series," and "thousands of women" and emphasize that the author will discuss something that occurred quickly.

12. C

The dash in the last sentence indicates that the author is providing a definition or an explanation. The information after the dash is simply a definition – it tells us what the author considers home to be.

13. D

The last sentence **illustrates** the **claim** that *our attachment to the past leads us to consume pop culture well past its shelf life* by providing examples of outdated pop culture that people use new technology to consume (*tickets to a revived 1950s musical, movie based on a comic book from the 1940s*).

14. 1B, 2D, 3D

14.1 The key sentence is the last sentence, which states that *This emotional affinity for the pastoral (i.e. the countryside) <u>shaped</u> Olmsted's vision for Central Park and many future works. Shaped = influenced.* The entire passage before the last sentence is primarily devoted to describing what what Olmsted saw in the English countryside.

14.2. The essential function of the second sentence is to illustrate the first sentence by providing quotations from Olmsted that demonstrate *the wide-eyed quality of an American in England*. While there is no answer that begins with a function word such as "illustrate," "support," or "exemplify," the answer does need to be something along those lines, and it almost certainly won't be something negative. That eliminates (C). (B) and (E) can also be eliminated because "simulate" and "advocate" virtually always indicate incorrect answers. That leaves (A) and (D). Let's go back to the passage: when we look at lines 2-4, we can notice that there are two exclamation points (*Ah, homely cottages! Ooh, blooming hawthorn!*) in the space of one line. The function of an exclamation point is to emphasize, hence (D). In addition, the quotes also serves to illustrate how Olmsted reacted, or **responded**, to his first encounter with the English countryside. In this case, the difficulty lies in the fact that word "reaction" or "response" is never explicitly stated in the passage – it is up to the reader to understand that the author is describing a response.

14.3 The key word is "observation." Observation = impression, hence (D). Note that this is fundamentally the same question as #2 above – if you understand that the passage is essentially describing Olmsted's reaction to the English countryside, and that all of the examples simply serve to illustrate what he thought of it (he was pretty impressed by it), then the answers to both questions are relatively straightforward.

15. E

The beginning of the passage states that until recently, scientists agreed on how the universe was most likely organized and that it could be reasonably assumed that they would soon prove that vision definitively. The last sentence of the passage points out (=highlights) that those scientists were actually incorrect and that there is no single theory. Since that is exactly the opposite of what scientists believed only a short time ago, it can reasonably inferred that such a finding was **unexpected**.

16. A

Lines 3-5 state that "viewing the acquisition and consumption of food as an ethical and moral act" *diminishes* the pleasure that food provides, indicating a negative point of view. That eliminates everything except (A) and (D), and the author is not *trivializing* the problem (suggesting that it is unimportant). On the other hand, he is definitely *criticizing* the belief that is detailed in lines 3-5.

17. E

What word is emphasized in lines 7-9? *Perfect*. That's a pretty strong word. And what idea is being expressed in those lines? The idea that the physical book is very important, much more important than electronic information. So why use a word as strong as *perfect* here? To underscore (emphasize) how *intensely* the author believes in that idea. Intense belief =conviction (the noun formed of "convinced").

18. C

How is the passage structured? It begins by describing one group of people (experimental scientists), then shifts course and describes how a second group of people (theoretical physicists) are different from (=contrast) the first group. The key phrase is "on the other hand," which indicates that the author is presenting a contrast.

19. A

What information is presented in the last sentence? That the result (=consequences) of Dwight Macdonald's self-criticisms (=a particular trait) was that he could never complete a full book.

20. 1A, 2D, 3E

20.1 The phrase "that is" indicates that the author is clarifying or **defining** the term "food miles" for the reader.

20.2 In line 13, Iceland is cited as an example of a place where it is not profitable to grow bananas, whereas Costa Rica is cited as a place where it *is* profitable to grow bananas. In other words, Costa Rica is presented as an **alternative** to Iceland.

20.3 Throughout the passage, the author discusses a problem: how to grow food in a way that is both profitable and good for the environment. In the last sentence, he suggests that the problem can be resolved by growing foods in the regions best suited to growing them. In other words, he proposes a solution.

21. B

The word "astronomical" functions both in its literal sense, "related to astronomy," and its more colloquial sense, "enormous." The author thus plays with words to highlight the fact that the enigma is related to astronomy, but that it is also a very, very big mystery. Be careful with (E) here – yes, the author is *describing* a paradox in the last sentence (scientists have lots of information but can't make any progress), but he's not resolving anything.

22. D

A machine is a physical object, but here it refers to dangerous types of computer code. Because the word "machine" is not used literally, it has a "specialized definition," given between the dashes in lines 11-13.

23. 1E, 2C

23.1 What happens literally in the passage? The author tells the story of how, right after she began acting school, she was stopped by a classmate who asked for a drink of water. The incident stuck out in her mind because 1) the woman was white and clearly treating her as an equal something very foreign to her since she had grown up "in segregation (line 23);" and 2) the woman's sense of urgency revealed to her the general importance of urgency in acting. So basically she's talking about why her meeting (=encounter) with the woman was so important (=significant), =significance of an encounter.

If you are unable to work this way, you can also work by process of elimination:

(A) Too broad. The author does discuss "authenticity" in the last paragraph, but only in relation to actors, not people in general.

(B) Too specific, off topic. The author isn't trying to encourage performers to do anything – she's simply describing her own experience. It's way too much of a leap to infer that she's trying

to get anyone else to make the same career choice that she made.

(C) Reads like a right answer but off topic. Again, the passage is about theater (=an art form), but it's about the author's own experience – she never discusses theater's *origins*.

(D) Segregation is mentioned in the passage, but it's a only a detail. The passage is about acting.

(E) Reads like a right answer (short, general) and accurately conveys the author's goal.

23.2 What's the point the author is making in the section where the word "segregation" appears? That she found the woman's behavior "odd" and that she was "stunned" by it because the woman was white – having grown up "in segregation," she was unaccustomed to the idea that any white woman, let alone one she had never met, would treat her like "a friend," "a sister." So the author mentions "segregation" to explain her surprise (=a reaction). So it's (C).

24. 1B, 2E, 3D

24.1 Think of this question in terms of "they say/I say." The first paragraph is "they say," as indicated by the first words: "Many readers." The second paragraph begins the "I say," the section in which the author explains why what "many readers" think is incorrect. That means the answer must be negative, eliminating (C) and (D). (A) is incorrect because the author is criticizing an idea rather than a work; (E) is incorrect because the theory isn't novel (new) – by definition, it's the conventional model. (B) is correct because the author is saying that what "many readers" think is wrong (=refuting). The rest of the passage is devoted to explaining that Thoreau was actually rather complex. Furthermore, if "many readers" have the same misconception, then it is by definition "common."

24.2 What is the assumption? That Thoreau was the sort of person who should have been alone. Why does the author mention it? Because the idea that Thoreau was a loner might stem from it. In other words, it might explain why people believe that Thoreau was a loner (=a particular belief).

24.3 The quotation *illustrates* the idea in the previous sentence (Thoreau "could be prickly to a fault") by showing that he resented being asked to openly appreciate his friends.

25. 1B, 2D, 3C, 4A, 5D

25.1 There are a couple of ways to approach this question. The fastest is to use the structure: old model vs. new model. That right there tells you that the point of the passage is to propose a new theory, a theory that "other people" probably don't agree with. And indeed, the author states not once but twice that the theory "may be hard for some people/scientists" to accept (=potentially controversial) because it completely overturns a model that's been around for a very long time.

Alternately, you can recognize that (B) is the shortest, most general answer, then check it out from there. If that doesn't work, you can always play process of elimination:

(A) Sounds vaguely plausible, but that's just not what's going on in the passage. The goal is to explain why the traditional model (classical theory) is wrong and why model-dependent realism is correct. The only mention of a particular phenomenon occurs when the authors allude to designing things "such as buildings and bridges" (lines 69-70), and that's by no means the focus of the passage.

(C) Exactly the opposite of what's happening in the passage – the author is arguing that model-dependent realism is the only way to understand the world.

(D) Too specific. There's no mention of any particular experiment conducted by Timothy Leary.

(E) Too extreme. Yes, the authors do believe that classical realism is inadequate to describe how reality actually functions, but they don't go so far as to discredit it or its underpinnings thoroughly. In fact, they state that *[classical physics] still serves us well when we design things such as buildings and bridges.*

25.2 To say that a problem is "academic" is to say that it is purely theoretical, without any real-world applications. To say that a problem is *not* academic is therefore to say that it is not strictly theoretical and does have applications in the real world, i.e. that it is *practical.*

25.3 The authors mention Timothy Leary when they introduce the "new model," which by definition goes against the accepted model. The phrase *alternative to a commonly accepted point of view* is a rephrasing of the phrase *another possibility* (line 33).

25.4 The authors use quotation marks around the word "realistic" in order to imply that people's "commonsense" understanding of the world (an understanding associated with classical physics, which the author believes is wrong) does not actually correspond to reality.

25.5 The authors mention "buildings and bridges" in lines 69-70 in order to point out that classical physics does still have some uses, that it should not be dismissed completely. In other words, they are **qualifying**, or making less harsh, their assertion that it is no longer a valid model for understanding reality.

Glossary of Function Words

Advocate – Synonym for *promote* and *encourage*.

Account for – Explain

Acknowledge (a point) – Recognize the merit or validity of an idea

Bolster – Support, provide additional evidence for an idea

Concede (a point) – Recognize the merit or validity of an opposing idea

Discredit – Disprove (literally, demonstrate a lack of credibility)

SAT passages are typically concerned with weighing evidence, considering prevailing theories, and proposing new explanations – while authors may have strong opinions about what is and is not true, passages do not, as a rule, contain sufficient information or evidence to definitively prove or disprove anything. *Discredit* is thus unlikely to appear as a correct answer choice.

Dismiss – Deny the importance or validity of an idea

Downplay – Deliberately understate, imply that something is unimportant

Evoke – To summon, call up (a memory, impression, etc.), recreate through description

Explicate – Explain in great detail

Highlight – Emphasize, call attention to

Jeer at – Make fun of in a cruel or harsh manner. More extreme synonym of *mock* and *scoff*. Typically signals a wrong answer.

Minimize – Deliberately understate the importance of an idea. Synonym for *downplay* and *trivialize* and, like those words, typically signals a wrong answer.

Mock – Make fun of

Qualify – Provide more information about a statement in order to make it seem less strong or blunt, or to indicate the conditions under which it would be true.

For example, a statement like, "The SAT is the worst test EVER" is extremely strong (not to mention a good example of a **hyperbole**).

To **qualify** it, however, you could say something like, "At least that's what it feels like when you're a junior in high school." That sentence reduces the impact of the first sentence, clarifies when and for whom it would be true, and makes it seem less **histrionic**.

It can be helpful to know that qualifying phrases are sometimes **parenthetical** – that is, they are found within parentheses or dashes – and are almost like asides to the reader. If you look back at the passage and see this kind of construction, "qualify" is almost certain to be correct. For example, consider the following passage:

> "In his discovery of the law of the gravity, which would transform the course of scientific thought, Newton was struck by – **if the story can be believed** – an apple that fell from a tree above the spot where he was reclining."

The phrase between the dashes is intended to suggest that this story may not in fact be true. In other words, it is intended to provide information about the truth of – to qualify – the idea that Newton was struck by an apple.

As discussed earlier, answer choices that contain familiar words used in unfamiliar ways are generally correct since the second meaning itself is being tested. Since "qualify" here is not being used in its most common sense of "to fulfill the required condition" (e.g. qualify for a job), it has a higher than average probability of being correct.

So here's a shortcut: If you have difficulty coming up with an answer on your own and see "qualify a statement" as an option, you should probably begin by taking a very close look at it. This is NOT to say that you should choose it without thinking – **sometimes it will in fact be wrong** – simply that you should consider it first, making sure to look back to the passage and see if it does in fact describe the function of statement or phrase in question.

Satirize – Make fun of by using irony, sarcasm, or parody

Scoff at – Make fun of, suggest that something is unworthy of serious consideration

Undermine – Weaken or attack the foundation of; subvert secretly.

Undermine is also unlikely to appear as a correct answer because SAT passages are not long enough to allow for the kind of in-depth evidence necessary to actually weaken a theory at its base.

Underscore – Call attention to. Synonym for *emphasize* and *highlight*.

Simulate – Recreate an experience

Since SAT passages are primarily analytical and argumentative and are not intended to recreate a particular experience for the reader, this answer choice makes no sense in virtually every instance that it appears.

Substantiate – Give evidence or support for, back up

Trivialize – Treat as trivial or unimportant. Synonym for *downplay* and *minimize* but more extreme and thus unlikely to appear as a correct answer.

8. Tone and Attitude

"Tone" and "attitude" questions ask about the feelings of either the author or a person mentioned in the passage toward a particular subject – most simply, whether those feelings are positive, negative, or neutral. These questions are typically phrased in the following ways:

-In line x, the author's tone/attitude can best be described/characterized as…

-The author would most likely view the events described in lines x-y as…

-The information in lines x-y suggests that the author would view advocates of Robertson's theory with…

-The individuals mentioned in line x would most likely view "the notion" (line y) with…

Note: although some tone and attitude questions can also be considered inference questions, I have chosen to discuss them here for the sake of consistency.

Avoiding Extremes

As a general rule, "extreme" answers to tone questions are incorrect, while correct answers are moderate. Thus, if an author views a subject positively, the correct answer is more likely to be "appreciative" rather than "reverent" or "awed;" if an author is clearly negative, the correct answer is more likely to be "skeptical" or "disdainful" than "hostile" or "furious;" and if an author employs very strong language, the correct answer is likely to be "emphatic" or "decisive" rather than an adjective that is strongly positive or negative.

There are several reasons for this pattern: first is that SAT passages themselves tend to be relatively measured – if not entirely neutral – in tone. Most positive passages are slightly positive, and most negative passages are slightly negative. **There are many exceptions, however, so you must ultimately consider each question on its own merits and choose the answer most directly supported by the passage.**

The second reason is that many of the passages that appear on the SAT are taken from works by professional scholars (neuroscientists, physicists, historians, anthropologists, theoretical physicists, etc.) – people who deal with theories that have often not yet been proven and that, in some cases, can never be definitively proven. If they go all out in favor of a theory that later turns out to be false, they risk losing a lot of their credibility. As a result, they have a serious incentive to avoid making overly strong statements. Rather than say that a given piece of evidence conclusively proves a new theory, they're therefore much more likely to use **qualifying statements** and say that the evidence *suggests* the theory *might* have some merit. The second statement is much, much more cautiously phrased than the first, and SAT answers tend to reflect that caution.

Neutral Tone, Definite Opinion

While many SAT questions use the terms "tone" and "attitude" interchangeably, they are not precisely the same thing, and it is important to understand the distinction between them.

An author can present information about a topic in a relatively neutral (or "objective" or "impartial") tone but still have a distinct opinion about it. A lack of strong language does not in any way imply a neutral attitude toward a subject; an author can believe that one idea is correct and another idea is incorrect, despite the decision to write in a deliberately straightforward, un-dramatic manner, and you are still responsible for determining what ideas the author agrees and disagrees with. While the language may be generally neutral, it will not be entirely devoid of opinion, and you will always have the information necessary to determine what the author thinks – that's why the passages are selected in the first place.

This is often the case for science passages, which have (perhaps deservedly so) a reputation for being the most boring passages on the SAT. Here, especially, it is important not to confuse a dry or objective tone with an absence of opinion or point of view. SAT passages are, for all intents and purpose, never just recitations of factual information but rather are chosen because they contain some sort of argument. More precisely, they frequently contain the "old idea vs. new idea" structure in which the author first discusses a prevailing theory, then at a certain point turns around and explains why it is no longer valid and why a new theory in fact provides a better explanation for a given phenomenon.

In such passages, the author's *attitude* will be generally negative toward the old explanation and generally positive toward the new explanation; while there will certainly be indications that the author rejects the former and embraces the latter, the overall *tone* may remain fairly neutral when discussing both.

For example, remember this passage?

Sometime near the end of the Pleistocene, a band
of people left northeastern Asia, crossed the Bering land
bridge when the sea level was low, entered Alaska and
became the first Americans. Since the 1930s, archaeologists
5   have thought these people were members of the Clovis
culture. First discovered in New Mexico in the 1930s, the
Clovis culture is known for its distinct stone tools, primarily
fluted projectile points. For decades, Clovis artifacts were
the oldest known in the New World, dating to 13,000 years
10   ago. But in recent years, researchers have found more and
more evidence that people were living in North and South
America before the Clovis.

   The most recently confirmed evidence comes from
Washington. During a dig conducted from 1977 to
15   1979, researchers uncovered a bone projectile point stuck in
a mastodon rib. Since then the age of the find has been
debated, but recently anthropologist Michael Waters and his
colleagues announced a new radiocarbon date for the rib:
13,800 years ago, making it 800 years older than the oldest
20   Clovis artifact. Other pre-Clovis evidence comes from a
variety of locations across the New World.

As discussed earlier, the passage follows a predictable pattern: it discusses an old theory (the Clovis people were the first people to inhabit North America) and a new theory (a group of people inhabited North America before the Clovis arrived).

When discussing these two theories, however, the author's *tone* remains relatively neutral and cautious; there is nothing in his language itself that screams at the reader that he approves of one idea and disapproves of the other. Instead of saying, for example, that the theory that the Clovis were the first inhabitants of North America is *absolutely* wrong, he simply states that "more evidence" has recently been found to suggest that it is not the case.

Here it is necessary to pay attention to *what* the author is saying rather than *how* he is saying it in order to determine what he believes. Sometimes content is more important than style. The correct answer to a question about the author's tone could therefore be *objective, neutral, detached, dispassionate*, or any general synonym for those words.

The Author Always Cares

While the tone of some passages will indeed be *objective* or *neutral*, as in the example above, it will also virtually never be *indifferent*, *apathetic*, or *diffident*. If you see one of these answers appear among the answer choices, you should generally begin by assuming that it is incorrect.

The reason for this is simple: authors generally care about the subject they're writing about. If they were indifferent, then pretty much by definition, they wouldn't bother to write about that subject. In addition, the texts for paired passages (which often include *indifferent* and its synonyms as answer choices to Passage 1/Passage 2 relationship questions) are chosen specifically because they have distinct points of view about a subject – often sharply differing points of view. It is generally possible to infer that the authors of these passages would either agree or disagree with one another's opinions. If there were no relationship, the passages simply wouldn't have been chosen in the first place.

The only real **exception** to this rule would be a question asking about a character in a fiction passage – in that (somewhat unlikely) scenario, a character could potentially exhibit a lack of interest. But the chances of that happening are relatively slim. ETS tends to pick passages about characters who have some level of engagement with the world around them – otherwise, there wouldn't be much to test.

Top Tone and Attitude Words

While there are theoretically thousands of possible answers to tone questions, the reality is that a relatively small number of answers – both correct and incorrect – tend to recur fairly frequently. The chart below lists some of the most common answer choices.

Important: the designation of "correct" or "incorrect" is intended to reflect <u>general</u> patterns only. You should therefore approach "incorrect" answers with a healthy dose of suspicion when they appear but nevertheless keep in mind that some of them have appeared as <u>correct</u> answers in the past.

Positive	Negative	Neutral
Correct:	**Correct:**	**Correct:**
Appreciative Approving Sympathetic Proud/Pride Agreement (P1/P2)	Disdainful Skeptical Sardonic	Emphatic/Decisive Objective/Impartial/Analytical Pragmatic/Prudent Reflective Wry
Incorrect:	**Incorrect:**	**Incorrect:**
Excited Reverent/Awed Accepting Amused Curious	Fearful Confused/Puzzled/Perplexed/Bewildered Apathetic/Indifferent Contemptuous Annoyed Nostalgic Resigned Envious/Resentful Hostile Impatient	Ambivalent Uncertain

Inferring Attitude

While the answers to many "attitude" questions are indicated directly in the passage, some questions will ask you to move a step beyond what is literally stated and infer what the author of the passage or a person/group discussed in the passage would be likely to think about a particular idea. Although answers to these questions cannot be directly found in the passage, they are always directly suggested and remain very close in meaning to the information that *is* explicitly stated. You should, however, work through them very methodically, breaking them into steps to avoid missing key information.

While these kinds of questions are always present in Passage 1/Passage 2 sets, they also accompany single passages that include or allude to multiple points of view. For example:

Sometime near the end of the Pleistocene, a band
of people left northeastern Asia, crossed the Bering land
bridge when the sea level was low, entered Alaska and
became the first Americans. Since the 1930s, archaeologists
5   have thought these people were members of the Clovis
culture. First discovered in New Mexico in the 1930s, the
Clovis culture is known for its distinct stone tools, primarily
fluted projectile points. For decades, Clovis artifacts were
the oldest known in the New World, dating to 13,000 years
10   ago. But in recent years, researchers have found more and
more evidence that people were living in North and South
America before the Clovis.
    The most recently confirmed evidence comes from
Washington. During a dig conducted from 1977 to
15   1979, researchers uncovered a bone projectile point stuck in
a mastodon rib. Since then the age of the find has been
debated, but recently anthropologist Michael Waters and his
colleagues announced a new radiocarbon date for the rib:
13,800 years ago, making it 800 years older than the oldest
20   Clovis artifact. Other pre-Clovis evidence comes from a
variety of locations across the New World.

The "researchers" (line 10) would most likely view
advocates of the theory described in lines 4-5 with

(A) admiration because they offer a novel perspective
(B) skepticism because they fail to acknowledge
       important new evidence
(C) hostility because they threaten to overturn decades
       of research
(D) suspicion because their methods are unreliable
(E) puzzlement because they focus on trivial factors

There are three steps to answering this question:

1. Define the theory.

2. Determine what the author thinks about the theory and why (agree/disagree).

3. Look for an answer that fits.

1) What's the theory in lines 4-5?

The Clovis were the first people in North America.

2) What do the researchers believe?

People were living in North and South America before the Clovis. (The Clovis were NOT the first people in North America.)

3) What's the relationship?

The information in steps 1 and 2 indicates opposing ideas, so they're going to disagree. That means we're going to look for something negative. Now, we're just going to look at the first word of each option.

(A) Admiration: positive. Cross out.
(B) Skepticism: negative, relatively neutral, usually indicates a correct answer. Keep it.
(C) Hostility: negative, too strong. Assume it's wrong.
(D) Suspicion: negative, relatively neutral. Keep it.
(E) Puzzlement: negative but off-topic. Cross it out.

Working this way, we're left with (B) and (D). (B) makes sense because someone who believed that the Clovis were the first people in the North America would be overlooking the evidence described in the second paragraph. (D) makes no sense in context; there's no information to suggest the "advocates" methods are unreliable.

So (B) is correct, as the wording suggested.

Reading Closely to Identify Tone and Attitude

While a familiarity with frequently correct and incorrect answers will certainly help you identify likely answers to tone questions faster, it won't always get you the answer itself. Unless you want to treat the SAT like a glorified guessing game, you need to know how to distinguish between choices when things aren't so clear cut. Although it is impossible to predict the exact phrasing that will appear on any given passage, there are some general types of words and phrases that tend to indicate particular tones and attitudes.

Important: because hearing how a passage *sounds* is a key element in identifying tone, it can help to read yourself the lines in question out loud (albeit very, very quietly). Recognizing which words are emphasized and which ones are less important can be very useful, especially for subtler answers like "wry," "pensive," and "ironic." Reading the text out loud will, however, only work if you are able to "translate" the words on the page into normal conversational speech, with the appropriate stresses and intonation. If you have difficulty using textual "clues" such as italics and quotation marks to understand how certain words would likely be spoken, this strategy is likely to be of limited help.

The lists below include both the common answers listed in the chart on the previous page as well some of their less frequent counterparts. Each group is divided into "moderate" and "extreme," with terms from the latter less likely to appear as correct answers. **"Moderate" answers unlikely to be correct are marked with an asterisk.**

Happiness and Approval

Moderate:

Appreciative
Approving
Sympathetic
Delighted
Pride
Optimistic
Encouraged
Amused*
Sanguine*
Mirthful*
Jovial*

Extreme:

Reverent
Awed
Magnanimous
Ecstatic
Excited

A passage whose tone corresponds to one of the above words will contain specific words and phrases that indicate the author's positive attitude. For example:

> Ideas **matter**. A relatively small number can be classed as **major** historical events. And many times, their **best, most eloquent** expression has been on paper, stamped in ink, sewn on one side, and bound between hard covers. In the beginning was the word, sure, but there's also **a lot to be said** for the book.

In this passage, the author's **positive tone** is revealed in a number of words and phrases:

> *ideas matter*
> *Major historical events*
> *best* and *most eloquent expression*
> *there's a lot to be said for the book.*

Taken together, all of these elements convey the overall impression that books and ideas are things that the author considers very important and holds in high regard.

Note, however, that although the author is distinctly positive toward his subject, he does not go overboard. He does not say that ideas *always* find their best expression in books, nor does he say that books are the *only* medium for conveying important ideas – instead, he uses **qualifying words** such as *relatively small* and *many times*. In addition, he understates his enthusiasm by saying *there's a lot to be said for the book* instead of *books are the best, most incredible, most amazing thing ever!*

His tone, therefore, would therefore most likely be characterized as *appreciative* on the SAT. It could also be described as *laudatory* (praiseworthy) or approving, but *appreciative* is simply more likely to appear. An extreme answer choice for this type of question would be *ecstatic*, *awed* or *reverent*, all of which imply a level of over-the-top enthusiasm that is simply not present in the passage.

Longing for the Past

Nostalgic
Wistful

Wistful and *nostalgic* are used more or less interchangeably, and you will never be asked to distinguish between them. A passage whose tone falls into this category will contain clear indication that the author misses the way things were in the past and regrets that they are now different. For example:

> No image **brings a tear to the eye of even the crustiest ink-on-paper romantic** like a **yellowing** photograph of the city room of a **deceased newspaper**. *The Journal-American* was once New York City's most widely read afternoon newspaper—yes, afternoon paper, a **once-grand tradition** of American journalism that has gone the way of the Linotype machine, the gluepot and the spike onto which editors would stick stories they deemed unworthy of publication.

There are a number of words and phrases in this passage that indicates that the author regrets the demise of the *New York Journal-American*. The phrase "brings a tear to the eye" and "once-grand" clearly indicates how sorry he is that it has disappeared, and the personification in the phrase "*deceased* newspaper" (a newspaper is not a living creature and thus cannot actually be deceased) further conveys his attachment to it. His tone is decidedly *wistful* or *nostalgic*.

Disagreement, Fear, and Anger

Moderate:	Extreme:
Skeptical	Angry
Wary	Hostile
Critical	Irate
Disparaging	Belligerent
Contentious	Outraged
Doubtful*	Incredulous
Unconvinced*	Accusatory
Dismissive*	Sullen
Fearful*	Envious/Resentful
Disbelief*	Furious
Argumentative*	Surly

As discussed earlier, one of the easiest ways to determine that an author's attitude toward a particular idea is negative is to use "they say/I say." By definition, the author's attitude toward what "other people" say will be negative, so if you recognize that a particular idea is associated with "them," you're already very close to the answer. Indeed, if a line reference begins with words like "those scientists," you can reasonably assume that the answer will be something like "skeptical" or "disdainful" – in such cases, the wording of the question itself provides an important clue to its likely answer. Many of the negative adjectives that appear as answer choices to tone questions are also relatively high-frequency "hard" words, though, so if you do not know the definitions of *derisive, indignant, contentious, ambivalent,* and *resentful,* you may encounter an extra layer of difficulty in determining correct answers.

If no "they say/I say" structure is present, or if you have difficulty recognizing it, you can also look for negative words and phrases that would indicate such an attitude. For example:

> String theory is dazzling **but unverified**. There is **no compelling proof** that it's true.

Here, for instance, the phrases *dazzling but unverified* and *no compelling proof* indicate that the author finds string theory interesting but of *questionable validity* – hence, she could be called *skeptical* or *critical*.

Authors will not always use explicitly negative wording, however. Rather, they may sometimes suggest their disagreement by using **rhetorical questions**. For example:

> Philosophy is in **trouble**. In search of something new, scholars are venturing down **back alleys** of thought. *Do readers truly need 60 pages about snobbery?*

Since the author has already told us that "philosophy is in trouble," we can easily infer that the answer to the rhetorical question would be a firm "no." The author clearly *doubts* that anyone would want to read 60 pages about snobbery – the rhetorical question indicates *skepticism* about the necessity of writing 60 pages on such a topic.

Remember, though, that context is key: a phrase that would logically seem positive when read out of context in the question may be regarded very differently by the author of the passage. For example, consider the following:

> Eating should be seen as pleasure and not penance; something that brings happiness and joy rather than anxiety. By viewing the acquisition and consumption of food as an ethical and moral act,
> 5   we **diminish** the fundamental pleasure that eating food provides us. By attaching social worth and political meaning to what we eat, and hoping that consumption can make the world a better place, we will not **only fail to improve** the world, but in the
> 10   process **lose the *essential* fact that eating should be about enjoyment**.

The author's attitude toward those who consider eating an "ethical and moral act" (line 4) could best be described as:

(A) sympathetic
(B) bewildered
(C) impatient
(D) critical
(E) ambivalent

If you encountered this question without reading the passage carefully, you might leap to the conclusion that since "ethical" and "moral" are clearly positive, the author would obviously have a positive attitude. And indeed, if we only looked at the wording of the question, we would have no reason to dispute that assumption.

This is where most people go wrong (or, in common parlance, get tricked). The question is not asking about the words themselves; instead, it is asking about the author's attitude toward those words. And in order to determine that, we need to start at the beginning of the sentence and read to the end of it. **To reiterate: do not ever start or stop reading halfway through a sentence – if you do so, you risk missing crucial information.**

If we read the entire sentence, we learn that according to the author, viewing the consumption of food (eating) as an ethical and moral act *diminishes* its pleasure. If we read further, we discover that eating this way ruins the *essential* purpose of eating. So we're looking for something negative, which means we can start by eliminating anything that's positive.

That definitely eliminates (A)… But unfortunately, everything else is negative. You can assume *ambivalent* is probably wrong since that's almost always the case. *Bewildered?* There aren't any questions, nor is there anything to suggest the author is confused. *Impatient?* That simply has nothing to do with the passage (usually the case when it appears as an answer choice). So it's (D), *critical*, which captures the idea that the author's attitude is negative, but not outrageously so.

Disdain and Arrogance

Moderate:	Extreme:
Disdainful	Contemptuous
Scornful	Self-Satisfied
Self-Deprecatory	Self-Congratulatory
	Pretentious
	Pompous
	Arrogant

The tone of a passage or portion of a passage can be described as **disdainful** when the author indicates that he or she looks down on a particular subject or person. For example:

> String theory is dazzling but unverified. There's zero proof that it's true. Yet, **like fringe cranks**, string theorists labor away, **unencumbered by reality**.

The author's assertion that string theorists are *fringe cranks* (charlatans or "hacks") and that these people feel *unencumbered* (unconstrained) *by reality*, indicates that the author looks down on them as fools. The tone could thus be described as *disdainful* or even *contemptuous*. Even though the latter word is fairly extreme, in this case it is an apt description because the language of the passage itself is quite extreme. Now let's look at a subtler example:

> For some activists, eating local foods is no longer just a pleasure—it is a moral obligation. Why? Because shipping foods over long distances results in the unnecessary emission of the greenhouse gases that are warming the planet. This concern
> 5   has given rise to the concept of "food miles," that is, the distance food travels from farm to plate. But food miles advocates fail to grasp the simple idea that food should be grown where it is most economically advantageous to do so. Relevant advantages consist of various combinations of soil, climate, labor, and other factors.
> 10   It is possible to grow bananas in Iceland, but Costa Rica really has the better climate for that activity.

The author's attitude toward the "advocates" (line 6) could best be described as

(A) somewhat perplexed
(B) highly irate
(C) mildly condescending
(D) generally appreciative
(E) strongly apathetic

Let's forget about the choices for a moment – since we're discussing arrogance and condescension here, the answer is clearly going to be (C). The question is *why*. Most of the passage is fairly neutral, but when we look at the sentence in which the word *advocates* appears, we see that the author accuses the "advocates" of "fail[ing] to grasp a *simple* idea." Stating that a group of people can't grasp a "simple" idea is a way of hinting that those people aren't particularly intelligent – so the author's tone could be called *mildly condescending*.

Defensiveness

A *defensive* tone indicates that an author feels that he or she is being unfairly criticized or accused, and feels the need to defend or justify a belief or action. For example, consider this passage from the opening of Kazuo Ishiguro's 2010 novel *Never Let Me Go*. It provides a stellar example of a defensive tone:

> My name is Kathy H. I'm thirty-one years old, and I've been a carer now for over eleven years… Now I know my being a carer so long **isn't necessarily because they think I'm fantastic at what I do…So I'm not trying to boast.** But then I do know for a fact they've been pleased with my work, and by and large, I have too. **Anyway, I'm not making any big claims for myself.** I know carers, working now, who are just as good and don't get half the credit. If you're one of them, **I can understand how you might get resentful.** But I'm not the first to be allowed to pick and choose, and I doubt if I'll be the last. **And anyway, I've done my share** of looking after donors brought up in every kind of place. By the time I finish, **remember**, I'll have done twelve years of this, and it's only for the last six they've let me choose.

Although we have no context for statements the narrator is making and have no information about what a "carer" is, we can discern that she feels she must protect herself against people who would think that she does not deserve her position.

How do we know this? Well, first of all, she spends quite a bit of time justifying herself: she tells us that *[she] hasn't necessarily lasted so long because she's fantastic at what [she] does*, then insists that she isn't bragging (*So I'm not trying to boast… Anyway, I'm not making any big claims for myself*) while simultaneously trying to prove her competence (*But then I do know for a fact they've been pleased with my work, and by and large, I have too.*)

Furthermore, she goes out of her way to remind the reader how much work she's put in to deserve her privileges (*By the time I finish, remember, I'll have done twelve years of this, and it's only for the last six they've let me choose*).

Clearly, she's anticipating being criticized and demonstrates a need to defend herself against that criticism at every turn.

Humor, Sarcasm, and Informality

Moderate:	**Extreme:**
Sardonic	Cynical
Wry	Disillusioned
Ironic	Frivolous
Irreverent	Jeering
Facetious	Caustic
Sarcastic	
Satirical	
Mocking	
Flippant	
Cavalier	
Conversational	
Humorous	
Jocular*	

Important: recognizing sarcasm and irony in written form is one of the most challenging skills that Critical Reading tests, and many of the most difficult questions involve the above tone words. Since questions that test them constitute such a common stumbling block, you are encouraged to pay particular attention to this section.

One common myth about the SAT is that Critical Reading passages are always written in exceedingly formal and proper prose. As a result, it simply doesn't occur to many test-takers that certain passages, or certain portions of passages, are actually intended to be amusing. To be fair, however, much of the humor that appears is not obvious, over-the-top, laugh-out-loud humor. Rather, it's based on **wordplay** that either involves **punning** on alternate meanings of words, or using words to mean exactly the **opposite** of what they normally mean (the literary equivalent of a kid who rolls his eyes and says "great" when he's asked to stop playing video games and take out the trash).

Unfortunately, humor and sarcasm can be difficult to recognize than other tones because there are no specific types of words that reliably signal their presence (although punctuation such as quotation marks can indicate that an author does not intend for a word to be understood literally). Words are used to mean the **opposite** of what they normally mean: negative becomes positive, and positive becomes negative. It is up to the reader to recognize that meanings are being flip-flopped *based on the context of the passage* and to connect those meanings to the author's tone.

One thing to be aware of is that humor often appears in Critical Reading passages when the author has a **negative attitude** and wants to criticize or mock what "they" say without being overly direct or heavy-handed. This stands in directly contrast to the usual positive associations that most people have with humor.

For example:

> The ethics of eating red meat have been **grilled** recently by critics who question its consequences for environmental health and animal welfare. But if you want to minimize animal suffering and promote more sustainable agriculture, adopting a vegetarian diet might be the worst possible thing you could do.

In the first line, the author puns on the word "grilled" by using it in its second meaning ("grill" means "question intensely") while simultaneously associating it with its first meaning (cooking food). The play on words creates a humorous or *irreverent* tone.

In context of the unexpected assertion that the author makes in the next sentence (being a **vegetarian** is bad for animals and agriculture – exactly the opposite of what most vegetarians would logically think), the play on words also establishes a tone of light *mockery* and *sarcasm* toward the "critics:" people who believe that eating **meat** is bad for animals and the environment.

Because the author introduces his critique through a clever play on words rather than simply announcing that it is wrong to believe that vegetarianism helps the environment, his tone could also be called *ironic, facetious, wry, sardonic,* or *satirical.* **Although it could be argued that there are subtle distinctions between these words, they are used interchangeably on the SAT, and you will never be asked to distinguish among them.**

If you didn't immediately pick up on the sarcasm in those couple of sentences, though, don't be too hard on yourself. Recognizing sarcasm, much more than is true for recognizing other kinds of tones, requires that you *hear* the words, with their accompanying intonation and emphases, as they would sound when spoken aloud. If someone were to read the passage on the previous page out loud, they would probably draw out or put special emphasis on the word "grilled" in order to make it clear that it was being used in an unexpected way. In the absence of such auditory cues, you must do your best to "translate" the words on the page into normal conversational speech. As mentioned earlier, you should read the words (very, very) quietly to yourself, thinking about which words a speaker would naturally stress or pay particular attention to. You may be able to recognize out loud what wasn't quite so apparent on paper.

Sometimes, however, authors will "tell" you what to pay attention to by using punctuation such as italics, quotation marks, and exclamation points, or rhetorical techniques such as repetition, to indicate that you should give special emphasis to a given word or phrase. In such cases, you must pay close attention to those features of the text and consider how they would "translate" into a spoken phrase. For example:

> Thoreau was capable of friendship, but on his own terms. He could be prickly to a fault. "I sometimes hear my Friends complain **finely** that I do not appreciate their **fineness**," he once wrote. "I shall not tell them whether I do or not. As if they expected a vote of thanks for every **fine** thing which they uttered or did."

In this passage, Thoreau plays with the word *fine* to mock what he considers his friends' unreasonable expectations. In the context of the larger point that the author is making (Thoreau "could be prickly to a fault"), the word acquires a distinctly negative connotation and conveys his irritation at being asked to constantly praise his friends for words and actions that he does not believe are worthy of praise.

One other way in which humor is expressed is through **register**, the level of formality or informality in an author's language. A person who is being irreverent or facetious will often use more casual or **conversational** language – language that more closely mimics everyday speech – than one who is being serious. Sometimes, that person will also use more casual language than would seem appropriate for a particular situation. For example, consider the last sentence of this excerpt:

> *Chicago Poems*, published in 1916, established Carl Sandburg's national reputation, creating a sensation with its frank imagery. The collection's keen sense of the Windy City's blue-collar environs grew out of Sandburg's years as a street reporter working his beat. Like his reportage, the poems often read like prose with a topical flair. They crackle with the authenticity of everyday experience, the texture of daily life. His poems from this period often have the vividness and urgency of a morning headline. **"Here is the difference between Dante, Milton and me," Sandburg would comment after Chicago Poems appeared. "They wrote about hell and never saw the place. I wrote about Chicago after looking the town over for years and years."**

The last sentence contains several features that indicate Sandburg is being deliberately and darkly (or **dryly**) humorous. First, there is a mismatch or **incongruity** between the content of his remark – he's comparing himself to Dante and Milton, two very serious poets who are recognized as absolute masters of their art – and the comparatively **lower** or **conversational register** of his language: he refers to hell as "the place" and uses the informal, almost slangy phrase "looking the town over" instead of a more formal phrase such as "observing the city." Furthermore, by comparing himself to two authors who wrote about hell and then mentioning Chicago, Sandberg is implicitly comparing Chicago to hell – a move that can be described as "dark humor," or humor that contains grim or unpleasant elements. The presence of that dark humor also makes Sandberg's comment seem somewhat **flippant** or **cavalier** – it gives the comparison between Chicago and hell a note of frivolousness in a slightly offhand and impertinent way.

Certainty and Directness

Moderate:

Certain	Frank
Emphatic	Candid
Decisive	Confessional
Vehement	
Resolute	
Conviction	

The fact that correct answers to SAT questions are rarely extreme does not mean that authors of SAT passages are necessarily moderate as well. While it is true that SAT authors are rarely over-the-top extreme, they do sometimes voice some very strong opinions. When this is the case, the answer is just as likely to be *emphatic* or *decisive*, or to contain the word *conviction* – terms that convey the strength of the author's beliefs rather than any positive or negative qualities – as it is to be a clearly positive or negative word such as *critical* or *optimistic*.

Writing that is *emphatic, decisive, vehement, resolute* or full of *conviction* tends to have some pronounced characteristics:

-It contains short, blunt, declarative statements (e.g. *There is no compelling proof that it's true).*

-It contains strong words and phrases such as *there is no doubt, certainly, indisputably, only*, and *most.*

-It generally lacks qualifying words or phrases such as *sometimes, frequently*, or *might* that would "soften" its meaning.

For example, compare the following two statements:

1) Books matter.

2) Under some circumstances, books have the potential to matter.

The two sentences deal with the same subject (the importance of books), but they do so in very different ways.

The first sentence is striking because it is so short and to-the-point – it simply says what it has to say, and that's that. Its tone could be described as **emphatic** or **decisive**.

The second sentence, on the other hand, is filled with **qualifying phrases** (*some, have the potential to be*) that tell us that the author wants to avoid making an overly strong statement. Its tone could be described as *tentative, hesitant*, or *cautious*.

Uncertainty and Confusion

Moderate:

Uncertain*
Puzzled*
Ambivalent*
Confused*
Equivocal*
Hesitant*

Extreme:

Perplexed
Baffled
Bewildered
Bemused
Incredulous
Indecisive

Examining Both Sides of an Argument ≠ Ambivalence

One very common point of confusion involving the word "ambivalent" stems from the fact that SAT authors often acknowledge the merits of arguments that they do not ultimately agree with. That does not, however, mean that those authors are uncertain about *their own* opinions. Even if they discuss other viewpoints extensively, they usually come down firmly on one side (albeit in ways that may strike you as unnecessarily subtle or confusing). As a result, "ambivalent" is virtually always incorrect, and you should start by assuming that it is wrong. For example, consider the following version of this passage:

> Several scholars vehemently refute the image of
> Thoreau as a misanthrope. Sandra Harbert Petrulionis, in her
> book, *Thoreau in His Own Time*, criticizes Emerson for
> flippantly immortalizing the term, "that terrible Thoreau."
> 5   Instead of focusing on "incidents of understandable local ire"
> against Thoreau, Petrulionis argues we should focus on the
> fact that "Thoreau engaged in a lifelong habit of serving and
> educating his community." **This is an important point.**
> Thoreau valued his community tremendously. And he valued
> 10   education and the dissemination of truth and knowledge.
>   **But I, for one, will <u>always</u> have a greater respect for**
> **Emerson, a man who worked within the difficult confines**
> **of the real world.** As it turns out, Thoreau had the longer-
> lasting and more powerful influence. His iconoclastic ideals
> 15   influenced some of the greatest men of the 20th century. But
> which is better, really? To fire the imaginations of men and
> women with inspiration during your own life, as Emerson did,
> or to retreat to the woods, doing comparatively little for those
> of your own generation, as Thoreau did? I'm not sure I know
> 20   the answer to that question. **But I do get the sense I would**
> **not have liked Thoreau had I met him. And he <u>certainly</u>**
> **would not have liked me**.

The author's attitude toward Thoreau can best be
characterized as

(A) appreciative
(B) critical
(C) ambivalent
(D) furious
(E) bewildered

This passage offers a stellar example of the sort of writing that frequently provokes confusion about tone. While the author's attitude toward Thoreau is clearly negative, he also acknowledges that Petrulionis is making an important point: Thoreau *did* help his community. It is, however, important to understand that the author's consideration of Petrulionis's argument does not by itself indicate that he has mixed feelings (i.e. is ambivalent) about Thoreau. While the author acknowledges that there is some truth to Petrulionis's point that Thoreau was an active member of his community, he still has a very clear opinion: Thoreau was a jerk. So (B) is the right answer.

If, on the other hand, we were to look at the actual beginning of the passage, our understanding of the author's attitude toward Thoreau would change a bit:

> **I vacillate on Thoreau.** I consider myself fairly well
> read when it comes to the writers of Concord…though
> certainly no expert. I love *Walden*. In my younger days, more
> times than I can count, I walked the same woods he walked
> 5 and was inspired by his love of simplicity and nature. I used
> to swim in Walden frequently and always enjoyed the quiet
> corner of the pond where his tiny dwelling once stood. "I went
> into the woods because I wished to live deliberately," he
> wrote of his two-year stint at Walden. "I did not wish to live
> 10 what was not life, living is so dear…I wanted to live deep
> and suck out all the marrow of life." How can you not admire
> passion like that?
>   Lately, however, I have been reading an interesting
> compilation of excerpts from his journals. The collection
> 15 highlights those journal entries in which Thoreau wrote spe-
> cifically about his fellow townsfolk: bits and pieces
> describing the inhabitants of Concord, their habits, their lives,
> and lots of fascinating period detail. But what struck me most
> about Thoreau's observations is his judgmental tone of
> 20 superiority. **As a younger man, poring over Walden, I
> believe I idealized Thoreau. Now I begin to wonder if he
> was, in fact, a misanthrope.**

In this version of the passage, the author is indicating that he is genuinely uncertain what to think about Thoreau because "to vacillate" means to waver or go back and forth. If we were to now see this question:

> The author's attitude toward Thoreau can best be
> characterized as
>
> (A) appreciative
> (B) impatient
> (C) ambivalent
> (D) contemptuous
> (E) bewildered

The answer would in fact be (C) because ambivalence is, by definition, the same thing as vacillating. Here the author genuinely comes across as torn. His overall *tone*, however, could be described as **confessional** because he is admitting to the reader that despite his youthful admiration of Thoreau, he is beginning to doubt whether that admiration was truly deserved.

In the first version of the passage on p. 233, the author's tone could also be called **uncertain** or **hesitant** when he states that he "is *not certain* whether [he] knows the answer" to the question of whether it is better to be renowned during one's lifetime (like Emerson) or to affect future generations (like Thoreau).

The presence of *rhetorical questions* can also indicate a lack of certainty. For example:

> In our time, reality stars can become "fame-ish" overnight; but the people of the nineteenth century bestowed fame on individuals—mostly male—who they felt had made significant contributions to history. **Why did the residents of Washington City, the members of government and their families, and, indeed, all of America declare Dolley the nation's "Queen"? What did they understand about Dolley Madison that we don't?**

The questions in the last three lines are key in identifying the author's tone: the fact that the author must ask *why* Dolley Madison was held in such high regard in the nineteenth century, and *what* people today *do not understand* about her indicates that confusion. Thus, we can say that the author is **puzzled** or **perplexed** or **bewildered**.

In addition, hypothetical words like *could, might, probably,* and *perhaps* frequently contribute to a tone of **uncertainty**. The words *guess* or *hypothesis* may also appear. For example:

> A better understanding of archaea's lifestyle and role in nitrogen cycles not only would rewrite ecology textbooks. It **could also have practical applications**, such as devising natural ways to boost a soil's nitrogen content without needing to use chemical fertilizers, or designing sewage treatment plants that employ microbes to remove nitrogenous waste more efficiently, or understanding which microbes produce global-warming gases such as nitrous oxide.

In this passage, the word *could* indicates that the author is **speculating** about the potential applications of knowledge regarding archaea's lifestyle and role in nitrogen cycles – that is, knowledge and applications that do not currently exist but that might exist in the future.

Objectivity and Neutrality

Moderate:

Objective
Evenhanded
Analytical
Neutral
Impartial
Detached
Disinterested
Pragmatic
Tempered
Moderate
Restrained

Extreme:

Apathetic
Indifferent
Diffident
Aloof
Resigned

While many SAT passages have a distinct tone or point of view, others (**particularly science passages**) will truly be neutral. An author who avoids strong language and who takes care to present both sides of an issue can be described as any of the above adjectives. To return to our earlier example:

> Sometime near the end of the Pleistocene, a band of people left northeastern Asia, crossed the Bering land bridge when the sea level was low, entered Alaska and became the first Americans. Since the 1930s, archaeologists have thought these people were members of the Clovis culture. First discovered in New Mexico in the 1930s, the Clovis culture is known for its distinct stone tools, primarily fluted projectile points. For decades, Clovis artifacts were the oldest known in the New World, dating to 13,000 years ago.

The passage is more notable for what it lacks than what it contains. The author employs no strong language or particular point of view – the language is dry and scholarly, the very opposite of **emotional**, and the emphasis is on dates and facts.

Thinking and Teaching

Moderate:	Extreme:
Pensive	Erudite
Reflective	Pedantic
Didactic	Moralistic
Scholarly	Philosophical

While Critical Reading passages will often be relatively serious or scholarly in tone, as is the case for the "Clovis" passage on the previous page, they will **not** be excessively so (e.g. *erudite* or *philosophical*). Critical Reading passages, while often challenging, are not intended to be overly abstruse or above the level of the very strongest high school readers. As discussed earlier, they are taken primarily from works written for a college-educated audience, but one that lacks highly specialized knowledge of particular fields. The inclusion of overly philosophical or erudite works would therefore contradict the essential framework of the test. If an original text includes terminology or references that would only be clear to more advanced readers, those references will be eliminated when the passage is adapted.

The test will, however, include passages whose tone is **reflective** or **pensive**. Unlike passages that are simply "analytical" or "detached," these passages are more personal and typically include phrases such as *I think, I believe,* and *it seems to me.* For example:

> I vacillate on Thoreau. I consider myself fairly well
> read when it comes to the writers of Concord…though
> certainly no expert. I love *Walden.* In my younger days, more
> times than I can count, I walked the same woods he walked
> and was inspired by his love of simplicity and nature. I used
> to swim in Walden frequently and always enjoyed the quiet
> corner of the pond where his tiny dwelling once stood. "I
> went into the woods because I wished to live deliberately," he
> wrote of his two-year stint at Walden. "I did not wish to live
> what was not life, living is so dear…I wanted to live deep
> and suck out all the marrow of life." How can you not admire
> passion like that?

This passage is filled with personal insights and could easily be described as **reflective** since the author is considering, or thinking through, his relationship to *Walden* and Thoreau.

A **didactic** tone is associated with the **second person** point of view, in which the narrator addresses the reader or another character directly in order to instruct them. For example:

> "Really Hopkins," said he, "I have high hopes for your
> career, but you must learn patience before rushing off
> to pursue the first conclusion which occurs to you.
> Examine every fact, test every link in your chain and only
> then take action.

The phrase "you must learn," and the commands "examine," "test," and "take" indicate that the narrator is instructing Hopkins. His tone could thus be called "didactic."

Tone and Attitude Exercises

1.   Math poses difficulties. There's little room for eyewitness testimony, seasoned judgment, a skeptical eye or transcendental rhetoric.

The author's tone could best be described as

(A) appreciative
(B) flippant
(C) bemused
(D) cynical
(E) frank

2.   To the degree that Audubon's prose has the shapely feel of a novel, it's because he was deft at crafting his observations into the stuff of story; the birds that he chronicles became not merely objects
5   of scientific data, but characters in a dramatic narrative.

The author's attitude toward "Audubon's prose" (line 1) is best described as

(A) puzzled
(B) skeptical
(C) approving
(D) defensive
(E) ardent

3.   Why is the connection between smells and memories so strong? The reason for these associations is that the brain's olfactory bulb is connected to both the amygdala (an emotion center) and to the hippocampus, which is involved
5   in memory. And, because smells serve a survival function (odors can keep us from eating spoiled or poisonous foods), some of these associations are made very quickly, and may even involve a one-time association.

Throughout the passage, the author's tone can best be described as

(A) baffled
(B) sympathetic
(C) ironic
(D) analytical
(E) skeptical

4.   Most people have so-called flashbulb memories of where they were and what they were doing when something momentous happened. (Unfort- unately, staggeringly terrible news seems to come out of the blue more often than staggeringly good
5   news.) But as clear and detailed as these memories feel, psychologists have discovered they are surprisingly inaccurate.

The "psychologists" (line 6) would most likely view the memories mentioned in line 1 with

(A) impatience
(B) dubiousness
(C) cautious acceptance
(D) amusement
(E) bewilderment

5.   Neuroscientists and humanists are tackling similar questions—by joining forces, they might vastly refine our understanding of the role that narrative plays in human cognition, for example,
5   or explore with empirical precision the power of literature to represent consciousness.

In lines 2-6 ("by joining...consciousness"), the author's tone can best be described as

(A) optimistic
(B) circumspect
(C) amused
(D) derisive
(E) apathetic

6.   Shakespeare in the world of ants, untroubled by any such war between honor and treachery, and chained by the rigid commands of instinct to a tiny repertory of feeling, would be able to write only
5   one drama of triumph and one of tragedy. Ordinary people, on the other hand, can invent an endless variety of such stories, and compose an infinite symphony of ambience and mood.

The author considers "ordinary people" (lines 5-6)

(A) appreciative
(B) diffident
(C) lamenting
(D) ironic
(E) relieved

238

7.   The Romans started making concrete more than 2,000 years ago, but it wasn't quite like today's concrete. They had a different formula, which resulted in a substance that was not as strong as the modern product. Yet
5   structures like the Pantheon and the Colosseum have survived for centuries, often with little to no maintenance. That resistance, or durability against the elements, may be due to one of the concrete's key ingredients: volcanic ash.

Throughout the passage, the author's tone can best be characterized as

(A) dismissive
(B) objective
(C) amused
(D) sympathetic
(E) nostalgic

8.   To be a woman in the Victorian age was to be weak: the connection was that definite. To be female was also to be fragile, dependent, prone to nerves and—not least—possessed of a mind that was several
5   degrees inferior to a man's. For much of the 19th century, women were not expected to shine either academically or athletically, and those who attempted to do so were cautioned that they were taking an appalling risk. Mainstream medicine was clear on this
10 point: to dream of studying at the university level was to chance madness or sterility, if not both. It took generations to transform this received opinion; that, a long series of scientific studies, and the determination and hard work of many thousands of women. For all
15 that, though, it is still possible to point to one single achievement, and one single day, and say: this is when everything began to change.

In lines 16-17 ("this is when…change"), the author's tone can best be described as

(A) ironic
(B) sympathetic
(C) nostalgic
(D) emphatic
(E) pensive

9.   In a speech given in 1963, the year after her World War I chronicle *The Guns of August* was published, Barbara Tuchman shared her research and writing process. When she started working
5   on a book, Tuchman surveyed secondary sources, which she considered "helpful but pernicious," then dived headfirst into primary sources. "Even an untrustworthy source is valuable for what it reveals about the personality of the author," she
10 told the audience. Published volumes of letters and telegrams were wonderful, but the real thing was better. "Nothing can compare with the fascination of examining material in the very paper and ink of its original."

The author's attitude toward an "untrustworthy source" (line 8) can best be characterized as

(A) skeptical
(B) ambivalent
(C) indifferent
(D) puzzled
(E) appreciative

10.   Until the past few years, physicists agreed that the entire universe is generated from a few mathematical truths and principles of symmetry, perhaps throwing in a handful of parameters like the mass of
5   the electron. It seemed that we were closing in on a vision of our universe in which everything could be calculated, predicted, and understood. However, two theories, eternal inflation and string theory, now suggest that the same fundamental principles from
10 which the laws of nature derive may lead to many different self-consistent universes, with many different properties.

In context of the passage, the author views the "vision" (line 6) as

(A) profound
(B) erroneous
(C) incomprehensible
(D) esoteric
(E) ingenious

11.   The book is a self-contained utterance. It is finished, the very opposite of a "slug" you encounter on a website casting about for visitors to contribute writing and research. It is much more than a slug, much
5   more than the most basic information readily available. The discrete physical embodiment of text, it makes the perfect gift, the perfect giveaway, the perfect method of saying, "Consider the following . . ." We often think of imaginative literature when we think of book-reading,
10   along with notional scenes of people entering other worlds through books, but the world we know, the communities to which we already belong, are reified and reinforced by books. Such is the incredible and incredibly flexible power of this primitive technology.

Throughout the passage, the author's attitude toward books could best be characterized as

(A) skeptical
(B) admonishing
(C) appreciative
(D) defensive
(E) irreverent

12.   With its collection of temples, stone kiosks, obelisks, a sacred lake, walls, and pylons built over fifteen hundred years and spread over more than six hundred acres—nearly twice the size of the National
5   Mall in Washington—Karnak is mind-bogglingly vast in both space and time. Even in partial ruin, Karnak provides a window into the formidable engineering and artistic abilities of ancient Egypt.
       The pyramids may be more stupendous and the
10   Parthenon more beautiful, wrote British adventurer Amelia Edwards in 1877 after wandering through the famous Hypostyle Hall which alone covers nearly 1.5 acres. "Yet in nobility of conception, in vastness of detail, in mystery of the highest order," she wrote, the
15   pillared space of Karnak at the heart of the complex surpasses them all. It was, she insisted without reservation, "the noblest architectural work ever designed and executed by human hands."

The passage indicates that Amelia Edwards viewed Karnak with

(A) awe
(B) cynicism
(C) perplexity
(D) apprehensiveness
(E) impatience

13.   For some activists, eating local foods is no longer just a pleasure—it is a moral obligation. Why? Because shipping foods over long distances results in the unnecessary emission of
5   the greenhouse gases that are warming the planet. This concern has given rise to the concept of "food miles," that is, the distance food travels from farm to plate.
       But food miles advocates fail to grasp the
10   simple idea that food should be grown where it is most economically advantageous to do so. Relevant advantages consist of various combinations of soil, climate, labor, and other factors. It is possible to grow bananas in Iceland, but Costa
15   Rica really has the better climate for that activity. Transporting food is just one relatively small cost of providing modern consumers with their daily bread, meat, cheese, and veggies. Concentrating agricultural production in the most favorable
20   regions is the best way to minimize human impacts on the environment.

1. The author's attitude toward growing "bananas in Iceland" (line 14) can best be described as

(A) outraged
(B) sympathetic
(C) skeptical
(D) excited
(E) defensive

2. In the last sentence, the author's tone can best be described as

(A) circumspect
(B) jocular
(C) fearful
(D) decisive
(E) fascinated

14.   More than two centuries ago, attempting to explain the formation of the Sun and its planets, Immanuel Kant proposed a "nebular hypothesis," according to which a swirling mass of gas and dust that surrounded our star-in-
5 formation condensed into clumps that became the planets. It its broad outlines, Kant's hypothesis remains the basis for modern astronomical approaches to planet formation, having triumphed over the concept, much in vogue during the first half of the twentieth century, that the Sun's
10 planets arose from a close passage of another star by the Sun. In that scenario, the gravitational forces between the stars would have drawn masses of gas from each of them, and some of this gas could then have cooled and con- densed to form the planets. This hypothesis, promoted
15 by the famed British astrophysicist James Jeans, had the defect (or the appeal, for those inclined in that direction) of making planetary systems extremely rare, because sufficiently close encounters between stars probably occur only a few times during the lifetime of an entire galaxy.
20 Once astronomers calculated that most of the gas pulled from the stars would evaporate rather than condense, they abandoned Jeans's hypothesis and returned to Kant's, which implies that many, if not most, stars should have planets in orbit around them.

1. The tone of the parenthetical information in line 16 can best be characterized as

(A) caustic
(B) hesitant
(C) impatient
(D) sympathetic
(E) wry

2. The author would most likely regard an astronomer who advocated "this hypothesis" (line 14) with

(A) sympathy
(B) resignation
(C) ambivalence
(D) disdain
(E) outrage

15.   By the middle of his life, Edmund Wilson was a fat, ferocious man: petty, pretentious, and petulant, a failure at many of the most ordinary tasks of life. But he could dance: through a poem, through a book,
5 through a library. He was the Nureyev at what he did—a genius, really: probably the greatest reader the United States has ever known.
    That's not to say he was the most influential figure of his time. Sometimes he got it wrong. His
10 prose was merely good enough—not sparkling; only clear and well organized—and he got nosebleeds whenever he tried to follow philosophy up into the stratosphere of metaphysics. For that matter, he never understood escapism, and so, in a golden age of
15 Hollywood screwball fluff, he condemned American movies as inferior to European—to say nothing of his famous essay that thundered against mystery novels.
    Mostly, though, he got it right. And if he seems lost to us now, that's not just because we have no
20 similar genius to occupy the space that he filled. It's also because that space has nearly disappeared. The magisterial critic has no role left in the United States, really. We appreciate, we enjoy, we peruse, we watch. But we don't define ourselves by reading
25 anymore. The novel, the premiere art form of western civilization over the last two hundred years, has ceased to be the mark of civilization. And so what need have we of Edmund Wilson—that fat, ferocious man, so nimble on his feet?

1. Throughout the passage, the author's attitude toward Edmund Wilson is one of

(A) reverence and celebration
(B) mild perplexity
(C) veiled envy
(D) qualified admiration
(E) cold detachment

2. The passage indicates that Edmund Wilson regarded "mystery novels" (line 17) with

(A) respect
(B) curiosity
(C) pride
(D) resentment
(E) contempt

3. In the last paragraph, the author's tone can best be characterized as

(A) defensive
(B) wistful
(C) impatient
(D) malicious
(E) aloof

16.   One of the first and most frequently repeated
        strategies used to cope with Berthe Morisot's
        position as a female member of a 'radical' art group
        participating in what is perceived as an exclusively
5   man's world has been to construct her as exceptional.
        Unlike other women artists, both before and during her
        time, she, it is claimed, does not fall into the inevitable
        traps which beset women artists. George Moore, writing
        in 1898, stated that Morisot's pictures 'are the only
10   pictures painted by a woman that could not be destroyed
        without creating a blank, a hiatus in the history of art.'
        In turn, her painting 'style,' Impressionism, is produced
        as a method which is suited to and the natural expression
        of an appropriately feminine temperament.
15   'Impressionism' is offered as the answer to the problem
        of Morisot's 'femininity,' the problem posed by a
        skilled and prolific professional woman painter in a
        world which deemed such activities to be 'unfeminine.'
        From as early as the 1870s Morisot's manner of
20   working was seen to reflect a naturally feminine
        sensibility; it was repeatedly called 'charming,' 'fem-
        inine,' and 'delicate' in a way which transposed onto
        the painting those characteristics most favored in the
        middle-class women of the time.

        Throughout the passage, the author's tone can best
        be characterized as

        (A) surly
        (B) ambivalent
        (C) incredulous
        (D) objective
        (E) amused

17.   Many readers, faced with Thoreau's enigmatic Yankee persona, have resorted to a kind of pop-culture shorthand for describing his life. As the capsule summary goes, Thoreau was an oddball loner who lived by a lake,

5   writing in praise of nature and against modern progress.

But the full story of Thoreau's life involves subtleties and contradictions that call his popular image into question. One idea that has persisted is that he was a hermit who cared little for others, yet he was active in his

10   community and responsible for circulating petitions for neighbors in need. In yet another way Thoreau was politically active, penning an essay, "Civil Disobedience," that would later inform the thinking of Mohandas Gandhi and the Rev. Martin Luther King Jr.

15   Despite his fame as a champion of solitude—a practice that he chronicled with wisdom and wit—Thoreau made no secret of the social life he indulged during his stay at Walden Pond from 1845 to 1847. In fact, one of the chapters of Walden, titled "Visitors," offers an extended

20   account of Thoreau's dealings with others. In fact, one of the chapters of Walden, titled "Visitors," offers an extended account of Thoreau's dealings with others. In fact, one of the chapters of Walden, titled "Visitors," the lifelong bachelor Thoreau lays out his rules for

25   entertaining:

I had three chairs in my house; one for solitude, two for friendship, three for society. When visitors came in larger and unexpected numbers there was but the third chair for them all, but they generally economized the

30   *room by standing up... I have had twenty-five or thirty souls, with their bodies, at once under my roof, and yet we often parted without being aware that we had come very near to one another.*

But even if Thoreau wasn't always averse to

35   human company, the idea that he was a loner might stem from the assumption that he was the kind of person who should have been alone. Thoreau was capable of friendship, but on his own terms. He could be prickly to a fault. "I sometimes hear my Friends complain finely that I

40   do not appreciate their fineness," he once wrote. "I shall not tell them whether I do or not. As if they expected a vote of thanks for every fine thing which they uttered or did."

Even those who liked him conceded that Thoreau could

45   be a cold fish. In a letter to his friend Daniel Ricketson in 1860, Thoreau addresses Ricketson's puzzlement over why he hasn't come to visit, telling Ricketson, without much ceremony, that he's had much better things to do. But after explaining himself, Thoreau continued to correspond with

50   Ricketson. Ralph Waldo Emerson, Thoreau's close friend and mentor, who came to grudgingly admire Thoreau's argumentative streak, famously described him as "not to be subdued, always manly and able, but rarely tender, as if he did not feel himself except

55   in opposition." In remembrance of Thoreau, Emerson offered this observation from one of Thoreau's friends: "I love Henry, but I cannot like him; and as for taking his arm, I should as soon think of taking the arm of an elm-tree."

1. The author's attitude toward "many readers" (line 1) could best be characterized as

(A) amused
(B) critical
(C) puzzled
(D) apathetic
(E) approving

2. Throughout the passage, the author's tone could best be described as

(A) confessional
(B) flippant
(C) dejected
(D) sardonic
(E) scholarly

3. In lines 39-43 ("I sometimes...did"), Thoreau's attitude can best be described as

(A) indignant
(B) sanguine
(C) furious
(D) apprehensive
(E) indifferent

18.   We were 210 students, all there to study identities, change identities, to learn to "be." There are a variety of ways to describe what acting is. "Being," "Seeming," "Becoming," "Lying," "Truth Telling," "Magic,"
5   "Transforming." We were new. Some among us had known the building for an hour longer than the others of us. No one ever arrives at the same time as everybody else. We were going to learn how to talk to each other onstage, and through all of this how to take our own
10 special message to the *world*.
      On one of the first days I was coming into the building, a tall, thin aristocratic-looking white woman who appeared to be about my age, and whom we ultimately referred to as the Katherine Hepburn among
15 us, came breathlessly down a narrow hallway, saying to me (whom she had never seen except in that one instant), "Do you know where I can get a drink of water?"
      She said this as if she had known me all my life, as if I were a sister, a brother, a friend. She may have
20 even grabbed my hand. I wasn't put off by the fact that she was a stranger. Her presence in that question made me feel in an instant as if I had known her all my life. Having grown up in segregation, I found it odd that a white person would approach me without her own barriers up,
25 and without the expectation that I would have barriers. I was so stunned by her presence that I didn't speak. Besides, I didn't know where to get a drink of water. Just as rapidly and as urgently, she vanished down the hallway and out into the street. I thought that perhaps this was
30 what acting was. Because, as real as it was, realer than real, it also seemed like a moment out of a scene from Chekhov's *Uncle Vanya*, or as if one of Tchaikovsky's symphonies had burst into speech. *Urgency* is the word. And it's one of the top ten in the vocabulary of acting.
35   Acting is the furthest thing from lying that I have encountered. It is the furthest thing from make-believe. It is the furthest thing from pretending. It is the most unfake thing there is. Acting is a search for the authentic. It is a search for the authentic by using
40 the fictional as a frame, a house in which the authentic can live. For a moment, because, yes indeed, real life inhibits the authentic.

1. The author's indicates that she reacted to the woman's "presence" (line 21) with

(A) indifference
(B) envy
(C) defiance
(D) surprise
(E) dismay

2. In lines 35-38 ("Acting is the...there is") the author's tone is most notable for its

(A) great conviction
(B) utter perplexity
(C) mild ambivalence
(D) jaunty optimism
(E) objective detachment

19. A few years ago the city council of Monza, Italy, barred pet owners from keeping goldfish in curved fishbowls. The sponsors of the measure explained that it is cruel to keep a fish in a bowl because the curved sides

5   give the fish a distorted view of reality. Aside from the measure's significance to the poor goldfish, the story raises an interesting philosophical question: How do we know that the reality we perceive is true? The goldfish is seeing a version of reality that is different from ours,

10 but can we be sure it is any less real? For all we know, we, too, may spend our entire lives staring out at the world through a distorting lens.

In physics, the question is not academic. Indeed, physicists are finding themselves in a similar

15 predicament to the goldfish's. For decades we have strived to come up with an ultimate theory of everything—one complete and consistent set of fundamental laws of nature that explain every aspect of reality. It now appears that this quest may yield not

20 a single theory but a family of interconnected theories, each describing its own version of reality, as if it viewed the universe through its own fishbowl.

This notion may be difficult for many people, including some working scientists, to accept. Most

25 people believe that there is an objective reality out there and that our senses and our science directly convey information about the material world. Classical science is based on the belief that an external world exists whose properties are definite and independent of the observer

30 who perceives them. In philosophy, that belief is called realism.

Those who remember Timothy Leary and the 1960s, however, know of another possibility: one's concept of reality can depend on the mind of the perceiver. That

35 viewpoint, with various subtle differences, goes by names such as antirealism, instrumentalism or idealism. According to those doctrines, the world we know is constructed by the human mind employing sensory data as its raw material and is shaped by the interpretive structure

40 of our brains. This viewpoint may be hard to accept, but it is not difficult to understand. There is no way to remove the observer— us—from our perception of the world. The way physics has been going, realism is becoming difficult to defend. In classical physics—the physics of Newton

45 that so accurately describes our everyday experience—the interpretation of terms such as object and position is for the most part in harmony with our commonsense, "realistic" understanding of those concepts. As measuring devices, however, we are crude instruments. Physicists have found

50 that everyday objects and the light we see them by are made from objects that we do not perceive directly. These objects are governed not by classical physics but by the laws of quantum theory. The reality of quantum theory is a radical departure from that of

55 classical physics. In the framework of quantum theory, particles have neither definite positions nor definite velocities unless and until an observer measures those quantities. Quantum physics also has important implications for our concept of the past.

60 In classical physics, the past is assumed to exist as a definite series of events, but according to quantum physics, the past, like the future, is indefinite and exists only as a spectrum of possibilities. Even the universe as a whole has no single past or history. So

65 quantum physics implies a different reality than that of classical physics—even though the latter still serves us well when we design things such as buildings and bridges.

These examples bring us to a conclusion that

70 provides an important framework with which to interpret modern science. In our view, there is no picture- or theory-independent concept of reality. Instead we adopt a view that we call model-dependent realism: the idea that a physical theory or

75 world picture is a model (generally of a mathematical nature) and a set of rules that connect the elements of the model to observations. According to model dependent realism, it is pointless to ask whether a model is real, only whether it agrees with

80 observation. If two models agree with observation, neither one can be considered more real than the other. A person can use whichever model is more convenient in the situation under consideration.

1. According to the author, some scientists are likely to regard "this notion" (line 23) with

   (A) amusement
   (B) uneasiness
   (C) fear
   (D) indifference
   (E) confusion

2. The author's attitude toward "realism" (line 31) can best be characterized as

   (A) doubtful
   (B) ambivalent
   (C) delighted
   (D) caustic
   (E) apathetic

3. In the last sentence, the attitude described by the author is one of

    (A) surprise
    (B) irrationality
    (C) amusement
    (D) despondence
    (E) pragmatism

4. Throughout the passage, the author's tone can best be described as

    (A) accepting
    (B) eager
    (C) analytical
    (D) fascinated
    (E) perplexed

Official Guide Tone and Attitude Questions

Test 1	Section 2	Question 14	p. 393
Test 1	Section 5	Question 14	p. 405
Test 1	Section 5	Question 15	p. 405
Test 1	Section 5	Question 16	p. 405
Test 1	Section 5	Question 18	p. 405
Test 1	Section 5	Question 21	p. 405
Test 2	Section 4	Question 10	p. 459
Test 2	Section 4	Question 18	p. 461
Test 2	Section 4	Question 19	p. 461
Test 2	Section 4	Question 22	p. 461
Test 2	Section 7	Question 15	p. 478
Test 2	Section 7	Question 24	p. 480
Test 2	Section 9	Question 18	p. 489
Test 3	Section 7	Question 10	p. 539
Test 3	Section 7	Question 14	p. 540
Test 3	Section 9	Question 7	p. 550
Test 3	Section 9	Question 9	p. 551
Test 3	Section 9	Question 10	p. 551
Test 3	Section 9	Question 18	p. 552
Test 4	Section 5	Question 10	p. 589
Test 4	Section 8	Question 13	p. 607
Test 4	Section 8	Question 19	p. 608
Test 5	Section 3	Question 23	p. 649
Test 6	Section 7	Question 10	p. 725
Test 6	Section 7	Question 12	p. 725
Test 6	Section 7	Question 20	p. 727
Test 7	Section 2	Question 8	p. 763
Test 8	Section 5	Question 20	p. 845
Test 9	Section 6	Question 15	p. 912
Test 9	Section 6	Question 22	p. 914
Test 9	Section 9	Question 15	p. 922
Test 9	Section 9	Question 16	p. 923
Test 9	Section 9	Question 17	p. 923
Test 10	Section 4	Question 9	p. 961
Test 10	Section 4	Question 12	p. 961
Test 10	Section 6	Question 15	p. 974
Test 10	Section 6	Question 17	p. 975

Explanations: Tone and Attitude Exercises

1. E

The tone can best be described as frank ("direct" or "candid") because the author makes a series of simple, straightforward statements that attempt to honestly explain why math is challenging. *Frank* is also the most neutral answer, and although the author acknowledges that math is indeed difficult, that fact is presented in a neutral, unemotional manner.

2. C

The author states that Audubon was *deft at crafting his observations into the stuff of story*. Since *deft* means "highly skilled," the author's attitude is positive. Only (C) and (E) are positive, and *ardent*, which means "burning" or "passionate," is too extreme.

3. D

Like many science passages, this passage is characterized by neutral, cautious scientific language (e.g. *some of these assumptions may even involve a one-time association*) and is largely fact-based and devoid of any strong language. (D) is therefore correct.

4. B

The passage states that psychologists have discovered flashbulb memories to be inaccurate. It is therefore logical that they would mistrust those memories, i.e. have a *dubious* (doubtful) attitude toward them.

5. A

The phrases "vastly refine our understanding" and "explore with empirical *precision*" indicate that the author believes that the partnership between neuroscientists and humanists is likely to have positive effects.

6. A

The author mentions "ordinary people" in order to contrast them with ants. What can "ordinary people" do that ants cannot? Compose *an endless variety of (complex) stories* — something positive. (A) is the only logical answer.

7. B

The passage presents information in a straightforward, neutral manner and is devoid of any strong language. It also contains many nouns (*substance, product, structures, resistance, durability, ingredient*), which give a tone of scholarly seriousness, and presents a balanced image of Roman concrete that takes into account its negatives (not as strong as modern concrete) as well as its positives (it was highly durable).

8. D

The repetition in the phrases *one single achievement* and *one single day* serves to emphasize the point that a change in how women were perceived academically occurred very quickly. Emphasize = emphatic

9. E

The passage indicates that Barbara Tuchman viewed untrustworthy sources as *valuable* because she believed that primary sources revealed information about their writers in ways that no secondary source could.

10. B

What is the "vision" in line 6? *That the entire universe is generated from a few mathematical truths and principles of symmetry, perhaps throwing in a handful of parameters like the mass of the electron.*

What does the author tell us about that vision? Two theories suggest that it's wrong. Wrong = erroneous.

11. C

Throughout the passage, the author exhibits a distinctly positive attitude toward the book: it *the perfect gift, the perfect giveaway, the perfect method of saying, etc.* So the answer must be positive. That eliminates (A) and (B). Although the author does at one point compare the book favorably to information that is "readily available," the predominant focus of the passage is simply on the book's positive qualities rather than on a longing for a pre-technological past – that eliminates (D). That leaves (C), which in this case is considerably more neutral than the language used in the passage.

12. A

This is an example of a passage whose wording truly does support an "extreme" answer. Amelia Edwards was, quite simply, overwhelmed by Karnak, and the heightened language she used clearly reflected that sense of awe ("mystery of the *highest order*," "the *noblest* architectural work *ever designed* and executed by human hands").

13. 1C, 2D

13.1 The author states that Costa Rica is a "better environment" than Iceland for growing bananas, indicating that he does not view Iceland as an ideal environment (i.e. he dismisses it). The answer must therefore be negative, eliminating (B) and (D). The author's tone throughout the passage is relatively neutral, however, making (A) and (E) far too extreme.

13.2 In lines 18-21, the author uses extreme language, stating that *Concentrating agricultural production in the most favorable regions is the best way to minimize human impacts on the environment.* Along with *emphatic, decisive* is an answer choice that will typically be correct when strong or extreme language is present in a passage.

14. 1E, 2D

14.1 The key to this question is to understand that Jeans's theory has been proven wrong because if it were true, planetary systems would be "extremely rare" – which of course they aren't. For most people, presumably, it would be a "defect" for planetary systems to be rare because no planetary systems = no earth = no life. Therefore, someone to whom the idea that planetary systems could only arise rarely *appealed* would essentially view the development of intelligent life as a bad thing – not a normal response! For that reason, the author's **aside** or **parenthetical comment** can be considered *wry* or *ironic*. **Shortcut:** when "wry" appears as an answer choice, there's a good chance it's right.

14.2 What does "this theory" refer to? Jeans's theory, namely that planets formed when a star passed close to the sun and gravitational forces sucked gas from each, which then cooled and turned into planets. What do we know about the theory? It's completely wrong. So the author would have a negative attitude toward an "advocate" of that theory. (B), (D), and (E) are negative, but "resigned" doesn't fit, and, and "outrage" is too strong.

15. 1D, 2E, 3B

15.1 Although the author focuses primarily on the positive aspects of Edmund Wilson's writing (*he was a genius at what he did…probably the greatest reader America has ever known*), he also **qualifies** his praise throughout the second paragraph by acknowledging that Wilson had flaws as well.

15.2 The passages tells us that Wilson "thundered against" mystery, which he condemned the way he condemned American movies. Although "contempt" is relatively extreme, it accurately describes his attitude.

15.3 Throughout the last paragraph, the author laments the fact that people no longer have a need for critics like Wilson because the novel (*the premiere art form of western civilization*) has lost its importance. The author clearly regrets this change, making "wistful" the correct answer.

16. D

Although the author is describing a belief with which she does not agree (Morisot's "Impressionism" was a result of her femininity), her *tone* can best be described as objective because it is devoid of any strong language.

17. 1B, 2E, 3A

17.1 What do "many readers" think? That Thoreau was an eccentric hermit who shut himself away in the woods and rejected all human company. What does that author think of that? It's not the whole story, i.e. it's wrong. His attitude can thus be described as "critical." In addition, the phrase "many readers" is almost by definition what "they" say. The answer must therefore be negative, leaving (B).

17.2 Although the author clearly believes that "many readers" are wrong to understand Thoreau's life in such simplistic terms, his overall tone is quite neutral and academic. He uses no strong language, presents multiple points of view, and cites specific examples to support each point about Thoreau's behavior.

17.3 The quotation is used to support the idea that Thoreau was "prickly to a fault," and in it, Thoreau demonstrates that he felt *offended* by his friends' insistence that he show thanks for the "fine things" that they did. In other words, he felt wronged, i.e. *indignant*.

18. 1D, 2A

18.1 In line 26, the author indicates that she was stunned by the woman's presence. "Stunned" is a synonym for "surprised," hence the answer is (D).

18.2 The repetition of the extreme word "furthest" conveys the author's strong belief in the importance of urgency. "Great conviction" is a synonym for "strong belief."

19. 1B, 2A, 3E, 4C

19.1 What's "the notion?" That there is no single theory that explains every aspect of reality but rather *a set of laws, each describing its own version of reality.*

What do the authors say about how some scientists are likely view that notion? That it may be *difficult for them to accept*. In other words, they will view be uncomfortable or **uneasy** with it. Note that a very fast way to answer this question is to use "they say/I say." If you recognize that "some scientists" and "many people" are phrases associated with "old model," you can assume immediately that the author's attitude will be one of skepticism.

19.2 What does the author think of realism? It's wrong (the "old model"). So the attitude must be negative. (B) is virtually always wrong and (D) is too extreme, leaving (A).

19.3 What is the attitude described in the last paragraph? That no model can describe all of reality, and that *a person can use whichever model is more convenient in the situation under consideration.* In other, words, a person can use whichever model is more practical, i.e. **pragmatic**.

19.4 This question requires you to distinguish between content and tone. Although the author is clearly arguing in favor of antirealism and against realism, the tone remains scientific and neutral throughout. (C) is correct because it is the most neutral answer.

9. Rhetorical Strategy

Of all the types of questions that appear in Critical Reading, rhetorical strategy questions probably come the closest to testing the sorts of things you've learned in English class. Unlike other kinds of reading questions, they require you to be familiar with specific terms and to recognize examples of them. They can ask about everything from several words to an entire passage, and they are typically phrased in the following ways:

-Which of the following rhetorical strategies does the author use in lines x-y?

-The main rhetorical strategy used throughout the passage is…?

-The opening paragraph makes use of which technique?

-A rhetorical strategy used by the author of Passage 1 but not by the author of Passage 2 is…

Although rhetorical strategy questions often appear quite challenging, in reality many of them are much more straightforward than they seem and can be answered quickly and often with minimal effort. Certain devices frequently appear as correct answers, while others are correct far less often, and in many cases it is only necessary to *look* at a passage to determine the correct answer.

Although the same few strategies tend to show up repeatedly as correct answers, I have nevertheless provided an extensive list of rhetorical devices in the glossary on p. 268 – there is no guarantee that a less-common term will never be used as a correct answer. Some of them you have probably discussed in English class, while others may be less familiar.

Provided that you have sufficient time to study you are of course better off being able to recognize all of the terms. **While the list may seem long, please note that all of the terms given have appeared as answer choices on administered exams.** That said, they are listed in approximate order in the frequency with which they appear on the SAT, so you should particularly focus on the first half or so of the terms listed.

Important: if you have a limited amount of time to study, you should know the following terms, which appear most frequently as correct answers, along with the shortcuts for recognizing them:

> **-Rhetorical question (question marks)**
> **-Direction citation/quotation (quotation marks)**
> **-Personal anecdote (the words "me" or "I")**

As a general rule, answers to rhetorical strategy questions should always be checked in order of most to least straightforward. If you see one of the terms listed above – terms that are both frequently correct and that have simple shortcuts – you need to check it first. (If more than one of the terms is listed, you can check them in the order of your choice.)

Let's look at an example:

> Ideas matter. A relatively small number can be classed
> as major historical events. And many times, their best, most
> eloquent expression has been on paper, stamped in ink,
> sewn on one side, and bound between hard covers. In the
> 5 beginning was the word, sure, but there's also a lot to be
> said for the book. Think of Abraham Lincoln's comment,
> one hundred and fifty years ago, upon meeting the creator of
> a book, "So, this is the little lady who made this big war." He
> was speaking to Harriet Beecher Stowe, the author of *Uncle*
> 10 *Tom's Cabin.* As we are asked to contemplate the
> disappearance of books as such, it's worth pausing over the
> astonishing range of personal, social, and political purposes
> that have been served by books: the liberation of individuals,
> the reinforcement of community, the expansion of self-
> 15 knowledge, the publication of scientific findings, the spread
> of lies and promulgation of facts. Vast are the aims served by
> books.

A rhetorical strategy used by the author is

(A) rhetorical questioning
(B) understatement
(C) allusion
(D) direct citation
(E) appeal to emotion

Now, if you could simply check the answers in order, but why waste your time? The first thing to notice is that (A) and (D) are both top answers *with shortcuts*, so you need to check them out first. You might as well just go in alphabetical order:

If you start with (A) and scan the passage for question marks, you'll see pretty fast that there aren't any. So (A) is gone.

Next we're going to look at (D). Sure enough, if you scan the passage, you'll see that there is in fact a direction quotation from Abraham Lincoln: "So this is the little lady who made this big war." So that's the answer. There, you're done. Not so bad, right?

Let's try another one:

> The vessel believed to have been Blackbeard's
> flagship is currently occupied by octopuses, which turn a
> pale, disgruntled green when nautical archaeologists
> approach. Black sea bass nip at the excavators' ears, and
> 5 moray eels spill out of the mouths of cannons, many of
> which are still loaded. But after nearly 300 years in the North
> Carolina shallows, the remains of what may be the Queen
> Anne's Revenge are surfacing, plank by worm-eaten plank.
>   The site, discovered in 1996, is 25 feet underwater,
> 10 less than a mile and a half from shore. But long weather
> delays during diving seasons and uncertain funding have
> slowed the excavation—this past fall's expedition was the
> first since 2008—and it can take years to clean and analyze
> artifacts corroded beyond recognition. Still, with objects
> 15 recovered from 50 percent of the site, archaeologists are
> increasingly confident that the wreck is the infamous frigate
> that terrorized the Caribbean and once blockaded Charleston,
> South Carolina, for a week before running aground in June
> 1718.

> Which of the following techniques is used in
> the first paragraph?

> (A) detailed description
> (B) comparison
> (C) rhetorical questioning
> (D) anecdote
> (E) euphemism

In this case, the first answer to check out is (C), but alas, a quick scan of the passage reveals no question marks. (You didn't think it was always going to be *that* easy, did you?) In this case, you have a couple of options:

1) Know your rhetorical devices well enough to spot the answer on your own.

Phrases like "pale, disgruntled green," "nip at the excavators' ears," and "spill out of" make the language in the first paragraph highly descriptive. So the answer is (A).

2) Check the other answers out one-by-one.

(B) There aren't any words such as *like* or *similar to* that would indicate comparison, so (B) is out.

(D) The passage is basically a straightforward description of a situation – there's no story.

(E) Euphemism involves replacing an offensive or unpleasant word with a nicer one. But there's nothing unpleasant here that's being replaced by something nicer. Besides, "euphemism" isn't usually a right answer.

For a glossary of rhetorical terms, please see p. 268.

Paragraph and Passage Organization

Questions that ask about the organization of ideas in a paragraph or entire passage are intended to test rhetorical strategies on a larger scale. They are typically phrased in the following ways:

-Which of the following best describes the organization
of this paragraph?

- Which of the following best describes the organization
of this passage?

-The statement in line x signals a shift from…

While such questions do not appear terribly often, they do appear often enough that not knowing how to do them (or how to do them quickly) can cost you both time and points. If you can recognize the main point and its location in the passage, however, you will have a much easier time determining just how the argument in a passage or paragraph is built around it.

To answer these types of questions correctly and quickly, you must therefore be able to identify places in the passage where key ideas and arguments are introduced, as well transition words that indicate the relationships of those ideas to one another.

If a question asks about the organization of a paragraph, you should begin by skimming for important transitions within that paragraph; then once you have identified those transitions, consider how they relate to one another (comparison/contrast, sequence, etc.).

If a question asks about the overall organization of a passage, you should focus on the last sentence of the first paragraph or the first sentence of the second paragraph (where the main point is most likely to be located) and the first (topic) sentence of each subsequent paragraph. Conclusions are generally not important for this type of question.

While you should be able to recognize how paragraphs and passages are organized, you should not generally worry about taking the time to label each section of a passage as you read it (although if you can do so quickly enough and find that strategy helpful, there is no reason for you *not* to do it). Questions that ask specifically about passage organization are fairly rare, and if you are already comfortable determining organization, you can most likely figure it out on the spot if and when you are asked to do so. As a preparation strategy, however, you may find it helpful to label the various parts of a passage (e.g. historical context, supporting example, counter-example, etc.) in order to become accustomed to viewing passages this way.

Let's look at some examples.

Paragraph Organization:

Theoretical physicists have **several hypotheses** about the identity of dark energy. **It may be** the energy of ghostly subatomic particles that can briefly appear out of nothing before self-annihilating and slipping back into the
5   vacuum. According to quantum physics, empty space is a pandemonium of subatomic particles rushing about and then vanishing before they can be seen. Dark energy **may also be** associated with an as-yet-unobserved force field called the Higgs field, which is sometimes invoked to explain why
10   certain kinds of matter have mass. (Theoretical physicists ponder things that other people do not.) **And in the models proposed by string theory**, dark energy may be associated with the way in which extra dimensions of space—beyond the usual length, width, and breadth—get compressed down
15   to sizes much smaller than atoms, so that we do not notice them.

Which of the following best describes the organization of this passage?

(A) an assertion followed by specific examples
(B) a description of a claim followed by an refutation of that claim
(C) a comparison of the strengths and weakness of several hypotheses
(D) a presentation of various explanations for a phenomenon
(E) a hypothesis followed by a description of an experiment

The bolded transitions reveal the structure of the paragraph: the first sentence tells us that there are "several hypotheses about the identity of dark energy," and the remainder of the passage is devoted to describing those hypotheses (first, the energy of ghostly subatomic particles; second, the association with the Higgs field; and third, extra dimensions of space). In other words, each section details a possible *explanation* for dark matter (*a phenomenon*). So the answer is (D).

Other questions will ask you to identify where a change or **shift** occurs in the passage. In order to answer these questions, you must be able to recognize key places in the development of the author's argument: where new or contradictory information is introduced, where important ideas are emphasized, and where the author moves from discussing a commonly held idea to introducing a challenge to that idea. We're going to take another look at this passage:

> A few years ago the city council of Monza, Italy, barred pet owners from keeping goldfish in curved fishbowls. The sponsors of the measure explained that it is cruel to keep a fish in a bowl because the curved sides give the fish a
> 5 distorted view of reality. Aside from the measure's significance to the poor goldfish, the story raises an interesting philosophical question: How do we know that the reality we perceive is true? The goldfish is seeing a version of reality that is different from ours, but can we be sure it is
> 10 any less real? For all we know, we, too, may spend our entire lives staring out at the world through a distorting lens.
>   In physics, the question is not academic. Indeed, physicists are finding themselves in a similar predicament to the goldfish's. *For decades we have strived to come up with*
> 15 *an ultimate theory of everything—one complete and consistent set of fundamental laws of nature that explain every aspect of reality.* **It now appears that this quest may yield not a single theory but a family of interconnected theories, each describing its own version of reality, as if it viewed**
> 20 **the universe through its own fishbowl.**

Lines 5-8 ("Aside from…true") signal a shift from

(A) a criticism of an explanation to an acknowledgment of its significance
(B) a discussion of a problem to a description of a possible solution
(C) an illustrative anecdote to a discussion of a general concern
(D) a presentation of a claim to a questioning of that claim
(E) an account of a personal experience to an objective analysis

Like many Critical Reading questions, this one appears to be considerably more difficult than it actually is. Look at the beginning of the passage: what is the author doing? He's *telling a story*. That much is pretty easy to figure out. Story = *anecdote*. That's all you need to know to answer the question. (C) is the only choice that includes that information. And indeed, those lines do mark the place where the author transitions from that story into the larger problem of the passage: perception vs. reality, and the relationship between that idea and physics.

Narrative Point of View

Questions that ask directly about narrative point of view are extremely rare, but they do occur, and you should therefore be familiar with the two most common types.

A **first person** narrative is written from the perspective of the narrator and includes the word "I." All personal anecdotes are, by definition, written in the first person. For example:

> On one of the first days I was coming into the building, a tall, thin aristocratic-looking white woman who appeared to be about my age, and whom we ultimately referred to as the Katherine Hepburn among us, came breathlessly down a narrow hallway, saying to me (whom she had never seen except in that one instant), "Do you know where I can get a drink of water?"
>
> She said this as if she had known me all my life, as if I were a sister, a brother, a friend. She may have even grabbed my hand. I wasn't put off by the fact that she was a stranger. Her presence in that question made me feel in an instant as if I had known her all my life.

A **third person** narrative, on the other hand, is written from an objective perspective and describes other people rather than the narrator him- or herself. For example:

> A few years ago the city council of Monza, Italy, barred pet owners from keeping goldfish in curved fish-bowls. The sponsors of the measure explained that it is cruel to keep a fish in a bowl because the curved sides give the fish a distorted view of reality. Aside from the measure's significance to the poor goldfish, the story raises an interesting philosophical question: How do we know that the reality we perceive is true?

Although this passage also contains an anecdote, it focuses on other people, not on the narrator. Note that unlike the first passage, its tone is much more neutral and detached. The majority of SAT passages are told from this perspective.

Second person narratives are written to "you" – they address the reader directly. Although passages in the second person can appear on the SAT, they do so very rarely, and the chance of your both encountering such a passage and being asked a question that requires you to identify its narrative point of view is extremely slim. For an example and discussion of the relationship between second person narrative and tone, please see p. 237.

Point of view questions can also ask about the narrator's perspective in terms of age or time. These questions tend to occur when passages discuss events that took place at different times, or when the narrator is looking back on an event. For example, look back at p. 244 for the full version of the first passage above. You could see a question like this:

This passage is narrated from the perspective of

(A) an adult recounting a significant childhood memory
(B) an adult recalling a memorable experience that
    occurred earlier in her adult life
(C) a student describing an individual who plays
    a significant role in her life
(D) an acting teacher trying to motivate her students
    to take more risks in their work
(E) a third-person narrator analyzing a story told to
    her by an acquaintance

Careful here. You can use the repeated appearance of the word "I" to eliminate (E) immediately, and you can probably also get rid of (D) without too much trouble since there's nothing in the passage to directly indicate that the narrator is talking to students, never mind trying to motivate them.

This is where things can get tricky. Let's start with (A). Yes, the passage is told by an adult recounting a significant memory, but careful – it's not a *childhood* memory. Although the author never comes out and states that she was an adult when this happened, we can directly infer from the fact that the "woman" she encounters is "about her age" that she's not a child. Now let's take (C) – if you're not thinking precisely, it's easy to jump to conclusions. After all, the author does talk about being a student, and she certainly does seem to be talking about someone who's made a big impact on her.

But think about what's really going on the passage: the author is an adult who's *looking back* on an even that occurred earlier in her life. Even though she's *describing* what happened when she was a student, she's no longer a student at the time she's telling the story. The entire action of the story takes place in the *past*, even if the author does switch into the present tense when she begins to reflect on the significance of the encounter. In addition, look at the tense of the verb in the answer choice: "plays" is in the present tense, implying an ongoing situation. The passage focuses on one single encounter, an encounter that's over. Nowhere does the passage directly suggest that the Katherine Hepburn-esque woman plays a significant role in the narrator's actual life beyond the theater. And no, we can't infer it – all we know is that she had a big impact in that one moment, and that her actions led to the narrator's understanding of the *concept* of urgency in acting. Anything beyond that is too much of a stretch. So which answer describes what's actually occurring in the passage? (B).

Rhetorical Strategy Exercises

1.   Why is the connection between smells and memories so strong? The reason for these associations is that the brain's olfactory bulb is connected to both the amygdala (an emotion center) and to the
5 hippocampus, which is involved in memory. And, because smells serve a survival function (odors can keep us from eating spoiled or poisonous foods), some of these associations are made very quickly, and may even involve a one-time association.

The last sentence includes which rhetorical strategy?

(A) digression
(B) detailed description
(C) rhetorical question
(D) speculation
(E) anecdote

2.   Most people have so-called flashbulb memories of where they were and what they were doing when something momentous happened. (Unfortunately, staggeringly terrible news seems to come out of the
5 blue more often than staggeringly good news.) But as clear and detailed as these memories feel, psychologists have discovered they are surprisingly inaccurate.

The passage contains which rhetorical strategy?

(A) generalization
(B) digression
(C) euphemism
(D) direct citation
(E) metaphor

3.   Shakespeare in the world of ants, untroubled by any such war between honor and treachery, and chained by the rigid commands of instinct to a tiny repertory of feeling, would be able to write only one drama of triumph
5 and one of tragedy. Ordinary people, on the other hand, can invent an endless variety of such stories, and compose an infinite symphony of ambience and mood.

The primary rhetorical strategy used in the first sentence is

(A) irony
(B) figurative language
(C) hyperbole
(D) appeal to emotion
(E) digression

4.   The Romans started making concrete more than 2,000 years ago, but it wasn't quite like today's concrete. They had a different formula, which resulted in a substance that was not as
5 strong as the modern product. Yet structures like the Pantheon and the Colosseum have survived for centuries, often with little to no maintenance. That resistance, or durability against the elements, may be due to one of the concrete's key ingredients:
10 volcanic ash.

In lines 7-8 ("That resistance…elements"), the author does which of the following?

(A) raises an objection
(B) concedes a point
(C) offers a solution
(D) makes an allusion
(E) defines a term

5.   Until the past few years, physicists agreed that the entire universe is generated from a few mathematical truths and principles of symmetry, perhaps throwing in a handful of parameters like the
5 mass of the electron. It seemed that we were closing in on a vision of our universe in which everything could be calculated, predicted, and understood. However, two theories, eternal inflation and string theory, now suggest that the same fundamental
10 principles from which the laws of nature derive may lead to many different self-consistent universes, with many different properties.

In lines 8-12, the author does which of the following?

(A) highlights a paradox
(B) exaggerates an effect
(C) concedes a point
(D) speculates about an outcome
(E) acknowledges a drawback

6.   Ideas matter. A relatively small number can be classed as major historical events. And many times, their best, most eloquent expression has been on paper, stamped in ink, sewn on one side, and bound between
5   hard covers. In the beginning was the word, sure, but there's also a lot to be said for the book. Think of Abraham Lincoln's comment, one hundred and fifty years ago, upon meeting the creator of a book, "So, this is the little lady who made this big war." He
10 was speaking to Harriet Beecher Stowe, the author of Uncle Tom's Cabin. As we are asked to contemplate the disappearance of books as books as such, it's worth pausing over the astonishing range of personal, social, and political purposes that have been served by books:
15 the liberation of individuals, the reinforcement of community, the expansion of self-knowledge, the publication of scientific findings, the spread of lies and promulgation of facts. Vast are the aims served by books.

Which of the following is a rhetorical strategy used in this passage?

(A) irony
(B) rhetorical question
(C) aside
(D) dry humor
(E) direct quotation

7.   The book is a self-contained utterance. It is finished, the very opposite of a "slug" you encounter on a website casting about for visitors to contribute writing and research. It is much more than a slug, much more than the
5   most basic information readily available. The discrete physical embodiment of text, it makes the perfect gift, the perfect giveaway, the perfect method of saying, "Consider the following . . ." We often think of imaginative literature when we think of book-reading, along with notional scenes
10 of people entering other worlds through books, but the world we know, the communities to which we already belong, are reified and reinforced by books. Such is the incredible and incredibly flexible power of this primitive technology.

1. The primary rhetorical strategy used in lines 1-8 ("The book…following")

(A) euphemism
(B) repetition
(C) rhetorical questioning
(D) appeal to authority
(E) metaphor

2. In lines 7-13, the author primarily makes use of

(A) broad generalization
(B) allusion
(C) understatement
(D) paradox
(E) irony

8.   Women's and African-American reading groups not only reinforced community bonds— and introduced countless readers to great works of literature—but indirectly and perhaps
5   unwittingly cleared a path to suffrage and other civil rights. In reading highbrow literature and discussing it in something like a classroom atmosphere, many women's reading groups created a rather formal semipublic arena for
10 women to grow intellectually. No wonder that in Texas clubwomen led efforts to establish a women's dormitory at the University of Texas at Austin, funded local and statewide scholarships for women, and were instrumental in
15 founding what is today Texas Women's University. And though reading groups might host visiting suffragist speakers, in general the reading groups tended to be too conservative for such reforms, even as they trained their
20 members in many a fine point of civic virtue.

Lines 1-6 ("Women's…civil rights") can best be characterized as

(A) an understatement
(B) an exclamation
(C) an assertion
(D) a concession
(E) an accusation

9.   Marie Curie was never easy to understand or
categorize. That was because she was a pioneer, an
outlier, unique for the newness and immensity of her
achievements. But it was also because of her sex. Curie
5 worked during a great age of innovation, but proper
women of her time were thought to be too sentimental to
perform objective science. She would forever be
considered a bit strange, not just a great scientist but a
great woman scientist. You would not expect the president
10 of the United States to praise one of Curie's male
contemporaries by calling attention to his manhood and
his devotion as a father. Professional science until fairly
recently was a man's world, and in Curie's time it was
rare for a woman even to participate in academic
15 physics, never mind triumph over it.

Which of the following best describes this passage?

(A) a description of a controversial figure followed by
     an impassioned defense of that figure
(B) a comparison of several figures followed by an
     analysis of one of the figures
(C) a general assertion followed by an explanation of
     that assertion
(D) a discussion of an injustice followed by a
     denunciation of that injustice
(E) an analysis of a historical figure followed by an
     appeal to the reader's sympathy

10.   There's a certain way jazz musicians from the
1930s pose for photographs, half-turned to face the
camera, symmetrically arrayed around the bandleader,
who can be identified by his regal smile and proximity
5 to the microphone. Publicity stills of the period were
the equivalent of English court paintings, hackwork
intended to exalt their subjects and attract admiration to
their finery. Bandleaders even took titles borrowed from
the aristocracy: Duke Ellington, Count Basie, Earl
10 Hines . . . well, Earl was actually the man's given name,
but he lived up to it in a way no tracksuited rap star
could approach, no matter how big the diamond in his
earlobe.

In lines 5-8 ("Publicity...finery"), the author makes use of

(A) euphemism
(B) cliché
(C) summary
(D) simile
(E) analogy

11.   I vacillate on Thoreau. I consider myself fairly
well read when it comes to the writers of
Concord…though certainly no expert. I love *Walden*.
In my younger days, more times than I can count, I
5 walked the same woods he walked and was inspired
by his love of simplicity and nature. I used to swim in
Walden frequently and always enjoyed the quiet
corner of the pond where his tiny dwelling once
stood. "I went into the woods because I wished to
10 live deliberately," he wrote of his two-year stint at
Walden. "I did not wish to live what was not life,
living is so dear…I wanted to live deep and suck out
all the marrow of life." How can you not admire
passion like that?
15   Lately, however, I have been reading an
interesting compilation of excerpts from his journals.
The collection highlights those journal entries in
which Thoreau wrote specifically about his fellow
townsfolk: bits and pieces describing the inhabitants
20 of Concord, their habits, their lives, and lots of
fascinating period detail. But what struck me most
about Thoreau's observations is his judgmental tone
of superiority. As a younger man, poring over
Walden, I believe I idealized Thoreau. Now I begin
25 to wonder if he was, in fact, a misanthrope.

1. Throughout the passage, the author makes use of

   (A) personification
   (B) metaphor
   (C) analogy
   (D) personal anecdote
   (E) appeal to emotion

2. Which of the following best describes the narrative
   point of view presented in this passage?

   (A) An author recognizes the influence of
        a particular writer on his work
   (B) An objective narrator analyzes the strengths
        and weaknesses of an argument
   (C) An adult reconsiders an opinion he held
        in his youth
   (D) A historian discovers new details about the
        life of an author
   (E) A biographer seeks to understand an author's
        life by reading that author's works

12.   In an essay in 1984—at the dawn of the personal computer era—the novelist Thomas Pynchon wondered if it was "O.K. to be a Luddite," meaning someone who opposes technological progress. A better question today
5 is whether it's even possible. Technology is everywhere, and a recent headline at an Internet humor site perfectly captured how difficult it is to resist: "Luddite invents machine to destroy technology quicker." Like all good satire, the mock headline comes perilously close to the
10 truth. Modern Luddites do indeed invent "machines"—in the form of computer viruses, cyberworms and other malware—to disrupt the technologies that trouble them.

The headline in lines 7-8 is an example of

(A) irony
(B) digression
(C) euphemism
(D) admonition
(E) historical allusion

13.   In our attempts to uncover the history of the cosmos, we have continually discovered that the segments most deeply shrouded in mystery are those that deal with origins – of the universe
5 itself, of its most massive structures (galaxies and galaxy clusters), and of the stars that provide most of the light in the cosmos. These mysteries arise in large part because during the cosmic "dark ages," when matter was just beginning to
10 organize itself into self-contained units such as stars and galaxies, most of this matter generated little or no detectable radiation. When we turn to the origin of planets, the mysteries deepen. We lack not only observations of the crucial, initial
15 stages of planetary formation but also successful theories of how the planets began to form.
    Astrophysicists may now have more data but they have no better answers than before. The beginnings of planet building pose a remarkably
20 intractable problem, to the point that one of the world's experts on the subject, Scott Tremaine, has elucidated (partly in jest) Tremaine's laws of planet formation. The first of these laws states that "all theoretical predictions about the prop-
25 erties of exosolar planets are wrong," and the second that "the most secure prediction about planet formation is that it can't happen." Tremaine's humor underscores the ineluctable fact that planets do exist, despite our inability to
30 explain this astronomical enigma.

The situation described in the last sentence can best be described as

(A) a paradox
(B) an allegory
(C) a cliché
(D) an allusion
(E) a metaphor

14.   By the middle of his life, Edmund Wilson was
a fat, ferocious man: petty, pretentious, and petulant,
a failure at many of the most ordinary tasks of life.
But he could dance: through a poem, through a
5 book, through a library. He was the Nureyev* at what
he did—a genius, really: probably the greatest reader
the United States has ever known.

      That's not to say he was the most influential
figure of his time. Sometimes he got it wrong.
10 His prose was merely good enough—not sparkling;
only clear and well-organized—and he got nosebleeds
whenever he tried to follow philosophy up into the
stratosphere of metaphysics. For that matter, he never
understood escapism, and so, in a golden age
15 of Hollywood screwball fluff, he condemned
American movies as inferior to European—to say
nothing of his famous essay that thundered against
mystery novels.

      Mostly, though, he got it right. And if he seems
20 lost to us now, that's not just because we have
no similar genius to occupy the space that he filled.
It's also because that space has nearly disappeared.
The magisterial critic has no role left in the United
States, really. We appreciate, we enjoy, we peruse, we
25 watch. But we don't define ourselves by reading
anymore. The novel, the premiere art form of western
civilization over the last two hundred years, has ceased
to be the mark of civilization. And so what need have
we of Edmund Wilson—that fat, ferocious man, so
30 nimble on his feet?

*Nureyev was a great twentieth century Russian ballet
  dancer.

1.   What is the primary rhetorical strategy
      used in lines 4-7?

    (A) understatement
    (B) allusion
    (C) cliché
    (D) euphemism
    (E) paraphrase

2. Lines 8-11 ("That's not...organized")
   can best be described as

    (A) qualification
    (B) hyperbole
    (C) digression
    (D) justification
    (E) appeal to emotion

3. Which rhetorical strategy does the author
   use in lines 11-13 ("and he...metaphysics"?

    (A) comparison
    (B) hyperbole
    (C) dry humor
    (D) allusion
    (E) extended analogy

4. Which rhetorical strategy does the author
   use in the last paragraph?

    (A) paradox
    (B) digression
    (C) analogy
    (D) allusion
    (E) rhetorical questioning

15.   Many readers, faced with Thoreau's enigmatic Yankee persona, have resorted to a kind of pop-culture shorthand for describing his life. As the capsule summary goes, Thoreau was an oddball loner who lived by a lake, writing

5   in praise of nature and against modern progress.

    But the full story of Thoreau's life involves subtleties and contradictions that call his popular image into question. One idea that has persisted is that he was a hermit who cared little for others, yet he was active in his

10   community and responsible for circulating petitions for neighbors in need. In yet another way Thoreau was politically active, penning an essay, "Civil Disobedience," that would later inform the thinking of Mohandas Gandhi and the Rev. Martin Luther King Jr.

15   Despite his fame as a champion of solitude—a practice that he chronicled with wisdom and wit—Thoreau made no secret of the social life he indulged during his stay at Walden Pond from 1845 to 1847. In fact, one of the chapters of Walden, titled "Visitors," offers an extended

20   account of Thoreau's dealings with others. In it, the lifelong bachelor Thoreau lays out his rules for entertaining:

    I had three chairs in my house; one for solitude, two
    for friendship, three for society. When visitors came in

25   *larger and unexpected numbers there was but the third*
    chair for them all, but they generally economized the
    room by standing up... I have had twenty-five or thirty
    souls, with their bodies, at once under my roof, and yet
    we often parted without being aware that we had come

30   *very near to one another.*

    But even if Thoreau wasn't always averse to human company, the idea that he was a loner might stem from the assumption that he was the kind of person who should have been alone. Thoreau was capable of

35   friendship, but on his own terms. He could be prickly to a fault. "I sometimes hear my Friends complain finely that I do not appreciate their fineness," he once wrote. "I shall not tell them whether I do or not. As if they expected a vote of thanks for every fine thing which they uttered or

40   did."

    Even those who liked him conceded that Thoreau could be a cold fish. In a letter to his friend Daniel Ricketson in 1860, Thoreau addresses Ricketson's puzzlement over why he hasn't come to visit, telling Ricketson, without much

45   ceremony, that he's had much better things to do. But after explaining himself, Thoreau continued to correspond with Ricketson. Ralph Waldo Emerson, Thoreau's close friend and mentor, who came to grudgingly admire Thoreau's argumentative streak, famously described him as "not to be

50   subdued, always manly and able, but rarely tender,

as if he did not feel himself except in opposition." In remembrance of Thoreau, Emerson offered this observation from one of Thoreau's friends: "I love Henry, but I cannot like him; and as for taking his

55   arm, I should as soon think of taking the arm of an elm-tree."

1. Which of the following rhetorical strategies does the author use in the passage?

    (A) understatement
    (B) direct quotation
    (C) irony
    (D) rhetorical questioning
    (E) analogy

2. In lines 31-34 ("But even...alone"), the author does which of the following?

    (A) qualifies an assertion
    (B) notes a paradox
    (C) introduces a digression
    (D) defines a term
    (E) offers a hypothesis

3. The author relies on which of the following in lines 41-47 ("Even those...Ricketson")?

    (A) anecdote
    (B) digression
    (C) oratory
    (D) euphemism
    (E) paradox

4. The quotation in lines 53-56 makes use of

    (A) analogy
    (B) anecdote
    (C) wry humor
    (D) exaggeration
    (E) cliché

Official Guide Rhetorical Strategy Questions

Test 1	Section 2	Question 7	p. 391
Test 1	Section 2	Question 15	p. 393
Test 1	Section 2	Question 23	p. 395
Test 1	Section 5	Question 22	p. 405
Test 1	Section 9	Question 16	p. 428
Test 2	Section 4	Question 25	p. 462
Test 2	Section 7	Question 17	p. 479
Test 3	Section 4	Question 15	p. 522
Test 3	Section 7	Question 9	p. 538
Test 3	Section 7	Question 23	p. 542
Test 4	Section 5	Question 22	p. 592
Test 4	Section 8	Question 16	p. 607
Test 5	Section 9	Question 7	p. 674
Test 6	Section 3	Question 16	p. 710
Test 6	Section 7	Question 17	p. 727
Test 7	Section 8	Question 7	p. 792
Test 9	Section 4	Question 13	p. 900
Test 9	Section 4	Question 15	p. 901
Test 9	Section 6	Question 11	p. 911
Test 10	Section 6	Question 11	p. 973
Test 10	Section 6	Question 16	p. 975
Test 10	Section 6	Question 24	p. 976

Explanations: Rhetorical Strategy Exercises

1. D

The last sentence states that *some of these associations may even involve a one-time association*, with the word "may" indicating that the author is describing a situation that could occur in the future or, in other words, speculating.

2. A

The author describes the phenomenon of "flashbulb memories" in broad, non-specific terms, using general phrases like "most people," "something momentous," "good news/terrible news" and providing no details.

3. C

The first sentence uses a variety of figurative devices such as personification (imagining Shakespeare as an ant) and metaphor (the *war* between honor and treachery, *chained* by rigid commands of instinct), making (C) the correct answer.

4. E

In line 8, the information between the commas (*or durability against the elements*) serves to define the word "resistance."

5. D

As in #1, the word "may" (*eternal inflation and string theory…may lead to many self-consistent universes*) indicates that the author is describing a hypothetical situation that could result from physicists' research, i.e. speculating.

6. E

The quotation marks in lines 8-9 indicate that the author is directly citing Abraham Lincoln.

7. 1B, 2A

7.1 The author repeats several words and phrases in these lines: *it is finished…it is much more than a slug, it makes the perfect gift, the perfect giveaway, the perfect method of saying…*

7.2 The repetition of the word "we" as well the broad references to "communities" and "worlds" indicate that the author is making a broad generalization.

8. C

The first sentence of the passage states the main point: it's an argument (i.e. an assertion) that the author goes on to spend the rest of the passage supporting.

9. C

Don't be distracted by the complexity of some of the answer choices. The passage is organized as a simple claim in the first sentence (*Marie Curie was never easy to understand or categorize*) followed by an explanation, as indicated by the word "because" in lines 2 and 4.

10. E

In lines 5-6, the author states that *publicity stills were the equivalent of English court paintings*. The word "equivalent" indicates that the author is comparing or drawing an *analogy* between the representations of jazz musicians and those of English aristocrats.

11. 1D, 2C

11.1 The fact that the passage consists of brief stories written in the first person ("I" and "my" appear repeatedly) indicates that the author's primary strategy is the personal anecdote.

11.2 Although the author "admired" Thoreau immensely in his "younger days" (implying that he is an adult), he now views Thoreau as unpleasant. In other words, he is reconsidering an opinion that he held in his youth.

12. A

In line 4, a Luddite is defined a someone who "opposes technological progress," and the headline plays with that idea. Although "destroying technology quicker" is something that a Luddite would logically want to do, inventing a machine (a form of technology) to do so is exactly the *opposite* of how such a person would go about it. Since irony can be defined as a situation whose outcome is the opposite of what one has been led to believe it will be, the headline can be considered ironic.

13. A

The situation described in the last sentence can be summarized as follows: the available data and models indicate that planets should not be able to form, but of course they do. So in other words, something exists when all the data says that it can't – a logical contradiction, i.e. a **paradox**.

14. 1B, 2A, 3C, 4E

14.1 In these lines, the author makes a reference, i.e. an allusion, to Nureyev.

14.2 In the first paragraph, the author makes a fairly extreme claim, namely that *[Wilson] was the greatest reader America has even known* – in line 9, he **qualifies** that claim, or makes it less absolute, by calling the reader's attention to Wilson's shortcomings (*Sometimes he got it wrong*).

14.3 In lines 11-13, the author uses a subtle, wry, i.e dry, humor to describe Wilson's difficulty in understanding philosophy – he plays on the idea that philosophy is an "elevated" subject by treating it as something *literally* high, using the image of a nosebleed (something that can occur when a person's body is unaccustomed to being at such a high altitude) to convey Wilson's puzzlement. Because the humor emerges from a subtle manipulation of ideas and associations, it can be called dry.

14.4 The question mark at the end of the last sentence indicates a rhetorical question.

15. 1B, 2E 3A, 4C

15.1 Lines 26-33 and 39-43 contain direct quotes from Thoreau. The easiest way to answer this question is simply to scan the passage for quotation marks.

15.2 The key word is *might* (*the idea that [Thoreau] was a loner might stem from the assumption that he was the kind of person who should have been alone*), which indicates that the author is suggesting a possible explanation (=a hypothesis) for why people believe that Thoreau was a loner.

15.3 In lines 45-49, the author uses the story or "anecdote" of Thoreau's letter to Ricketson in order to illustrate Thoreau's lack of warmth toward his friends.

15.4 The dry humor emerges from Emerson's play on word: he uses the word "arm" to refer to both a person's arm and the branch of a tree. By punning on that word, Emerson subtly but pointedly conveys Thoreau's aloofness and lack of warmth.

Glossary of Rhetorical Terms

Whenever possible, I have listed shortcuts for recognizing rhetorical terms.

Terms that are likely to appear as correct answers are marked with an **asterisk**.

*(Personal) Anecdote – A brief story. A *personal* anecdote is simply a story from the author's experience.

Shortcut: I, my, me

Personal pronouns (*I, my, me*) will always appear, sometimes multiple times, when the correct answer is "personal anecdote." If that answer is listed among the choices, you should immediately scan the passage for these words. If they appear, it is usually unnecessary to look at the other answers.

Example:

On a mid-August day with a heat index of 115 degrees, in a rental car with slow pickup, **I** drive through the Orlando suburbs searching for Eatonville, a three-square-mile town of 2,400 residents. **I** keep getting lost. Finally a brown "Eatonville Historic District" sign appears, and fifteen miles later it dawns on **me** that **I** have gone too far. I turn back, find the city limits, and enter Eatonville. At the "Welcome to Maitland" sign, **I** realize **I** have driven through the entire town. It took three minutes.

*Rhetorical Question – A question asked without expectation of response, usually for dramatic effect or to emphasize a point.

Shortcut: question marks

When "rhetorical question(s)" appears as an answer choice, you should scan the passage for question marks. If they are present, it will be the correct answer; otherwise, it can be quickly eliminated.

You do not have to worry about the SAT tricking you by including non-rhetorical questions in a passage – virtually any question asked by the author of an SAT passage will be a rhetorical question, so if a question marks appears, you can choose that answer without hesitation.

Example:

In our time, reality stars can become "fame-ish" overnight; but the people of the nineteenth century bestowed fame on individuals—mostly male—who it felt had made significant contributions to history. **Why did the residents of Washington City, the members of government and their families, and, indeed, all of America declare Dolley the nation's "Queen"? What did they understand about Dolley Madison that we don't?**

(Direct) Citation/Quotation – word-for-word transcription of words spoken or written by someone other than the author.

Shortcut: quotation marks

Quotation marks will always be used to indicate that the author is including someone else's words or thoughts verbatim. Whenever you see "direct citation" or "direct quotation" listed among the answer choices, simply scan the passage for quotes.

Example:

Make no mistake—Dolley Madison was as fiercely partisan as any male politician. Her declaration, **"I confess I do not admire contention in any form, either political or civil"** is often cited by historians as proof of her pacific nature. The second half of the statement reveals more – **"I would rather fight with my hands than my tongue"**… During his presidency, James Madison was hampered by what Dolley called "a Capricious Senate," whose objections she characterized as "almost treason." Still, she subsumed her feelings, so that one guest declared, **"By her deportment in her own house you cannot discover who is her husband's friends or foes."**

*Allusion – Reference

An allusion is simply a reference, usually to a work of art, literature, or well-known story or place. While it appears very frequently among the answer choices to rhetorical strategy questions, it appears less frequently as a correct answer than either "anecdote" or "rhetorical questioning."

Shortcut: footnotes

Occasionally, ETS will provide a footnote for a reference that high school students cannot be expected to be familiar with – if the answer "allusion" appears in regard to a footnoted section of the passage, it's probably correct.

Example:

The United States recently crossed a digital **Rubicon***: for the first time, more data was sent over wireless devices than by telephone.

*The Rubicon is a river in Northern Italy, and the phrase "crossing the Rubicon" means "passing a point of no return" because Julius Caesar crossed it with his army in 49 A.D. and began a civil war.

Important: If the answer "obscure allusions" appears, it is almost certainly wrong.

ETS deliberately avoids using passages that include such references because they would not be understood by most test-takers. If a passage does include a (single) reference that most high school students cannot reasonably expected to be familiar with, a footnote will be provided.

Assertion – Declarative statement or argument.

In SAT passages, statements of assertion are usually topic sentences and/or located at key places within an argument (e.g. the last sentence of the first paragraph). Assertions are typically blunt and are characterized by a tone of great confidence; they do not include support or explanations.

Example:

Ideas matter. A relatively small number can be classed as major historical events. And many times, their best, most eloquent expression has been on paper, stamped in ink, sewn on one side, and bound between hard covers.

Appeal (to Emotion) – An urgent plea for the reader's sympathy or attention.

Because the tone of most SAT passages is relatively measured and neutral, **"appeal" (or "appeal to emotion") will nearly always be wrong** when it appears among the answer choices.

Comparison – Discussion of the similarities between two people or two things.

Shortcut: like, similar to

Example:

Just like human beings, chimpanzees can share a joke but they are also capable of sharing laughter even when they don't find something particularly funny. A recent study of wild chimpanzees has found that laughter occurs not just when chimps are enjoying themselves but also when they want to promote social bonding – **much like** human smiles help people relate to one another in a conversation.

Contrast – Discussion of the differences between two people or two things

Shortcut: unlike, in contrast to

Example:

The **essential difference** between literary and scientific style is the use of metaphor. What counts in science is the importance of the discovery. Lyrical expression in literature, **on the other hand**, is a device to communicate emotional feeling directly from the mind of the writer to the mind of the reader. There is **no such goal** in scientific reporting, where the purpose of the author is to persuade the reader by evidence and reasoning of the validity and importance of the discovery.

Comparisons may include either literal (as in the above example) or **figurative language**. Types of comparisons that use figurative language include **similes**, **metaphors**, and **personification** (described later in this section).

On the SAT, either "figurative language" itself OR a specific rhetorical device (e.g. metaphor), may be listed as an answer choice. You will never, however, see both "figurative language" *and* a specific rhetorical device appear as answers to the same question.

Metaphor – Comparison that does not use "like" or "as" but that instead states that something **is** something else.

> **Example:**
>
> The dance **revolution** was fought on many fronts, but the **key battle** took place at Vermont's Bennington College.

Simile – Comparison using "like" or "as"

> **Example:**
>
> Named after the Greek Island of Lefkada, artist and author Lafcadio Hearn was **like** an island unto himself.

*Analogy – Comparison, typically in the form "x is to y" but also in the form of either a simile or a metaphor. Similes and metaphors are types of analogies.

> On the SAT, the terms "analogy" and "simile" are used more or less interchangeably; the former appears as an answer choice much more frequently than the latter, and you will not be asked to decide between them.
>
> **Example:**
>
> [Zora Neale Hurston] was not a joiner of movements or trends. **Like her hometown, Hurston was iconoclastic.**

An **Extended Analogy** is an analogy that continues beyond a single comparison. While it is highly unlikely that the SAT would include an extended analogy that lasted the length of a full passage, you could see one that lasted several sentences or even a paragraph.

> **Example:**
>
> The dance **revolution** was fought on many fronts, but the **key battle** took place at Vermont's Bennington College. It was here in the 1930s, amid the cow farms in the bucolic Green Mountains, that the giants of modern dance—Graham, Humphrey, Holm, Weidman—fine-tuned their techniques and trained their **dancer armies** to **spread the revolution** across the country.

Allegory – An allegory is a story in which the main elements (characters, settings, etc.) all function as symbols for something else. Although an allegory may be discussed or referred to in an SAT passage, passages themselves are highly unlikely to contain allegories.

Personification – Describing an inanimate object as if it possessed human characteristics

Example:

Five-fingered ferns hung over the water and **dropped** spray from their **fingertips**… The high mountain wind coasted, **sighing** through the pass and **whistled** on the edges of the big blocks of broken granite.

Euphemism – Replacement of an offensive or unpleasant word with a less offensive one.

Example:

The early years of the telephone brought concerns over the unwanted entry—via telephone line—of **unsavory characters** into the home, and some people called for laws to regulate criminal use of the phone.

In the sentence above, the more refined phrase "unsavory characters" replaces the much blunter-sounding "criminals."

(Detailed) Description – (Vivid) account or recollection of a person, object, event, etc.

Shortcut: lots of adjectives

Example:

There's a picture of Hines with his band on the stage at the Pearl Theater in Philadelphia, exuding swank. Their suit pants, which bear stripes of black satin down the seams, break perfectly over their gleaming shoes; their jacket lapels have the span of a Madagascar fruit bat; their hair is slicked. They were on top of their world.

Also see Rhetorical Strategy "Blackbeard" passage, first paragraph, p. 253.

*Hyperbole/Exaggeration – Overstated or over-the-top language employed for dramatic or humorous effect.

Example:

By the middle of his life, Edmund Wilson was a fat, ferocious man: petty, pretentious, and petulant, a failure at many of the most ordinary tasks of life. But he could dance: through a poem, through a book, through a library. He was the Nureyev at what he did—a genius, really: probably **the greatest reader America has ever known**.

*Understatement – Opposite of hyperbole. Use of deliberately restrained, un-dramatic language. Form of irony and dry/wry humor, often used to satirize or mock.

> **Example:**
>
> William Shakespeare is an author who has become **rather well known** for his theatrical writing.

Since Shakespeare is probably the best-known English dramatist in history, saying that he is "rather well known" constitutes a massive understatement.

Wordplay – Verbal wit or punning, often involving double meanings of words.

> **Example:**
>
> Food is at the center of our anxieties about science and modernity, yet the truth is that it has become a scapegoat, or perhaps I should say *scapetofu*, for a host of imaginary sins we associate with technology.

Understanding the tone of this passage requires that you recognize the play on words involved in *scapetofu*. A scape*goat* is an innocent person who gets blamed for someone else's problem or crime – and here the author is saying that people blame food for problems they wrongly believe technology has created. By altering the original word and replacing *goat* (an animal and type of meat) with *tofu* (a meat substitute that vegetarians are often made fun of for eating), the author is implicitly mocking the people who subscribe to this belief. In addition, the phrase "or should I say…" is deliberately coy and understated, the literary equivalent of a wink. His tone could thus be described as *wry*, or *facetious*, or *ironic*.

Paradox – Statement or situation that appears illogical or contradictory but that may reveal an underlying truth.

> **Example:**
>
> The case of Henry Thoreau stands as proof for the whole notion of human inscrutability. **This man told us more of himself than perhaps any other American writer, and still he remains beyond fathoming**.

Irony – Incongruity (gap) between what would logically be expected from a situation and what actually occurs

> The example for "paradox" above also describes a situation that is ironic. Because Thoreau "told us more of himself than perhaps any other American writer," it is logical to assume that people would have a clear idea of him as a person. That, however, is not the case. Instead, "he remains beyond fathoming" (incomprehensible). We thus have a clear contradiction between expectations (we would expect to know a lot about Thoreau based on all he wrote) and outcome (we don't know much at all).

Dry/Wry Humor – Form or subtle, often dark, humor that is frequently based on wordplay, irony, or sarcasm.

Example:

In our attempts to uncover the history of the cosmos, we have continually discovered that the segments most deeply shrouded in mystery are those that deal with origins…The beginnings of planet building pose a remarkably intractable problem, to the point that one of the world's experts on the subject, Scott Tremaine, has elucidated (partly in **jest**) Tremaine's laws of planet formation. **The first of these laws states that "all theoretical predictions about the properties of exosolar planets are wrong," and the second that "the most secure prediction about planet formation is that it can't happen."** Tremaine's **humor** underscores the ineluctable fact that planets do exist, despite our inability to explain this astronomical enigma.

When you read that little excerpt, it's probably safe to assume that you didn't immediately start howling with laughter. You might not even have been sure why it was supposed to be funny. (If, on the other hand, you did collapse into giggles, you probably don't have much trouble identifying this kind of humor.)

Although the words "jest" (kidding) and "humor" in this case directly indicate that Tremaine's "laws" are supposed to be funny, you need to think about what they're actually saying in order to understand the humor. Tremaine is making fun of the difficulty scientists have in understanding the beginning of the universe by using typically dry, scientific language to state complete absurdities. It is of course ridiculous to suggest that "the most secure prediction about planet formation is that it can't happen" because if that were true, there would be no Earth and no people. Tremaine himself wouldn't exist, and he certainly couldn't have written this passage!

Even if you are not rolling with laughter at this point or do not even find that excerpt particularly funny, you still need to be willing to understand that the *author's intention* is for it to be amusing. And to reiterate: it is irrelevant if you don't *feel* that those lines are funny; the author's deliberate use of scientific language to state something that's logically impossible indicates that *he* intends for them to be funny. **And the author's intention is the only thing that counts.**

Cliché – Trite saying that expresses a common or banal idea.

Example:

A bird in the hand is worth two in the bush.
What goes around comes around.
As light as a feather.
Every cloud has a silver lining.

Because SAT passages tend to be taken from relatively serious authors who go out of their way not to include clichés in their writing, this answer is highly unlikely to be correct.

Generalization – Broad statement or assertion.

Example:

Studies show that when **we** read nonfiction, **we** read with our shields up. **We** are critical and skeptical. But when **we** are absorbed in a story, **we** drop our intellectual guard. **We** are moved emotionally, and this seems to make **us** rubbery and easy to shape. But perhaps the most impressive finding is just how fiction shapes **us**. Fiction enhances **our** ability to understand other people; it promotes a deep morality.

Qualification – Inclusion of additional information to "soften" a blunt or harsh statement, or to provide a more detailed understanding of a generalization.

Shortcut: dashes, parentheses

Example:

[General Statement] There is nothing so stimulating for the hands and the mind as studying a musical instrument. **[Qualification]** The journey to mastery demands focus, discipline, lightness of touch, musical intuition, and persistence.

In the above example, the general statement is quite extreme: it states that *nothing* is as stimulating for the hands and the mind as studying an instrument. The second statement qualifies it by providing an explanation and giving examples of the various ways in which it stimulates the mind and the hands.

Important: because "qualification" is being used in its second meaning, it has a high chance of being correct when it appears. If you see it among the answer choices, you should therefore check it first.

Hypothesis/Speculation – Prediction about an outcome or assumption.

Example:

Why did nineteenth century American women feel obliged to wear thin slippers at all times and in all seasons when English women apparently felt free to match their shoes to their circumstances? It **may be** that the very fluidity of American class structure increased the pressure on women to be dependent and ladylike.

Digression – Off-topic discussion

Because Critical Reading passages are by nature very limited in length, they are generally unlikely to even have *space* to contain digressions. When this answer choice appears, it is therefore very likely to be incorrect.

Acknowledgment – Recognition of an alternate (opposing) point of view.

Concession – Acknowledgment that an opposing view or argument is valid or that part of one's argument is wrong.

Example (acknowledgment and concession):

I can't help but fixate on [Thoreau's] condemnations of those he deemed to be worthless…He seemed to believe that he possessed the true compass as to what was good and noble as he looked at other men, coldly assessing their worth and disturbingly certain as to his judgment. **[But] it would be unjust if I did not mention that several scholars vehemently refute this image of Thoreau.** Sandra Harbert Petrulionis, in her book, *Thoreau in His Own Time*…argues we should focus on the fact that "Thoreau engaged in a lifelong habit of serving and educating his community." **This is an important point.** Thoreau valued his community tremendously. And he valued education and the dissemination of truth and knowledge.

In the above passage, the author begins by making a claim (Thoreau could be cold and judgmental), then uses the phrases "It would be unjust if I did not mention," and "This is an important" point to indicate that he is making a **concession** and **acknowledging** the other side of his argument: Thoreau cannot be considered entirely bad because he valued education and knowledge, and was active in his community.

Exclamation – A brief, forceful outcry or utterance.

Shortcut: exclamation point

Example:

"…Then he cried loudly, his face turned toward the door, causing the walls of the room to echo: **"They are approaching!"**

Because they deviate from the cautious, analytical tone of most Critical Reading passages, exclamations are most likely to be found in fiction passages, if at all.

Repetition – Use of a word/phrase multiple times within a sentence or group of sentences.

Parallel Structure – Repetition of the same word or group of words at the same place (usually the beginning) in consecutive sentences. Parallel structure can also be a form of repetition – you will never be asked to distinguish between those two devices.

Example (repetition and parallel structure):

As we are asked to contemplate the disappearance of books as such, it's worth pausing over the astonishing range of…purposes that have been served by books: **the** liberation **of** individuals, **the** reinforcement **of** community, **the** propagation **of** orthodoxy, **the** expansion **of** self-knowledge, **the** publication **of** scientific findings, education and delectation, insult and calumny, **the** spread **of** lies and promulgation of facts, public good and private satisfaction.

Paraphrase – Shortened restatement of a passage or text, usually for clarification.

   Shortcut: That is (to say), In other words

Aside – Parenthetical remark used to offer commentary or addresses the reader directly.

   Shortcut: Parentheses

   Example:

…Kant's hypothesis remains the basis for modern astronomical approaches to planet formation, having triumphed over the concept…that the Sun's planets arose from a close passage of another star by the Sun. In that scenario, the gravitational forces between the stars would have drawn masses of gas from each of them, and some of this gas could then have cooled and condensed to form the planets. This hypothesis, promoted by the famed British astrophysicist James Jeans, had the defect **(or the appeal, for those inclined in that direction)** of making planetary systems extremely rare, because sufficiently close encounters between stars probably occur only a few times during the lifetime of an entire galaxy.

Accusation – Charge of guilt or wrongdoing.

Since accusations generally include a kind of strong, inflammatory language that is at odds with the more neutral tones of most SAT passages, this answer choice will generally be incorrect when it appears.

Oratory – Dramatic and rousing speech.

By definition, "oratory" is typically too extreme and inconsistent with most SAT passages to appear as a correct answer.

Tribute – Testimonial praising a person's accomplishments or positive qualities.

Anachronism – A person/object that is out of place in its time period and belongs to a different era.

Flashback – Insertion of an earlier event into a narrative, jumping back in time.

Because most passages are not long enough to have space for flashbacks and because this device is inconsistent with the analytical content of most passages, this choice will generally be incorrect. If a flashback did occur, it would be most likely to appear in a fiction or memoir passage.

10. Inferences

Inference questions test what a particular section of a passage **suggests** or **implies** rather than what it directly states. They are typically phrased in the following ways:

-In lines x-y, the author suggests that...

-In lines x-y, the author implies that...

-The author would most likely argue that the artists mentioned in lines x-y are...

-It can be inferred that the author considers "those scientists" (lines x-y)...

Because inference questions ask you to take a step beyond what the author is literally saying, you should not expect the answer to be stated word-for-word in the passage. Even though the correct answer may be close to what is stated (often closer than what you are expecting), you should be prepared to work your way very carefully through these questions and avoid leaping to conclusions. That is of course true everywhere, but it is even more true here.

One of the reasons that inference questions tend to be so difficult is that most of the people who take the SAT have never been exposed to basic formal logic, at least in a non-mathematical context, and consequently have no idea of the rules that the SAT is playing by. While Critical Reading is by nature more subjective than Math, the basic kinds of reasoning that govern the two sections are fundamentally quite similar, and nowhere is this more apparent than on inference questions.

According to that all-encompassing source of knowledge, *Wikipedia*, **inference** can be defined as "the act of drawing a conclusion by deductive reasoning from given facts," and the rules governing the types of conclusions that can be logically drawn from a given statement are very strict.

For any given assertion, "if x, then y," only two valid inferences can be made:

1) the statement itself

2) its **contrapositive**: if not y, then not x.

So, for example, from the statement, "If a creature is a dog, then it is an animal," we can make the valid inferences that:

- A creature that is a dog is an animal (rephrasing of the original statement)

- All dogs are animals (rephrasing of the original statement)

- If a creature is not an animal, then it is not a dog (contrapositive)

- All creatures that are not animals are not dogs (rephrasing of contrapositive)

This is the essential type of reasoning on which SAT inference questions are based. **Correct answers to inference questions will therefore often do nothing more than reword the original statement from a different angle.**

Important: Make sure that you pay close attention to answer choices that are phrased negatively (ones that contain the word "not") or that contain double negatives (e.g. not impossible = possible). Unless you carefully work out what this type of wording actually means, it is very easy to become confused by answers that contain it.

Fallacies

Statements that go outside the bounds of what can be determined logically from a given assertion are known as **fallacies**; incorrect answer choices to inference questions are fallacies, and they involve various types of faulty reasoning.

Fallacies based on the assertion "if a creature is a dog, then it is an animal" would include:

- Some types of dogs are not animals

- Dogs are the most popular type of domestic animal

- Both dogs and cats are animals

- Dogs make better pets than other kinds of animals

It's fairly easy to see that those statements have little to do with the original assertion. On the SAT, however, fallacies can be more difficult to identify because you are required to sift through so much information, some of which is relevant and some of which is not.

The key to dealing with inference questions is to make sure that you are absolutely clear about the literal meaning of the lines in questions. Ideally, you should take a couple of seconds, make sure you understand them, **jot down a quick (3-4 word) summary**, then look for the answer closest in *overall meaning* to that statement. That answer should be correct.

Because the right answer might be phrased in a way you're not expecting, though, it is crucial that you not eliminate any answer without making sure you really understand what it says and how it relates to the lines in question. Knowing how to recognize a couple of common fallacies can also help you identify incorrect answers more easily.

One very common type of fallacy involves **speculation**: that is, it *could* be true based on the information in the passage, but usually there simply isn't enough information to judge whether it is *actually* true. Some of these answers are quite obviously wrong because they are so far outside the bounds of what is discussed in the passage that they are patently absurd, while others sound so plausible that it seems that they should be true. In fact, some of them may in fact be true – they just won't be supported by the passage.

Another common type of fallacy involves the reasoning, "if x is true in one case, then x is true in all cases," or "if x is true for one member of a group, then it is true for all members of that group." In reality, the only thing that x being true in one case suggests is that x is true in that particular case. It does not automatically mean that x will be true in any other case or for any other person.

Such fallacies are characterized by **extreme words** such as *always*, *never*, *all*, and *only*. To be sure, there are cases in which a given statement will imply that a particular fact applies to all situations/people, but such statements are comparatively rare. To look at how those fallacies might play out in a set of answer choices, let's take another look at this passage:

> Edgar Allan Poe should have become a lawyer. A brilliant, inventive mind with an eye for detail, Poe could have spotted the need for copyright protections, the absence of which made it difficult for him to prosper as a writer. The
> 5 alternative would have had other benefits as well. It would have been acceptable to his foster father, as law was an appropriate profession for a Virginia gentleman, and it would have allowed Poe to manage the family import-export business in his spare time. Perhaps, also, the city of Rich-
> 10 mond would today be honoring a favorite son with a statue with the inscription "Edgar Allan Poe, fortunate son of Virginia, graduate of the University, and creator of the international legal system that endures to this day." Edgar Allan Poe, Esq. probably would thus be memorialized in
> 15 stone, just as the actual Mr. Edgar Allan Poe, writer, is not.

It can be inferred from lines 1-9 ("Poe could have…spare time") that

(A) a lack of legal protection impeded Poe's ability to profit from his work
(B) Poe's relationship with his foster father was characterized by great turbulence
(C) Poe's choice of profession caused him to become an outcast
(D) writers would be more likely to prosper if they became lawyers.
(E) Poe's entire family strongly disapproved of his choice of profession

(B), (C), and (E) all fall into the category of speculation – they sound plausible enough, but they're just outside the bounds of what can be logically inferred.

For (B), the author tells us that Poe's foster father would have considered law an "acceptable" career, implying that he considered writing an "unacceptable" career. That *could have* (and presumably did) cause some tension between them, but we cannot extend that presumption to their relationship in general. It might seem reasonable, but there's nothing to directly support it, and so it's too far out of bounds.

(C) contains the same problem: the author alludes to the idea that writing was not respectable but says nothing about Poe becoming an outcast because he chose to write. He does tell us that Poe "failed to prosper," but not making money is something very different from being rejected by society. The fact that Poe historically was in fact something of an outcast is completely irrelevant here. It may be factually true, but if it isn't directly supported by the passage, it isn't a valid inference.

(E) is incorrect because the passage only suggests what Poe's foster father thought – it tells us nothing about what any other member of Poe's family thought, biological or otherwise, and so we cannot make any assumptions about their attitude.

(D) contains the fallacy "if x is true for one person, then x is true for everyone." The passage discusses exactly one writer: Edgar Allan Poe. The author certainly suggests that *Poe* would have been more successful had he become a lawyer – that's the point of the passage – but he does nothing to suggest that anything about Poe's situation could be extended to any other writer, never mind writers in general. So it's too broad.

(A) is **correct** because it simply restates what the passage says: as a lawyer, Poe "could have spotted the need for copyright protections, the absence of which made it difficult for him to prosper as a writer."

The difficulty lies in the syntax of the sentence (the wording "the absence of *which*" is likely to throw some people off), not necessarily the idea itself.

We could, however, rewrite this sentence in a more straightforward manner: Poe wasn't successful because his work wasn't protected by copyright (or, **if** there had been copyright protections, **then** Poe would have been more successful as a writer). What does it mean to be protected by copyright? That people aren't allowed to copy your work. Which is exactly what (A) says.

Now let's take a look at another example, one that does in fact make a much broader generalization than the previous passage. While it may seem short, many inference questions are based on only a few lines, and thus the overall context is often not very important.

> Kurt Vonnegut had been trying to shape the material that became *Slaughterhouse-Five* for twenty years. Rare for writers—rare **for anybody**—this most formative experience may have befallen him not as a child, but in young manhood.

It can be inferred from the passage that

(A) Kurt Vonnegut spent more time writing *Slaughterhouse-Five* than he spent writing any other book
(B) the most influential event in a person's life does not typically occur in adulthood
(C) Kurt Vonnegut had more difficulty writing *Slaughterhouse-Five* than he had writing any other book
(D) writers often undergo their most formative experiences as adults
(E) some of the events in *Slaughterhouse-Five* were based on Kurt Vonnegut's childhood experiences

As usual, there are a couple of different ways to approach this type of question:

1) The short way: answer it in your own words, then look for an option that matches

The first thing to notice is that the second sentence contains dashes with a parenthetical statement inside (*rare for anybody*). Since a construction like this nearly always signals important information, the logical starting place would be that sentence. What does that place in the passage tell us?

> -It is **rare** for a writer to have his most formative experience *not as child, but in young manhood* (i.e. adulthood).

> -In other words, it is **common** (the opposite of rare) for writers to have their most formative experience as *children*.

> -The information between the dashes tells us that the above fact extends to people in general (*anybody*).

> -Thus, people in general (most people) undergo their most formative (=influential) experiences when they are children. If they are children, that means they are NOT adults. **Which is what (B) says. It's just phrasing the idea the opposite way.**

2) The long way: check all the answers one-by-one, in order

(A) The passage tells us Vonnegut spent 20 years writing *Slaughterhouse-Five*. That's a long time, but we have no idea how much time he spent writing any other book. It **could** be true, but we just don't have enough information. So (A) is out.

(B) See above

(C) Same problem as (A). We have nothing to compare Vonnegut's experience of writing *Slaughterhouse-Five* to. Could be true, but not enough information. The phrase "any other" is also pretty extreme, which suggests that the answer is incorrect.

(D) The passage states exactly the opposite: writers *rarely* undergo their most formative experience as adults.

(E) All we know is that Vonnegut's most formative experience, one he had as an adult, shaped *Slaughterhouse-Five*. The passage gives us no information about whether his childhood experiences shaped the book in any way. Could be true, but not enough information.

Alternately, the correct answer could be phrased this way:

> Kurt Vonnegut had been trying to shape the material that became *Slaughterhouse-Five* for twenty years. Rare for writers—rare for anybody—this most formative experience may have befallen him not as a child, but in young manhood.

It can be inferred from the passage that:

(A) Kurt Vonnegut spent more time writing *Slaughterhouse-Five* than he spent writing any other book
(B) the most influential event in a person's life typically occurs before adulthood
(C) *Slaughterhouse-Five* was Kurt Vonnegut's most difficult book to write
(D) Writers often undergo their most formative experiences as adults
(E) Some of the events in *Slaughterhouse-Five* were based on Kurt Vonnegut's childhood experiences

Again, start with the information between the dashes; that approach would hold true even if the passage were 85 lines long. The basic assertion is that most people undergo formative experiences in childhood, which is by definition not adulthood. Look for the answer that most nearly matches that general idea, keeping in mind that it might be phrased from an unexpected angle – that's (B), which states that most formative events take place **before** adulthood (i.e. childhood).

When I walk someone through this strategy, their usual question is "But how did you know that the answer would be between the dashes?" Well, I didn't, not for sure. But dashes are almost always important, especially when it comes to inference questions, because they contain information that's easily overlooked. So there was already an exceedingly high probability that paying attention to that place would point me toward the answer. If it hadn't worked, I'd simply have checked the answers one by one.

Working through Critical Reading questions is sometimes a process of trial-and-error. You make an assumption based on how texts are usually put together and how the test is typically constructed, and much of the time it'll turn out to be right (it is a *standardized* test, after all). If it's not, then your job is to reexamine your original assumption and try to work through the question from a different angle. The SAT is a reasoning test – if you're a strong reader with a good vocabulary and approach the exam with the attitude that you can reason your way systematically through each question, you'll eventually hit on the answer.

"Main Point" Inference Questions

Some inference questions are based less on formal logic and more on understanding how texts are organized and what role specific pieces of information play within an argument.

Although these questions are phrased as inference questions, they are more dependent on an understanding of how texts are usually arranged – on the fact that an author typically opens with a broad statement that is then supported throughout a paragraph. We can use the same passage to illustrate this type of question:

> Kurt Vonnegut had been trying to shape the material
> that became *Slaughterhouse-Five* for twenty years. Rare for
> writers—rare for anybody—this most formative experience
> may have befallen him not as a child, but in young manhood.

It can be inferred that, for the author of the passage, *Slaughterhouse-Five* (line 2) is a work that

(A) promotes an artistic vision incompatible with reality
(B) does not succeed in shaping its material effectively
(C) exemplifies a common literary tendency
(D) draws more on Vonnegut's adult experiences than on his childhood ones
(E) reveals the difficulty Vonnegut faced in writing about his childhood experiences

The primary mistake most people make when attempting to answer a question such as this is that they only read the lines (or, at best, the sentence) in which *Slaughterhouse-Five* is mentioned. If we read those lines, we learn exactly one piece of information: the book took twenty years for him to write. That could easily lead us to assume that the answer is (E).

The problem, however, is that the next sentence makes clear that Vonnegut was not writing about his childhood experiences but rather about those that "[befell] him…in young manhood." So (E) doesn't work so well after all. This is where a lot of people start to get confused and then decide to guess.

The key to answering a question such as this is to realize that we are being asked to understand the writing of *Slaughterhouse-Five* in the context of the second sentence, whose function is to explain or support the first sentence (main idea). So now we need to think about what those two sentences say:

- #1 tells us that Vonnegut spent almost 20 years writing *Slaughterhouse-Five*.

- #2 tells us that Vonnegut was unusual because he underwent his most formative experience as an adult.

What makes this an inference question is the fact that the author never spells out the relationship between the two sentences. Based on our (presumed) knowledge of where explanations are typically situated in relation to the larger ideas they support, we must make the logical jump that the author mentions formative experiences in adulthood as unusual *because* these are the experiences on which Vonnegut based *Slaughterhouse-Five*.

The missing link, the one that the reader is expected to supply, is that *Slaughterhouse-Five* is about Kurt Vonnegut's most formative experience, and that that experience occurred during Kurt Vonnegut's young manhood, i.e. when he was an adult.

Thus, *Slaughterhouse-Five* is about an experience that Vonnegut had when he was an adult.

So the answer is (D).

We could, of course, also check out each answer individually:

(A) Completely off topic. The passage gives no indication whatsoever that *Slaughterhouse-Five* – or any other work – is incompatible with reality. Besides, "promote" is usually wrong.

(B) All we know is that *Slaughterhouse-Five* took Kurt Vonnegut a very, very long time to write. The author gives no indication of believing that it was not a successful work.

(C) The "vague" answer. Answers that shift from the specifics of a passage to making a statement in the abstract are frequently correct, but in this case, the answer describes a situation that is exactly the *opposite* of that described in the passage. *Slaughterhouse-Five* was unusual because Vonnegut, unlike most authors, based it on experiences he had as an adult; it therefore exemplifies an *unusual* rather than a common literary tendency.

(D) See above

(E) Half-right, half-wrong. Yes, it reveals the difficulty Vonnegut had in writing the work, but since that work was based on events experienced in adulthood rather than childhood, the answer cannot be correct.

Inference Exercises

1.   Around the middle of the 20th century, science dispensed with the fantasy that we could easily colonize the other planets in our solar system. Science fiction writers absorbed the new reality: soon, moon and
5 asteroid settings replaced Mars and Venus.

The author suggests that that colonizing "other planets" (line 3) would be

(A) a difficult endeavor
(B) an exciting challenge
(C) a straightforward process
(D) a controversial experiment
(E) a futile undertaking

2.   Most people have so-called flashbulb memories of where they were and what they were doing when something momentous happened. (Unfortunately, staggeringly terrible news seems to come out of the
5 blue more often than staggeringly good news.) But as clear and detailed as these memories feel, psychologists have discovered they are surprisingly inaccurate.

The parenthetical information in lines 3-5 implies that flashbulb memories

(A) frequently involve unpleasant recollections
(B) occur in a relatively small number of people
(C) are the least accurate type of memory
(D) are often vague and lacking in detail
(E) illustrate the limits of psychological research

3.   Shakespeare in the world of ants, untroubled by any such war between honor and treachery, and chained by the rigid commands of instinct to a tiny repertory of feeling, would be able to write only one drama of
5 triumph and one of tragedy. Ordinary people, on the other hand, can invent an endless variety of such stories, and compose an infinite symphony of ambience and mood.

The author suggests that "Shakespeare in the world of ants" (line 1) would be

(A) incomprehensible to most people
(B) a tragic figure
(C) similar to a symphonic composer
(D) caught between honor and treachery
(E) fundamentally limited

4.   Why is the connection between smells and memories so strong? The reason for these associations is that the brain's olfactory bulb is connected to both the amygdala (an emotion center) and to the hippocampus, which is
5 involved in memory. And, because smells serve a survival function (odors can keep us from eating spoiled or poisonous foods), some of these associations are made very quickly, and may even involve a one-time association.

It can be inferred from the passage that

(A) the amygdala and the hippocampus are the only brain structures involved in both smell and memory
(B) the brain can rapidly process information necessary for survival
(C) memories involving smell are stronger than any other type of memory
(D) the hippocampus is primarily responsible for alerting people to the presence of poisonous foods
(E) the hippocampus is one of the most important regions of the brain

5.   It may be small and hard to find, but Eatonville is important for two reasons: It was the first all-black incorporated town in the United States, and it was the childhood home of Zora Neale Hurston. Much of
5 Hurston's writing is set here, and a number of her characters are thinly disguised versions of actual residents.

In the last sentence, the author suggests that

(A) Eatonville's residents were responsible for encouraging Zora Neale Hurston to become a writer
(B) Zora Neale Hurston went to great lengths to disguise the inspiration for her characters
(C) Zora Neale Hurston first began to write as a child growing up in Eatonville
(D) Eatonville was the only all-black incorporated town to serve as the backdrop for an author's works
(E) many of Zora Neale Hurston's characters are not entirely fictional creations

6.   A quick glance through one of the many books that Herman Melville owned and studied—his copy of *The Poetical Works of William Wordsworth*, or *Don Quixote*, for example—reveals tangible evidence of his
5 creative approach to reading: the pages are covered with markings and annotations. There are vertical scores, underlines, brackets, checks, double- and triple-checks, x's, circles, as well as words, phrases, fragments of poetry, and even whole paragraphs of prose. Despite his
10 well-documented propensity for collecting fine editions of old books, Melville evidently had no qualms about picking up his pencil—or, in some rare instances, his crayon—and inscribing his thoughts in their margins.

It can be inferred from the passage that Herman Melville

(A) was unconcerned with preserving any of his property
(B) viewed reading as an interactive process
(C) found it difficult to understand many of the books that he read
(D) preferred works of poetry to works of fiction
(E) only collected high-quality editions of old books

7.   Frederick Law Olmsted's *Walks and Talks* has all the wide-eyed quality of an American in England for the first time: Ah, homely cottages! Ooh, blooming hawthorn! He even marvels at the sight of a "real"
5 (unimported) Hereford cow over the hedge," though he had surely seen a cow before. But tucked into the breathless prose is naturalist poetry. His observation, for instance, of "mild sun beaming through the watery atmosphere, and all so quiet" captures how
10 achingly beautiful the softly lit English countryside is. This emotional affinity for the pastoral shaped Olmsted's vision for Central Park and many future works.

The passage supports which of the following statements about Frederick Law Olmsted?

(A) he was famous for his poetry as well as his landscape designs
(B) he never been exposed to rural life before arriving in England
(C) his voyage to England marked the first time he had left the United States
(D) his impressions of the English countryside had a lasting effect on his career
(E) he tried in vain to hide his enthusiasm for the English countryside

8.   Until the past few years, physicists agreed that the entire universe is generated from a few mathematical truths and principles of symmetry, perhaps throwing in a handful of parameters like the mass of
5 the electron. It seemed that we were closing in on a vision of our universe in which everything could be calculated, predicted, and understood. However, two theories, eternal inflation and string theory, now suggest that the same fundamental principles
10 from which the laws of nature derive may lead to many different self-consistent universes, with many different properties.

The author implies that "physicists" (line 1) now believe

(A) the universe can be understood through the principles of symmetry
(B) studying the mass of the electron may lead to new insights about the formation of the universe
(C) the universe is more complex than scientists previously thought
(D) string theory cannot explain the fundamental laws of nature
(E) eternal inflation and string theory are incompatible with the principles of scientific research

9.   Experimental scientists occupy themselves with observing and measuring the cosmos, finding out what stuff exists, no matter how strange that stuff may be. Theoretical physicists, on the other
5 hand, are not satisfied with observing the universe. They want to know why. They want to explain all the properties of the universe in terms of a few fundamental principles and parameters. These fundamental principles, in turn, lead to the "laws of
10 nature," which govern the behavior of all matter and energy.

Lines 1-8 suggest that

(A) theoretical physicists have no interest in observing the universe
(B) the universe is too complex to reduce to a set of fundamental principles
(C) experimental scientists are frequently unprepared for their discoveries
(D) experimental scientists are less concerned with explanations than are theoretical physicists
(E) experimental scientists and theoretical physicists hold conflicting views about the laws of nature

10.   For some activists, eating local foods is no longer just a pleasure—it is a moral obligation. Why? Because shipping foods over long distances results in the unnecessary emission of the green-house gases that are
5   warming the planet. This concern has given rise to the concept of "food miles," that is, the distance food travels from farm to plate.
        But food miles advocates fail to grasp the simple idea that food should be grown where it is most econ-
10 omically advantageous to do so. Relevant advantages consist of various combinations of soil, climate, labor, and other factors. It is possible to grow bananas in Iceland, but Costa Rica really has the better climate for that activity. Transporting food is just one relatively small cost
15 of providing modern consumers with their daily bread, meat, cheese, and veggies. Concentrating agricultural production in the most favorable regions is the best way to minimize human impacts on the environment.

In the second paragraph (lines 8-18), the author implies that

(A) transportation is not the most important factor in determining the cost of food
(B) concentrating agricultural production can be detrimental to the environment
(C) growing crops in warm climates is the most cost-effective means of producing food
(D) bananas should be grown in Iceland as well as Costa Rica
(E) food miles advocates should take more responsibility for agricultural production

11.   Sometime near the end of the Pleistocene, a band of people left northeastern Asia, crossed the Bering land bridge when the sea level was low, entered Alaska and became the first Americans.
5   Since the 1930s, archaeologists have thought these people were members of the Clovis culture. First discovered in New Mexico in the 1930s, the Clovis culture is known for its distinct stone tools, primarily fluted projectile points. For decades,
10 Clovis artifacts were the oldest known in the New World, dating to 13,000 years ago. But in recent years, researchers have found more and more evidence that people were living in North and South America before the Clovis.
15   The most recently confirmed evidence comes from Washington. During a dig conducted from 1977 to 1979, researchers uncovered a bone projectile point stuck in a mastodon rib. Since then the age of the find has been debated, but recently
20 anthropologist Michael Waters and his colleagues announced a new radiocarbon date for the rib: 13,800 years ago, making it 800 years older than the oldest Clovis artifact. Other pre-Clovis evidence comes from a variety of locations across the New World.

It can be inferred that the "band of people" (line 2)

(A) obtained most of their food from hunting
(B) were primarily known for their fluted projectile points
(C) settled in New Mexico before migrating into South America
(D) first arrived in the New World about 13,000 years ago
(E) inhabited the New World earlier than the Clovis people did

12.   Many readers, faced with Thoreau's enigmatic
Yankee persona, have resorted to a kind of pop-culture
shorthand for describing his life. As the capsule summary
goes, Thoreau was an oddball loner who lived by a lake,
5   writing in praise of nature and against modern progress.
But the full story of Thoreau's life involves subtleties
and contradictions that call his popular image into question.
     One idea that has persisted is that he was a hermit
who cared little for others, yet he was active in his
10   community and responsible for circulating petitions
for neighbors in need. In yet another way Thoreau was
politically active, penning an essay, "Civil Disobedience,"
that would later inform the thinking of Mohandas Gandhi
and the Rev. Martin Luther King Jr.
15   Despite his fame as a champion of solitude—a
practice that he chronicled with wisdom and wit, Thoreau
made no secret of the social life he indulged during his
stay at Walden Pond from 1845 to 1847. In fact, one of the
chapters of Walden, titled "Visitors," offers an extended
20   account of Thoreau's dealings with others. But even if
Thoreau wasn't always averse to human company, the
idea that he was a loner might stem from the assumption
that he was the kind of person who should have been
alone. Thoreau was capable of friendship, but on his own
25   terms. He could be prickly to a fault. "I sometimes
hear my Friends complain finely that I do not appreciate
their fineness," he once wrote. "I shall not tell them
whether I do or not. As if they expected a vote of thanks
for every fine thing which they uttered or did."

1. The author suggests that the view held by "many
   readers" (line 1) is

   (A) somewhat puzzling
   (B) highly unconventional
   (C) arrogant
   (D) cynical
   (E) shortsighted

2. In lines 20-24 ("But…alone"), the author implies that
   Thoreau

   (A) was unable to maintain close friendships
   (B) was more of a loner than is generally acknowledged
   (C) did not entirely reject other people's company
   (D) was often ungrateful to his friends
   (E) was wrong to reject his friends' offers of assistance

13.   By the middle of his life, Edmund Wilson was
a fat, ferocious man: petty, pretentious, and petulant,
a failure at many of the most ordinary tasks of life.
But he could dance: through a poem, through a book,
5   through a library. He was the Nureyev at what he
did—a genius, really: probably the greatest reader the
United States has ever known.
     That's not to say he was the most influential
figure of his time. Sometimes he got it wrong. His
10   prose was merely good enough—not sparkling, only
clear and well-organized—and he got nosebleeds
whenever he tried to follow philosophy up into the
stratosphere of metaphysics. For that matter, he never
understood escapism, and so, in a golden age of
15   Hollywood screwball fluff, he condemned American
movies as inferior to European—to say nothing of his
famous essay that thundered against mystery novels.
     Mostly, though, he got it right. And if he seems
lost to us now, that's not just because we have no
20   similar genius to occupy the space that he filled. It's
also because that space has nearly disappeared. The
magisterial critic has no role left in the United States,
really. We appreciate, we enjoy, we peruse, we
watch. But we don't define ourselves by reading
25   anymore. The novel, the premiere art form of western
civilization over the last two hundred years, has
ceased to be the mark of civilization. And so what
need have we of Edmund Wilson—that fat, ferocious
man, so nimble on his feet?

In lines 9-14 ("Sometimes…escapism") the author
suggests that Edmund Wilson

   (A) had a limited comprehension of certain subjects
   (B) preferred Hollywood movies to European ones
   (C) found mystery novels puzzling
   (D) was frequently in poor health
   (E) had a strong interest in metaphysics

14.   In our attempts to uncover the history of the cosmos,
we have continually discovered that the segments most
deeply shrouded in mystery are those that deal with
origins – of the universe itself, of its most massive
5   structures (galaxies and galaxy clusters), and of the stars
that provide most of the light in the cosmos. These
mysteries arise in large part because during the cosmic
"dark ages," when matter was just beginning to organize
itself into self-contained units such as stars and galaxies,
10   most of this matter generated little or no detectable
radiation. When we turn to the origin of planets, the
mysteries deepen. We lack not only observations of the
crucial, initial stages of planetary formation but also
successful theories of how the planets began to form.
15   Astrophysicists may now have more data but they
have no better answers than before. The beginnings of
planet building pose a remarkably intractable problem, to
the point that one of the world's experts on the subject,
Scott Tremaine, has elucidated (partly in jest) Tremaine's
20   laws of planet formation. The first of these laws states that
"all theoretical predictions about the properties of exosolar
planets are wrong," and the second that "the most secure
prediction about planet formation is that it can't happen."
Tremaine's humor underscores the ineluctable fact that
25   planets do exist, despite our inability to explain this
astronomical enigma.

In the second paragraph (lines 15-26), the author
implies that

(A) existing information about planetary formation
     provides limited insight
(B) current conditions make it impossible for new
     planets to form
(C) the Earth may have more in common with
     exosolar planets than was originally thought
(D) scientists have given up all hope of
     understanding planetary formation
(E) breakthroughs in technology could lead to
     the discovery of new planets

Official Guide Inference Questions

Test 1	Section 2	Question 6	p. 391
Test 1	Section 2	Question 9	p. 391
Test 1	Section 2	Question 20	p. 395
Test 1	Section 5	Question 23	p. 406
Test 1	Section 9	Question 8	p. 427
Test 1	Section 9	Question 9	p. 427
Test 1	Section 9	Question 13	p. 428
Test 1	Section 9	Question 15	p. 428
Test 1	Section 9	Question 19	p. 428
Test 2	Section 4	Question 24	p. 462
Test 2	Section 7	Question 14	p. 478
Test 2	Section 7	Question 18	p. 480
Test 2	Section 7	Question 19	p. 480
Test 2	Section 7	Question 22	p. 480
Test 2	Section 9	Question 11	p. 489
Test 2	Section 9	Question 14	p. 489
Test 3	Section 7	Question 6	p. 538
Test 3	Section 7	Question 21	p. 542
Test 3	Section 9	Question 12	p. 551
Test 3	Section 9	Question 15	p. 551
Test 4	Section 2	Question 9	p. 577
Test 4	Section 2	Question 11	p. 577
Test 4	Section 2	Question 19	p. 577
Test 4	Section 2	Question 13	p. 579
Test 4	Section 5	Question 11	p. 589
Test 4	Section 5	Question 12	p. 589
Test 4	Section 5	Question 14	p. 590
Test 4	Section 5	Question 18	p. 591
Test 4	Section 8	Question 12	p. 607
Test 5	Section 3	Question 7	p. 645
Test 5	Section 3	Question 8	p. 645
Test 5	Section 3	Question 11	p. 646
Test 5	Section 3	Question 17	p. 647
Test 5	Section 3	Question 18	p. 647
Test 5	Section 3	Question 21	p. 649
Test 5	Section 3	Question 22	p. 649
Test 5	Section 7	Question 16	p. 665
Test 5	Section 9	Question 8	p. 674
Test 5	Section 9	Question 13	p. 674
Test 5	Section 9	Question 16	p. 674
Test 6	Section 3	Question 20	p. 711
Test 6	Section 3	Question 21	p. 711
Test 6	Section 3	Question 24	p. 711
Test 6	Section 9	Question 9	p. 736
Test 6	Section 9	Question 10	p. 736
Test 6	Section 9	Question 11	p. 736

Explanations: Inference Exercises

1. A

The author states that in the mid-20th century, *science dispensed with* (got rid of) *the fantasy that we could easily colonize other planets*, implying that colonizing other planets would be a **difficult** project or **endeavor**. (A) states that directly. (E) is too extreme because the passage only indicates that colonizing other planets would be difficult, not **impossible**.

2. A

The information in the parentheses indicates that people tend to learn of "staggeringly terrible" news suddenly more often than they learn of good news suddenly. Since flashbulb memories are formed of news that is learned suddenly, it can be inferred that those memories frequently involve bad news. The logic involved in this question is essentially a syllogism:

A: Flashbulb memories are formed of momentous events
B: Momentous events are frequently bad
C: Thus, flashbulb memories are frequently bad

This is not a form of logic that the SAT routinely tests, and thus it is not covered in the chapter, but it is well within the bounds of what could appear on the exam. It can also be helpful to keep in mind when you encounter a question that asks about parenthetical information.

3. E

The author presents ants as *chained by the rigid commands of instinct to a tiny repertory of feeling* and *capable of writing only one drama*. They are also presented in direct opposition to people with their *endless variety of stories*. The opposite of "endless" is limited, and because they are "chained by instinct," their limits are an essential (=fundamental) part of what they are.

4. B

The passage states that *Because smells serve a survival function, some of these associations [between smells and memory] are made very quickly*, implying that when a particular kind of sensory information is necessary for a person to survive, that brain can rapidly form connections (=process information) to make survival possible.

5. E

The answer is a simple rephrasing of the passage from a slightly different angle. The last sentence states that Hurston's characters were *thinly disguised versions of actual residents*, meaning that Hurston did not invent her characters from scratch, i.e. they are **not** entirely fictional.

6. B

The passage details the many, many ways that Herman Melville recorded his responses in his books as he read them. He is described as a reader who was actively engaged with his books rather than one who simply sat back and absorbed them passively.

7. D

The last sentence states that Olmsted's *affinity for the pastoral* (i.e. the English countryside) *shaped* (=had a strong impact on) *his vision for Central Park and many future works* (= his career).

8. C

The passage states the string theory and eternal inflation have **overturned** the relatively simple, straightforward vision of the universe, *generated from a few mathematical truths*, in which *everything could be calculated, predicted, and understood*, and that they now believe there are *many different self-consistent universes with many different properties*. The repetition of the word "many" indicates that the new vision of the universe is much more complex than the old.

9. D

This is essentially a main point/structure inference question. How is the passage organized? It first describes what experimental scientists do (observe things) and then contrasts them with theoretical physicists, who want to *understand* how things work. The entire point of the passage is that theoretical physicists are **more** interested in explanations than experimental scientists – i.e. experimental scientists are **less** interested in explanations than are theoretical physicists.

10. A

In the second paragraph, the author states that *Transporting food is just one relatively small cost of providing modern consumers with their daily bread, meat, cheese, and veggies*. If transportation is "just one relatively small cost," then logically there must be other, larger costs, which by definition are more important. Therefore, it can be inferred that transportation is **not** the most important cost of producing food.

11. E

The point of the passage is the Clovis people *were not* the first people in the New World. "The band of people" mentioned in line 2 refers to the people who *were* the first to arrive in the New World, coming *before* the Clovis. Since the Clovis are believed to have arrived 13,000 years ago, the discovery of spear points dating back to

13,800 years ago indicates that the Clovis were not the first Americans. What makes this question potentially difficult is that after mentioning the "band of people," the author introduces the Clovis people – a different group. It is up to the reader to keep the two groups straight and follow what researchers believe about each one.

12. 1E, 2C

12.1 Because the readers understand Thoreau's life through a "pop-culture shorthand," they miss the "subtleties and complexities" that truly comprised his life and view it as simpler than it actually was. That is essentially the definition of "shortsighted."

12.2 In line 21, the author states that Thoreau *wasn't always averse to human company*, which means that he was *sometimes* not averse to human company. To be "averse" means to dislike it or reject it, so to be "not averse" means to "not reject entirely," and that is exactly what (C) says. Note that (D) is also supported by information in the third paragraph, but the question asks only about lines 20-24.

13. A

What does the author discuss in the second paragraph? The areas in which Wilson fell short (*Sometimes he got it wrong*) – so the correct answer must match that idea. Furthermore, the author states that Wilson *never understood escapism* (= limited comprehension)...*and so he condemned American movies* (=certain subjects) *as inferior to European ones*.

14. A

In lines 15-16, the author states that *Astrophysicists may now have more data but they have no better answers than before*. In other words, the data that astrophysicists have acquired has **not** helped them understand how the planets formed. Not understanding = limited insight.

11. Assumptions, Generalizations, and Claims

"Assumption" and "generalization" questions ask you to recognize the underlying logic or identify a general rule that can be inferred from a particular section of a passage. These questions do not appear very frequently, but when they do, they are usually phrased in the following ways:

-An important assumption in the passage is that...

-The author's assumption in lines x-y is that...

-The underlying assumption in lines x-y is that

-An (important) assumption shared by the authors
of Passage 1 and Passage 2 is that...

-Which generalization is best supported by the passage?

Although these questions are phrased differently, they test essentially the same skill, and they are both types of inference questions. As is true for correct answers to inference questions, correct answers to assumption questions typically rephrase the lines provided in the question from a slightly different standpoint or in a somewhat more general manner.

They are also like function questions in that they test your ability to move from specific information to abstract concepts. As a result, correct answers are not always easy to identify and will often bear little obvious relationship to the information in the passage.

Incorrect answers, on the other hand, will go beyond the bounds of what can reasonably be inferred from the passage. They may include information that is factually true but irrelevant to the lines in question. They may also use some of the same wording that is found in the passage and alter it just enough so that it means something different from what it means in the passage.

Let's look at an example. You're probably familiar with this passage by now, but we're only going to work with part of it right now.

In classical physics— the physics of Newton that so accurately describes our everyday experience—the interpretation of terms such as object and position is for the most part in harmony with our commonsense, "realistic"

5 understanding of those concepts. As measuring devices, however, we are crude instruments. Physicists have found that everyday objects and the light we see them by are made from objects that we do not perceive directly. These objects are governed not by classical physics but

10 by the laws of quantum theory. The reality of quantum theory is a radical departure from that of classical physics. In the framework of quantum theory, particles have neither definite positions nor definite velocities unless and until an observer measures those quantities. Quantum

15 physics also has important implications for our concept of the past. In classical physics, the past is assumed to exist as a definite series of events, but according to quantum physics, the past, like the future, is indefinite and exists only as a spectrum of possibilities. Even the universe as

20 a whole has no single past or history. So quantum physics implies a different reality than that of classical physics— even though the latter still serves us well when we design things such as buildings and bridges.

The underlying assumption in lines 10-14 ("The reality ...those quantities") is that

(A) the position of certain types of particles can never be conclusively determined
(B) scientific findings are sometimes influenced by human behavior
(C) quantum physics and empirical observation are thoroughly incompatible
(D) the behavior of everyday objects is governed by neither classical physics nor quantum theory
(E) measurements of particle velocity and position are frequently inaccurate

If you looked at the answer choices, thought that (B) had nothing whatsoever to do with the passage, and eliminated it immediately, then congratulations: you just fell into the exact same trap that 90% or so of test-takers would fall into – that's exactly the assumption that the College Board is playing on. In reality, the answers to many hard questions will be those that initially seem **least** likely to be correct – that's what makes them hard questions. If you know that upfront, however, it's a lot easier to catch yourself before you jump to eliminate answers without really considering what they're saying.

So, for the record, why is the answer (B)?

Well, let's work through the question for real:

1) Re-read the lines in question, only the lines in question, and nothing but the lines in question.

> *The reality of quantum theory is a radical departure from that of classical physics. In the framework of quantum theory, particles have neither definite positions nor definite velocities unless and until an observer measures those quantities.*

2) Figure out the basic idea and put it in your own words.

Without an observer present, particles don't have definite positions or velocities. They only acquire those things IF someone is watching.

That's it. That's all we have to work off of. The correct answer must have something to do with this fact.

3) Consider the implications.

If particles behave differently when people are watching them than they do when no one is watching them, then scientists can **only** learn how particles behave when those particles are being observed. (It's not as if they can set up a video camera and see what happens when they're not around!). In other words, the scientists' behavior is going to influence how those particles behave, and their findings will reflect that. Hence (B).

Otherwise, you can always go through the answers one-by-one.

(A) the position of certain types of particles can never be conclusively determined

No. The passage states that the positions and velocities of particles **can** be determined when observers are watching. It says nothing about an exception for certain types of particles. It could be true, but we don't have enough information. Besides, the word "never" is extreme and typically signals an incorrect answer.

(B) scientific findings are sometimes influenced by human behavior

See above.

(C) quantum physics and empirical observation are thoroughly incompatible

Again no. The passage states that quantum physics accepts that the velocity and position of particles can be determined by an observer (= empirical observation).

(D) the behavior of everyday objects is governed by neither classical physics nor quantum theory

No. The passage states that the behavior of everyday objects is governed by quantum theory.

(E) Measurements of particle velocity and position are frequently inaccurate

Not enough information. There's absolutely nothing in those lines to either support or refute that idea.

The question also could have been phrased this way:

> Which of the following generalizations could be made from lines 10-15?
>
> (A) most scientific theories are controversial when they are first proposed
> (B) the position and velocity of unobserved particles can never be determined
> (C) quantum physics and empirical observation are generally incompatible
> (D) scientific theories are sometimes unable to explain to explain the behavior of everyday objects
> (E) measurements of particle velocity and position are frequently inaccurate

In this case, you might assume that the word "never" in choice (B) would automatically eliminate the answer from consideration, but unfortunately you'd be wrong. Here's why:

The passage states that particles **only** have definite position and velocity when they are being observed – phrased the opposite way, particles cannot (i.e. *never*) have definite position or velocity when they are *not* being observed.

Remember: the fact that extreme answers will *usually* be wrong means exactly that – very occasionally, answers containing words such as "only," "never," and "always" will in fact be right. The College Board is under no obligation to play by its own rules, and if your goal is truly to answer every single question correctly, you need to recognize that general patterns will only get you so far.

Supporting and Undermining Claims

Questions that ask you to identify information that would either strengthen or weaken an argument have the same basis as "assumption" questions but require you to take the process a step further.

Questions that ask you to support/strengthen a claim are testing your ability to recognize what sort of information would be **consistent** with an argument or idea discussed in the passage.

Questions that ask you to undermine/challenge/weaken a claim are testing your ability to recognize what sort of information would be **inconsistent** with an argument or idea discussed in the passage.

These questions are typically phrased in the following ways:

-Which of the following would best support the argument in lines x-y?

-Which of the following would most undermine the author's claim in lines x-y?

-Which of the following, if true, would most weaken the argument in lines x-y?

-Which of the following would challenge the assertion in lines x-y?

-Which of the following examples would be best to add in lines x-y?

In order to infer whether the information presented in the answer choices would strengthen, weaken, or simply be irrelevant to a particular idea or argument, you must first understand the logic on which the argument is based.

While there certainly is an effective method for approaching these questions, there is no – I repeat no – real shortcut to solving them. If you're going to tackle them, you had better be ready; if you're not really certain what a support/undermine question is asking, OR you don't feel that you can focus properly, you are better off simply skipping it. If you feel confident in your ability to answer the question, you can always return to it later – *after* you've already answered everything that's more straightforward.

If you try to work through it when your head isn't completely clear, at a certain point you'll almost certainly break down and guess, and then probably get the answer wrong. This is not the place to count on being a lucky guesser – these questions are hard, and you shouldn't even attempt to answer them unless you really do know what you're doing.

How to Work Through Support/Undermine Questions

In order to answer support/undermine questions, you must be unfailingly precise and willing to solve them step-by-step, much like you'd solve a math or science problem. As a matter of fact, many times these questions essentially test *scientific reasoning* – it's not an accident that they frequently accompany science passages. They are about logic, not interpretation or literary analysis.

1) Reread the lines in question

In order to answer them, you must first understand the exact idea described in the lines given. This is one place where you cannot only use the main point, nor should you rely on what you think you remember the author saying. Go back and read, word-for-word.

2) Sum up the claim in your own words

Once you have reread the lines, you must make sure you understand the claim or assertion. Stop, take a moment, and put it in your own words. This is important – you can't evaluate whether a particular scenario would strengthen or weaken an argument unless you clearly understand what the argument is.

3) Determine what sort of information would be (in)consistent with the claim

It is important that you at least attempt to do this on your own and not assume you'll be able to recognize the information from the answer choices. Chances are they'll be phrased too obscurely.

4) Look at the answers

When you try identify the scenario that would either strengthen or weaken the claim in question, keep in mind that it may be phrased in a manner that you are not fully expecting. Even more so here than on inference questions, you must truly be willing to consider what each answer choice is actually saying and avoid jumping to eliminate options because they are phrased in ways that sound confusing or unrelated to the passage itself.

If you do in fact understand what a passage is saying, are willing to break the process down carefully, and, very importantly, are willing to write down each step as you go along in order to avoid confusion, these questions can become quite straightforward. *But you can't get impatient, and you can't skip steps, no matter how much you want to just get the answer.*

Let's look at an example. We're just going to consider a portion of a passage we've already seen. It's exactly the type of passage on which you're likely to see a support/undermine question appear.

The reality of quantum theory is a radical departure from that of classical physics. In the framework of quantum theory, particles have neither definite positions nor definite velocities unless and until an observer measures those quantities. Quantum physics also has important implications for our concept of the past. In classical physics, the past is assumed to exist as a definite series of events, but according to quantum physics, the past, like the future, is indefinite and exists only as a spectrum of possibilities. Even the universe as a whole has no single past or history. So quantum physics implies a different reality than that of classical physics—even though the latter still serves us well when we design things such as buildings and bridges.

Which of the following examples would be best to add in line 14?

(A) automobiles
(B) musical instruments
(C) electron microscopes
(D) book covers
(E) surgical lasers

Before we can figure out which example would be most logical to add, we have to figure out what idea they're supporting in the first place. When we back up a few lines to the beginning of the sentence, we find that information:

> So quantum physics implies a different reality than that of classical physics—even though the latter still serves us well when we design things such as buildings and bridges.

So classical physics is useful for building things like buildings and bridges – large-scale, complex objects necessary for everyday life. The correct example must fit that definition:

(A) automobiles – yes, cars are big, complex creations that people rely on in daily life. So that fits. Leave it.

(B) musical instruments – those *could* certainly be complex to build, but they're relatively small and not a crucial part of daily life. Eliminate it.

(C) electron microscopes – electron microscopes are certainly complex to build, but they're highly specialized objects only used in laboratory settings. Eliminate it.

(D) book covers – they're everyday objects, but they're not huge and complex. Eliminate it.

(E) lasers – same problem as (B). Eliminate it too.

So the answer is (A).

Now let's try something a bit harder:

It was once thought that light pollution only
affected astronomers, who need to see the night sky
in all its glorious clarity. And, in fact, some of the earliest efforts to control light pollution were made to protect
5   the view from Lowell Observatory. Unlike astronomers,
most of us may not need an undiminished view of the
night sky for our work, but like most other creatures we do
need darkness. Darkness is as essential to our internal
clockwork as light itself. The regular oscillation of waking
10   and sleep in our lives is nothing less than a biological
expression of the regular oscillation of light on Earth. So
fundamental are these rhythms to our being that altering
them is like altering gravity.

Which of the following would most undermine the author's
claim in lines 9-13?

(A) Even brief periods of exposure to light pollution have
      been shown to cause insomnia.
(B) Some people report changes in their sleeping habits
      when the seasons change.
(C) Once established, sleep patterns become so ingrained that
      they are nearly impossible to change.
(D) People who work at night often have little difficulty
      remaining awake at late hours.
(E) Attempts to introduce laws prohibiting some kinds of
      light pollution are rarely successful.

Looking at the answer choices, you're probably struck by how little any of them have to do with the passage itself. It also might seem as if more than one of the choices is plausible.

Very carefully and very methodically, however, we're going to work through it.

1) Go back to the passage and reread the given lines:

> *Darkness is as essential to our internal clockwork as light itself. The regular oscillation of waking and sleep in our lives is nothing less than a biological expression of the regular oscillation of light on Earth. So fundamental are these rhythms to our being that altering them is like altering gravity.*

2) Sum up the claim presented in those lines

People's waking/sleeping cycles reflect the fact that light = day, dark = night ("the regular oscillation of life on earth"), and that changing that relationship is profoundly unnatural ("like altering gravity").

Notice that there are two major stumbling blocks built into this question: first, you either have to know what "oscillation" means or figure it out from context. The second is that the syntax of the last sentence is inverted: you must recognize that "these rhythms" is the subject in order to make sense out of the sentence. (If it were rearranged, it would read, "These rhythms are so fundamental to our being that altering them is like altering gravity").

3) Figure out what would undermine that claim

If the claim is that normal sleep patterns (day = awake, night = sleep) reflect the fact that it's light during the day and dark at night, then we're looking for something to interrupt that relationship – something that suggests darkness is NOT necessarily related to sleep and that light is NOT necessarily linked to wakefulness. That's it. The opposite of the original claim.

4) Go one by one through the answers

(A) Even brief periods of exposure to light pollution have been shown to cause insomnia.

If having a normal sleep cycle must depend on one's exposure to **natural** light and dark, then logically, exposure to light pollution (fake light) would disturb that cycle and cause people to remain awake (insomnia) when they should be asleep. So (A) is consistent with the claim presented in the passage.

(B) Some people report changes in their sleeping habits when the seasons change.

The passage never explicitly discusses seasons, but still it's fairly reasonable to infer that changing seasons = changing patterns of light and dark. Since light and dark determine waking and sleeping, it's reasonable that changing the natural patterns of lightness and darkness would alter people's sleep patterns. That's generally consistent with the claim in the passage, and we're looking for something to contradict it. So no.

(C) Once established, sleep patterns become so ingrained that they are nearly impossible to alter.

At first glance, this might seem to work. The passage states that altering normal sleep patterns is like "altering gravity," i.e. virtually impossible. But the answer never specifies what *kind* of sleep patterns become ingrained – abnormal sleeping patterns could become just as ingrained as normal sleeping. More importantly, the answer never deals with the central claim: that altering people's exposure to normal light cycles is profoundly unnatural. Besides, the extreme word *impossible* suggests that the answer is wrong.

(D) People who work at night often have little difficulty remaining awake at late hours

Working at night (when it is dark, when people should be sleeping) is a violation of the natural order because darkness = sleep. Logically, people who work at night should be tired then. But if they have *little* difficulty, if it's easy for them, that would violate the claim in the passage. So this works. Note the double negative: *little difficulty*. If you miss the word "little," you miss the entire meaning of the answer choice.

(E) Attempts to introduce laws prohibiting some kinds of light pollution are rarely successful.

No. This has absolutely nothing whatsoever to do with the relationship between light, darkness, and sleep.

So through a combination of process of elimination and logical thinking, we've determined that the answer must be (D).

Assumptions, Generalizations, and Claims Exercises

1.   Most people have so-called flashbulb memories of where they were and what they were doing when something momentous happened. (Unfortunately, staggeringly terrible news seems to come out of the blue
5 more often than staggeringly good news.) But as clear and detailed as these memories feel, psychologists have discovered they are surprisingly inaccurate.

1. The passage supports which of the following generalizations?

  (A) unpleasant memories are easier to recall than pleasant ones
  (B) people only form flashbulb memories that involve terrible news
  (C) momentous occasions most frequently involve happy news
  (D) the clarity of a memory is not a reliable indicator of its accuracy
  (E) memories of recent occurrences are more detailed than those of distant events

2. In context of the passage, which of the following situations would most likely be preserved as a flashbulb memory?

  (A) a young women reunites with a friend after the two have not seen each other for several months
  (B) a recent college graduate begins his first day at a new job
  (C) a woman unexpectedly learns that she has won an enormous sum of money in the lottery
  (D) a boy leaves for a short trip with his grandfather
  (E) a student receives a poor grade on a test for which he did not study

2.   For Egyptologists, Karnak offers a treasure trove of data on Egypt's evolution into an international power with great wealth, a unique and mysterious religion, and a way of life centered on the ebb and
5 flow of the Nile, which coursed through the country's heart. One relief, for example, which lists pharaohs stretching back to the Old Kingdom, provides scholars with important information on the ruling class. Even destruction tells a tale: Some pharaohs chiseled away
10 their predecessors' names in an attempt to wipe out any memory of their existence and accomplishments.

1. An underlying assumption in the last sentence is that

  (A) Egyptian rulers sought to consolidate their power by any means possible
  (B) many Egyptian pharaohs' names have been lost
  (C) pharaohs often succeeded in eliminating all traces of their predecessors
  (D) scholars can gain insight into a culture by studying objects that have been poorly preserved
  (E) scholars have difficulty learning about the pharaohs whose names were chiseled away

2. Which of the following would be best to add as an examples in lines 9-11 ("Some...accomplishments")

  (A) Some pharaohs wore elaborate headdresses decorated in red and white.
  (B) Some pharaohs ascended the throne when they were still children.
  (C) Some pharaohs overturned the laws made by previous rulers.
  (D) Some pharaohs commissioned pyramids to be constructed in their honor.
  (E) Some pharaohs owned hundreds of slaves.

3.　Are we overwhelmed by the new or trapped in the old? The digital age bombards us with technological wonders. And yet, our attachment to the past leads us to consume pop culture well past its shelf life. The iPod
5　may have revolutionized how we listen to music, but many people are using it to listen to tunes that hit the big time half a century ago—or using their iPads to book tickets for a revived 1950s Broadway musical or for the latest movie based on a comic book from the 1940s.

The passage best supports which of the following generalizations?

(A) new technologies are fundamentally incompatible with outdated popular culture
(B) some forms of popular cultures should be opposed on moral grounds
(C) people are often reluctant to give up familiar forms of entertainment
(D) individuals should be discouraged from becoming overly attached to the past
(E) new technologies will continue to revolutionize life in the twenty-first century

4.　Ideas matter. A relatively small number can be classed as major historical events. And many times, their best, most eloquent expression has been on paper, stamped in ink, sewn on one side, and bound between
5　hard covers. In the beginning was the word, sure, but there's also a lot to be said for the book. Think of Abraham Lincoln's comment, one hundred and fifty years ago, upon meeting the creator of a book, "So, this is the little lady who made this big war." He was
10　speaking to Harriet Beecher Stowe, the author of *Uncle Tom's Cabin*. As we are asked to contemplate the disappearance of books as such, it's worth pausing over the astonishing range of personal, social, and political purposes that have been served by books: the liberation
15　of individuals, the reinforcement of community, the expansion of self-knowledge, the publication of scientific findings, the spread of lies and promulgation of facts. Vast are the aims served by books.

Based on Abraham Lincoln's comment, which example would the author most likely add to the list in lines 14-18?

(A) the emancipation of women
(B) the incitement of military conflicts
(C) the creation of friendships
(D) the election of politicians
(E) the revelation of secrets

5.　In an era when few men and no woman received such international renown, Dolley Madison's stature has puzzled historians and modern Americans (who associate her name with ice cream and a line of
5　packaged pastries). In our time, reality stars can become "fame-ish" overnight; but the people of the nineteenth century bestowed fame on individuals—mostly male—who they felt had made significant contributions to history. Why did the residents
10　of Washington City, the members of government and their families, and, indeed, all of America declare Dolley the nation's "Queen"? What did they understand about Dolley Madison that we don't?

1. Which generalization about Dolley Madison does the passage support?

(A) she behaved in a condescending manner
(B) she failed to make significant contributions to United States history
(C) she has generated a great deal of scholarly controversy
(D) she was more famous than any man of her era
(E) she was a highly exceptional woman

2. An underlying assumption of the passage is that

(A) women commonly earned fame in the nineteenth century
(B) nineteenth century Americans were justified in holding Dolley Madison in such great esteem
(C) reality television is responsible for the destruction of older forms of entertainment
(D) women in the United States were forced to struggle for equality with men during the nineteenth century
(E) historians have underestimated the importance of women's political contributions in the nineteenth century

6.　　The book is a self-contained utterance. It is
finished, the very opposite of a "slug" you encounter
on a website casting about for visitors to contribute
writing and research. It is much more than a slug, much
5　more than the most basic information readily available.
The discrete physical embodiment of text, it makes the
perfect gift, the perfect giveaway, the perfect method of
saying, "Consider the following . . ." We often think of
imaginative literature when we think of book-reading,
10　along with notional scenes of people entering other
worlds through books, but the world we know, the
communities to which we already belong, are reinforced
by books. Such is the incredible and incredibly flexible
power of this primitive technology.

The passage best supports which generalization?

(A) books will eventually be replaced by newer forms
　　of technology
(B) books are powerful only because they allow people
　　to enter other worlds
(C) books serve a powerful social function
(D) books and electronic resources are equally powerful
　　tools for research
(E) books have little effect on existing communities

7.　　The Romans started making concrete more than
2,000 years ago, but it wasn't quite like today's concrete.
They had a different formula, which resulted in a substance that was not as strong as the modern product.
5　Yet structures like the Pantheon and the Colosseum
have survived for centuries, often with little to no
maintenance. That resistance, or durability against the
elements, may be due to one of the concrete's key
ingredients: volcanic ash.

Which of the following, if true, would most strengthen
the author's claim in lines 7-9 ("That resistance…ash")?

(A) volcanic ash was also used in construction by the
　　Etruscans, who inhabited Italy before the Romans
(B) access to parts of the Colosseum is now restricted
　　because of damage to the structure
(C) volcanic ash rarely needs to be ground in order to
　　reduce the size of its particles
(D) volcanic ash is used in a wide variety of modern
　　products, including toothpaste and cleaning agents
(E) buildings reinforced with volcanic ash withstand
　　natural disasters better than buildings reinforced
　　with other substances

8.　　The vessel believed to have been Blackbeard's
flagship is currently occupied by octopuses, which
turn a pale, disgruntled green when nautical
archaeologists approach. Black sea bass nip at the
5　excavators' ears, and moray eels spill out of the
mouths of cannons, many of which are still loaded.
But after nearly 300 years in the North Carolina
shallows, the remains of what may be the Queen
Anne's Revenge are surfacing, plank by worm-eaten
10　plank. The site, discovered in 1996, is 25 feet
underwater, less than a mile and a half from shore. But
long weather delays during diving seasons and
uncertain funding have slowed the excavation—this
past fall's expedition was the first since 2008—and it
15　can take years to clean and analyze artifacts corroded
beyond recognition. Still, with objects recovered from
50 percent of the site, archaeologists are increasingly
confident that the wreck is the infamous frigate that
terrorized the Caribbean and once blockaded
20　Charleston, South Carolina, for a week before running
aground in June 1718.

Lines 16-21 ("Still…1718") are based on the
assumption that

(A) severely damaged artifacts can nevertheless
　　provide important insights
(B) objects from the remaining half of the site will
　　probably soon be recovered
(C) the frigate that terrorized the Carribean could only
　　have belonged to Blackbeard
(D) archaeologists can make reasonable conjectures
　　based on incomplete evidence
(E) the excavation of the Queen Anne's Revenge
　　took place too far underwater to be affected by
　　the weather

9.	For some activists, eating local foods is no longer just a pleasure—it is a moral obligation. Why? Because shipping foods over long distances results in the unnecessary emission of the greenhouse gases that are
5	warming the planet. This concern has given rise to the concept of "food miles," that is, the distance food travels from farm to plate.

But food miles advocates fail to grasp the simple idea that food should be grown where it is most
10	economically advantageous to do so. Relevant advantages consist of various combinations of soil, climate, labor, and other factors. It is possible to grow bananas in Iceland, but Costa Rica really has the better climate for that activity. Transporting food is just
15	one relatively small cost of providing modern consumers with their daily bread, meat, cheese, and veggies. Concentrating agricultural production in the most favorable regions is the best way to minimize human impacts on the environment.

Which of the following most nearly undermines food Miles advocates' claim about the "moral obligation" (line 2)?

(A)	greenhouses used to grow food in cold climates produce more harmful gases than do the airplanes used to transport food
(B)	when shipped internationally, food is typically accompanied by other products
(C)	airplanes used to transport foods now release larger quantities of greenhouse gas than they did a decade ago
(D)	the rate at which greenhouse gases are warming the atmosphere has slowed because of international legislation
(E)	the majority of crops grown in the world are not consumed by local inhabitants

10.	There's a certain way jazz musicians from the 1930s pose for photographs, half-turned to face the camera, symmetrically arrayed around the band-leader, who can be identified by his regal smile and
5	proximity to the microphone. Publicity stills of the period were the equivalent of English court paintings, hackwork intended to exalt their subjects and attract admiration to their finery. Bandleaders even took titles borrowed from the aristocracy:
10	Duke Ellington, Count Basie, Earl Hines . . . well, Earl was actually the man's given name, but he lived up to it in a way no tracksuited rap star could approach, no matter how big the diamond in his earlobe.

Which of the following should be added to the list in line 10?

(A)	Fats Waller
(B)	Charlie Parker
(C)	Thelonius Monk
(D)	King Oliver
(E)	Max Roach

11. Sometime near the end of the Pleistocene, a band of people left northeastern Asia, crossed the Bering land bridge when the sea level was low, entered Alaska and became the first Americans. Since the 1930s, archaeologists have thought these people were members of the Clovis culture. First discovered in New Mexico in the 1930s, the Clovis culture is known for its distinct stone tools, primarily fluted projectile points. For decades, Clovis artifacts were the oldest known in the New World, dating to 13,000 years ago. But in recent years, researchers have found more and more evidence that people were living in North and South America before the Clovis.

The most recently confirmed evidence comes from Washington. During a dig conducted from 1977 to 1979, researchers uncovered a bone projectile point stuck in a mastodon rib. Since then the age of the find has been debated, but recently anthropologist Michael Waters and his colleagues announced a new radiocarbon date for the rib: 13,800 years ago, making it 800 years older than the oldest Clovis artifact. Other pre-Clovis evidence comes from a variety of locations across the New World.

Which of the following statements, if true, would most strengthen the author's argument in the last sentence of the first paragraph (lines 9-12)?

(A) Fluted projectiles dating to 11,800 years ago have been discovered in a remote South American location
(B) The projectile point found during the 1977-1979 dig is the same age as the mastodon rib
(C) Members of the Clovis culture were discovered to have lived in many different locations across the Southwestern United States
(D) Bone projectile points dating to 14,800 years ago have been found throughout northeastern Asia
(E) Michael Waters and his colleagues may have significantly overestimated the age of the mastodon rib

12. More than two centuries ago, attempting to explain the formation of the Sun and its planets, Immanuel Kant proposed a "nebular hypothesis," according to which a swirling mass of gas and dust that surrounded our star-in-formation condensed into clumps that became the planets. In its broad outlines, Kant's hypothesis remains the basis for modern astronomical approaches to planet formation, having triumphed over the concept, much in vogue during the first half of the twentieth century, that the Sun's planets arose from a close passage of another star by the Sun. In that scenario, the gravitational forces between the stars would have drawn masses of gas from each of them, and some of this gas could then have cooled and condensed to form the planets. This hypothesis, promoted by the famed British astrophysicist James Jeans, had the defect (or the appeal, for those inclined in that direction) of making planetary systems extremely rare, because sufficiently close encounters between stars probably occur only a few times during the lifetime of an entire galaxy. Once astronomers calculated that most of the gas pulled from the stars would evaporate rather than condense, they abandoned Jeans's hypothesis and returned to Kant's, which implies that many, if not most, stars should have planets in orbit around them.

Which of the following most weakens the "concept" mentioned in line 9?

(A) "close passage of another star by the Sun" (lines 11-12)
(B) "gravitational forces between the stars" (lines 12-13)
(C) "this gas could have cooled and condensed to form planets" (lines 14-15)
(D) "most of the gas pulled from the stars would evaporate" (lines 22-23)
(E) "Jeans's hypothesis" (line 24)

Official Guide Assumptions, Generalizations, and Claims Questions

Test 2	Section 7	Question 13	p. 478
Test 3	Section 4	Question 13	p. 522
Test 3	Section 4	Question 18	p. 522
Test 3	Section 4	Question 14	p. 523
Test 3	Section 4	Question 17	p. 523
Test 3	Section 7	Question 20	p. 542
Test 4	Section 2	Question 17	p. 577
Test 4	Section 2	Question 21	p. 579
Test 4	Section 5	Question 20	p. 592
Test 4	Section 5	Question 23	p. 592
Test 5	Section 3	Question 13	p. 647
Test 5	Section 3	Question 15	p. 647
Test 5	Section 3	Question 24	p. 649
Test 5	Section 7	Question 11	p. 663
Test 5	Section 7	Question 19	p. 665
Test 5	Section 7	Question 24	p. 666
Test 6	Section 7	Question 11	p. 725
Test 7	Section 2	Question 19	p. 767
Test 7	Section 2	Question 20	p. 767
Test 9	Section 4	Question 19	p. 901
Test 10	Section 4	Question 15	p. 963
Test 10	Section 6	Question 13	p. 973

Explanations: Assumptions, Generalizations, and Claims
Exercises

1. 1D, 2C

1.1 The passage indicates that flashbulb memories are "clear and detailed" but that they are also "surprisingly inaccurate." In other words, just because a memory is clear does not mean that it is true, i.e. *the clarity of a memory is not a reliable indicator of its accuracy.*

1.2 What type of situation is likely to become a flashbulb memory? One in which something momentous occurs "out of the blue." The key word is thus "unexpectedly" in (C), which describes a momentous piece of news (winning an enormous sum of money).

2. 1D, 2C

2.1 What's the point of the last sentence? The part before the colon: *even destruction tells a tale.* In context of the passage, which describes Karnak as a "treasure trove of data" about ancient Egypt, it indicates that even artifacts that have been destroyed (=poorly preserved), can help Egyptologists (=scholars) better understand ancient Egypt (=a culture).

Choices (A), (B), (C), and (E) are all too extreme: the passage only indicates one method by which some pharaohs tried to erase the names of their predecessors – it says nothing about whether they succeeded in eliminating all traces. It also says nothing about other ways in which they tried to consolidate their power, let alone that they would do it "by any means necessary." Furthermore, the passage indicates that scholars have learned from the pharaohs' attempts to erase their predecessors' names, and it is entirely possible that scholars could have other ways of learning about those predecessors.

2.2 What's the point? That pharaohs tried to erase the memories of their predecessors. The correct answer must therefore add to that idea. The word "overturned" in (C) is key because it indicates that some pharaohs sought to get rid of something their predecessors had accomplished.

3. C

The passage indicates that people have reacted to new technologies by clinging to "outdated pop culture" such as musicals and comic books (=forms of entertainment) from the 1940s and '50s. The fact that they hold on to these things means, by definition, that they are *reluctant to relinquish them.*

4. B

What was Abraham Lincoln's comment? "So, this is the little lady who made this big war." A "military conflict" is simply another way of saying "war," and since the author provides that quote as support for the idea that books are powerful, he would logically add it to the list in lines 14-18.

5. 1E, 2B

5.1 The passage indicates that Dolley Madison was one of the most well-known, beloved figures in the United States during an era when *few men and no women received such international renown*, and when *the people… bestowed fame on individuals – mostly male – who they felt had made significant contributions to history.* It can therefore be inferred that if Dolley Madison was famous during that era, she must have been an extremely unusual (=highly exceptional) woman.

5.2 By asking what nineteenth century Americans knew that historians today do not, the author implies that nineteenth century Americans *did* in fact have knowledge of Dolley Madison that has been lost. In addition, the author clearly indicates in lines 6-9 that nineteenth century Americans did not bestow fame lightly, directly implying that they must have had very good reason (=been justified) for elevating Dolley Madison in such an unusual manner.

6. C

In lines 11-13, the author states that *the world we know, the communities to which we already belong, are reinforced by books.* Reinforcing communities to which people already belong = playing a role in society, i.e. *having a social function.*

7. E

What is the author's claim in lines 7-9?

Roman concrete may have lasted so long despite being weaker than modern concrete because it contained volcanic ash.

So the correct answer must contain information supporting the idea that volcanic ash makes buildings stronger. (E) fulfills that requirement since it suggests that houses (i.e. buildings) built with volcanic ash are stronger than houses not built with it. All of the other answers are irrelevant to the argument.

8. D

The passage indicates that although objects have been recovered from only 50% of the site (line 17), archaeologists are "increasingly confident" that the ship they found did in fact belong to Blackbeard. In other words, they were able to formulate a hypothesis they believe is likely to be true (=make reasonable a conjecture) about the ship's identity without having access to the entire site. In other words, they did so based on *incomplete evidence.*

9. A

Why do food miles advocates claim that people have a moral obligation to consume locally grown foods? *Because shipping foods over long distances results in the unnecessary emission of the greenhouse gases that are warming the planet.*

So the correct answer must somehow interrupt the idea that growing food locally is better than importing it because the transportation process leads to higher levels of greenhouse gas emissions than growing it locally does.

(A) is the correct answer because it suggests that growing food locally can actually lead to higher rates of greenhouse gas emissions than importing it would. (B) and (E) are entirely unrelated to the original argument. In (B), the fact that food is accompanied by other products when it is shipped provides no information about the amount of greenhouse gases released in the shipping process; likewise, in (E) it does not matter whether most crops are consumed by local inhabitants or not – the answer fails to address the central relationship of the question, that between shipping and the emission of greenhouse gases. (C) would strengthen rather than weaken the argument: if emissions have increased, that would be a reason to encourage people to consume locally-grown food. (D) falls into the category of "not enough information:" even if the rate at which greenhouse gases are warming the atmosphere has slowed, it could still be sufficiently harmful to cause serious environmental damage. The answer says nothing about emissions slowing to a rate at which it would NOT be environmentally harmful to ship food over long distances.

10. D

What's the point of the list in line 10? That jazz musicians of the 1930s often took names that denoted royalty. All of the names listed (*Count, Duke, Earl*) are names that are also royal titles, so the correct name must also be a royal title. *King* is the only choice that is clearly associated with royalty.

11. B

What's the argument in lines 10-13? That there were in people living in the Americas *before* the Clovis. The oldest known Clovis artifact is 13,000 years old, indicating that the Clovis arrived in the Americas around 13,000 years ago. If older artifacts exist, then, they were most likely not produced by the Clovis but rather by some other people who arrived earlier. So to **strengthen** the idea that other people were in the Americas before the Clovis, the correct answer must be related to the idea that pre-Clovis artifacts exist.

(B) is the correct answer because it supports exactly that idea: we know that the mastodon rib is 13,800 years old, and if the projectile point were the same age, it could not have been made by the Clovis because they did not arrive until 800 years later.

(A) does not strengthen the argument since the Clovis were known to have arrived 13,000 years ago – something found 11,800 years ago would not be surprising. (C) is irrelevant to the argument. (D) is as unsurprising as (A) because the Clovis came from northeastern Asia and therefore would have inhabited that region well before they came to the Americas. (E) would weaken the argument because it suggests that the projectile have been made *after* the Clovis arrived.

12. D

What is the "concept" mentioned in line 9? *...the Sun's planets arose from a close passage of another star by the Sun. In that scenario, the gravitational forces between the stars would have drawn masses of gas from each of them, and some of this gas could then have cooled and condensed to form the planets.*

Remember that the author states that this theory ("Jeans's hypothesis") has been disproven, and that Kant's theory is now the accepted model. So anything related to Jeans's hypothesis can be eliminated. (A), (B), (C), and (E) all describe elements of Jeans's hypothesis, whereas (D) states the evidence that scientists used to *disprove* Jeans's hypothesis – namely that any gas that was pulled from the Sun and stars as they passed one another could not have condensed into planets because it would have evaporated immediately.

12. Analogies

When the SAT was revised in 2005, one of the biggest alterations was the elimination of the analogy section. What most people fail to realize, however, is that analogy questions were not eliminated entirely. While there are no longer vocabulary-based analogy questions, there are still passage-based analogy questions. The College Board didn't change things nearly as much as is commonly believed.

I think it's pretty safe to say that analogy questions are among the most hated questions on the Critical Reading section (if you happen to like them, consider yourself lucky). They're also among the most difficult: people already scoring around 700 often find that analogy questions are one of the few remaining types of questions that regularly give them trouble. The good news is that analogy questions show up relatively infrequently – you won't even find them on every test, and when they do appear, there's usually only one. The bad news, of course, is they do crop up sometimes, and you have to be prepared to handle them when that happens.

Recognizing Analogy Questions

Analogy questions can be phrased in several ways: most frequently, you will be asked to identify the scenario from among the answer choices that is most *analogous* (similar) to the scenario described in several lines of the passage. You may also be asked to identify the answer choice that is *most like* or *most similar to* a scenario described in the passage. Either way, the answer choices will describe a series of situations and people completely unconnected to the passage itself. You are responsible for drawing the connection between the specific wording in the passage and the more general situation it describes, and for recognizing which of the answers describes the same essential situation.

Solving Analogy Questions

Like inference questions, analogy questions have no simple solution: while there are tools you can use to recognize the correct answer confidently and efficiently, the answer will never be spelled out in any obvious way in the passage and there is often no way to solve them without systematically considering each answer choice. Unfortunately, there are no general key words that regularly appear in answer choices to indicate either correct or incorrect responses. While the correct answer will typically contain a synonym or synonyms for words in the passage, you must identify those words on your own.

For that reason, the kind of systematic, step-by-step approach that on other kinds of questions can sometimes be jettisoned is required here. Provided that you're willing to stick to it closely, however, analogy questions can be... well, I wouldn't go so far as to say pleasant, but definitely manageable enough to not make you want to rip your test in half whenever you see one.

1) Go back to the passage and read the exact lines provided in the question.

Analogy questions are not context-based questions. Provided you understand the general point of the passage well enough for those lines to make sense, you should be able to answer the question based only on the lines given. Reading anything else will most likely confuse you.

2) Quickly rephrase the scenario presented

Take a moment and reiterate for yourself exactly what's going on in those lines. Who is the person in question, what is that person doing, and what's the outcome?

3) Sum up the scenario <u>in general terms</u>. Write it down.

This is the crucial step – you have to understand what's going on in more abstract terms in order to draw the analogy. What you write can be very short and simple, but if you don't have something to look at to keep you focused, you'll usually have much more difficulty recognizing the answer when you see it.

4) Check the answers one by one, in order

As you read each answer, think about whether it matches the general "template" for the scenario you've established in step 3. If it clearly doesn't match, cross it out; if there's any chance it could work, leave it. If you're left with more than one answer, think about which one matches the template more closely – that will be the correct answer.

It is important to reiterate that going through these steps need not be time-consuming. On the contrary, it is possible to do them very, very quickly. But you should do your best to avoid skipping steps. If you don't define the relationships precisely upfront, it's very easy to get confused and to forget exactly what you're looking for.

Let's look at an example:

> Up close, amid the confusion of broken and standing
> stones, it still seems smaller than its reputation, notwith-
> standing the obvious feat represented by the erection of
> the famous sarsen stones; the largest weighs as much as
> 5   50 tons. Unique today, Stonehenge was probably also
> unique in its own time, some 4,500 years ago—a stone
> monument modeled on timber precedents. Indeed, its
> massive lintels are bound to their supports by joints taken
> straight from carpentry, an eloquent indication of just how
> 10 radically new this hybrid monument must have been. It is
> this newness, this assured awareness that nothing like it
> had existed before, this revelatory quality that is still pal-
> pable in its ruined stones. The people who built Stonehenge
> had discovered something hitherto unknown, hit upon
> 15 some truth, turned a corner—there is no doubt that the
> purposefully placed stones are fraught with meaning.

Which of the following is most analogous to the situation described in lines 11-14?

(A) A newspaper reporter exposes a major scandal and
     receives an award for her work.
(B) A well-known classical musician successfully releases
     an album of contemporary songs.
(C) An artist invents a revolutionary painting technique and
     creates a work demonstrating its significance.
(D) An archaeologist is praised by his colleagues for
     his detailed studies of an ancient civilization.
(E) A politician commissions the construction of a large-scale
     public works project.

Now we're going to apply the process described above to figure out the solution:

1) Reread only the lines in question

Lines 11-14 state:

The people who built Stonehenge had discovered something hitherto unknown, hit upon some truth, turned a corner—there is no doubt that the purposefully placed stones are fraught with meaning.

2) Reiterate lines in your own words

Builders of Stonehenge discovered something wildly, incredibly new that changed the way they understood their world, then built Stonehenge as a monument to that discovery.

If you feel that it helps to write this part down and you can do so quickly, write it down. If it will take too much time or doesn't seem necessary skip it.

3) Rephrase #2 in a more general way

Discover smthg new, change outlook, do smthg to show off

Notice the shorthand here. This is similar to a "main point" exercise – the goal is to capture the general idea as simply and quickly as possible.

4) See which answer matches the summary in #3

One by one, we're going to check the answers in order.

(A) A newspaper reporter exposes a major scandal and receives an award for her investigation.

No. Exposing something bad and being rewarded for it is not the same thing as discovering something new that changes one's outlook on the world and then creating something to convey that discovery.

The answer could maybe work if you stretched it – after all, exposing is sort of like discovering, and that experience *could* change someone's outlook on the world, but the answer gives no indication of the latter, and the two situations are not fundamentally the same. If we really wanted to, we could leave the answer, but only with the assumption that there's probably something better.

(B) A well-known classical musician successfully releases an album of contemporary songs.

No. Successfully switching from one kind of music to another is not at all the same thing as making an entirely new discovery. So (B) is out.

(C) An artist stumbles on a revolutionary technique and creates a work demonstrating its significance.

It could work: the answer describes a person who makes an important discovery that alters their perception, then creates something that is based on that discovery and that is intended to convey its importance. Maybe the situation described in the answer choice isn't quite as extreme as the one in the passage, but still, it captures the same general idea.

Besides, we also have synonyms for words/ideas in the passage: *discovered = stumbles upon, something hitherto unknown, hit upon some truth, turned a corner = revolutionary*, and *meaning = significance*.

So we keep (C).

**(D) An archaeologist is praised by his colleagues for
his detailed studies of an ancient civilization.**

No. There's nothing in here that goes along with the idea of discovering something new,
only studying something in detail – not at all the same thing. The fact that the archeologist is
praised is irrelevant.

This is the "trick" answer because it plays on a phenomenon known as "associative
interference." Stonehenge was built by an ancient civilization, and archaeologists study
ancient civilizations, so if you don't really understand what the question is asking, it is easy to
automatically assume that an answer that mentions people studying ancient civilizations
would be correct. But there's no relationship.

**(E) A politician commissions the construction of a large-scale
public works project.**

No. Again, associative interference. Yes, Stonehenge was a large project – the passage makes
that much clear – but the lines in question tell us nothing about who commissioned it.
Instead, they focus on the fact that it was constructed to convey some new truth about the
world that its builders had discovered. That doesn't mean it couldn't have been
commissioned, but we have no information about that.

So the answer is (C) since it comes the closest to replicating the general scenario described in
the passage. It might not be 100% perfect, but it's close enough.

You may also be asked to identify an analogy within the passage itself. Such questions are not strictly analogy questions but rather questions that test your ability to keep track of a concept throughout a passage and to recognize when the same idea is being discussed in different words. For example:

> In our attempts to uncover the history of the cosmos, we have continually discovered that the segments most deeply shrouded in **mystery** are those that deal with origins – of the universe itself, of its most massive structures
> 5 (galaxies and galaxy clusters), and of the stars that provide most of the light in the cosmos. These mysteries arise in large part because during the cosmic "dark ages," when matter was just beginning to organize itself into self-contained units such as stars and galaxies, most of this
> 10 matter generated little or no detectable radiation. When we turn to the origin of planets, **the mysteries deepen**. We lack not only observations of the crucial, initial stages of planetary formation but also successful theories of how the planets began to form.
> 15   Astrophysicists may now have more data but they have no better answers than before. The beginnings of planet building pose a remarkably intractable problem, to the point that one of the world's experts on the subject, Scott Tremaine, has elucidated (partly in jest) Tremaine's laws of planet
> 20 formation. The first of these laws states that "all theoretical predictions about the properties of exosolar planets are wrong," and the second that "the most secure prediction about planet formation is that it can't happen." This underscores the ineluctable fact that planets do exist, despite our inability to
> 25 explain **this astronomical enigma**.

Which of the following is most like the "astronomical enigma" (line 25)?

(A) "stars that provide most of the light in the cosmos" (lines 5-6)
(B) "little or no detectable radiation" (line 10)
(C) "successful theories of how the planets began to form" (lines 13-14)
(D) "the properties of exosolar planets" (line 21)
(E) "the ineluctable fact" (line 24)

The "astronomical enigma" refers to the fact that scientists **do not know** how planets formed and what their early existence was like. If you back up and read the full sentence in which (C) appears, you discover that scientists **lack** successful theories. So the answer is (C). It is of course possible to check all the answers out one-by-one; however, the answer choices tell you that you're looking for something explicitly stated in the passage, which means that if you take the time to define the "enigma" for yourself upfront, you can probably spot what it refers to in the passage pretty quickly.

Analogy Exercises

1.   Around the middle of the 20th century, science dispensed with the fantasy that we could easily colonize the other planets in our solar system. Science fiction writers absorbed the new reality: soon, moon and
5 asteroid settings replaced Mars and Venus.

Which of the following is most analogous to the situation described in the passage?

(A) A college student who wants to become a doctor earns poor grades in science and decides to study English instead
(B) A pilot is forced to make an emergency landing because of dangerous weather conditions
(C) A writer continues to publish novels despite receiving unfavorable reviews
(D) a physicist wins an important award after making a groundbreaking discovery
(E) a politician retires from office after becoming involved in a scandal

2.   Our psychological habitat is shaped by what you might call the magnetic property of home, the way it aligns everything around us. Perhaps you remember a moment, coming home from a trip, when the house you
5 call home looked, for a moment, like just another house on a street full of houses. But then the illusion faded and your house became home again. That, I think, is one of the most basic meanings of home—a place we can never see with a stranger's eyes for more than a
10 moment.

The situation described in lines 3-7 ("a moment… again") is most analogous to which of the following?

(A) a mother briefly fails to recognize her child when she arrives to pick him up from school
(B) a student walks past the friend he planned to meet because the friend's appearance has changed
(C) a doctor greets a patient warmly because she is happy that he has been cured
(D) a teacher has difficulty distinguishing a boy from his identical twin brother
(E) an architect is praised by her colleagues for her innovative design of a house

3.   Why is the connection between smells and memories so strong? The reason for these associations is that the brain's olfactory bulb is connected to both the amygdala (an emotion
5 center) and to the hippocampus, which is involved in memory. And, because smells serve a survival function (odors can keep us from eating spoiled or poisonous foods), some of these associations are made very quickly, and may even involve a one-
10 time association.

The connection between smells and memories is most like which of the following?

(A) a driver avoids an intersection after narrowly avoiding a crash
(B) a child develops a preference for a particular food after repeatedly refusing to eat it
(C) a young woman inexplicably develops an allergy to a common household item
(D) a man has difficulty eating after an illness compromises his sense of smell
(E) a food manufacturer develops a technology to prevent its products from spoiling

4.   Experimental scientists occupy themselves with observing and measuring the cosmos, finding out what stuff exists, no matter how strange that stuff may be. Theoretical physicists, on the other
5 hand, are not satisfied with observing the universe. They want to know why. They want to explain all the properties of the universe in terms of a few fundamental principles and parameters. These fundamental principles, in turn, lead to the "laws
10 of nature," which govern the behavior of all matter and energy.

The theoretical physicists' goal, as indicated in the passage, is most similar to which of the following?

(A) a biologist observing changes in a specimen over an extended period of time
(B) an astronaut flying to a distant planet
(C) a family working together to construct a new home for one of its members
(D) an astronomer observing the stars through a telescope
(E) a linguist seeking to discover underlying features common to all languages

5.   A quick glance through one of the many books that Herman Melville owned and studied—his copy of *The Poetical Works of William Wordsworth*, or *Don Quixote*, for example—reveals tangible evidence of his
5   creative approach to reading: the pages are covered with markings and annotations. There are vertical scores, underlines, brackets, checks, double- and triple-checks, x's, circles, as well as words, phrases, fragments of poetry, and even whole para-
10 graphs of prose. Despite his well-documented propensity for collecting fine editions of old books, Melville evidently had no qualms about picking up his pencil—or, in some rare instances, his crayon—and inscribing his thoughts in their margins.

Which of the following is most similar to the situation described in the last sentence (lines 10-14)

(A) a teacher writes encouraging comments on a student's paper
(B) a person makes loud comments during a movie and disturbs other people in the theater
(C) a conductor acquires an original score and then covers every page with markings
(D) a man accidentally spills water on an expensive painting given to him by a friend
(E) the new owner of a house paints its door a bright shade of orange

6.   Frederick Law Olmsted's *Walks and Talks* has all the wide-eyed quality of an American in England for the first time: Ah, homely cottages! Ooh, blooming hawthorn! He even marvels at the sight of a "real
5   (unimported) Hereford cow over the hedge," though he had surely seen a cow before. But tucked into the breathless prose is naturalist poetry. His observation, for instance, of "mild sun beaming through the watery atmosphere, and all so quiet" captures how achingly
10 beautiful the softly lit English countryside is. This emotional affinity for the pastoral shaped Olmsted's vision for Central Park and many future works.

As described in lines 1-6, Olmsted's reaction to England is most analogous to which of the following?

(A) an archaeologist publishes a paper about an object found at an excavation site
(B) a grandfather tells his grandson about a trip that he took as a young man
(C) a young woman travels to an unfamiliar city and excitedly describes her experience in a postcard
(D) an exchange student struggles to adapt to a new culture
(E) an artist travels to a foreign country and sketches a statue in a museum

7.   In our attempts to uncover the history of the cosmos, we have continually discovered that the segments most deeply shrouded in mystery are those that deal with origins – of the universe itself, of its
5   most massive structures (galaxies and galaxy clusters), and of the stars that provide most of the light in the cosmos. These mysteries arise in large part because during the cosmic "dark ages," when matter was just beginning to organize itself into self-contained
10 units such as stars and galaxies, most of this matter generated little or no detectable radiation. When we turn to the origin of planets, the mysteries deepen. We lack not only observations of the crucial, initial stages of planetary formation but also successful theories of
15 how the planets began to form.
    Astrophysicists may now have more data but they have no better answers than before. The beginnings of planet building pose a remarkably intractable problem, to the point that one of the world's experts on the
20 subject, Scott Tremaine, has elucidated (partly in jest) Tremaine's laws of planet formation. The first of these laws states that "all theoretical predictions about the properties of exosolar planets are wrong," and the second that "the most secure prediction about planet
25 formation is that it can't happen." Tremaine's humor underscores the ineluctable fact that planets do exist despite our inability to explain this astronomical enigma.

The astrophysicists' predicament, as described in lines 16-17, is most analogous to which of the following?

(A) an astronomer observes a planet whose existence was not predicted by any model
(B) mathematicians are perplexed by a problem that scholars have tried for decades to solve
(C) a group of researchers discovers that the data supporting its hypothesis is invalid
(D) chemical analysis of a meteorite reveals that it contains an isotope not found on Earth
(E) an accepted scientific theory is unexpectedly challenged by new evidence

Official Guide Analogy Questions

Explanations: Analogy Exercises

1. A

What is the scenario described in the passage? Science fiction writers realized that it was not realistic for the Earth to easily colonize other planets, so they changed their works to incorporate that new reality by focusing on asteroids and the moon.

General scenario: realize x is unrealistic, adjust expectations to do y

The key word in (A) is *instead*. The answer describes a person who realizes that a goal is unrealistic (it's pretty hard to become a doctor when you get bad grades in science class) and changes plans accordingly (studies English instead).

In (B), the pilot is *forced* to land, whereas the science fiction writers make a choice to focus on something that reflects the reality of their situation. (C) describes the opposite of the original scenario because the writer *continues* to write when faced with discouragement; (D) simply has no relation to the original scenario; and in (E), the politician does not realize that something specific is unrealistic and replace his/her career with a new one but rather abandons the career altogether.

2. A

What's the situation described in lines 3-7? Not recognizing a very familiar place for a moment – a place that it is virtually impossible not to recognize.

General scenario: not recognize x, when x is something that you *always* recognize.

(A) is the correct answer because a child is someone whose appearance a parent *cannot* forget (at least under normal circumstances),

and the parent only fails to recognize the child *briefly* (=for a moment).

(B) is not correct because the friend's appearance has changed – the passage says nothing about the house looking different; (C) is unrelated to the passage; in (D) the focus is on someone who cannot distinguish between two things that look the same, not on someone who does not recognize one familiar thing; and (E) is unrelated to the passage.

3. A

What defines the relationship between smells and memories? It's very strong because it serves a survival function: things that smell bad are more likely to be harmful, and thus people learn to avoid things associated with that smell.

General scenario: x is potentially harmful, so avoid x.

(A) is correct because it describes a situation in which a person was exposed to a potentially harmful situation (narrowly avoiding a crash) and as a result goes out of her way not to put herself in that situation again because she has made a connection between that situation and its possible negative consequences. (B) is not correct because the passage only discusses the connection between smells and negative consequences – it says nothing about changing one's preferences; (C) is not correct because the passage makes clear that bad smells can indicate harmful substances – there is nothing "inexplicable" about that association; (D) plays on associative interference by using the word "smell," which appears in the passage, but the situation described is otherwise entirely unrelated to it; and (E) is entirely unrelated to the passage.

4. E

What is the theoretical physicists' goal? *They want to know why. They want to explain all the properties of the universe in terms of a few fundamental principles and parameters.* (lines 6-8)

General scenario: want to know the general rules governing a particular phenomenon

(E) is correct because the linguist wants to "uncover the *underlying* features" of all languages. (A) describes what experimental scientists do, *not* theoretical physicists; science theme aside, (B) and (D) are entirely unrelated to the passage (theoretical physicists come up with theories, they don't go flying off to distant planets or spend their time observing things; (C) is incorrect because the passage says nothing about collaboration.

5. C

What's the situation described in lines 10-14? Melville acquired "fine editions of old books" and proceeded to annotate every inch of them with all sorts of markings.

General scenario: person gets something old and presumably expensive, ruins it deliberately by commenting all over it.

(C) is correct because a first edition of a music score is usually old and presumably expensive, and proceeds to deliberately mark it up – just like Melville did to his books. In (A), a student's paper is not something old and expensive; (B) describes something disturbing, but bothering people in a movie theater is not the same thing as marking a physical object; in (D), the painting is not ruined *deliberately*; and (E) describes a situation in which one feature (the door) is decorated in an unbecoming manner, rather than the whole thing – we also do not know whether the house is old and/or expensive.

6. C

What was Olmsted's reaction to England? He was incredibly ("breathlessly") excited about it and wrote all about how excited he was.

General scenario: go someplace new, get really excited about it, write something to show that excitement.

(C) is the answer because it describes a person who does precisely the above. (A) is completely off-topic. (B) involves a trip, but the recollection of a trip that happened a long time ago, whereas the passage describes Olmsted's reaction to England while he was there; (D) describes someone in a new place, Olmsted did not "struggle to adapt"; and (E) again refers to someone in a new place but says nothing about that person's *reaction* to that place.

7. B

What is the astrophysicists' predicament? They just can't figure out how planets get formed, despite having lots of data.

General scenario: have lots of information about a problem but still can't find a solution.

(B) fits the scenario above – if mathematicians have tried for decades to solve the problem, it can be assumed that there's lots of data about it, yet they're still "stumped."

(A) and (D) are incorrect because the passage describes a problem that has no apparent solution, not the discovery of something new; (C) is incorrect because the passage does not indicate that the scientists' data is invalid, just that it is not helpful; and (E) is incorrect because the passage does not discuss a theory that has been challenged but rather the seeming impossibility of formulating a theory in the first place.

13. Fiction Passages

Fiction passages are drawn from an exceedingly wide range of sources – while some are excerpted from works written well over a century ago by authors such as Charlotte Brontë and Charles Dickens, others come from contemporary novels by authors such as Amy Tan, Jhumpa Lahiri, and Gabriel Garcia Marquèz. Many contemporary passages will be minority-themed, or at least by minority (African-American, Hispanic, Asian-American) authors and will revolve around themes such as assimilation, the conflict between new and old cultures, family relationships, etc. Such passages can be treated more or less identically to the non-fiction excerpts that often deal with identical themes – aside from the fact that those themes will often be hinted at indirectly rather than spelled out for the reader, the fact that they are taken from works of fiction rather than from actual experiences is not terribly important.

Passages drawn from works of fiction dating from the nineteenth or early twentieth centuries are often far more challenging because they typically contain language more complex and situations less familiar than those contained in more contemporary works. That said, when such passages do appear, the questions tend to be relatively straightforward and are primarily designed to gauge whether you have understood the basic scenario described in the passage. You should, however, be aware that the test-writers sometimes alter the original works to make them fit into 85 or so lines, with the result that passages can be truncated awkwardly. That, in addition to the fact that they must be read entirely out of context, can make it very difficult to figure out just what is happening. You must, however, rely only on the information provided by the author and not attempt to speculate about any larger symbolism or meaning for what you are reading; doing so can get you in a lot of trouble. What matters is your ability to understand the literal events of the passage, and how the author's choice of words and use of specific rhetorical figures convey those events. That's it.

If you do go looking for some larger symbolism or start to make assumptions not explicitly supported by the passage, you can easily lose sight of the basics. In fact, most people have problems with passages like these not because there's an esoteric interpretation that can only be perceived through some quasi-mystical process, but rather because they aren't sufficiently *literal*.

Fiction Passages and Main Point

Because fiction passages are not based on arguments but instead revolve around characters' actions/reactions and relationships, their "main points" can often be challenging to identify. They do, however, generally convey an essential idea, character trait, or relationship that essentially functions as the point; provided that you can identify that idea, you should be able to answer many of the questions without too much difficulty. While fiction passages do sometimes contain more "detail" questions (e.g. vocabulary-in-context, tone in particular lines) and fewer logic-based question (e.g. inference, supporting/undermining claims) than do other types of passages, many correct answer choices will also rephrase the central conflict, character trait, etc. that the passage describes, so it is very much in your interest to take a moment and underline it/write it down before you look at the questions.

Unfortunately, there is no single most common passage structure: sometimes the main idea or relationship of the passage will, as in other types of passages, be found in the last sentence of the first paragraph or in the last sentence of the passage (you should always pay attention to those places just in case); other times, the main idea may be located somewhere else entirely or may never be explicitly stated at all. So while it is often possible to skip over large swaths of text in a passage dealing with, say, Frederick Douglass during an initial read-through, **you should generally plan to read fiction passages in their entirety**, trying to get a sense of the overall idea they convey and being careful not to waste too much time on unfamiliar words or turns of phrase.

As is true for all other types of passages, you should pay careful attention to major transitions, unusual punctuation, and strong language because they will virtually always appear at key places in the passage.

Important: always read the italicized blurb above a fiction passage!

While you should always plan to read the blurb before each passage, it is particularly important that you do so for fiction passages because it will sometimes provide important contextual information without which the passage will not make sense. (No introduction will, however, be provided for short fiction passages.)

Let's start by looking at a very short fiction passage.

> Occasionally a postcard would arrive in Seattle, where Ruma and Adam and their son Akash lived. The postcards showed the facades of churches, stone fountains, crowded piazzas, terra cotta rooftops mellowed by late afternoon sun. Nearly fifteen years had
> 5   passed since Ruma's only European adventure, a month-long EuroRail holiday she'd taken with two girlfriends after college, with money saved up from her salary as a paralegal. She'd slept in shabby pensions, practicing a frugality that was foreign to her at this stage of her life, buying nothing but variations of the same postcards her
> 10   father sent now. Her father wrote succinct, impersonal accounts of the things he had seen and done: "Yesterday the Uffizi Gallery. Today a walk to the other side of the Arno. A trip to Siena scheduled tomorrow." Occasionally there was a sentence about the weather. But there was never a sense of her father's presence in those places.

When most people consider the point of a passage like this, they tend to get confused, primarily because they get caught up in all the details. Typically, when I ask someone what the point of a passage like this is, I tend to get a response like, "Well, so the passage is talking about this person, Ruma, and then, like, describing how she went to Europe and stuff, and then, um like, it talks about her father…" As established earlier, this is the sort of thinking that you want to avoid at all cost. Stop for a moment, think rationally, and focus on the part of the passage most likely to provide you with key information: the end.

And indeed, if you forget about the description in the middle and just focus on the end, the author actually spells out the point that all that description is leading up to: the postcards were "impersonal" and "revealed nothing about [Ruma's father's] presence. That's it – that all you want to focus on.

Then, if you encounter a question like the following (which is pretty likely), the answer becomes a lot easier to figure out:

> The passage indicates that the "postcards" (line 2) were
>
> (A) surprising
> (B) exotic
> (C) dispassionate
> (D) thrilling
> (E) idealistic

Do not under any circumstances get distracted by the reference to line 2. Although the postcards are mentioned there, we don't find out their significance until the last sentence. The word "dispassionate" simply rephrases the idea expressed there, namely that the cards were impersonal, so the answer is (C).

The question could also be asked about from this angle:

> The description in lines 11-12 ("Yesterday…tomorrow") primarily serves to
>
> (A) highlight the similarities between the postcards sent by
>   Ruma and those sent by Ruma's father
> (B) provide a detailed description of the sites visited by
>   Ruma's father
> (C) illustrate the detached nature of the descriptions on
>   the postcards
> (D) criticize the succinctness of Ruma's father's writing
> (E) offer an analysis of Ruma's father's personality

Because this is a function question, you need to consider it in context of the surrounding sentences. What do those sentences reveal? That Ruma's father's postcards were "impersonal" and "revealed nothing about his presence." Impersonal = detached nature, which again leads you to (C).

Now we're going to look at a somewhat longer passage. It's by Amy Tan, a well-known Chinese-American author whose work has been used by ETS in the past.

Fiction Passage Exercises

The following passage is taken from a novel published in 2005. The protagonist, Ruth Young, is a writer; Art is her boyfriend.

In the coauthoring trade, "Ruth Young" was the small-type name that followed "with," that is, if it appeared at all. After fifteen years, she had nearly thirty-five books to her credit. Most of her early work had
5 come from corporate communications clients. Her expertise had woven its way into communication in general, then communication problems, behavioral patterns, emotional problems, mind-body connections, and spiritual awakening. She had been in the business
10 long enough to see the terms evolve from "chakras" to "ch'i," "prana," "vital energy," "life force," "biomagnetic force," "Bioenergy fields," and finally back to "chakras." In bookstores, most of her clients' words of wisdom were placed in the light or popular
15 sections Self-Help, Wellness, Inspirational, New Age. She wished she were working on books that would be categorized as Philosophy, Science, Medicine.

By and large, the books she helped write were interesting, she often reminded herself, and if not, it was
20 her job to *make* them interesting. And though she might pooh-pooh her own work just to be modest, it irked her when others did not take her seriously. Even Art did not seem to recognize how difficult her job was. But that was her fault. She preferred to make it look easy. She
25 would rather others discern themselves what an incredible job she did in spinning gold out of dross. They never did, of course. They didn't know how hard it was to be diplomatic, to excavate lively prose from incoherent musings. She had to assure clients that her
30 straightforward recasting of their words still made them sound articulate, intelligent, and important. She had to be sensitive to the fact the authors saw their books as symbolic forms of immortality, believing that their words on the printed page would last far longer than
35 their physical bodies. And when the books were published, Ruth had to sit back quietly at parties while the clients took credit for being brilliant. She often claimed she did not need to be acknowledged to feel satisfied, but that was not exactly true.

1. Lines 1-4 suggest that Ruth

   (A) has written more books than most of her colleagues
   (B) is a well-respected member of her profession
   (C) is not always given credit for her work
   (D) prefers to write books related to communications
   (E) is frequently ignored by the authors with whom she collaborates

2. Lines 13-17 ("In bookstores…Medicine") suggest that the books Ruth coauthors

   (A) are not financially lucrative
   (B) are featured prominently in bookstores
   (C) are of no interest to her friends and family
   (D) are unlikely to be taken seriously
   (E) only appeal to communications specialists

3. In line 25, "discern" most nearly means

   (A) perceive
   (B) clarify
   (C) elicit
   (D) discuss
   (E) differentiate

4. Based on the information in lines 20-24 Ruth's attitude toward her work can best be described as

   (A) resentful
   (B) dismissive
   (C) cynical
   (D) self-deprecatory
   (E) flippant

5. In line 26, "dross" is most like

(A) "words of wisdom" (line 14)
(B) "an incredible job" (lines 25-26)
(C) "incoherent musings" (line 29)
(D) "symbolic forms of immortality"
    (line 33)
(E) "the clients" (line 37)

6. In line 28, "excavate" most nearly means

(A) dig
(B) extract
(C) revise
(D) hollow out
(E) expose

7. The author uses the phrase "incoherent musings" (line 29) in order to

(A) criticize a particular type of literature
(B) challenge a popular notion
(C) defend an attitude
(D) describe a result
(E) emphasize the difficulty of a task

8. Lines 29-31 suggest the "authors" held what assumption?

(A) Their writing was badly in need of
    additional editing.
(B) Their work would only be considered
    important during their lifetimes.
(C) Their writing would be incomprehensible
    to the general public.
(D) Ruth's job was much more difficult than
    most people believed it to be.
(E) Readers would not respect them if they
    wrote in a clear and direct manner.

9. Which of the following is most analogous to situation in lines 32-35 ("the authors saw… physical immortality")

(A) An author is praised by critics for her
    groundbreaking novel.
(B) A composer writes a symphony that
    continues to be performed for many
    centuries.
(C) An editor rejects a novel by a young
    novelist because she believes it will
    not appeal to readers.
(D) An established artist is unable to sell
    his most recent painting.
(E) A journalist enjoys a brief period of
    popularity after publishing an article
    in a major newspaper.

10. Ruth's attitude toward "sitting back" (line 36) is primarily one of

(A) resigned apathy
(B) intense loathing
(C) wry amusement
(D) tacit discomfort
(E) analytical detachment

The following passage, in which the narrator describes her first day at a new school, is taken from a novel by a Caribbean-American author

It was the first day of a new term, Miss Nelson said, so we would not be attending to any of our usual subjects; instead, we were to spend the morning in contemplation and reflection and writing something she
5 described as an "autobiographical essay." In the afternoon, we would read aloud to each other our auto-biographical essays. (I knew quite well about "autobiography" and "essay," but reflection and contemplation! A day at school spent in such a way! Of
10 course, in most books all the good people were always contemplating and reflecting before they did anything. Perhaps in her mind's eye she could see our future and, against all prediction, we turned out to be good people.) On hearing this, a huge sigh went up from the girls.
15 Half the sighs were in happiness at the thought of sitting and gazing off into clear space, the other half in unhappiness at the misdeeds that would have to go unaccomplished. I joined the happy half, because I knew it would please Miss Nelson, and, my own
20 selfish interest aside, I liked so much the way she wore her ironed hair and her long-sleeved blouse and box-pleated skirt that I wanted to please her.

The morning was uneventful enough: a girl spilled ink from her inkwell all over her uniform; a
25 girl broke her pen nib and then made a big to-do about replacing it; girls twisted and turned in their seats and pinched each other's bottoms; girls passed notes to each other. All this Miss Nelson must have seen and heard, but she didn't say anything—only kept reading her
30 book: an elaborately illustrated edition of the *The Tempest*, as later, passing by her desk, I saw. Midway in the morning, we were told to go out and stretch our legs and breathe some fresh air for a few minutes; when we returned, we were given glasses of cold lemonade
35 and a slice of bun to refresh us.

As soon as the sun stood in the middle of the sky, we were sent home for lunch. The earth may have grown an inch or two larger between the time I had walked to school that morning and the time I went
40 home to lunch, for some girls made a small space for me in their little band. But I couldn't pay much attention to them; my mind was on my new surroundings, my new teacher, what I had written in my nice new notebook with its black-all-mixed-up-with-white cover and
45 smooth lined pages (so glad was I to get rid of my old notebooks, which had on their covers a picture of a wrinkled-up woman wearing a crown on her head and a neckful and armfuls of diamonds and pearls—their pages so coarse, as if they were made of cornmeal). I flew
50 home. I must have eaten my food. By half past one, we were sitting under a flamboyant tree in a secluded part of our schoolyard, our auto-biographical essays in hand. We were about to read aloud what we had written during our morning of contemplation
55 and reflection.

In response to Miss Nelson, each girl stood up and read her composition. One girl told of a much revered and loved aunt who now lived in England and of how much she looked forward to one day
60 moving to England to live with her aunt; one girl told of her brother studying medicine in Canada and the life she imagined he lived there (it seemed quite odd to me); one girl told of the fright she had when she dreamed she was dead, and of the matching fright she
65 had when she woke and found that she wasn't (everyone laughed at this, and Miss Nelson had to call us to order over and over); one girl told of how her oldest sister's best friend's cousin best friend (it was a real rigmarole) had gone on a Girl Guide
70 jamboree held in Trinidad and met someone who millions of years ago had taken tea with Lady Baden-Powell; one girl told of an excursion she and her father had made to Redonda, and of how they had seen some booby birds tending their chicks. Things
75 went on in that way, all so playful, all so imaginative. I began to wonder about what I had written, for it was the opposite of playful and it was the opposite of imaginative. What I had written was heartfelt, and, except for the very end, it was all too true. The
80 afternoon was wearing itself thin. Would my turn ever come? What should I do, finding myself in a world of new girls, a world in which I was not even near the center?

It was a while before I realized that Miss Nelson
85 was calling on me. My turn at last to read what I had written. I got up and started to read, my voice shaky at first, but since the sound of my own voice had always been a calming potion to me, it wasn't long before I was reading in such a way that, except for
90 the chirp of some birds, the hum of bees looking for flowers, the silvery rush-rush of the wind in the trees, the only sound to be heard was my voice as it rose and fell in sentence after sentence. At the end of my reading, I thought I was imagining the upturned faces
95 on which were looks of adoration, but I was not; I I thought I was imagining, too, some eyes brimming over with tears, but again I was not. Miss Nelson said that she would like to borrow what I had written to read for herself, and that it would be placed on the
100 shelf with the books that made up our own class library, so that it would be available to any girl who wanted to read it.

1. Line 2, "attending to" most nearly means

   (A) accompanying
   (B) serving
   (C) taking charge of
   (D) devoting time to
   (E) scrutinizing

2. As characterized by the narrator, the "good people" (line 10) are

   (A) whimsical and capricious
   (B) mysterious and intriguing
   (C) moralistic and disdainful
   (D) circumspect and prone to reverie
   (E) kindly and magnanimous

3. The parenthetical statement in lines 7-13 serves to convey the narrator's

   (A) delight
   (B) curiosity
   (C) envy
   (D) indifference
   (E) bewilderment

4. The author states that Miss Nelson "kept reading her book" (lines 29-30) in order to

   (A) emphasize Miss Nelson's love of Shakespeare
   (B) suggest that the narrator had acquired her love of contemplation from her teacher
   (C) highlight the central role of literature in the narrator's classroom
   (D) suggest that Miss Nelson had a tendency to ignore her students
   (E) illustrate a pose of deliberate indifference

5. In lines 41-50 ("But I...food"), the narrator's attitude is one of

   (A) amusement
   (B) exasperation
   (C) cautious interest
   (D) abject terror
   (E) eager anticipation

6. Based on the description in lines 56-74 which of the following best characterizes the students' compositions?

   (A) convoluted and scholarly
   (B) whimsical and entertaining
   (C) wry and ironic
   (D) comedic and impudent
   (E) grandiose and condescending

7. In line 76, "wonder about" most nearly means

   (A) question
   (B) interrogate
   (C) gaze
   (D) speculate
   (E) marvel

8. In line 80, the phrase "wearing itself thin" is used to emphasize the narrator's

   (A) hostility
   (B) obstinacy
   (C) impatience
   (D) hesitation
   (E) capriciousness

9. Lines 80-83 reveal the narrator's sense of

   (A) dejection
   (B) uncertainty
   (C) facetiousness
   (D) determination
   (E) self-importance

10. The narrator indicates that she viewed her "own voice" (line 87) as

    (A) a warning
    (B) a rebuke
    (C) a paradigm
    (D) a balm
    (E) a premonition

11. The primary rhetorical device used by the author in lines 88-93 is

    (A) understatement
    (B) euphemism
    (C) parallel structure
    (D) cliché
    (E) direct citation

The following passage is taken from a novel published in the nineteenth century. Here, the narrator pays a visit to his friend, a detective.

One night I was returning from a journey to a patient, when my way led me through Baker Street. As I passed the well-remembered door, I was seized with a keen desire to see Holmes again, and to know
5   how he was employing his extraordinary powers. His rooms were brilliantly lit, and, even as I looked up, I saw his tall, spare figure pass twice in a dark silhouette against the blind. He was pacing the room swiftly, eagerly, with his head sunk upon his chest and
10   his hands clasped behind him. To me, who knew his every mood and habit, his attitude and manner told their own story. He was at work again. I rang the bell and was shown up to the chamber which had formerly been in part my own.
15   His manner was not effusive. It seldom was; but he was glad, I think, to see me. With hardly a word spoken, but with a kindly eye, he waved me to an armchair. Then he stood before the fire and looked me over in his singular introspective fashion.
20   "Wedlock suits you," he remarked. "I think, Watson, that you have put on seven and a half pounds since I saw you."

"Seven!" I answered.

"Indeed, I should have thought a little more. Just
25   a trifle more, I fancy, Watson. And in practice again, I observe. You did not tell me that you intended to go into harness."

"Then, how do you know?"

"I see it, I deduce it. How do I know that you
30   have been getting yourself very wet lately?

"My dear Holmes," said I, "this is too much. You certainly would have been burned, had you lived a few centuries ago. It is true that I had a country walk on Thursday and came home in a dreadful mess, but as I
35   have changed my clothes, I fail to see how you work it out."

"It is simplicity itself," said he; "my eyes tell me that on the inside of your left shoe, just where the firelight strikes it, the leather is scored by six almost
40   parallel cuts. Obviously they have been caused by someone who has very carelessly scraped round the edges of the sole in order to remove crusted mud from it. Hence, you see, my deduction that you had been out in vile weather As to your practice, if a
45   gentleman walks into my rooms smelling of iodo-form, with a black mark of nitrate of silver upon his right forefinger, and a bulge on the right side of his top-hat to show where he has secreted his stethoscope, I must be dull, indeed, if I do not pronounce him to be
50   an active member of the medical profession."

I could not help laughing at the ease with which he explained his process of deduction. "When I hear you give your reasons," I remarked, "the thing always appears to me to be so ridiculously simple that I could
55   easily do it myself, though at each successive instance of your reasoning I am baffled until you explain your process. And yet I believe that my eyes are as good as yours."

"Quite so," he answered. "You see, but you do not
60   observe. The distinction is clear. For example, you have frequently seen the steps which lead up from the hall to this room."

"Frequently."

"How often?"
65   "Well, some hundreds of times."

"Then how many are there?"

"How many? I don't know."

"Quite so! You have not observed. And yet you have seen. That is just my point. Now, I know that
70   there are seventeen steps, because I have both seen and observed. By-the-way, since you are interested in these little problems, and since you are good enough to chronicle one or two of my trifling experiences, you may be interested in this." He threw over a
75   sheet of thick, pink-tinted note-paper which had been lying open upon the table. "It came by the last post," said he. "Read it aloud."

The note was undated, and without either signature or address.
80   "There will call upon you to-night, at a quarter to eight o'clock," it said, "a gentleman who desires to consult you upon a matter of the very deepest moment. Your recent services to one of the royal houses of Europe have shown that you are one who
85   may safely be trusted with matters which are of an importance which can hardly be exaggerated. This account of you we have from all quarters received. Be in your chamber then at that hour, and do not take it amiss if your visitor wears a mask.
90   "This is indeed a mystery," I remarked. "What do you imagine that it means?"

"I have no data yet. It is a capital mistake to theorize before one has data. Insensibly one begins to twist facts to suit theories, instead of theories to suit
95   facts.

1. In the first paragraph, Watson determines that Holmes is "at work" (line 12) based on Holmes'

   (A) reserved manner
   (B) physical conduct
   (C) detailed narration
   (D) eccentric behavior
   (E) inexplicable silence

2. Based on the description in lines 15-19, Holmes' could best be described as

   (A) gregarious and outgoing
   (B) sly and cunning
   (C) reserved and laconic
   (D) jovial and sanguine
   (E) brooding and mercurial

3. Lines 37-50 indicate that Holmes

   (A) does not hold doctors in particularly high regard
   (B) spends less time outdoors than the narrator does
   (C) enjoys associating with members of the medical profession
   (D) considers the narrator careless in his personal habits
   (E) bases his observations on more than one of his senses

4. In line 48, "secreted" most nearly means

   (A) exuded
   (B) concealed
   (C) examined
   (D) insinuated
   (E) disguised

5. In line 49, "dull" most nearly means

   (A) dimwitted
   (B) blunt
   (C) uninteresting
   (D) stagnant
   (E) common

6. As described by Watson, Holmes makes a "distinction" (line 60) between

   (A) observing visually and observing aurally
   (B) behavior in public and behavior in private
   (C) the act of perceiving and the act of reflecting on what one has perceived
   (D) reasoning based on logic and reasoning based on intuition
   (E) the act of entering and the act of departing

7. Lines 83-88 suggest that Holmes is known for his

   (A) keen intelligence
   (B) belligerence
   (C) magnanimity
   (D) irreverence
   (E) discretion

8. Lines 86-87 ("This...received") indicate that Holmes' reputation is

   (A) unjustified
   (B) widespread
   (C) controversial
   (D) inexplicable
   (E) exaggerated

9. In lines 92-95, Holmes' attitude toward "theorizing" could best be described as

   (A) cynical
   (B) novel
   (C) flippant
   (D) prudent
   (E) impatient

10. In line 93, "insensibly" most nearly means

    (A) unfeelingly
    (B) eccentrically
    (C) imperceptibly
    (D) irrationally
    (E) unresponsively

11. Throughout the passage, Watson's attitude toward Holmes could best be described as one of

    (A) reverence
    (B) bewilderment
    (C) indifference
    (D) admiration
    (E) ambivalence

The following passage is excerpted from a nineteenth century British novel. The narrator, who is on a journey, has run out of money and must sell his coat.

Feeling that I could go but a very little way that day, I resolved to make the sale of my jacket its principal business. Accordingly, I took the jacket off; and carrying it under my arm, began to inspect

5 shops. It was a likely place to sell a jacket; for the dealers in second-hand clothes were numerous. But as most of them had among their stock an officer's coat or two, I was rendered timid by the costly nature of their dealings, and walked about for a long

10 time without offering my merchandise.

This modesty directed my attention to the marine-store shops in preference to the regular dealers. At last I found one that I thought looked promising, at the corner of a dirty lane, ending in an

15 enclosure full of stinging-nettles. Into this shop, which was low and small, and which was darkened rather than lighted by a little window, I went with a palpitating heart; which was not relieved when a man with the lower part of his face all covered with

20 a stubbly grey beard, rushed out of a dirty den behind it, and seized me by the hair.

'Oh, what do you want?' grinned this old man, in a fierce, monotonous whine. 'Oh, my eyes and limbs, what do you want? Oh, my lungs and liver,

25 what do you want? Oh, goroo, goroo!'

I was so much dismayed by these words, and particularly by the repetition of the last unknown one, which seemed to emerge from his throat, that I could make no answer; hereupon the old man, still

30 holding me by the hair, repeated:

'Oh, what do you want? Oh, my eyes and limbs, what do you want? Oh, my lungs and liver, what do you want? Oh, goroo!' - which he screwed out of himself, with an energy that made his eyes

35 start in his head.

'I wanted to know,' I said, trembling, 'if you would buy a jacket.'

'Oh, let's see the jacket!' cried the old man. 'Oh, my heart on fire, show the jacket to us! Oh, my eyes

40 and limbs, bring the jacket out!'

With that he took his trembling hands, which were like the claws of a great bird, out of my hair; and put on a pair of spectacles.

'Oh, how much for the jacket?' cried the old

45 man, after examining it. 'Oh - goroo! - how much for the jacket?'

'Half-a-crown,' I answered, recovering myself. 'Oh, my lungs and liver,' cried the old man, 'no! Oh, my eyes, no! Oh, my limbs, no! Eighteen-pence.

50 Goroo!'

Every time he uttered this ejaculation, his eyes seemed to be in danger of starting out; and every sentence he spoke, he delivered in a sort of tune, always exactly the same, like a gust of wind, which

55 begins low, mounts up high, and falls again.

'Well,' said I, glad to have closed the bargain, 'I'll take eighteenpence.'

'Oh, my liver!' cried the old man, throwing the jacket on a shelf. Oh, my lungs, get out of the

60 shop! Oh, my eyes and limbs - goroo! - don't ask for money; make it an exchange.' I never was so frightened in my life; but I told him that nothing other than money was of any use to me, but that I would wait for it outside, as he desired, and had no

65 wish to hurry him. So I went outside, and sat down in the shade in a corner. And I sat there so many hours, that the shade became sunlight, and the sunlight became shade again.

He made many attempts to induce me to

70 consent to an exchange; at one time coming out with a fishing-rod, at another with a fiddle, at another with a cocked hat. But I resisted all these overtures; each time asking him, with tears in my eyes, for my money or my jacket. At last he began

75 to pay me in halfpence at a time; and was full two hours getting by easy stages to a shilling.

'Oh, my eyes and limbs!' he then cried, peeping hideously out of the shop, after a long pause, 'will you go for twopence more?'

80 'I can't,' I said; 'I shall be starved.'

'Oh, my lungs and liver, will you go for threepence?'

'I would go for nothing, if I could,' I said, 'but I want the money badly.'

85 'Oh, go-roo!' 'will you go for fourpence?'

I was so faint and weary that I closed with this offer; and taking the money out of his claw, not without trembling, went away more hungry and thirsty than I had ever been. But at an expense of

90 threepence I soon refreshed myself; and, being in better spirits, limped seven miles upon my road.

Stop!

If you were a little confused when you read this, don't be surprised. Taken out of context, the narrator's goal and his interaction with the eccentric (to put it mildly) shopkeeper can easily seem baffling and leave many people wondering whether they missed something important about the significance of the encounter. The significance of the passage, however, is completely irrelevant. We're only interested in its literal meaning and how the author (Dickens, in case you're wondering) goes about conveying that meaning.

So let's consider what we know:

-The narrator is on a journey and wants to sell his jacket.

-He doesn't think it's worth a lot of money, so he looks around for a shop where he won't embarrass himself by trying to sell it.

-He finds a run-down shop, goes in, and is confronted by an apparently crazy shopkeeper, who grabs him by the hair and makes strange sounds. Understandably, he's pretty freaked out.

-He tries to sell the jacket but the shopkeeper wants him to exchange it instead.

-He goes outside and waits a really long time for the shopkeeper to give in.

-Finally, the shopkeeper offers to pay him, but a lot less money than he wants.

-Eventually, the narrator gets sick of haggling and decides to accept the shopkeeper's offer because he needs the money.

The narrator is so exhausted and hungry/thirsty from waiting for the shopkeeper to back down that he immediately goes and spends some of the money to make himself feel better, then continues on his journey.

For the record, it is NOT necessary that you write all this out on the SAT – that would constitute a massive waste of time. You must, however, keep the literal events of the passage in mind as you read the questions and not attempt to impose an explanation on them.

For a **"main point,"** the goal is simply to write something that captures the central conflict:

> **Narrator = sell, crazy shopkeeper = trade**

OR

> **Narrator vs. crazy shopkeeper, must sell jacket!**

Now look at the questions.

1. In lines 7-11, the narrator's attitude can best be described as one of

   (A) cheerful amusement
   (B) apprehensiveness and hesitancy
   (C) overwhelming fear
   (D) bewilderment and perplexity
   (E) apathy and resignation

2. In context of the passage, the narrator's statement in lines 8-9 ("I was rendered…dealings") implies that

   (A) he had never before entered an expensive shop
   (B) he was intimidated by the presence of soldiers
   (C) his believed that his coat lacked monetary value
   (D) he regarded the act of selling his coat as morally corrupt
   (E) he was frightened of the shopkeepers' odd behavior

3. In line 14, the narrator's use of the word "promising" can best be described as

   (A) ironic
   (B) philosophical
   (C) cavalier
   (D) vitriolic
   (E) enigmatic

4. Lines 15-17 contain an example of

   (A) euphemism
   (B) paradox
   (C) hyperbole
   (D) metaphor
   (E) oratory

5. In line 18, "relieved" most nearly means

   (A) exhausted
   (B) undermined
   (C) absolved
   (D) becalmed
   (E) interrupted

6. The comparison in line 42 primarily serves to

   (A) suggest that the shopkeeper is keeping wild animals on the premises
   (B) call attention to the shopkeeper's overwhelming sense of anxiety
   (C) emphasize the shopkeeper's menacing appearance
   (D) highlight the contrast between the shopkeeper and the narrator
   (E) dramatize the fundamental struggle between good and evil

7. In line 52, "starting out" most nearly means

   (A) beginning
   (B) protruding
   (C) wondering
   (D) departing
   (E) disturbing

8. The "tune" (line 53) can best be described as

   (A) monotonous
   (B) grating
   (C) intermittent
   (D) exotic
   (E) repetitive

9. Lines 62-68 primarily serve to emphasize the narrator's

   (A) callowness and immaturity
   (B) capriciousness and whimsicality
   (C) misanthropy and foolishness
   (D) sympathy and good humor
   (E) obstinacy and determination

10. In line 69, "induce" most nearly means

    (A) cajole
    (B) threaten
    (C) facilitate
    (D) defy
    (E) elicit

11. The humor in the last paragraph primarily results from

    (A) the contrast between the narrator's naiveté and the shopkeeper's world-weariness
    (B) the narrator's reluctance to acknowledge the eccentricity of the shopkeeper's actions
    (C) the narrator's exaggerated claims about the extremity of his hunger and thirst
    (D) the narrator's inexplicable fear when he accepts the money from the shopkeeper
    (E) the rapidity with which the narrator spends the payment he has worked so hard to obtain

Answers are located at the end of this chapter.

Official Guide Fiction Passages

Explanations: Fiction Passage Exercises

Passage #1: Ruth

1. C

In lines, 2-3, the phrase "that is, if [Ruth's name] appeared at all" indicates that Ruth's name did not always appear on the books she co-authored, i.e. that she was not always given credit for her work. Careful with (E) – it doesn't actually express the same idea as (C). The passage only indicates that Ruth's name doesn't always appear on the books she helps write; it says nothing about the authors actually ignoring her, and there's nothing to directly support an inference that they do.

2. D

Line 14 indicates that the books Ruth works on are considered "light" or "popular," which by definition are not "serious."

3. A

Because Ruth prefers to "make [her work] look easy," the word in question must mean something like "figure out." In addition, although the question only refers to line 25, a synonym for "discern," "recognize," is actually given in line 23. In both cases (A) is closest in meaning.

4. D

Line 21 indicates that Ruth dismissed her own work in order to be "modest," which is a synonym for "self-deprecating" (putting oneself down).

5. C

The phrase "spinning gold out of dross" means to take something ugly and turn it into something beautiful, with "dross" literally referring to the original versions of the books Ruth is given to rewrite, and "gold" referring to the revised products. Since "incoherent musings" also refers to the authors' original work, (C) is correct.

6. B

What is Ruth's job? She has to take the "incoherent musings" that the authors give her and turn them into something that makes sense. In other words, she has to pull out the ideas contained in the original, get rid of the messy parts, and make them interesting to readers. "Extract" conveys that idea most clearly." The remaining answer don't make grammatical sense when they're plugged back into the sentence – you can't dig, revise, hollow out, or expose something from something else.

7. E

The word "incoherent" is fairly strong -- it implies that what the authors originally wrote made no sense whatsoever. Why mention that fact? To emphasize "how hard" (line 27) Ruth's job was. Hard job = difficulty of a task.

8. E

Lines 29-31 state that Ruth "had to assure clients that her straightforward recasting of their words still made them sound articulate, intelligent, and important." In other words, the authors thought that if they were **not** straightforward (= writing in a clear and direct manner), then they **would** sound important. We can rewrite that statement as follows: if the authors **were** straightforward, then they **would not** sound important. Which is essentially the idea that (E) expresses.

9. B

What's described in lines 32-35? The authors saw "their books as symbolic forms of immortality, believing that their words on the printed page would last far longer than their physical bodies."

What's the general scenario? Produce a creative work that outlasts you.

Which situation fits that criteria? (B) because the symphony is performed "for centuries" after it is composed.

10. D

The last sentence indicates that Ruth is not happy (=uncomfortable) about the lack of acknowledgment she receives for her work, and the entire passage indicates that she is silent (=tacit) about her unhappiness.

Passage #2: Autobiographical Essay

1. D

If you were to plug in your own word, you might say something like "spending time on" or "working on," which would most likely give you the answer quickly. (The word "spend," which appears in line 4, is also used as a synonym for "attend to.") Alternately, you could plug in each word. You can't "accompany" or serve" a subject, so (A) and (B) are out, and "taking charge of" doesn't really make sense. It is possible to "scrutinize" a subject (examine it very closely), but there's nothing to indicate that the students would need to do so.

2. D

What do we know about the "good people?" They were always "contemplating and reflecting before they did anything." What does it mean to be contemplative? To have a tendency to get lost in one's thoughts and be a bit dreamy, i.e. be "prone to reverie." "Circumspect" means

"cautious," which goes along with the idea of thinking about things before taking action.

3. A

The exclamation points in line 9, along with the fact that the narrator associated contemplation with "good people" in books, reveal the narrator's positive attitude. In this context, "delight" is the only possible answer.

4. E

Remember that this is a function question, which means that you need to consider the context of the lines referenced. The information you need to answer the question comes *before* the dash – the fact that Miss Nelson "must have seen and heard" indicates that she's aware of her students' mischief but pretending not to care. In other words, she's deliberately being indifferent to what they're doing.

5. E

In the first paragraph, the narrator makes clear her excitement about writing her essay and reading it aloud. Lines 41-50 illustrate that excitement (she can't pay attention, "flies" home, and can barely remember eating).

6. B

Although the question refers you to a very long set of lines, you can actually save yourself a lot of time by spotting the words "playful and imaginative" in lines 77-78, which the narrator uses to describe the compositions. That tells you the right answer must be something similar, so (A), (C), and (E) are out. In (D), "comedic" could work, but "impudent" (rude) doesn't fit. The fact that all the students "laughed until Miss Nelson called [them] to order" indicates that they were entertained, and the fact that some of the compositions were slightly outrageous and not particularly serious indicates whimsicality.

7. A

If you were to plug in your own word, you might say something like "doubt" because the narrator's composition was so different from other students' and she's starting to worry a little. "Question" is the word that comes closest in meaning to "doubt" because it can carry a connotation of uncertainty, and none of the other options make sense in context.

8. C

Consider the context: the narrator has been waiting her turn for a long time, listening to all of her classmates read. She's getting nervous and growing tired of waiting for her turn. In addition, the question "Would my turn ever come?" directly reveals her impatience.

9. B

The rhetorical questions as well the phrase "what should I do?" indicate that the narrator is unsure of how to proceed. Although her concern about being "not even near the center" may lead you to think that she is self-important and pick (E), the lines only convey her worry over not fitting in and give no indication that she considers herself to be above anyone else.

10. D

A balm is something that is used to soothe, and the narrator states that her voice had "always been a calming potion to [her]."

11. C

The lines in question make use of parallel structure because they contain multiple clauses with the "noun + of + noun" structure ("chirp **of** some birds," "hum **of** bees," "rush-rush **of** the wind").

Passage #3: Sherlock Holmes

1. B

The narrator states that Holmes' attitude and manner "told their own story," i.e. they indicated that Holmes was at work. What did that attitude and manner consist of? Holmes "pacing the room swiftly, with his head sunk upon his chest and his hands clasped behind him." The emphasis is on Holmes' physicality and movement.

2. C

Holmes is described as being "seldom [effusive]" and "introspective," and as speaking "hardly a word." "Reserved" is the opposite of "effusive," and laconic = not talkative.

3. E

Holmes observes both with his eyes (line 37), and his nose ("if a gentleman walks into my room smelling of iodoform..." lines 44-46).

4. B

The bulge in the top-hat would indicate that the stethoscope is placed there, but since it is not visible, it must be hidden. The word in question must therefore be a synonym for "hidden," and that applies only to (B).

5. A

Holmes is describing his "simple" process of logical deduction, explaining why things are utterly obvious to him. In this context, "dull" must mean something like "stupid" or "foolish," and "dimwitted" is a synonym for those words.

6. C

Holmes distinguishes between his type of seeing, which involves thinking carefully about what he has perceived visually (he knows that there are seventeen steps leading up to the room) and Watson's, which involves only receiving information with his eyes but not actually thinking about that information. (Watson only knows that there are stairs leading up to the room but does not know how many.)

7. E

The letters states that Holmes is one "who may safely be trusted with matters which are of an importance which can hardly be exaggerated." In other words, he can keep a secret – and that's what "discretion" means.

8. B

The letter states that Holmes reputation for secret-keeping (=this account) has been "from all quarters received," i.e. from everywhere. Everywhere = widespread.

9. D

What information do we have about Holmes' view of theorizing? He doesn't want propose any theories too early because he might twist the facts to fit them instead of relying on the facts themselves. In other words, he thinks it's dangerous to jump to conclusions, i.e. he's being cautious and practical, = prudent.

10. D

The entire process that Holmes is describing is one of logical deduction, and twisting "facts to suit theories" rather than "theories to suit facts" is highly illogical. So "insensibly" must mean something like illogical, and "irrational" is a synonym for "illogical."

11. D

Throughout the passage, the author clearly has a positive attitude toward Holmes. He refers to his "extraordinary powers," has a "keen desire to see him again," and is amazed at the simplicity of Holmes' reasoning. So the answer has to be positive, leaving only (A) and (D). There is, however, no extreme or over-the-top language in the passage to suggest that he worships Holmes – that his attitude is one of reverence – so "admiration" is correct.

Passage #4: Crazy Shopkeeper

1. B

What information does the narrator provide in lines 7-11? He was "timid" and walked around for a long time before entering a shop. In other words, he was nervous and a little scared (=apprehensive) and not eager (=hesitant) to try to sell his coat.

2. C

The phrase *I was rendered timid by the costly nature of their dealings* indicates that the narrator was intimidated by the expensive items he saw in the shops, implying that he did not believe his coat to be worth as much money as those items.

3. A

The narrator's description of the store as dirty, dark, and in an enclosure "full of stinging nettles" indicates that the word "promising," which typically is used in regard to something positive, is here being used in regard to something just the opposite. Although the narrator does in fact regard the store as "promising" because he believes that it is the only one where he has a chance of selling his coat, the choice of that word is ironic because its connotations are exactly the opposite of those contained in the passage.

4. B

By definition, the function of a window is to bring light into a building, but the shop is *darkened rather than lighted by a little window* – a seeming contradiction or **paradox**.

5. D

Because the narrator's nervousness does not decrease when he enters the shop, the statement that his *palpitating heart was not "relieved"* indicates that his heart continued to pound. So "relieved" must mean something like "made better" or "calmed down." Although the word "becalmed" may be unfamiliar, you should be able to recognize that it contains the word "calm" and make the connection.

6. C

What's the essential idea that the narrator wants to convey through his description of the shopkeeper? He's frightening or **menacing** (we know because the narrator tells us that he's trembling). The comparison between the shopkeeper's hands and "the claws of a great bird" – a frightening image – therefore serves to support that idea.

7. B

The narrator indicates that the shopkeeper has worked himself into a frenzy, and when someone is in that state, their eyes typically bulge out. The word closest in meaning to "bulge" is "protrude," so (B) is correct.

8. E

What information do we have about the tune? That it was *always exactly the same*. In other words, it was repetitive.

9. E

The narrator states that he sat under the tree for more than a day (*for so many hours until shade became sunlight, and the sunlight became shade again*), suggesting that he is extremely stubborn, i.e. "obstinate and determined."

10. A

The narrator describes the various objects (fishing rod, hat, fiddle) that the shopkeeper brings in order to tempt him into an exchange. The word "induce" therefore must have a relatively positive connotation and mean something like "persuade." Of the choices, "cajole" ("coax by means of flattery") is the closest in meaning.

11. E

The humor in the last paragraph results from the fact that the narrator has worked so hard to sell his jacket to the shopkeeper rather than trade it for another object, then must immediately spend three-quarters of his earnings "refreshing himself" because he is so exhausted from insisting on being paid actual money.

14. Paired Passages

Paired passage sets come in two types: short and long. Most frequently, short paired passages (about 15 lines each, 4 questions) will be found in either the first or the second twenty-five minute Critical Reading section, while long paired passages (about 45 lines each, 10-12 questions) will appear during the final Critical Reading section. There are, however, exceptions, so you should not be overly surprised if the passages appear in a different order.

Regardless of where they show up, paired passages – especially long paired passages – are many people's least favorite part of Critical Reading. They hit you just when you don't have anything more to give, and they demand a level of focus that goes even beyond that required for the rest of Critical Reading. Instead of asking you to deal with one or two major viewpoints, they can sometimes ask you to deal with three or four: not only what the author of each passage thinks but sometimes also what the author of each passage says that *other people* think (got that straight?).

While Passage 1/Passage 2 relationship questions are often among the most difficult on the SAT, they are also the most direct embodiment of the "they say/I say model" and come closest to asking you to do the kind of reading you'll do in college. When you write research papers, you will in fact be asked to consider multiple interpretations or points of view regarding an event or phenomenon. The ability to understand differences between arguments, even subtle ones, is crucial to your being able to analyze them and formulate a coherent argument of your own in response.

While it isn't necessarily possible to make the process of reading and answering questions about paired passages easy, there are nevertheless some strategies that you can use to make it more straightforward and manageable.

How to Read Paired Passages

Above all, remember this: *your job is to deal with the smallest amount of information possible at any given time*. If you can focus on only what is necessary to focus on, and forget about everything else, the process becomes least manageable. Furthermore, the more work you do in terms of determining each author's argument and point of view upfront, the less work you'll have to do on the actual questions. Those things are true everywhere on the SAT, but they're especially true here. So in a nutshell:

1. Read Passage 1: write main point + tone

2. Do questions for Passage 1

3. Read Passage 2: write main point + tone, AND relationship to Passage 1

4. Do questions for Passage 2

5. Do Passage 1/Passage 2 relationship questions

When you work this way, breaking down every part of the question and working through each step separately, the chances of you becoming confused are greatly reduced.

Important: Questions about only one passage are often interspersed with questions asking about both passages. **When you skip over questions asking about both passages, remember to mark those questions so that you remember to come back to them. Make your marks huge and obvious.**

Common Passage 1/Passage 2 Relationships

Both P1 and P2 will *always* revolve around the same basic idea or event, even if it isn't always immediately obvious how the two passages relate to one another. The most common P1/P2 relationship simply involves two authors with conflicting views on or interpretations of an idea or event; however, there are a handful of other relationships that can occur.

- Passage 1 and Passage 2 present opposing views of the same topic (P1 = positive, P2 = negative or vice-versa).

- Passage 1 and Passage 2 agree but have different focuses or stylistic differences (e.g. P1 is written in third person and P2 is written in first person).

- Passage 1 and Passage 2 discuss different aspects of the same event or idea (e.g. P1 focuses on how an event was perceived by the press, P2 focuses on how it affected women).

- Passage 2 provides an example of an idea described generally in Passage 1.

- Passage 2 provides an explanation for a phenomenon discussed in Passage 1.

Why is it so important to determine the relationship between the passages? First, because long paired passages will almost always include a question that explicitly asks you to identify the relationship between the passages, and short paired passages will often include one of these questions as well. If you've already defined the relationship, you've essentially answered the question before you've even looked at it.

It is also crucial to determine the relationship between the passages because you generally cannot infer what the author of one passage would likely think of an idea in the other passage without knowing whether the authors agree or disagree. When the authors of the two passages disagree, most of the answers to relationship questions will be negative, and you can often automatically eliminate any positive or neutral answer just by reading the first word or two. Likewise, when the authors agree, most correct answers will be positive.

You should, however, be aware that some questions will ask you to identify a statement with which both authors would clearly agree, even when the passages indicate that they hold conflicting opinions. (Conversely, you may also be asked to identify a point of disagreement for two authors who clearly agree with one another.)

In such cases, you must proceed very carefully. Very often, the answers to such questions will often be based on an easily-overlooked detail in one or both of the passages. Sometimes that detail will in fact be located in a key place in one of the passages (introduction, last sentence, topic sentence of one of the paragraphs, close to a major transition or a dash/colon), but sometimes it will not. Because it is very unlikely that you will remember the information necessary to answer the question, you should always plan to return to the passages and reread as necessary. You should also make sure that you do not eliminate any answer unless you are really and truly certain that it is incorrect. I repeat: do not even try to rely on your memory. Just read.

Relationship Questions are Inference Questions

Because there is absolutely no difference between questions that ask about only one passage in a P1/P2 set and any other question about a single passage elsewhere on the test, there is absolutely no difference in how you should approach questions asking about single passages.

For most people, the real challenge is the relationship questions, the vast majority of which ask you to infer what one author would think about a particular idea in the other passage. In such cases, you must break down the question, making sure to define each idea separately and clearly before you attempt to determine the relationship between them.

As a general rule, such questions should be broken down in the following way:

1) Re-read the lines in question and sum up the idea in your own words.

2) Reiterate for yourself the main point of the other passage.

3) Determine whether the authors would agree or disagree.

4) Look at the answer choices: if the authors would agree, cross out all negative answers; if the authors would disagree, cross off all positive answers.

   Important: as discussed earlier, answers that indicate a lack of interest on the part of one author (e.g. *apathetic, indifferent, diffident*) are virtually guaranteed to be incorrect. Passages are chosen precisely because there is a specific relationship between their ideas, so by definition those words cannot be right.

5) Think carefully about the remaining answers. You should be down to two, three at the most.

Let's look at some examples:

Passage 1

In recent years, we've seen an explosion of
scientific research revealing precisely how positive
feelings like happiness are good for us. We know that
they motivate us to pursue important goals and over-
5   come obstacles, protect us from some effects of stress,
connect us with other people, and even stave off
ailments. The science of happiness has spawned a
small industry of motivational speakers and research
enterprises. Clearly, happiness is popular. But can
10   feeling too good ever be bad? Researchers are just
starting to seriously explore these questions, with
good reason: By recognizing the potential pitfalls of
happiness, we enable ourselves to understand it more
deeply and we learn to better promote healthier and
15   more balanced lives.

Happiness, it turns out, has a cost when experienced
too intensely. For instance, we often are told that
happiness can open up our minds to foster more creative
thinking and help us tackle problems or puzzles. This is
20   the case when we experience moderate levels of
happiness. But according to Mark Alan Davis's 2008
analysis of the relationship between mood and creativity,
when people experience intense and perhaps overwhelming amounts of happiness, they no longer
25   experience the same creativity boost. **What's more,
psychologist Barbara Fredrickson has found that too
much positive emotion—and too little negative
emotion—makes people inflexible in the face of new
challenges.**

Passage 2

30   **In reality, there is no clear-cut answer yet on
Whether being upbeat can keep you healthy or cure
anything.** For some diseases, which may build over
decades, the relationship between patients' attitudes
and their prognosis is dubious at best. For other diseases,
35   though, the scientific outlook is sunnier. There's
evidence that mood can predict whether someone who
has had one heart attack will have another.

Little research has been done on the biological basis
of positive thinking as a therapeutic treatment for illness,
40   but scientists know the brain and the immune system
communicate. Given that scientists also know the immune
system plays a role in inflammation of the arteries, which
can play a role in heart attacks, it's reasonable to think that
heart attacks could be tied back to things going on in
45   the brain.

It's not an accident that the main point of each passage is located in a key place: focusing on
the last sentence of the first passage and the first sentence of the second is often a quick way
to identify the relationship between the passages, and you can sometimes save yourself a lot
of time by paying extra attention to those places from the start.

So what do we have in terms of main point and tone?

Passage 1

Main Point: too much happiness = bad
Tone: objective/neutral

Passage 2

Main Point: happiness **might** help health BUT not sure
Tone: objective/cautiously optimistic

Relationship: Disagree

Notice that even though the authors disagree, the two passages don't contradict each other in the most straightforward way possible – that is, one author does not say that happiness is good while the other says happiness is bad. The relationship is a bit subtler than that. The first author doesn't talk about the negative effects of happiness in and of itself but rather *excessive* happiness, and the second author doesn't say that happiness is always a good thing but rather than it *might* have a positive impact on people's health. That information will become very important when you answer certain questions.

Let's start by looking at something fairly straightforward in terms of relationship, though:

> The author of Passage 2 would most likely respond to the argument in lines 3-6 ("We know…stave off illness") by
>
> (A) claiming that the immune system rather than the brain is responsible for staving off illness
> (B) insisting that positive thinking is less important than biology in predicting the development of disease
> (C) downplaying the potential of positive thinking as a therapeutic response
> (D) questioning whether enough information was available to determine the benefits of positive thinking
> (E) suggesting that researchers who study positive thinking are subject to unconscious biases

If you read through all of the answer choices individually, you're likely to get confused – and then stuck. (If you can always recognize the correct answer, you probably don't need to be reading this.) You'll probably be able to eliminate two or three possibilities, but chances are you'll get down to a few answers and then not know how to choose the correct one. You might have an inkling that one of the answers is right and choose it based on gut instinct, or you might simply take a wild guess. You might also leave it blank because you're really not sure. Regardless of what you do, you'll probably end up spending a lot of time on the question.

Although it may seem somewhat counterintuitive, the fastest way to narrow down the choices and respond to the question is to forget the answer choices entirely. Instead, you're going to answer at least part of the question on your own. For real.

1) Re-read and sum up the lines in question from Passage 1

> *We know that [positive feelings] motivate us to pursue important goals and overcome obstacles, protect us from some effects of stress, connect us with other people, and even stave off ailments.*

So basically, positive feelings have been shown to help people with a whole bunch of things, including improving their health. That's a good thing.

2) Look at the main point (1st sentence) of Passage 2

> *In reality, there is no clear-cut answer yet on whether being upbeat can keep you healthy or cure anything.*

That's not an overwhelmingly negative statement, but still… it's saying we don't know. So it's very mildly negative.

3) Consider the implications

P1 = Positive, P2 = Negative

The two passages clearly disagree on this point, so we're looking for a negative answer. We're going to start by just looking at the beginning of each answer choice.

> (A) claiming
> (B) insisting
> (C) downplaying
> (D) questioning
> (E) suggesting

(A), (B), and (E) are all neutral, so we're going to make an educated guess, assume they're wrong, and cross them out – if nothing else works, we can always erase the lines through them (that's why working in pencil is so important!).

Next we're going to consider the remaining answers:

(C) downplaying the potential of positive thinking as a therapeutic response

This answer does not fit with the main point because the author of P2 believes that it is possible for positive thinking to be an effective therapy and would thus be unlikely to downplay it.

(D) questioning whether enough information was available to determine the benefits of positive thinking

Logically, if the author of P2 believes that not enough research has been done on the relationship between happiness and health, then there's no way we can "know" whether happiness does in fact allow people to "stave off (resist) ailments." In other words, we don't have sufficient information. So this makes sense. The answer is in fact (D).

Alternately, however, choice (D) could have been written this way:

(D) expressing skepticism about the power of positive thinking to help people resist illness

In that case, looking at only the first word of the answer choice would not help you – you'd have to read slightly further to get to the key word, *skepticism*.

This question could also be asked more explicitly as an attitude question:

> The author of Passage 2 would most like view what "we know" (line 3) with
>
> (A) appreciation
> (B) apprehension
> (C) impatience
> (D) skepticism
> (E) loathing

Since either *appreciation* or *skepticism* is generally correct when it appears, you can begin by assuming that either (A) or (D) is the correct answer. From there, the process for determining the answer would be identical: define what "we know" (that positive thinking can help people resist illness), then see what the author of P2 thinks (not enough info to know whether positive thinking helps people resist illness). Since the relationship is negative, the answer must be (D).

You could also easily see a question such as this:

> Compared to the author of Passage 1, the author of Passage 2 is less
>
> (A) certain
> (B) jovial
> (C) impulsive
> (D) ironic
> (E) exasperated

The author of Passage 2 opens by saying that "there is no clear-cut answer," which immediately indicates a lack of certainty and points directly to (A).

Or, you could also see a question like this:

> Unlike the author of Passage 2, the author of Passage 1
>
> (A) describes biological principles
> (B) refers to specific research
> (C) discusses the role of the immune system
> (D) proposes a solution to a problem
> (E) offers a personal anecdote

We want to start by considering the answers that correspond to the most obvious elements in the text – those that can be identified with a minimum of effort. The easiest answer to check is (E) because whenever a personal anecdote is involved, the word "I" will pretty much always appear. It's not there, so (E) can be eliminated.

Next we want to want to look at (B) because the phrase "specific research" is, well, specific and therefore easy to check. The first passage mentions two studies, one by Mark Allan David and another one by Barbara Fredrickson. So yes, that checks out. The second passage includes the word "research" (line 38) but, unlike P1, never mentions a specific study. So the answer is (B).

As mentioned earlier, you're just as likely to see a question that asks about what the passages have in common. Much to the surprise of many test-takers, such questions occur very frequently when the passages present conflicting viewpoints.

Remember: questions are often targeted to test your understanding of the complexities or **nuances** of the relationship between the two passages – that is, the fact that an author can agree with part of someone else's argument and disagree with another part. As discussed earlier, this is one way in which professional writing tends to differ signficantly from the kind of writing that is encouraged in high school: most adult authors are not focused on proving their point at the expense of everything else. They consider contradictory evidence, weigh its merits and flaws, and often recognize that it is at least partially valid before attempting to draw a conclusion.

Sure enough, the author of the first passage does in fact acknowledge the positive effects of happiness – something that's easy to forget if you get too caught up in the information at the end of the passage.

Practically speaking, that means recognizing the overall relationship between the passages is *not* sufficient to answer all of the questions. For example:

> Which generalization is supported by both passages?
>
> (A) the detrimental aspects of happiness often outweigh
>   the more beneficial aspects
> (B) the relationship between the brain and the immune
>   system can be affected by a person's mental state
> (C) a person's mood is the most important factor in
>   predicting illness
> (D) happiness may play a role in allowing some people
>   to remain healthy
> (E) people who understand the pitfalls of happiness
>   remain healthier than those who do not

If you're trying to answer the question based only off the main points (too much happiness = bad vs. is happiness good or bad?), you'd probably be likely to cross out (D) immediately. After all, the author of Passage 1 focuses on the *negative* aspects of happiness, so it seems reasonable to assume that he wouldn't discuss how happiness allows people to resist illness – something that is clearly positive.

This, however, is where most people's memories fail them – and it illustrates perfectly why you shouldn't try to rely on your memory in the first place! The key is that while the author of Passage 1 does in fact *focus* on the negative aspects of happiness, he doesn't ignore its positive aspect entirely. As a matter of fact, he states that *"positive feelings...[can] even stave off ailments"* (lines 2-7). In other words, they may allow some people not to get sick, i.e. *remain healthy*. So the answer is (D).

You could also see a question that asks about the similarity in tone:

The tone of both passages could best be described as

(A) philosophical
(B) analytical
(C) cavalier
(D) indifferent
(E) disparaging

It's pretty easy to get rid of (C) and (E), as well as (D) if you remember that "indifferent" is basically always wrong. That leaves you with (A) and (B). It might be easy to talk yourself into (A), but remember: these are science passages. They're moderate, stick to the facts, and avoid grand theorizing. They don't discuss any great moral issues or ponder the reasons people might persist in clinging to happiness, even in dire circumstances. "But I feel like the tone is kind of philosophical" is not enough justification to make (A) the correct answer.

But, you might say, the main point of Passage 2 is negative: how can its tone be neutral? Well, remember: an author can have a definite (positive/negative) point of view, yet express that point of view in relatively neutral language. This is one of those instances in which content and tone do not match.

The author is clearly saying that too much happiness is a bad thing, but the *manner* in which that information is conveyed is not particularly negative. As a matter of fact, even though the two passages express generally opposite ideas, *there is no significant difference in their tone.* Both are typical of scientific passages in that they are careful to recognize both sides of the issue at hand and use moderate, cautious language (e.g. *"there is no clear-cut answer"*). Their common tone exists apart from their differences in opinion.

Now let's look at a longer set of passages:

*In line 105, *au courant* is a French expression meaning "current."

354

Passage 1

Is fiction good for us? We spend huge chunks of our lives immersed in novels, films, TV shows, and other forms of fiction. Some see this as a positive thing, arguing that made-up stories cultivate our
5 mental and moral development. But others have argued that fiction is mentally and ethically corrosive. It's an ancient question: Does fiction build the morality of individuals and societies, or does it break it down?

10 This controversy has been flaring up — sometimes literally, in the form of book burnings — ever since Plato tried to ban fiction from his ideal republic. In 1961, Newton Minow famously said that television was not working in "the public interest" because its
15 "formula comedies about totally unbelievable families, blood and thunder, mayhem, western bad men, western good men, private eyes, gangsters, and cartoons" amounted to a "vast wasteland." And what he said of TV programming has also been said, over
20 the centuries, of novels, theater, comic books, and films: They are not in the public interest.

Until recently, we've only been able to guess about the actual psychological effects of fiction on individuals and society. But new research in
25 psychology and broad-based literary analysis is finally taking questions about morality out of the realm of speculation.

This research consistently shows that fiction does mold us. The more deeply we are cast under a story's
30 spell, the more potent its influence. In fact, fiction seems to be more effective at changing beliefs than nonfiction, which is designed to persuade through argument and evidence. Studies show that when we read nonfiction, we read with our shields up. We are
35 critical and skeptical. But when we are absorbed in a story, we drop our intellectual guard. We are moved emotionally, and this seems to make us rubbery and easy to shape.

But perhaps the most impressive finding is just
40 **how fiction shapes us. Fiction enhances our ability to understand other people; it promotes a deep morality.** More peculiarly, fiction's happy endings seem to warp our sense of reality. They make us believe in a lie: that the world is more just than it
45 actually is. But believing that lie has important effects for society — and it may even help explain why humans tell stories in the first place.

Passage 2

I've been a devoted, even fanatical reader of fiction my whole life, but sometimes I feel like I'm wasting
50 time if I spend an evening immersed in Lee Child's newest thriller, or re-reading *The Great Gatsby*. Shouldn't I be plowing through my in-box? Or getting the hang of some new productivity app? Or catching up on my back issues of The Economist?
55 That slight feeling of self-indulgence that haunts me when I'm reading fake stories about fake people is what made me so grateful to stumble on a piece in *Scientific American Mind* by cognitive psychologist Keith Oatley extolling the practical benefits to be
60 derived particularly from consuming fiction.

Over the past decade, academic researchers have gathered data indicating that fiction-reading activates neuronal pathways in the brain that measurably help the reader better understand real human emotion —
65 improving his or her overall social skillfulness. It turns out that when Henry James, more than a century ago, defended the value of fiction by saying that "a novel is a direct impression of life," he was more right than he knew.

70 Theory of mind, the ability to interpret and respond to those different from us is plainly critical to success, particularly in a globalized economy. The imperative to try to understand others' points of view — to be empathetic — is essential in any
75 collaborative enterprise. Emotions also have an impact on the bottom line. A 1996 study published in the journal Training and Development assessing the value of training workers at a manufacturing plant in emotional management skills — teaching employees
80 to focus on how their work affects others rather than simply on getting the job done — found that union grievance filings were reduced by two-thirds while productivity increased substantially.

And if you want your diet of fiction to be
85 specifically relevant to work, there is a body of great literature about business and organizational behavior. For instance, Anthony Trollope's *The Way We Live Now*, inspired by 19th century financial scandals among the British elite, resonates powerfully today.
90 In his autobiography, Trollope wrote that "a certain class of dishonesty, dishonesty magnificent in its proportions, and climbing into high places, has become at the same time so rampant and so splendid that there seems to be reason for fearing that men and
95 women will be taught to feel that dishonesty, if it can become splendid, will cease to be abominable. If dishonesty can live in a gorgeous palace with pictures on all its walls, and gems in all its cupboards, with marble and ivory in all its corners, and can give
100 Apician dinners, and get into Parliament, and deal in millions, then dishonesty is not disgraceful, and the man dishonest after such a fashion is not a low scoundrel. Instigated, I say, by some such reflections as these, I sat down in my new house to write "The
105 Way We Live Now." Seems fairly *au courant** to me.

The first thing you're likely to notice about this set of passages is that it's considerably more challenging than the first set. The relationship is also a lot less obvious, and figuring it out is going to take some work.

Let's start by considering the main point and tone of each passage:

Passage 1

Main point: fiction = important b/c helps us understand other people
Tone: extremely positive

Even though the information is not located in an obvious place (e.g. last sentence of first paragraph), we know that this is the point because the author tells us that it is the *most impressive finding*. The sentence in which it appears also begins with a major transition: *but*.

Passage 2

Main point: fiction helps ppl succeed in business
Tone: positive

Now let's think about the **relationship**: the passages are agreeing, and they're basically saying the same thing. They're just doing so from different perspectives.

The first passage discusses why fiction is important, namely that it can improve society by helping people understand one another.

In the second passage, the author focuses on a specific **application** of fiction, namely the application of fiction to business. Why can fiction help people succeed in business? Because it encourages **empathy** – exactly what the author of Passage 1 says that fiction does. So if the following question appeared:

Which of the following best describes the relationship between Passage 1 and Passage 2?

The answer could easily be:

Passage 2 describes the practical application of an idea discussed in Passage 1

Now we're going to think about style. When two passages describe the same idea or phenomenon and generally agree, there will usually be a significant difference in style or tone between them – a difference that is virtually guaranteed to be tested.

For example, you could see a question that looks like this:

Unlike Passage 1, Passage 2 makes use of

(A) colloquialism
(B) personal anecdote
(C) euphemism
(D) understatement
(E) irony

Provided that you have noted upfront that the second passage contains sections written in the first person, (B) should immediately leap out at you.

Or the question could be asked in this way:

Compared to the tone of Passage 1, the tone of
Passage 2 is more

(A) speculative
(B) impatient
(C) analytical
(D) puzzled
(E) personal

The answer to this question basically comes down to the fact that the author of Passage 2 uses the first person pronoun *I* whereas Passage 1 is written from a neutral, objective point of view. Passage 2 contains sections that are neutral and analytical in tone, but it is also "bookended" by the author's discussion of her personal experience with fiction.

You might also see a question that asks about a stylistic *similarity* between the two passages, which you might not expect since they appear to be so different:

A rhetorical strategy used by the authors of both
Passage 1 and Passage 2 is

(A) historical allusion
(B) rhetorical questioning
(C) appeal to emotion
(D) comparison and contrast
(E) direct citation

This question looks much more difficult than it actually is. If you remembered to check the answers in order of most to least concrete, you would start with (E) and scan the passage for quotation marks. Sure enough, there is a quote from Newton Minnow in the first passage and one from Trollope's *The Way We Live Now* in the second. So that's the answer. You don't even have to look at anything else. Over, done with, all in about five seconds. Now try the following question on your own:

The author of Passage 2 would most likely react
to the statement in lines 35-38 of Passage 1
("But when ...shape") with

(A) mild skepticism
(B) total indifference
(C) outright hostility
(D) complete agreement
(E) cautious acceptance

Re-read lines 35-38 and put in your own words

_____

_____

_____

Main Point of Passage 2:

_____

_____

_____

Relationship:

_____

_____

Answer:

_____

_____

The answer and explanation are located at the end of the chapter.

Paired Passage Exercises

Passage 1

It started with newspapers ten years ago, and
now it's afflicting television as well: just as millions of
readers abandoned the morning newspaper, many
viewers are now turning their backs on network
5   television. Although media experts argue that television
itself is drawing more viewers than ever, the way
people in the United States watch TV is changing. An
increasing number of people now tune in with digital
devices (so they can avoid advertisements) or
10   on-demand videos and programming accessible online,
either through computers or a variety of other devices.

But are these new and innovative ways to watch
television the only reason for the overall decline in
network audiences? Television executive Susan
15   Ellison says that might not be the case. She claims that
the ratings decline could actually be caused by a dearth
of programming that appeals strongly to viewers. "The
issue no one mentions is that the major networks no
longer seem to be producing mega-hits that draw
20   millions of loyal viewers," Ellison points out. "As a
result, I would say that it's too early to either write off
television entirely or conclude that this is just a phase."

Passage 2

Having survived more than a few pronounce-
ments of its impending death during the last
25   couple of decades, television is at another crossroads.
That, despite the fact that the evening broadcasts still
draw more than all the cable news programs combined.
Even if it is the biggest draw, it's clear that
lifestyle changes (nobody home at 6:30 P.M., younger
30   viewers turning away from traditional TV) have
impacted viewership. Tom Rosenstiel, head of the
Project for Excellence in Journalism, says, "The
networks may have so much audience for conventional
television that it is watched at 6:30 in the traditional
35   manner that they may not see the rush to innovate."
That would be a mistake, he warns. "I don't think we
know if people are going to watch a twentieth-century
TV news program on the giant digital table that's
hanging on their wall or watch something entirely
different."

1. An assumption shared by the authors of both
passages is that

   (A) contemporary viewers find most network
      programs unappealing
   (B) cable news channels represent the future of
      television programming
   (C) the future of television viewership is
      somewhat uncertain
   (D) television viewers' habits are increasingly
      shaped by their desire to avoid programming
      interruptions
   (E) network news is unlikely to remain the most
      popular form of television

2. Susan Ellison (Passage 1) would most likely
respond to Tom Rosenstiel's assertion in lines
36-40 ("I don't think...different") by arguing that

   (A) twenty-first century viewers will have no
      interest in twentieth-century forms of
      programming
   (B) the form in which a program is accessed is less
      important than its ability to attract viewers
   (C) the shift to digital devices is no more than a
      temporary phase
   (D) digital devices will eventually replace
      conventional television sets completely
   (E) the increasing diversity of television audiences
      has made the development of successful
      programs much more difficult

3. The tone of both passages can best be described
as

   (A) didactic
   (B) sympathetic
   (C) caustic
   (D) neutral
   (E) amused

4. Unlike Passage 2, Passage 1

   (A) offers an alternative explanation
   (B) cites an authority
   (C) mentions a new form of technology
   (D) acknowledges a drawback
   (E) defines a term

Passage 1

Our food now travels an average of 1,500 miles before ending up on our plates. This globalization of the food supply has serious consequences for the environment, our health, our communities and our
5   taste buds. The distance from which our food comes represents our separation from the knowledge of how and by whom what we consume is produced, processed, and transported. And yet, the quality of a food is derived not merely from its genes and the
10 greens that fed it, but from how it is cared for. If the production of what we eat is destructive of the land and of human community – as it very often is – how can we understand the implications of our own participation in the global food system when those
15 processes are obscured from us? How can we act responsibly and effectively for change if we do not understand how the food system works and our own role within it?

Passage 2

For some activists, eating local foods is no longer
20 just a pleasure – it is a moral obligation. Why? Because shipping foods over long distances results in the unnecessary emission of the greenhouse gases that are warming the planet. This concern has given rise to the concept of "food miles," that is, the distance food
25 travels from farm to plate. Activists particularly dislike air freighting foods because it uses relatively more energy than other forms of transportation. Food miles are supposed to be a simple way to gauge food's impact on climate change.
30   But food miles advocates fail to grasp the simple idea that food should be grown where it is most economically advantageous to do so. Relevant advantages consist of various combinations of soil, climate, labor, and other factors. It is possible to grow
35 bananas in Iceland, but Costa Rica really has the better climate for that activity. Transporting food is just one relatively small cost of providing modern consumers with their daily bread, meat, cheese, and veggies. Concentrating agricultural production in the most
40 favorable regions is the best way to minimize human impacts on the environment.

1. Compared to the tone of Passage 2, the tone of Passage 1 is less

   (A) skeptical
   (B) anxious
   (C) erudite
   (D) inquisitive
   (E) certain

2. The author of Passage 1 would most likely respond to the assertion in lines 31-32 of Passage 2 ("Food should...do so") with

   (A) skepticism
   (B) enthusiasm
   (C) perplexity
   (D) fury
   (E) sympathy

3. Which rhetorical strategy is used by the author of both Passage 1 and Passage 2?

   (A) appeal to emotion
   (B) allusion
   (C) aside
   (D) rhetorical questioning
   (E) anecdote

4. Unlike the author of Passage 1, the author of Passage 2 focuses on

   (A) ethical considerations
   (B) scientific innovations
   (C) financial concerns
   (D) nutritional consequences
   (E) social relationships

Passage 1

Many readers, faced with Thoreau's enigmatic Yankee persona, have resorted to a kind of pop-culture shorthand for describing his life. As the capsule summary goes, Thoreau was an oddball loner who lived by a lake, writing in praise of nature and against modern progress.

But the full story of Thoreau's life involves subtleties and contradictions that call his popular image into question. One idea that has persisted is that he was a hermit who cared little for others, yet he was active in his community and responsible for circulating petitions for neighbors in need. In yet another way Thoreau was politically active, penning an essay, "Civil Disobedience," that would later inform the thinking of Mohandas Gandhi and the Rev. Martin Luther King Jr.

Despite his fame as a champion of solitude—a practice that he chronicled with wisdom and wit—Thoreau made no secret of the social life he indulged during his stay at Walden Pond from 1845 to 1847. In fact, one of the chapters of Walden, titled "Visitors," offers an extended account of Thoreau's dealings with others. In it, Thoreau lays out his rules for entertaining:

I had three chairs in my house; one for solitude, two for friendship, three for society. When visitors came in larger and unexpected numbers there was but the third chair for them all, but they generally economized the room by standing up

But even if Thoreau wasn't always averse to human company, the idea that he was a loner might stem from the assumption that he was the kind of person who should have been alone. Thoreau was capable of friendship, but on his own terms. He could be prickly to a fault. "I sometimes hear my Friends complain finely that I do not appreciate their fineness," he once wrote. "I shall not tell them whether I do or not. As if they expected a vote of thanks for every fine thing which they uttered or did."

Even those who liked him conceded that Thoreau could be a cold fish. In a letter to his friend Daniel Ricketson in 1860, Thoreau addresses Ricketson's puzzlement over why he hasn't come to visit, telling Ricketson, without much ceremony, that he's had much better things to do. But after explaining himself, Thoreau continued to correspond with Ricketson. Ralph Waldo Emerson, Thoreau's close friend and mentor, who came to grudgingly admire Thoreau's argumentative streak, famously described him as "not to be subdued, always manly and able, but rarely tender, as if he did not feel himself except in opposition." In remembrance of Thoreau, Emerson offered this observation from one of Thoreau's friends: "I love Henry, but I cannot like him; and as for taking his arm, I should as soon think of taking the arm of an elm-tree."

Passage 2

I vacillate on Thoreau. I consider myself fairly well read when it comes to the writers of Concord …though certainly no expert. In my younger days, I walked the same woods he walked and was inspired by his love of simplicity and nature. Lately, however, I have been reading a compilation of excerpts from his journals, and what struck me most about Thoreau's observations is his judgmental tone of superiority. As a younger man, poring over Walden, I believe I idealized Thoreau. Now I begin to wonder if he was, in fact, a misanthrope.

I'm certainly not the first person to ponder this matter. Journalist Alex Beam wrote an article about Thoreau in the *New York Times* saying, "Over the years I have called him a misanthrope, a slob, a loser, 'a world-class mooch,' and a 'tree-hugging pyromaniac.'" Other contemporaries noted this too. Perhaps no one more than Ralph Waldo Emerson, one of Thoreau's dearest friends and admirers, who wrote frankly of Thoreau's judgmental attitude, what I might call misanthropy.

The prevailing theme of Thoreau's journal entries is Thoreau's ability to find nobility, beauty, even poetry in the lives of simple, virtuous men. That's fine, I suppose. But, I can't help but fixate on his condemnations of those he deemed to be worthless. What made Thoreau so sure in his judgments? He seemed to believe that he possessed the true compass as to what was good and noble as he looked at other men, coldly assessing their worth and disturbingly certain as to his judgment.

Several scholars vehemently refute this image of Thoreau. Sandra Harbert Petrulionis, in her book, *Thoreau in His Own Time*, criticizes Emerson for flippantly immortalizing the term, "that terrible Thoreau." Instead of focusing on "incidents of understandable local ire" against Thoreau, Petrulionis argues we should focus on the fact that "Thoreau engaged in a lifelong habit of serving and educating his community." This is an important point. Thoreau valued his community tremendously. And he valued education and the dissemination of truth and knowledge.

But I, for one, will always have a greater respect for Emerson, a man who worked within the difficult confines of the real world. As it turns out, Thoreau had the longer lasting and more powerful influence. His iconoclastic ideals influenced some of the greatest men of the 20th century. But which is better, really? To fire the imaginations of men and women with inspiration during your own life, as Emerson did, or to retreat to the woods, doing comparatively little for those of your own generation, as Thoreau did? I'm not sure I know the answer to that question. But I do get the sense I would not have liked Thoreau had I met him. And he certainly would not have liked me.

1. Which of the following statements best describes the relationship between Passage 1 and Passage 2?

   (A) The author of Passage 1 describes a novel theory about Thoreau, whereas the author of Passage 2 rejects that theory.
   (B) The author of Passage 1 attempts to provide a balanced perspective of Thoreau, whereas the author of Passage 2 focuses on a personal reaction.
   (C) The author of Passage 1 finds Thoreau unpleasant as an individual, whereas the author of Passage 2 acknowledges his contributions to his community.
   (D) The author of Passage 1 praises Thoreau's literary achievements, whereas the author of Passage 2 questions their importance.
   (E) The author of Passage 1 is primarily interested in how Thoreau was viewed by his contemporaries, whereas the author of Passage 2 is more interested in his enduring cultural significance.

2. Compared to the tone of Passage 2, the tone of Passage 1 is more

   (A) reflective
   (B) apathetic
   (C) defensive
   (D) objective
   (E) critical

3. Compared to the tone of Passage 1, the tone of Passage 2 is less

   (A) puzzled
   (B) hostile
   (C) formal
   (D) impatient
   (E) resigned

4. Sandra Harbert Petrolionis (Passage 2) would most likely consider supporters of "one idea" (line 8)

   (A) groundbreaking
   (B) short-sighted
   (C) perplexing
   (D) pretentious
   (E) nostalgic

5. Based on the characterization in lines 64-68, the author of Passage 1 would most likely respond to Alex Beam (Passage 2) by

   (A) praising him for acknowledging an aspect of Thoreau's personality that scholars often ignore
   (B) criticizing him for promoting a vision of Thoreau that has no basis in reality
   (C) accusing him of oversimplifying a complex individual
   (D) defending Thoreau's need for nature and solitude
   (E) insisting that Thoreau's works occupy a central place in the literary canon

6. Which of the following is used by the author of Passage 2 but not by the author of Passage 1?

   (A) rhetorical question
   (B) direct citation
   (C) historical allusion
   (D) digression
   (E) figurative language

7. The authors of both passages would most likely agree that Thoreau's ideas

   (A) outweigh his personal shortcomings
   (B) do not reflect his misanthropic tendencies
   (C) are less important than those of Emerson
   (D) were largely inspired by his love of nature
   (E) had a significant influence on later generations

8. Thoreau's response to Daniel Ricketson (lines 40-42) can be cited as support for which idea in Passage 2?

   (A) "I walked the same woods he walked and was inspired by his love of simplicity and nature." (lines 55-57)
   (B) "what struck me most about Thoreau's observations is his judgmental tone of superiority" (lines 59-60)
   (C) "several scholars vehemently refute this image of Thoreau" (lines 83-84)
   (D) "And he valued education and the dissemination of truth and knowledge" (lines 92-93)
   (E) "His iconoclastic ideals influenced some of the greatest men of the 20th century." (lines 97-99)

Official Guide Paired Passage Questions*

Test 1	Section 2	Question 16	p. 394	Literal Comprehension
Test 1	Section 2	Question 17	p. 394	
Test 1	Section 2	Question 22	p. 395	Literal Comprehension
Test 1	Section 2	Question 24	p. 395	Literal Comprehension
Test 1	Section 5	Question 9	p. 403	
Test 1	Section 5	Question 11	p. 403	
Test 1	Section 5	Question 12	p. 403	
Test 2	Section 4	Question 9	p. 459	
Test 2	Section 4	Question 11	p. 459	
Test 2	Section 4	Question 12	p. 459	Literal Comprehension
Test 2	Section 9	Question 7	p. 489	
Test 2	Section 9	Question 12	p. 489	
Test 2	Section 9	Question 17	p. 490	
Test 2	Section 9	Question 18	p. 490	Tone
Test 3	Section 4	Question 9	p. 521	
Test 3	Section 4	Question 10	p. 521	Literal Comprehension
Test 3	Section 4	Question 11	p. 521	Attitude
Test 3	Section 7	Question 14	p. 541	
Test 3	Section 7	Question 15	p. 541	
Test 3	Section 7	Question 19	p. 542	
Test 3	Section 7	Question 21	p. 542	
Test 3	Section 7	Question 22	p. 542	Literal Comprehension
Test 3	Section 7	Question 23	p. 542	Rhetorical Strategy
Test 3	Section 7	Question 24	p. 542	
Test 4	Section 2	Question 21	p. 579	Assumptions, Generalizations & Claims
Test 4	Section 2	Question 22	p. 580	
Test 4	Section 2	Question 23	p. 580	Tone
Test 4	Section 2	Question 24	p. 580	
Test 4	Section 5	Question 6	p. 588	
Test 4	Section 5	Question 7	p. 588	Tone
Test 4	Section 5	Question 8	p. 588	
Test 4	Section 5	Question 9	p. 588	Rhetorical Strategy
Test 5	Section 7	Question 9	p. 663	Generalization
Test 5	Section 7	Question 10	p. 663	Literal Comprehension
Test 5	Section 7	Question 11	p. 663	Assumptions, Generalizations & Claims
Test 5	Section 7	Question 12	p. 663	Function
Test 5	Section 7	Question 13	p. 665	
Test 5	Section 7	Question 22	p. 666	Literal Comprehension
Test 5	Section 7	Question 23	p. 666	Literal Comprehension
Test 5	Section 7	Question 24	p. 666	Assumptions, Generalizations & Claims

*When paired passage questions fall into an additional category, that category is listed in the right-hand column.

Explanations: Paired Passage Exercises

"Importance of Fiction" Passages

Answer: D

Lines 40-42 in Passage 1 and lines 61-65 in Passage 2 both clearly indicate that reading fiction can produce profound emotional effects in people. The fact that the extreme word "complete" appears is irrelevant. Extreme answers are sometimes correct, and in this case (D) is fully supported by the passage.

"Television Viewership" Passages

1. C

The final sentence of each passage provides a quotation stating that the impact of societal and technological changes on television-viewing habits is still unknown. (A) is supported only by the author of Passage 1; (B) is supported by neither passage – the author of Passage 2 explicitly states that "evening broadcasts draw *more* viewers than all the cable news programs combined"; (D) is supported by Passage 1 but not by Passage 2; and (E) is incorrect because the author of Passage 1 never mentions network news.

2. B

What does Susan Ellison think? That people aren't watching television because the programs aren't good enough to make it worth watching, not because there are so many new devices on which they can watch it on.

What does Tom Rosenstiel think? That media executives shouldn't be complacent just because lots of people are still watching television, and that it's impossible to know how new devices will change how people watch in the twenty-first century.

So how would Ellison probably respond? That he's focusing on the wrong issue – the problem isn't that devices themselves are responsible for the decline in viewership but rather the lack of interesting programming.

(A) is supported by neither author, and the phrase "no interest" indicates that the answer is too extreme; likewise, (C) is supported by neither author – Susan Ellison simply states that it's too soon to know whether declining TV viewership, not the shift to digital device, is temporary; (D) seems like a reasonable assumption, but both passages only indicate that a shift towards digital devices is occurring. It cannot be inferred that the authors believe they will replace television completely; and there is no information about the diversity of TV audiences in either passage that would support (E).

3. D

Both passages are written in quintessential journalistic style: snappy, to-the-point, and careful not to take sides or draw any extreme conclusions. "Neutral" is therefore correct.

4. A

In Passage 1, Susan Ellison suggests (=offers an explanation) that the decline in television viewership (=a problem) might be caused by a lack of appealing programming rather than by the emergence of new devices on which people can watch television (=an alternative explanation).

"Food Production" Passages

1. E

The author of Passage 2 is pretty sure that there's one best way to approach the problem of transporting food: "Concentrating agricultural production in the *most favorable* regions is the best way to minimize human impacts on the environment." In comparison, the author of Passage 1 is much less certain; the extended rhetorical questions suggest he is genuinely searching for an answer.

2. A

What do lines 31-32 say? "Food should be grown where it is most economically advantageous to do so."

What does the author of Passage 1 think? That shipping food hundreds of miles has pretty bad consequences for the environment, health, and even taste buds.

So the answer is going to be negative, eliminating everything except (A) and (D), and (D) is way too extreme: it simply doesn't fit with the author of Passage 1's relatively measured, concerned tone.

3. D

The question marks in lines 15 and 18 of Passage 1, and in line 20 of Passage 2, indicate the presence of rhetorical questions.

4. C

The answer is essentially the main point of Passage 2: "Food should be grown where it's most economically advantageous to do so." The author of Passage 1 does not address the monetary aspect of food production anywhere in the passage.

"Thoreau" Passages

1. B

The length of the answer choices makes this question seem much more difficult than it actually is. The key is in the passages' different points of view: Passage 1 is written in the third person in a neutral, objective style, and attempts to examine the complexities (good and bad aspects) of Thoreau, while Passage 2 is written in the first person (as indicated by the numerous appearances of the word "I"). While the author of Passage 2 does take different points of view into account, his focus is primarily on his own reaction to Thoreau – that is, although he recognizes the importance of Thoreau's ideas, he also cannot surmount his personal dislike of the author himself.

2. D

This is essentially the same question as #1, just asked from a slightly different standpoint. Passage 2 is written in the first person by an author with a very particular take on Thoreau; the author of Passage 1 is more objective because he seeks to examine all sides of the argument without making a firm judgment himself.

3. C

Again, the author of Passage 2 is writing in the first person, which almost by definition gives his style a more personal, i.e. less formal, tone.

4. B

What does Sandra Harbert Petrolionis think? That the negative aspects of Thoreau's personality should be overlooked because he did wonderful things for his community.

What is "one idea?" That "he was a hermit who cared little for others."

So supporters of "one idea" would believe exactly the opposite of what Sandra Harbert Petrulionis believes, meaning that the answer must 1) be negative, and 2) mean something like "wrong." That eliminates (A) because "groundbreaking" is a good thing. (C) doesn't make sense because "perplexing" doesn't mean "wrong"; in (D), pretentious means "pompous," which doesn't mean "wrong" either; and in (E), "nostalgic" means longing for the past, which doesn't make sense in context. "Short-sighted" is the correct answer because it indicates that the supporters hold a simplistic view of Thoreau, one that fails to take into account his more positive aspects.

5. C

What does Alex Beam think about Thoreau? That he was "a slob, a loser…a misanthrope," etc. Not a very nice guy.

What's the main point of Passage 1? That Thoreau wasn't just "an oddball loner who lived by a lake, writing in praise of nature and against progress" (how Beam sees him), and that the reality is more complex. So the answer has to be negative.

(A), (D), and (E) can all be eliminated because they're positive. (B) might look tempting, but look carefully at the wording: the answer states that Beam's vision has *no* basis in reality when in fact the author of Passage 1 is careful to point out that it is understandable why someone would believe Thoreau was a hermit and a misanthrope. (C) is correct because the author of Passage 1 clearly states that Thoreau's

life was "full of subtleties and complexities." To see Thoreau as one-sided the way Beam does is therefore to oversimplify him.

6. A

The question marks in lines 81, 101, and 105 of Passage 2 indicate rhetorical questions, and there are no question marks in Passage 1.

7. E

Both authors mention that Thoreau's ideas had an impact on 20th century thinkers (lines 11-14 in Passage 1, and lines 98-101 of Passage 2). (A) is incorrect because for the author of Passage 2, Thoreau's unlikeability is clearly more important than his ideas; (B) is incorrect because both authors agree that Thoreau's writings reveal his dislike for people; (C) is incorrect because the author of Passage 1 does not mention Emerson's ideas at all, only his impressions of Thoreau, and the author of Passage 2 only says that he find Emerson as a person more likable while acknowledging the importance of Thorea's ideas; and (D) is incorrect because neither author states or suggests that nature was Thoreau's only influence.

8. B

What was Thoreau's response to Ricketson? That he had "much better things to do" than socialize with him. What idea is the quote used to support? That Thoreau was a "cold fish" who was "prickly" even to his friends. So the correct answer must be related to that idea. Only (B) fits. The other answer are all used to illustrate Thoreau's more positive aspects.

Appendix A: Official Guide Questions by Test

Test	Section	#	Type
Test 1			
1	2	6	Inference
1	2	7	Rhetorical Strategy
			Literal Comprehension
1	2	8	Function
1	2	9	Inference
1	2	10	Function
1	2	11	Literal Comprehension
1	2	12	Function
1	2	13	Vocabulary in Context
1	2	14	Tone and Attitude
1	2	15	Rhetorical Strategy
1	2	16	P1/P2 Relationship/
			Literal Comprehension
1	2	17	P1/P2 Relationship
1	2	18	Literal Comprehension
1	2	19	Function
1	2	20	Inference
1	2	21	Vocabulary in Context
1	2	22	P1/P2 Relationship/
			Literal Comprehension
1	2	23	Rhetorical Strategy
1	2	24	P1/P2 Relationship/
			Literal Comprehension
1	5	9	P1/P2 Relationship
1	5	10	P1/P2 Relationship
1	5	11	P1/P2 Relationship
1	5	12	P1/P2 Relationship
1	5	13	Vocabulary in Context
1	5	14	Tone and Attitude
1	5	15	Tone and Attitude
1	5	16	Tone and Attitude
1	5	17	Function
1	5	18	Tone and Attitude
1	5	19	Function
1	5	20	Vocabulary in Context
1	5	21	Tone and Attitude
1	5	22	Rhetorical Strategy
1	5	23	Inference
1	5	24	Function
1	9	7	Literal Comprehension
1	9	8	Inference
1	9	9	Inference
1	9	10	Literal Comprehension
1	9	11	Literal Comprehension
1	9	12	Literal Comprehension
1	9	13	Inference
1	9	14	Literal Comprehension
1	9	15	Inference
1	9	16	Rhetorical Strategy
1	9	17	Literal Comprehension
1	9	18	Literal Comprehension
1	9	19	Inference
Test 2			
2	4	1	Vocabulary in Context
2	4	9	P1/P2 Relationship
2	4	10	Tone and Attitude
2	4	11	P1/P2 Relationship
2	4	12	P1/P2 Relationship
			Literal Comprehension
2	4	13	Vocabulary in Context
2	4	14	Function
2	4	15	Vocabulary in Context
2	4	16	Vocabulary in Context
2	4	17	Literal Comprehension
			Vocabulary in Context
2	4	18	Tone and Attitude
2	4	19	Tone and Attitude
2	4	20	Literal Comprehension
2	4	21	Function
2	4	22	Tone and Attitude
2	4	23	Vocabulary in Context
2	4	24	Inference
2	4	25	Rhetorical Strategy
2	7	6	Function
2	7	7	Literal Comprehension
2	7	8	Vocabulary in Context
2	7	9	Vocabulary in Context
2	7	10	Function
2	7	11	Function
2	7	12	Function
2	7	13	Assumptions, Generalizations & Claims

2	7	14	Inference
2	7	15	Tone and Attitude
2	7	16	Vocabulary in Context
2	7	17	Rhetorical Strategy
2	7	18	Inference
2	7	19	Inference
2	7	20	Literal Comprehension
2	7	21	Literal Comprehension
2	7	22	Inference
2	7	23	Literal Comprehension
2	7	24	Tone and Attitude
2	9	7	P1/P2 Relationship
2	9	8	Vocabulary in Context
2	9	9	Literal Comprehension
2	9	10	Function
2	9	11	Inference
2	9	13	Function
2	9	14	Inference
2	9	15	Vocabulary in Context
2	9	16	Literal Comprehension
2	9	17	P1/P2 Relationship
2	9	18	P1/P2 Relationship/ Tone

Test 3

3	4	9	P1/P2 Relationship
3	4	10	P1/P2 Relationship/ Literal Comprehension
3	4	11	P1/P2 Relationship
3	4	12	Function
3	4	13	Assumptions, Generalizations, & Claims
3	4	14	Assumptions, Generalizations, & Claims
3	4	15	Rhetorical Strategy
3	4	16	Literal Comprehension
3	4	17	Literal Comprehension
3	4	18	Assumptions, Generalizations, & Claims
3	4	19	Function
3	4	20	Vocabulary in Context
3	4	21	Literal Comprehension
3	4	22	Assumptions, Generalizations, & Claims
3	4	23	Literal Comprehension
3	4	24	Function
3	7	6	Inference

3	7	7	Literal Comprehension
3	7	8	Function
3	7	9	Rhetorical Strategy
3	7	10	Tone and Attitude / Vocabulary in Context
3	7	11	Vocabulary in Context
3	7	12	Function
3	7	13	Literal Comprehension
3	7	14	Tone and Attitude
3	7	15	P1/P2 Relationship
3	7	16	Vocabulary in Context
3	7	17	Function
3	7	18	Function
3	7	19	P1/P2 Relationship
3	7	20	Assumptions, Generalizations, & Claims
3	7	21	Inference
3	7	22	P1/P2 Relationship/ Literal Comprehension
3	7	23	P1/P2 Relationship/ Rhetorical Strategy
3	7	24	P1/P2 Relationship
3	9	1	Vocabulary in Context
3	9	7	Tone and Attitude
3	9	8	Literal Comprehension
3	9	9	Tone and Attitude
3	9	10	Tone and Attitude
3	9	11	Literal Comprehension
3	9	12	Inference
3	9	13	Literal Comprehension
3	9	14	Function
3	9	15	Inference
3	9	16	Function
3	9	17	Vocabulary in Context
3	9	18	Tone and Attitude
3	9	19	Function

Test 4

4	2	9	Inference
4	2	10	Function
4	2	11	Inference
4	2	12	Literal Comprehension
4	2	13	Inference
4	2	14	Vocabulary in Context
4	2	15	Literal Comprehension
4	2	16	Literal Comprehension

4	2	17	Assumptions, Generalizations, & Claims
4	2	18	Vocabulary in Context
4	2	19	Inference
4	2	20	Vocabulary in Context
4	2	21	P1/P2 Relationship/ Supporting a claim
4	2	22	P1/P2 Relationship
4	2	23	P1/P2 Relationship
4	2	24	P1/P2 Relationship
4	5	10	Tone and Attitude
4	5	11	Inference
4	5	12	Inference
4	5	13	Literal Comprehension
4	5	14	Inference
4	5	15	Literal Comprehension
4	5	16	Main Point
4	5	17	Vocabulary in Context
4	5	18	Inference
4	5	19	Function
4	5	20	Assumptions, Generalizations, & Claims
4	5	21	Literal Comprehension
4	5	22	Rhetorical Strategy
4	5	23	Assumptions, Generalizations, & Claims
4	5	24	Main Point
4	8	7	Literal Comprehension
4	8	8	Vocabulary in Context
4	8	9	Main Point
4	8	10	Function
4	8	11	Literal Comprehension
4	8	12	Inference
4	8	13	Tone and Attitude
4	8	14	Literal Comprehension
4	8	15	Literal Comprehension
4	8	16	Rhetorical Strategy
4	8	17	Vocabulary in Context
4	8	18	Literal Comprehension
4	8	19	Tone and Attitude
4	8	20	Literal Comprehension

Test 5

5	3	6	Vocabulary in Context
5	3	7	Inference
5	3	8	Inference
5	3	9	Literal Comprehension

5	3	10	Function
5	3	11	Inference
5	3	12	Function
5	3	13	Function/Assumptions, Generalizations & Claims
5	3	14	Literal Comprehension
5	3	15	Assumptions, Generalizations, & Claims
5	3	16	Function
5	3	17	Inference
5	3	18	Inference
5	3	19	Literal Comprehension
5	3	20	Vocabulary in Context / Literal Comprehension
5	3	21	Inference
5	3	22	Inference
5	3	23	Tone and Attitude
5	3	24	Assumptions, Generalizations, & Claims
5	7	9	P1/P2 Relationship
5	7	10	P1/P2 Relationship
5	7	11	P1/P2 Relationship/ Assumptions, Generalizations & Claims
5	7	12	P1/P2 Relationship/ Function
5	7	13	P1/P2 Relationship
5	7	14	Literal Comprehension
5	7	15	Function
5	7	16	Inference
5	7	17	Vocabulary in Context
5	7	18	Function
5	7	19	Assumptions, Generalizations, & Claims
5	7	20	Literal Comprehension
5	7	21	Literal Comprehension
5	7	22	P1/P2 Relationship / Literal Comprehension
5	7	23	P1/P2 Relationship/ Literal Comprehension
5	7	24	P1/P2 Relationship/ Assumptions, Generalizations & Claims
5	9	7	Rhetorical Strategy
5	9	8	Inference
5	9	9	Literal Comprehension
5	9	10	Function
5	9	11	Vocabulary in Context

5	9	12	Vocabulary in Context
5	9	13	Inference
5	9	14	Literal Comprehension
5	9	15	Literal Comprehension
5	9	16	Inference
5	9	17	Literal Comprehension
5	9	18	Literal Comprehension
5	9	19	Literal Comprehension

Test 6

6	3	6	P1/P2 Relationship/Attitude
6	3	7	P1/P2 Relationship/Rhetorical Strategy
6	3	8	P1/P2 Relationship Literal Comprehension
6	3	9	P1/P2 Relationship
6	3	10	Vocabulary in Context
6	3	11	Literal Comprehension
6	3	12	Literal Comprehension
6	3	13	Literal Comprehension
6	3	14	Literal Comprehension
6	3	15	Function
6	3	16	Rhetorical Strategy
6	3	17	Literal Comprehension
6	3	18	Literal Comprehension
6	3	19	Main Point
6	3	20	Inference
6	3	21	Inference
6	3	22	Vocabulary in Context
6	3	23	Vocabulary in Context
6	3	24	Inference
6	7	9	Literal Comprehension
6	7	10	Tone and Attitude
6	7	11	Assumptions, Generalizations, & Claims
6	7	12	Tone and Attitude
6	7	13	Vocabulary in Context
6	7	14	Literal Comprehension
6	7	15	Vocabulary in Context
6	7	16	Function
6	7	17	Rhetorical Strategy
6	7	18	Literal Comprehension
6	7	19	Function
6	7	20	P1/P2 Relationship/Attitude
6	7	21	P1/P2 Relationship
6	7	22	P1/P2 Relationship
6	7	23	P1/P2 Relationship
6	7	24	P1/P2 Relationship
6	9	7	Literal Comprehension
6	9	8	Vocabulary in Context
6	9	9	Inference
6	9	10	Inference
6	9	11	Inference
6	9	12	Vocabulary in Context
6	9	13	Inference
6	9	14	Inference
6	9	15	Inference
6	9	16	Inference
6	9	17	Literal Comprehension
6	9	18	Literal Comprehension
6	9	19	Literal Comprehension

Test 7

7	2	6	Function
7	2	7	Analogy
7	2	8	Tone and Attitude
7	2	9	Main Point
7	2	10	Function
7	2	11	Function
7	2	12	Main Point
7	2	13	Main Point
7	2	14	Vocabulary in Context
7	2	15	Function
7	2	16	Function
7	2	17	Vocabulary in Context
7	2	18	Function
7	2	19	Assumptions, Generalizations, & Claims
7	2	20	Assumptions, Generalizations, & Claims
7	2	21	Inference
7	2	22	Literal Comprehension
7	2	23	Function
7	2	24	Inference
7	5	9	P1/P2 Relationship
7	5	10	P1/P2 Relationship
7	5	11	P1/P2 Relationship/Tone
7	5	12	P1/P2 Relationship
7	5	13	P1/P2 Relationship/Literal Comprehension
7	5	14	Function

7	5	15	Literal Comprehension
7	5	16	Analogy
7	5	17	Literal Comprehension
7	5	18	Function
7	5	19	P1/P2 Relationship
7	5	20	Function
7	5	21	Vocabulary in Context
7	5	22	Main Point
7	5	23	Function
7	5	24	P1/P2 Relationship/ Function/Rhetorical Strategy
7	8	7	Rhetorical Strategy
7	8	8	Inference
7	8	9	Literal Comprehension
7	8	10	Inference
7	8	11	Inference
7	8	12	Literal Comprehension
7	8	13	Vocabulary in Context
7	8	14	Inference
7	8	15	Literal Comprehension
7	8	16	Vocabulary in Context
7	8	17	Vocabulary in Context
7	8	18	Inference Literal Comprehension
7	8	19	Vocabulary in Context

Test 8

8	2	10	Inference
8	2	11	Literal Comprehension
8	2	12	Literal Comprehension
8	2	13	Main Point Literal Comprehension
8	2	14	Literal Comprehension
8	2	15	Function
8	2	16	Literal Comprehension
8	2	17	Inference
8	2	18	Literal Comprehension
8	2	19	Literal Comprehension
8	2	20	Literal Comprehension
8	2	21	Vocabulary in Context
8	2	22	Inference
8	2	23	Literal Comprehension
8	2	24	Inference
8	5	9	Inference
8	5	10	Vocabulary in Context
8	5	11	Inference
8	5	12	Vocabulary in Context

8	5	13	Vocabulary in Context
8	5	14	Literal Comprehension
8	5	15	Literal Comprehension
8	5	16	Inference
8	5	17	Literal Comprehension
8	5	18	Literal Comprehension
8	5	19	Literal Comprehension
8	5	20	Tone and Attitude
8	5	21	P1/P2 Relationship
8	5	22	P1/P2 Relationship/ Literal Comprehension
8	5	23	P1/P2 Relationship
8	5	24	P1/P2 Relationship
8	8	7	Inference
8	8	8	Inference
8	8	9	Literal Comprehension
8	8	10	Literal Comprehension
8	8	11	Literal Comprehension
8	8	12	Vocabulary in Context
8	8	13	Vocabulary in Context
8	8	14	Function
8	8	15	Literal Comprehension
8	8	16	Inference
8	8	17	Literal Comprehension
8	8	18	Literal Comprehension
8	8	19	Literal Comprehension

Test 9

9	4	9	P1/P2 Relationship/ Literal Comprehension
9	4	10	Inference
9	4	11	P1/P2 Relationship
9	4	12	P1/P2 Relationship
9	4	13	Rhetorical Strategy
9	4	14	Function
9	4	15	Rhetorical Strategy
9	4	16	Vocabulary in Context
9	4	17	Function
9	4	18	Literal Comprehension
9	4	19	Assumptions, Generalizations, & Claims
9	4	20	Vocabulary in Context
9	4	21	Function
9	4	22	Literal Comprehension
9	4	23	Inference
9	4	24	Main Point
9	6	6	Vocabulary in Context

9	6	7	Inference
9	6	8	Literal Comprehension
9	6	9	Literal Comprehension
9	6	10	Function
9	6	11	Rhetorical Strategy
9	6	12	Function
9	6	13	Inference
9	6	14	Inference
9	6	15	Tone and Attitude
9	6	16	Literal Comprehension
9	6	17	Literal Comprehension
9	6	18	Literal Comprehension
9	6	19	Vocabulary in Context
9	6	20	Literal Comprehension
9	6	21	Vocabulary in Context
9	6	22	Tone and Attitude
9	6	23	Literal Comprehension
9	6	24	Inference
9	9	7	P1/P2 Relationship/ Literal Comprehension
9	9	8	P1/P2 Relationship
9	9	9	P1/P2 Relationship Literal Comprehension
9	9	10	P1/P2 Relationship
9	9	11	Literal Comprehension
9	9	12	Literal Comprehension
9	9	13	Function
9	9	14	P1/P2 Relationship/ Function
9	9	15	Tone and Attitude
9	9	16	Tone and Attitude
9	9	17	Tone and Attitude
9	9	18	Function
9	9	19	P1/P2 Relationship

Test 10

10	4	9	Tone and Attitude
10	4	10	Inference
10	4	11	Function
10	4	12	Tone and Attitude
10	4	13	Literal Comprehension
10	4	14	Inference
10	4	15	Assumptions, Generalizations, & Claims
10	4	16	Function
10	4	17	Inference
10	4	18	Main Point
10	4	19	Inference
10	4	20	Inference
10	4	21	Literal Comprehension
10	4	22	Vocabulary in Context/ Literal Comprehension
10	4	23	Literal Comprehension
10	4	24	Function
10	6	6	P1/P2 Relationship
10	6	7	P1/P2 Relationship
10	6	8	P1/P2 Relationship/Attitude
10	6	9	Literal Comprehension
10	6	10	Function
10	6	11	Rhetorical Strategy
10	6	12	Vocabulary in Context
10	6	13	Assumptions, Generalizations, & Claims
10	6	14	Vocabulary in Context
10	6	15	Tone and Attitude
10	6	16	Rhetorical Strategy
10	6	17	Tone and Attitude
10	6	18	Vocabulary in Context
10	6	19	Literal Comprehension
10	6	20	Vocabulary in Context
10	6	21	Literal Comprehension
10	6	22	Function
10	6	23	Analogy
10	6	24	Rhetorical Strategy
10	9	7	P1/P2 Relationship
10	9	8	P1/P2 Relationship/ Literal Comprehension
10	9	9	Inference
10	9	10	Literal Comprehension
10	9	11	Analogy
10	9	12	Vocabulary in Context
10	9	13	Vocabulary in Context
10	9	14	Inference
10	9	15	P1/P2 Relationship
10	9	16	P1/P2 Relationship
10	9	17	P1/P2 Relationship
10	9	18	P1/P2 Relationship
10	9	19	P1/P2 Relationship/ Literal Comprehension

Suggested Reading

Gerald Graff, Cathy Birkenstein, and Russell Durst: *They Say/I Say: The Moves that Matter in Academic Writing*, 2nd Edition. New York: W.W. Norton and Company, 2009.

Periodicals:

The New York Times
The Economist
The New Yorker
The Atlantic Monthly
Wilson Quarterly
Humanities Magazine
Smithsonian Magazine
Boston Review
Dissent
The Times Literary Supplement
Scientific American
National Geographic
The New Republic
Reason Magazine

For links to many additional resources for SAT-level material, please visit Arts and Letters Daily: http://www.aldaily.com

Books and Articles:

Barbara Arrowsmith-Young	*The Woman Who Changed Her Brain*
Nikolai Gogol	*The Overcoat*
Temple Grandin	*Thinking in Pictures* *Animals in Translation* (with Catherine Johnson)
Ann Fadiman	*The Spirit Catches You and You Fall Down*
Brian Greene	*The Elegant Universe* *The Hidden Reality* *The Fabric of the Cosmos*
Stephen Hawking	*The Elusive Theory of Everything* (with Leonard Mlodinow) *The Grand Design* (with Leonard Mlodinow) *A Brief History of Time*
Alexandra Horowitz	*Inside of a Dog: What Dogs See, Smell, and Know*

Jhumpa Lahiri	*Interpreter of Maladies*
	The Namesake
	Unaccustomed Earth
	The Lowland
Linda Nochlin	"Why Have There Been No Great Women Artists?"
	(http://www.bakeru.edu/faculty/adaugherty/wc/module5/
	artists.html, click on #1, "Women Artists")
Steven Pinker	*The Stuff of Thought*
	How the Mind Works
	The Blank Slate
Michael Pollan	*The Botany of Desire*
	The Omnivore's Dilemma
	In Defense of Food
Lisa Randall	*Warped Passages: Unraveling the Mysteries of the*
	Universe's Hidden Dimensions
	Knocking on Heaven's Door: How Physics and Scientific
	Thinking Illuminate the Universe and the Modern World
Oliver Sacks	*Awakenings*
	The Man Who Mistook His Wife for a Hat
	Musicophilia
	Uncle Tungsten
	Hallucinations
Anna Deaveare Smith	*Talk to Me: Listening Between the Lines*
Leonard Susskind	*The Black Hole War*
	The Cosmic Landscape
Tom Vanderbilt	"The Traffic Guru," *Wilson Quarterly*, Summer 2008.
	http://www.wilsonquarterly.com/article.cfm?AID=1234

Reprints and Permissions

Sally Adee: From "Roughnecks in Space: Moon Mining in Science Fiction," *New Scientist*, 27 April 2012, 3:39 PM (http://www.newscientist.com/gallery/moon-mining).

Jerry Adler: From "Jazz Man," *Smithsonian Magazine*, September 2005.

Kathy Adler and Tamar Garb: Adapted from *Berthe Morisot: Correspondences*, compiled and edited by Denis Rouart. Moyer Bell, 1987. Reprinted with permission of the authors.

Caroline Alexander: From "If Stones Could Speak," *National Geographic*, June 2008

Catherine Allgor: From "The Politics of Love," *Humanities*, January/February 2010, Vol. 31, Number 1.

Mike Archer: From "Ordering the vegetarian meal? There's more animal blood on your hands." *The Conversation*, 16 December 2011, 6.34am (http://theconversation.edu.au/ordering-the-vegetarian-meal-theres-more-animal-blood-on-your-hands-4659).

Ronald Bailey: Adapted from "The Food Miles Mistake," Reason.com, 4 November 2008. (http://reason.com/archives/2008/11/04/the-food-miles-mistake).

Sven Birkerts: From "Vertigo," *Agni Online*, April 2012 (http://www.bu.edu/agni/essays/print/2012/75-birkerts.html)

Patrick Brown: Adapted from "Thoreau the Misanthrope." Originally published on the blog *Historical Digression*, 13 July 2012. (http://historicaldigression.com/2012/07/13/thoreau-the-misanthrope/). Reprinted with permission from the author.

Richard Conniff: From "What the Luddites Really Fought Against," *Smithsonian Magazine*, March 2011. Reprinted with permission of the author.

Callie Crossman: From "Making the News" by Callie Crossman, *Wellesley Magazine*, Fall 2012. Reprinted with permission of the author.

Mike Dash: From "The Woman Who Bested the Men at Math," Smithsonian.com, 28 October 2011 (http://blogs.smithsonianmag.com/history/2011/10/the-woman-who-bested-the-men-at-math/).

David Dubal: From "Let's Tickle the Ivories," *The New Criterion*, February 2012

Julie DesJardins: From "Madame Curie's Passion," *Smithsonian Magazine*. Reprinted with permission from the author.

Charles Dickens: Adapted from *The Personal History of David Copperfield*. London: Bradbury and Evans, 1850, pp. 131-133. Accessed from Google Books: (http://books.google.com/books?id=nmIVAAAAQAAJ&printsec=frontcover&dq=the+personal+history+of+david+copperfield&hl=en&sa=X&ei=R4G8UYHrNO_F0AHZ4oGACQ&ved=0CDgQ6AEwAA#v=onepage&q=goroo&f=false),

Franklin Foer: From "The Browbeater," *The New Republic*, 23 November 2011. Reprinted with permission of the publisher.

Henry Louis Gates: From *The Signifying Monkey*. New York: Oxford University Press, 1989. pp. 3-4.

Jonathan Gottschall: From "Why Fiction is Good for You," *The Boston Globe*, 29 April 2012. Reprinted with permission of the author.

Stephen Hawking and Leonard Mlodinow: From "The Elusive Theory of Everything," *Scientific American*, September 2010. Reprinted with permission of the authors.

Danny Heitman: From "Audubon the Writer," *Humanities*, November/December 2012, vol. 32 no. 6.
From: "Let Us Now Praise James Agee," *Humanities*, July/August 2012, Vol. 33, Number 4

Hannah Hickey: From "In Praise of Scum: Planet's Nitrogen Cycle Overturned by 'Tiny Ammonia Eaters of the Seas,'" University of Washington website, 2/1/2009. (http://www.washington.edu/news/2009/10/01/in-praise-of-scum-planets-nitrogen-cycle-overturned-by-tiny-ammonia-eater-of-the-seas/)

Meredith Hindley: From "The Dramatist," *Humanities*, September/October 2012 | Vol. 33, Number 5

Kazuo Ishiguro: From *Never Let Me Go*. Toronto: Vintage Canada (Random House), 2005, pp. 3-4.

Sam Kean: From "Fields Apart," *The American Scholar*. Winter 2012. Reprinted with permission of the author.

Jamaica Kincaid: Excerpt from "Gwen" from ANNIE JOHN by Jamaica Kincaid. Copyright © 1985 by Jamaica Kincaid. Reprinted by permission of Farrar, Straus and Giroux, LLC.

David Kipen: From "Unhappy Camper," Humanities, January/February 2012, Vol. 33, Number 1.

Verlyn Klinkenborg: Adapted from "Our Vanishing Night," *National Geographic*, November 2008. Reprinted with permission of the author.

Maggie Koerth-Baker: From "The Power of Positive Thinking," Truth or Myth? *Live Science*, 29 August 2008, 5:20 AM, 05:20 (http://www.livescience.com/2814-power-positive-thinking-truth-myth.html).

Anne Kreamer: Adapted and condensed from "The Business Case for Reading Novels," Harvard Business Review Blog, 1/11/12. Original version available at http://blogs.hbr.org/2012/01/the-business-case-for-reading/).

Jhumpa Lahiri: From "Unaccustomed Earth," *Unaccustomed Earth*, New York: Random House, 2008. pp. 3-4

Edward Lawrence: From "Poe Man's Immortality," *Humanities*, September/October 2008, Vol. 29, Number 5.

Kirk Leech: From "Why Moralism Spoils the Appetite," *Spiked Review of Books*. No. 53, February 2012.

Alan P. Lightman: From "The accidental universe: Science's crisis of faith," *Harpers*, December 2011.

Wilfred W. McClay: From "Lincoln the Great," *Humanities*, January/February 2009, Vol. 30, Number 1

David McConnell: From "Playing with Infinity on Riker's Island," *Prospect*, February 2012.

Greg Miller: From "How Our Brains Make Memories," Smithsonian.com, May 2010.

Fred Pearce: From "Climate Migration is a Solution, Not Desperation," *New Scientist*, 3 April 2012, 4:50 PM. (http://www.newscientist.com/article/dn21664_climate-migration-is-a-solution-not-desperation.html).

Ronald Riggio: From "Why Certain Smells Trigger Positive Memories," *Psychology Today*, 1 May 2012. Reprinted with permission of the author.

Michael Shapiro: From "The Newsroom Rush of Old," *Smithsonian Magazine*, March 2011. Reprinted with permission of the author.

David Skinner: From "The Ubiquitous Book, *Humanities*, September/October 2010: Vol. 31, Number 5.

Anna Deaveare Smith: From TALK TO ME by Anna Deavere Smith, copyright © 2000 by Anna Deaveare Smith. Used by permission of Random House, Inc

Janet Mansfield Soares: From "Grassroots Modern, *Humanities*, September/October 2010: Vol. 31, Number 5

Amy Tan: From *The Bonesetter's Daughter* by Amy Tan, copyright © 2001 by Amy Tan. Used by permission of G.P. Putnam's Sons, a division of Penguin Group (USA) Inc.

Anne Trubek: From "Zora's Place," *Humanities*, November/December 2011, Vol. 32, Number 6.

Abigail Tucker: From "Did Archaeologists Uncover Blackbeard's Treasure?," *Smithosonian Magazine*, March 2011

Neil Degrasse Tyson and Donald Goldsmith: From *Origins: Fourteen Billion Years of Cosmic Evolution*. New York: W.W. Norton and Co., 2005. Reprinted with permission of W.W. Norton and Co.

Tom Vanderbilt: From "The Call of the Future," *Wilson Quarterly*, Spring 2012

Erin Wayman: From "Homonid Hunting," Smithsonian magazine online blogs, 28 November 2011 (http://blogs.smithsonianmag.com/hominids/2011/11/the-first-americans/); from: "The Secrets of Ancient Rome, Smithsonian.com, 16 November 2012. (http://www.smithsonianmag.com/history-archaeology/The-Secrets-of-Ancient-Romes-Buildings.html#ixzz1tkUUqvz).

James Williford: From "Humanities on the Brain, *Humanities*. January/February 2012, Vol. 33, Number 1.

Acknowledgments

There are a number of people I need to thank for helping me bring this often overwhelming project to fruition. First, I owe an enormous debt of gratitude to Catherine Johnson, host of the *Kitchen Table Math* blog and SAT-author extraordinaire, for introducing me to *They Say/I Say: The Moves that Matter in Academic Writing*. The concepts outlined in the book provided me with a framework for both understanding how Critical Reading is structured and for explaining the differences between high school and college reading. Second, I need to thank Debbie Stier for pointing out the importance of teaching students to "read the test" critically. Her comments forced me to examine closely the unconscious assumptions with which I approached Critical Reading, and to elucidate those assumptions in order to better explain how the exam works. I also need to thank my wonderful proofreader, Jenny Hill for catching the many, many typos and inconsistencies that I had overlooked; my fellow tutor Stacey Howe-Lott for helping me categorize Critical Reading questions and pointing out those that I had originally overlooked; and Elizabeth Foster for saving me from having to write an additional seventy-five explanations. Finally, I need to thank the authors who were generous enough to allow me to adapt their work for inclusion in this book: Leonard Mlodinow, Cathy Adler and Tamar Garb, Verlyn Klinkenborg, Patrick Brown, Michael Shapiro, Julie DesJardins, Richard Conniff, Ronald Riggio, Jonathan Gottschall, and Callie Crossman.

About the Author

Since 2007, Erica Meltzer has worked as a tutor and test-prep writer, helping numerous students raise their SAT, ACT, GRE, and GMAT Verbal scores and gain acceptance to their top-choice schools. In addition to *The Critical Reader*, she is also the author of *The Ultimate Guide to SAT Grammar* (2011) and *The Complete Guide to ACT English* (2014). Her books have been widely praised as the most effective resources available for the verbal portions of the SAT and ACT, and are used by tutors and test prep companies across the United States. A graduate of Wellesley College, she is based in New York City. You can visit her online at http://www.thecriticalreader.com.

22246091R00214

Made in the USA
San Bernardino, CA
26 June 2015